THE MURDER
and THE TRIAL

THE MURDER
and THE TRIAL

BY

Edgar Lustgarten

EDITED AND WITH AN INTRODUCTION BY

Anthony Boucher

New York · CHARLES SCRIBNER'S SONS

FOR
Edana Romney

Contents

Introduction

THE proper study of mankind is man, killing. The true illuminator of man's inner self is the murderer, fresh-steeped in the deep damnation of a taking-off.

We all live in what the Requiem Mass calls "the certain condition of death to come" . . . but in God's time. The man who arrogates to himself the life-taking power of God (or, if you will, Fate), who takes in his own hands the shears of Atropos, shows us ourselves as we might be but for the grace of God (or the chance of conditioning). His motives and impulses are ours, magnified to such a scale that we may read them as never before.

It takes the Bible only 88 verses to reach murder. This is, indeed, the second sin recorded in that history, and the first which is *malum in se* rather than *malum prohibitum*—an evil in and of itself, rather than an act which becomes evil because it violates a high behest. And ever since Cain was very wroth at the rejection of his sacrifice, murder has been inextricably associated with the esthetic and ethical peaks of literature.

There is no need to stress the prevalence of murder in the Greek tragedy, the Elizabethan drama or the Victorian novel. It is only the Twentieth Century that has considered murder a debasing rather than an elevating topic—a view which future ages may rank with such other of our concepts as the distinction between popular and serious literature, or the belief that there is a democratic road to knowledge.

Cain, Oedipus, Macbeth, Lizzie Borden, the faceless Ripper, Leopold and Loeb—these are among the towering symbol-figures of culture, who teach us more about ourselves than most of the leaders, the saints, the poets and even the lovers.

But the great murder studies of the past were fictional or dramatized; and it remained for this century, despite its sociological priggishness, to develop the art of factual crime-writing.

ix

The Elizabethans wrote a little true crime—at least enough to furnish material to their poets: Shakespeare's murder tragedies stem, of course, from factual chronicles; and two great anonymous plays sometimes attributed to him—*Arden of Feversham* and *The Yorkshire Tragedy*—were more up to the factual minute than the recent dramatization of *Compulsion*. The Eighteenth Century had Defoe and the Nineteenth the splendid pioneer essays of De Quincey; but modern fact-crime may be justly dated from J. B. Atlay's *Famous Trials of the Century* (1899). In 1906 William Roughead, who acknowledged a great debt to Atlay, published his first book (*Trial of Dr. Pritchard*) and the Golden Century of true murder was well under way.

Fact-crime writing in today's sense—as distinguished from the sensational journalism of most "true crime" magazines—demands four qualities from its maker: *literacy,* at least as polished as that of the essayist or novelist; *scholarship* and dogged research, to establish every exact fact of the case considered; *insight* into human character and motives, as precise as that of the psychologist, as intuitive as that of the creative writer; and, lest we be overwhelmed by what that insight reveals, a feeling of *irony,* of relish—what James Bridie, in the case of Roughead, has termed "that bright sense of the incongruous sometimes called humour."

The masters of true murder have been a varied lot: a foreign correspondent (William Bolitho), a bibliophile (Edmund Pearson), two lady novelists (F. Tennyson Jesse and Rebecca West), a daily book-reviewer (Joseph Henry Jackson) and even an actor-manager (H. B. Irving). But the profession of the law can claim, among the moderns, the first (Atlay), the greatest (Roughead), and the latest to enter the very first ranks: Edgar Lustgarten.

A second-generation lawyer, Lustgarten practiced in Manchester for ten years before the War. His wartime activities in counter-propaganda for the BBC (as "Brent Wood") disclosed his talents as writer and broadcaster. In 1947 he brought out his first novel, *A Case to Answer* (in America, *One More Unfortunate*), one of the most satisfactory debuts in the history of the suspense novel—a highly persuasive study of a murder trial which anticipates all the qualities of his non-fiction. After a second novel in quite another genre (*Blondie Iscariot,* 1948, which successfully resembles an English W. R. Burnett), he published in 1950 *Verdict in Dispute,* a collection of six essays on debatable murder trials; and readers instantly acknowledged a new and authoritative master of true crime.

Lustgarten possesses, as you will see, all of the four qualities of literacy, scholarship, insight and irony, and possesses each to such a degree as to mark him the indisputable successor to Roughead as the foremost living writer in the field. And to these he adds a quality peculiarly his own, unmatched by any previous analyst in the field: a magnificently subtle sense of what he has called "the architectonics of advocacy," the manner in which the niceties of courtroom technique may determine life and death—plus an unmatched skill in making these niceties completely clear to the lay reader.

The pieces here chosen represent, regretfully, only about half of the published essays of Edgar Lustgarten. Omissions are (I admit to anticipate protests) grievous; but the only satisfactory "selection" from Lustgarten would be *The Complete Works*, an impractically huge volume.

In addition to full-scale essays from earlier collections, this book includes a number of briefer items, most of them hitherto unknown in America. For Lustgarten is the only fact-crime writer since Edmund Pearson to be as great in the short (or even short-short) essay as when he writes with no limitations on length. His selectivity and economy are as notable as his other skills: he can convey the essential significance of even a major and complex case in two thousand words or less.

Three of the pieces here (Seddon, Pigott and Borden) are from Lustgarten's *Prisoner at the Bar* broadcasts for the BBC's Light Programme. Inevitably they represent spoken rather than written English, but are so clear and lively that one reads them with delight . . . and with envy of the BBC audience.

Of the essays here included, you might particularly notice the Bartlett-Wood-Barney trilogy for its wonderful contrast of periods, both in crime and in advocacy; Borden (Lustgarten's only treatment of an American case) for its fresh analysis of a turning-point in an otherwise familiar trial; Pigott and Blitz for startling examples of brilliant advocacy; Smith and Wilde for dry sexual humor; Thorne for its relation to Lustgarten's first novel (which develops a different solution to a similar situation); Thompson and Wallace as superbly definitive treatments of standard classics; and Jones and Hulten (one of Lustgarten's few essays on relatively recent crime) as evidence that even a brutal callous killing in today's world of post-war violence can have its meaning as part of the proper study.

ANTHONY BOUCHER

Berkeley, California
December, 1957

THE MURDER
and THE TRIAL

I

Edith Thompson

THE case of Edith Thompson caught the British legal system on its weakest side. That system is an admirable instrument for ascertaining *facts;* it is much less efficient in dealing with psychology. The fault lies less with the machinery itself than with those who operate and supervise it. Imagination is the lawyer's bugbear and literalism his occupational disease. For him life is governed not by passions but by statutes, and he likes to interpret individual actions as if each had its origin in icy reason. The dismal consequences may be seen in a string of bad decisions. The human mind cannot be read like a charter-party or a bill of sale.

Great advocates, of course, are in a class apart. Their success with witnesses and their command over juries are based upon the most penetrating insight. A Carson or a Russell, a Hastings or a Birkett, possesses powers to grasp and understand the thoughts of others which sometimes seem to verge on the uncanny. But in any generation great advocates are few, while stereotyped lawyers are always two a penny. Rigid, narrow, formalistic and self-righteous, they are particularly ill-suited to present or sit in judgment on a case which calls for sympathetic knowledge of the world.

Edith Thompson was charged with murdering her husband, but not by direct act, and not alone. At no time was it suggested that she played a physical part; the Crown acknowledged that she did not lift a finger. Their case was that she urged murder on her lover; that the latter in her presence carried out the wicked deed; and that these two factors taken in conjunction made her under English law a principal in the crime.

3

Much of this thesis was not seriously contested. The lover at least admitted having fought and stabbed the husband; Mrs. Thompson admitted being present when he did; the legal proposition was unarguably sound. So if, as appeared likely all along, Mrs. Thompson's lover was found guilty of murder, her own neck would be forfeit if the jury were convinced that she had spurred him to it with malice and design. This in its turn depended upon whether, in their estimation, words that she had used constituted—and were *meant* to constitute—incitement.

Words exist to communicate a meaning. But the meaning inferred by the listener or the reader is not always that intended by the speaker or the writer. There are primary and secondary senses; there are overtones and undertones that are idiosyncratic; there is hyperbole and satire; there is untrammelled fantasy and deliberate make-believe. It is absurd to suppose that every phrase should be literally construed. The man who says "I thought I'd die" when talking of an illness may well mean that he really anticipated death, but the man who says "I thought I'd die" about a comic story is merely conveying that it gave him a good laugh. It is only by reference to the character of their author and to the circumstances in which they were employed that one can hope to extract the true significance of words. They must be related, not only to the dictionary, but to life.

The lawyers in the Thompson trial brought dictionaries to court, but carefully closed the doors upon the teeming life outside.

Few are unfamiliar with the outline of the tragedy that cast a City bookkeeper and Ilford housewife for a rôle befitting Bernhardt or Réjane. Beneath a commonplace plot of jealousy and intrigue lay hidden drama of such spiritual intensity that it fascinates even those most repelled by crime. The story has been told by many practised pens, and several works of fiction owe to it their inspiration. But the latter, not improperly, have claimed artistic license; recapitulation of the facts may not be out of place.

Late in the evening of October 3rd, 1922, Mrs. Thompson was walking along a quiet road in Ilford with her husband, a respectable shipping clerk, at her side. They were returning from a visit to a West End theatre. As they neared their home, a man overtook them; he pushed Mrs. Thompson to one side, stabbed her husband several times and swiftly disappeared. Mrs. Thompson shrieked and ran for help. A doctor lived near by; he hurried to the spot, but Percy Thompson was already beyond aid.

The police arrived, the body was removed, and a Sergeant escorted

Mrs. Thompson home. She was much distressed and apparently bewildered. She spoke as though her husband had had some kind of fit, and made no mention of an attack or an attacker.

But meanwhile at the mortuary they were examining the corpse. Natural death could be instantly ruled out. There were cuts in the ribs, on the chin and lower jaw, and at the right elbow on the inside of the arm. At the back of the head there were two vicious-looking stabs, one of which had severed a great artery in the neck. It was this last wound that had caused Percy Thompson's death and established beyond doubt that the hapless man was murdered.

Taking all into account, it was difficult to believe that Mrs. Thompson had told them the whole truth. Not unnaturally the police began to wonder whether the murder had its roots in her domestic life.

An enquiry on these lines immediately bore fruit. It led them to a young man by name of Frederick Bywaters, a P. and O. employee of excellent repute. They discovered, with commendable energy and speed, that this boy—he was but twenty—had been linked with Mrs. Thompson in one form or another for a considerable time. He had known her family since he was a schoolboy. In 1921 he had been on holiday with the Thompsons and afterwards had stayed with them for several weeks at Ilford. He had left as a result of a dispute with Percy Thompson about the latter's behaviour to his wife. Since then he had corresponded with Mrs. Thompson when he was at sea and seen her surreptitiously when he was at home. He had in fact met her in an Aldersgate Street tea shop less than seven hours before the murder was committed.

The police concluded—and their conclusion was well founded—that Frederick Bywaters was Edith Thompson's lover. He was obviously a man who "might be able to assist them in their investigations." On the evening of October 4th Bywaters was taken to the police station for questioning.

When he got there he found, among others, Mr. Wensley—Inspector Wensley of the Steinie Morrison case, much older now and more exalted in the hierarchy, but just as shrewd and eagle-eyed as ever. While Bywaters denied all connection with the crime and adopted an aggressive, irritated air, Wensley was scrutinising him minutely. "There are spots on the sleeve of your overcoat," he suddenly remarked. "They look to me like blood."

The overcoat was confiscated for chemical examination (which ultimately confirmed the detective's diagnosis) and Bywaters, still protesting, was provisionally detained.

A little later the same evening the police brought Mrs. Thompson to the station. She was not officially placed under restraint, but, in Superintendent Wensley's felicitous phrase, "it was *convenient* to have her at hand while we were looking for something that would give us a line." So, unbeknown to each other, in the interests of "convenience," lover and mistress slept under the same roof.

Mrs. Thompson had not implicated Bywaters at all. Next day, when she was invited to give "further information," she still maintained she had seen nobody approach. Bywaters for his part made no change in his attitude. The enquiry, which had opened with such impetus and promise, was now merely ticking over and showed signs of being stalled.

Late that afternoon, though, an incident occurred that set the wheels back again in motion. It has been described by Wensley as "a dramatic interlude" and by at least one famous lawyer as "a little trap." Whether by accident or whether by design, Mrs. Thompson was conducted along a corridor where, through an open doorway, she caught a glimpse of Bywaters.

The shock cracked her nerve. She broke down, crying, "Oh God, oh God, what can I do? Why did he do it? I did not want him to do it." Mrs. Thompson was at this moment admittedly hysterical and it is not without interest to dwell upon her words. "Why did he do it? *I did not want him to do it.*" That could not have been a calculated stratagem; that was uttered in the agony of impulse, a cry wrung against her will out of the woman's heart. Yet one would be hard put to it to draft another sentence expressing so precisely the gist of her defence.

But, understandably, the police were not concerned with her defence; they were only concerned with the effect of this on Bywaters. "Why did he do it?" That was all the lead required. The notebooks were whipped out, the formal warning given, and within a few minutes Mrs. Thompson signed a statement naming Bywaters as the man who had "scuffled" with her husband.

From that moment Bywaters was halfway to the gallows. Faced with this complete reversal of the situation, he made a further statement from which he never struggled free.

"I waited," he said, "for Mrs. Thompson and her husband. . . . I pushed her to one side, also pushing him further up the street. I said to him, 'You have got to separate from your wife.' He said, 'No.' I said, 'You will have to.' We struggled. I took my knife from my pocket and we fought and he got the worst of it. Mrs. Thompson must have been spellbound for I saw nothing of her during the fight. I ran away. . . . The reason I fought Thompson was because he never acted like a man to his wife. He always seemed several degrees lower than a snake. I loved her and could not go on seeing her leading that life. I did not intend to kill him. I only meant to injure him." Bywaters prefaced this statement with an important affirmation: "Mrs. Edith Thompson was not aware of my movements on Tuesday evening, October 3rd."

It may have been true, but one should say this about Bywaters; he tried his best to shield Mrs. Thompson (and continued to do so gallantly, though clumsily, to the end).

His efforts, however, met with no success. The police had made their minds up to bring them both to trial, and each was duly charged with Percy Thompson's murder.

The case against Bywaters was simple, factual and tolerably clear. Apart from noting that on trial he introduced somewhat belatedly the theme of self-defence, it need not concern us further.

The case against Mrs. Thompson had at first been nonexistent. All that could be said against her was that she had lied in a futile attempt to protect and cover Bywaters. That might make her an accessory after the fact. It could not bring her into danger of the rope.

What could? At the Old Bailey the judge was to express it in these words, "You will not convict her," he enjoined the jury, "unless you are satisfied that she and he *agreed* that this man should be murdered when he could be, and she *knew* he was going to do it, and *directed* him to do it, and *by arrangement between them* he was doing it."

There had been nothing whatever in Mrs. Thompson's conduct to suggest that she possessed foreknowledge of the crime. She had seemed serene and normal to companions at the theatre. She had made frantic exertions to procure medical aid. Most striking touch of all, a householder who lived close by the scene of the assault had heard her cry, "Oh don't! Oh don't!" in a most piteous tone. If that was merely play-acting to impress an unseen audience, to dissociate herself from Bywaters' attack, why did she say afterwards she had seen nobody there?

How could the police prove Mrs. Thompson's complicity? How could they establish the existence of a plot? How could they show, with the material available, that Bywaters had acted at her bidding and direction? The answer is, they couldn't; and if nothing had turned up the prosecution of the woman would have been quietly withdrawn. No self-respecting counsel would have agreed to open it.

But something did turn up. In a routine inspection of Bywaters' belongings the police unearthed and seized sixty-five letters written by Mrs. Thompson to her lover and sometimes couched in extraordinary terms.

These letters became the salient feature of the trial and were certainly the arbiter of Edith Thompson's fate. One must now turn aside from the action of the story. It is the letters one must study—the letters and their writer, for they throw light on her just as she throws light on them.

Edith Thompson was no ordinary woman of the suburbs, occupied and satisfied by the dreary daily round. She was a remarkable and complex personality, endowed with signal attributes of body and of mind. She had intelligence, vitality, a natural grace and poise, sensitiveness, humour and—illumining all these—that quintessential femininity that fascinates the male. If the list had only ended there her tale would have been different; she might not have found happiness, she would not have met her doom. But there was one further element in Edith Thompson's make-up; she had the instincts of an artist and, lacking the artist's outlet, she used them in a manner that led to her undoing.

The friends and acquaintances of her own social circle doubtless envied Edith Thompson the good fortune of her lot. She had a sober, thrifty husband; a pleasant little home; a responsible and well-paid job she had held for several years. Indeed, she earned as much or perhaps more than did her husband, which could hardly fail to gratify her taste for independence. "She is a very capable woman," said her employer at the trial. "With her business capacity she could get employment anywhere."

But the comfortable monotony of Ilford and the City did not appease the restlessness in Edith Thompson's soul. There was nothing in either to fire imagination, as the artist in her so avidly desired. Her existence was prosaic and uneventful; her husband unresponsive and humdrum. She lived in and through novels which she devoured till they were part of her; but what were other people's novels, after all? Time was slipping by; in 1921 she had been married six whole years; soon, all too soon, she would be an old, old woman without even the solace of remembered joys. Unconsciously but ardently she sought some focus, some rallying point and symbol of her appetite for life.

She found it in Bywaters. He was eight years her junior; hardly more than a youth, but conspicuously virile and handsome in a heavy, sensual way. She raised this earthy lover to the heights. She breathed into their love a flame so fierce that even Bywaters was transported and transfigured. It was Antony and Cleopatra, it was Romeo and Juliet, it was every great romance in the chronicles of time.

Fact and reality were no more than a cue for the exuberant fancy of Edith Thompson's mind. When the true story fell short she improved it in her letters, until it was a story worth an artist's while; a story replete with sacrifice and violence, with colourful suitors and relentless poisoning wives, with all the trappings of the novels she had read and all the delirium of the love she had imagined. This was the driving force behind the famous letters which the prosecution used to get their writer hanged.

One does not seek to whitewash Mrs. Thompson nor to try to gloss over whatever were her sins. But none can understand her who fails to realise that she was a woman of quality whose talents were frustrated.

A notion has found currency that Mrs. Thompson's letters contained little else but equivocal and sinister allusions. This notion runs quite contrary to the fact.

From August 1921 to October 1922 she wrote to Bywaters several scores of times. The letters she received from him during the same period were, with three exceptions, prudently destroyed. Of the sixty-five from her remaining in existence, more than half were not introduced in evidence by the Crown—because there was nothing in them, no reference, no phrase, which could possibly be quoted to Mrs. Thompson's detriment. Of those that were exhibited—thirty-two in all—only fractions consisted of disputable stuff; more than nine-tenths was as transparently innocent of crime as is the private talk of lovers anywhere on earth.

Most love letters, however skilled the writer, are unreadable except by those to whom they are addressed. In making herself an exception to this rule, Mrs. Thompson gave a further proof of her peculiar gifts. Sometimes she looked forward to Bywaters' return:

> It is four whole weeks today since you went and there is still another four more to go—I wish I could go to sleep for all that time and wake up just in time to dress and sit by the fire—waiting for you to come in on March 18th. I don't think I'd come to meet you darlint it always seems so ordinary and casual for me to see you after such a long time in the street, I shall always want you to come straight to our home and take me in both your arms.

Sometimes she looked back into the past, half gratified, half fearful:

I'll always love you—if you are dead—if you have left me—even if you don't still love me—I shall always love you. . . . If things should go badly with us, I shall always have this past year to look back upon and feel that "Then I lived!" I never did before and never shall again.

Sometimes she is despondent and reproachful: he does not write (or "talk" as she always calls it) often or expansively enough.

What an utterly absurd thing to say to me, "Don't be too disappointed."

You can't possibly know what it feels like to wait and wait each day —every little hour—for something that means life to you and then not get it.

You told me from Dover that you were going to talk to me for a long time at Marseilles and now you put it off to Port Said.

You force me to conclude that the life you lead away from England is all absorbing, that you haven't time nor inclination to remember England or anything England holds.

There were at least five days you could have talked to me about—if you only spared me five minutes out of each day. But what is the use of me saying all this—it's the same always—I'm never meant to have anything I expect or want. If I am unjust—I'm sorry—but I can't feel anything at present—only just as if I have had a blow on the head and I'm stunned—the disappointment—no, more than that—the utter despair is too much to bear—I would sooner go under today than anything.

All I can hope is that you will never feel like I do today. . . . Perhaps I ought not to have written this, but how I feel and what I think I must tell you always.

There is no mistaking the dynamic of her passion, nor her untutored power of conveying it in words.

Let's be ourselves—always darlingest there can never be any misunderstandings then—it doesn't matter if it's harder—you said it was our Fate against each other—we only have will power when we are in accord, not when we are in conflict—tell me if this is how you feel. With you darlint there can never be any pride to stand in the way—it melts in the flame of a great love—I finished with pride, oh a long time ago.

The City bookkeeper's pen flew over the paper; she was buoyant, depressed, ecstatic, apprehensive. But over and over again a bogey rose to scare her. He was twenty. She was twenty-eight.

My veriest own lover, I always think about "the difference." . . . Sometimes when I'm happy for a little while I forget—but I always remember very soon. . . . Shall I always be able to keep you? Eight years is such a long time—it's not now—it's later—when I'm Joan and you're not grown old enough to be Darby. When you've got something that you've never had before and something that you're so happy to have found—you're always afraid of it flying away—that's how I feel about your love.

Don't ever take your love away from me darlint. I never want to lose it and live.

Life, it is clear, inflicted many torments on this burning spirit with aspirations unfulfilled. But there was always one escape.

Aren't books a consolation and a solace? We ourselves die and live in the books we read while we are reading them and then when we have finished, the books die and we live—or exist—just drag on through years and years, until when? Who knows—I'm beginning to think no one does—no, not even you and I, we are not the shapers of our destinies.

I'll always love you darlint.

"We are not the shapers of our destinies." It has a terrible and prophetic ring.

She wrote always a great deal about the books she was reading or wanted him to read. She did not merely tell him whether she had enjoyed them; she did not even confine herself to mentioning the theme; but habitually made minute analyses of the characters and discussed the motive springs that underlay their actions. She formed and ventilated fervid views about these fictional creations.

The man Lacosta in *The Trail of '98* . . . he was so vile I didn't think of him at all, and I'd rather not now darlint.

I enjoyed John Chilcote ever so much, I admire the force in the man that made him tackle such a position against such odds.

No I don't agree with you about Bella Donna darlint—I hate her —hate to think of her—I don't think other people made her what she was—that sensual pleasure-loving greedy Bella Donna was always there. If she had originally been different—a good man like Nigel would have altered her darlint—she never knew what it was to be denied anything—she never knew "goodness" as you and I know it —she was never interested in a good man—or any man unless he could appease her sensual nature. . . . She doesn't seem a woman to me—she seems abnormal—a monster.

A reply to some stricture on the ending of a novel shows the depth of her absorption in imaginary worlds.

The endings are not the story. . . . Do as I do. Forget the end, lose yourself in the characters and the story, *and in your own mind make your own end.*

Such was the prevailing mental climate of these letters that are passed down to posterity as the effusions of a murderess. One must now examine a few specific passages selected by the Crown as indicative of guilt. These passages of course should not be read in isolation. They ought to be read—as the lawyers did not read them—within the context of the letters as a whole. Then and only then one has a chance of judging whether, according to the precept she herself laid down, it was in her own mind that Mrs. Thompson made her end.

The compromising words, faithfully copied into counsels' briefs by thrilled and awestruck typists, were singularly artless if they ministered to crime. Does a cold-blooded conspirator, pondering every move, ignore the risk of letters getting lost or going astray? Does a party to a plot, receiving reckless letters, studiously preserve the evidence of guilt?

Such modifying reflections usually come as afterthoughts. First interpretations are rigorously literal. One can well imagine detective eyes popping out of detective heads when they originally lighted upon passages like this.

> I used the "light bulb" three times, but the third time—he found a piece—so I have given it up—until you come home.

Who is "he"? Who could it be except the lady's husband? What was the "light bulb" and in what way was it used? The light bulb; he found a piece. Wasn't powdered glass a familiar form of poisoning?

As they read on, letter after letter, Scotland Yards's suspicions deepened into certainty.

> I was buoyed up with the hope of the "light bulb" and I used a lot —big pieces too—not powdered—and it has no effect—I quite expected to be able to send that cable—but no, nothing has happened from it. . . . I know I feel I shall never get him to take a sufficient quantity of anything bitter.

References to a bitter taste frequently recur.

> He puts great stress on the fact of the tea tasting bitter "as if something had been put in it," he says. Now I think whatever else I try in it again will still taste bitter—he will recognise it and be more suspicious still and if the quantity is still not successful it will injure any chance I may have of trying when you come home.

Though other extracts gained equal prominence at the trial, one surmises that in the initial stage these furnished the key. They laid a firm-looking foundation for a practicable theory which was confidently applied to unriddle ambiguities. By the aid of this explanatory touchstone, each could be resolved to favour the Crown case.

> This time really will be the last you will go away—like things are, won't it? We said it before darlint I know and we failed . . . but there will be no failure this next time darlint, there mustn't be—I'm telling you—if things are the same again then I'm going with you— wherever it is—if it's to sea—I am coming too—and if it's to nowhere —I'm also coming darlint. You'll never leave me behind again, never, *unless things are different.*

What did Mrs. Thompson mean, "unless things are different"? Obvious, said the Crown; she meant, unless we've done the murder.

> I ask you again to think out all the *plans and methods* for me.

What did Mrs. Thompson mean, "plans and methods"? Obvious, said the Crown; she meant ways and means of murder.

> Yes, darlint, you are jealous of him—but I want you to be—he has the right by law to all that you have the right to by nature and by love —yes darlint be jealous, so much that you will *do something desperate.*

What did Mrs. Thompson mean, "do something desperate"? Obvious, said the Crown; she meant, brace yourself for murder.

If some of these inferences seem prejudiced or forced, this must be said in fairness to the Crown: make one assumption, and it is true that all else follows. If what one terms the key passages are taken at face value; if every statement in them is accepted as a fact; if each of the incidents described by Mrs. Thompson is assumed to have occurred exactly as she says—then there can be only one possible conclusion. Mrs. Thompson had herself tried to kill her husband and had been imploring Bywaters to succeed where she had failed.

That was the conclusion, granted the assumption. But was the assumption justified that Mrs. Thompson never indulged in flights of fancy and that all her reporting was meticulously exact?

The trial, so far as she was personally concerned, became a committee of inquiry to decide this single point.

The case of The King against Bywaters and Thompson began at the Old Bailey on December 6th, 1922. A row of well-known counsel faced Mr. Justice Shearman. Sir Henry Curtis Bennett, then rivalling Marshall Hall in public esteem as a defender, was instructed to appear on behalf of Mrs. Thompson. Mr. Cecil Whiteley, an agile-minded and energetic advocate, undertook the well-nigh hopeless task of representing Bywaters. The Crown had thought fit to nominate a Law Officer—a move which secured for them the right to the last word. Their choice fell on Thomas Inskip, a learned abstract lawyer, who in the whirligig of politics had been made Solicitor-General. This case was not, one may conjecture, an assignment Inskip relished. His capacities were misemployed, his shortcomings exposed. He displayed as little grasp of human impulses and frailties as he later did of strategy when Minister of Defence.

Interest in the trial was not confined to those who, through craving for sensation or mere prurient curiosity, can never resist the double bait of murder and of sex. The unusual issue that had to be determined; the fact that the solution lay in the temper of a mind; a feeling that Mrs. Thompson was a highly gifted woman who, innocent or otherwise, would repay attentive study—this made a gulf between the case and the average murder trial like the gulf between the average thriller and one by Graham Greene. The best, as well as the worse, were attracted into court, and some notable figures from literature and Fleet Street took their place among the audience assembled for the drama.

The drama opened in most undramatic circumstances.

The scene had been set and the characters introduced. Bywaters and Mrs. Thompson had been brought into the dock and eyed from every angle like a pair of movie stars. The twelve who were to try them had answered to their names and all had seemed in readiness for a great forensic battle.

Then Sir Henry Curtis Bennett spoke in quiet, even tones. The judge gave a brief order. An official led the puzzled jury out of court. The defence were raising a preliminary objection; they wished to argue on a point of law.

This argument took place, as such arguments do, in a deceptive atmosphere of academic calm. Points of law are not contrived to gratify the public thirst for clamour and excitement. They may be as fateful, though, as contests more spectacular. The routine seldom varies. An erudite submission by one counsel, an erudite counter-submission by another, much reading out of large books, a Latin tag or two—and then a gentle pronouncement by the judge, which may create a precedent and terminate a life.

The significance of Sir Henry's point of law cannot be overstated. He was contending that the letters, the all-important letters, were not admissible as evidence and should be excluded from the trial.

The rules governing the admissibility of evidence are something of a mystery to the man in the street, who is apt to think of them as lawyers' hocus-pocus. This view is unwarranted. Though they sometimes seem—and sometimes are—mechanical and arbitrary in operation, such rules are based on long and rich experience of what is required to protect the individual. Reliance upon them betrays neither guilt nor weakness; it is a claim upon the birthright of a British citizen.

To invoke the aid of any rule which might shut out the letters was the plain duty of Mrs. Thompson's counsel. Success in this would be decisive. There would be no evidence, no need for further argument, no element of risk. If the Crown could be deprived of the right to read and use the Correspondence bundle in Sir Thomas Inskip's brief the case against Mrs. Thompson would be virtually at an end.

Curtis Bennett's submission was necessarily technical, and interesting only to scholars of the law. Briefly, he said this: that the letters, by their nature, could only throw light upon *intent;* that intent is not an issue unless there is an *act* to be explained; that the Crown could not prove, and did not set out to prove, that Mrs. Thompson committed any act in the murder. Hence, said Curtis Bennett, the letters were irrelevant; hence they ought not to be admitted into evidence.

"But," said the judge, "it is alleged that the lady was present at the murder. Are the letters not *then* evidence of her felonious intent?"

"No, my lord," said Curtis Bennett, "not on this indictment. I agree," he added, "that I should not be able to object to the letters on the *second* indictment."

(In fact five separate charges stood against Mrs. Thompson— charges of murder, of soliciting to murder, of inciting to conspire to murder, of administering poison with intent to murder, and of administering a destructive thing with intent to murder. The last four had been deferred pending the verdict on the first, though it might be assumed that in the event of an acquittal the Crown would not proceed with the subsidiary charges.)

Cecil Whiteley who, at Bywaters' desire, accorded all support throughout to Mrs. Thompson's case, also objected to the admission of the letters. In reply, the Solicitor-General said that the letters were evidence not merely of intent, but of incitement. "This is a crime," he declared, "where one hand struck the blow, and we want to show by these letters that Mrs. Thompson's mind conceived and incited it."

The judge accepted this submission and rejected those of the defence. "The question is a very difficult one," he said, "but I think that these letters are admissible."

It was a decision firmly based in law, but it proved in the long run inimical to justice.

So the letters were "in," as lawyers say colloquially, and the Crown exploited them down to the last syllable. The Solicitor-General made them the burden of his somewhat undistinguished opening address. At the prosecution's close they were read in their entirety—a proceeding which occupied most of the second day. They were put piecemeal to the prisoners when they went into the box; not only to Mrs. Thompson, but to Bywaters as well. She was invited to explain what she had meant, he to explain what he had taken her to mean.

In the course of this repetitive and time-consuming process the jury could have learnt the key passages by heart, together with the innuendoes proffered by the Crown. But there was another consequence that favoured the defence. As the background gradually filled in and a fuller, clearer picture of the tragedy took shape, much that had been quoted acquired a fresh perspective.

It transpired, for instance, that the lovers, faced with the barrier of Mrs. Thompson's marriage, had together discussed the possibility of suicide. One strongly suspects that this was just another piece of Mrs. Thompson's mania for self-dramatisation, and that there was no real intention of carrying it out. But the vital point to mark is that it was at least *discussed;* there were expressions in the letters not susceptible of any other meaning.

> All I could think about last night was that compact we made. Shall we have to carry it through? Don't let us darlint. *I'd like to live* and be happy—not for a little while but for all the while you still love me. Death seemed horrible last night—when you think about it darlint, *it does seem a horrible thing to die, when you have never been happy really happy for one little minute.*

They had also canvassed the idea of persuading Percy Thompson to separate from his wife.

> I said exactly what you told me to and he replied that he knew *that's what I wanted and he was not giving it to me*—it would make things far too easy for both of you (meaning you and me) especially for you he said.

Mrs. Thompson had been ready—or had said that she was ready—to run away without warning from her husband and her home.

Darlingest find me a job abroad. I'll go tomorrow and not say I was going to a soul and not have one little regret.

Suicide. Separation. Leaving England with her lover. Might it have been these objects, and not murder at all, that had taken such a grip of Mrs. Thompson's mind? "I ask you to think out the plans and methods for me." Plans and methods for killing her husband—or herself? "You'll never leave me again unless things are different." Different because Percy Thompson had been killed—or because he had at last agreed to separation? "Be jealous so that you will do something desperate." Murder the husband—or take away the wife? It became glaringly, almost embarrassingly, apparent that many of the phrases which the Crown had singled out were open to quite credible alternative constructions.

But this merely trimmed the edges of the sprawling, straggling case which the Solicitor-General had placed before the jury. The key passages were not affected nor dislodged. "I used the light bulb three times, but the third time he found a piece." "I feel I shall never get him to take a sufficient quantity." "Whatever else I try in it will still taste bitter." No stretching of the sense could make these refer to suicide, or matrimonial separation, or slipping off abroad. For these there was but one excuse conformable with innocence—that they were fabulous, air-drawn, fantastical inventions, the figments of Mrs. Thompson's over-fertile brain.

This in a sentence was the case for the defence. It was not a case that could be built up far in cross-examination. It was not a case that could be tested much by pondering the facts. The problem was to estimate a woman's imagination, and to solve it the jury were thrown back upon their own.

There were, however, two solid tangible realities to guide them in their psychopathological explorations.

The first was more revealing of her character than anything Mrs. Thompson could have said about herself.

In one of her letters she had treated Bywaters to a particularised description of a family upset. Her sister Avis had informed her, she declared, that her indignant husband had been down to see her father and told him "everything—about all the rows we have had over you. But"—observe the painstaking reverence for detail—"she did not mention he said anything about the first real one on August 1st—so I suppose he kept that back to suit his own ends."

Mrs. Thompson's father (Avis was alleged to have reported) had expressed an intention of "talking to" his daughter. "But I went down and nothing happened. . . . I told Avis I should tell them off if they said anything to me."

Now Mrs. Thompson's father and sister were witnesses at the trial— the latter for the defence, the former for the Crown. Curtis Bennett questioned them both about this highly circumstantial story.

"Did Thompson," he asked the father, "ever come to you and make a complaint about the conduct of Bywaters with your daughter?"

"Never," was the reply. "That is the purest imagination."

"Is there any truth whatever in this story?"

"There is none. As a matter of fact, I had no idea that my daughter and her husband were not on good terms."

The sister in turn was equally emphatic. Curtis Bennett read aloud the passage from the letter with its constant and plausible mention of herself. "I rang Avis. . . ." "Dad was going to talk to me, Avis said. . . ." "I told Avis I should tell them off. . . ."

"Is there any truth in that at all?" Curtis Bennett enquired of Avis.

"There is none whatever."

"Did you ever tell her anything like that?"

"I did not."

"Did it ever happen?"

"It did not."

It had never happened and Avis had never told her. Yet Mrs. Thompson's account of this imaginary incident has a realism few can infuse into the truth. What a little miracle of unconscious art prompted that reference to "the first real row" in August! Who could believe that a story so minutely related wasn't true? Almost certainly it half convinced its author, and this I have no doubt was its principal design. More important than anything, more important even than her hold upon her lover, was the endless romantic tale that Edith Thompson spun, and deep in the heart of which she lived a life apart.

The second signpost was erected by a witness of great influence whose word was magical with juries.

There had been an exhumation of Percy Thompson's body with the express object of examining for poison. Bernard Spilsbury conducted the post-mortem.

He found precisely nothing. There was no trace or sign of any poison. There was no trace or sign of any glass. There was no indication that either one or the other had ever been administered.

The Crown produced this tremendous piece of evidence in a shabby, grudging, discreditable way. They tried to make it seem that the post-mortem was nugatory by stressing that all traces might have disappeared. But the exhumation wasn't made without hope of finding something; the most famous of pathologists had said that there was nothing; and the Crown would have done better to have faced up to the fact and not tried to look as though they expected nothing anyway.

All those pieces of glass ("I used quite a lot"), all those light bulbs, all that stuff that tasted bitter. Like the story about Avis and the family upset, its unaffected naturalness insisted on belief. But Science—unimpressionable Science—using its steely, material approach, could find no evidence that this transpontine melodrama had ever been performed except in Mrs. Thompson's mind.

The Crown case had closed. Bywaters had given evidence with the pugnacity of despair and tightened the noose already slung around his throat. Now Curtis Bennett faced a grave and vexing question. Ought Mrs. Thompson to go into the box?

Criminal charges must be strictly proved. It is not enough for the Crown to say, "Look, we have kicked up a great dust of suspicion; you, the accused, are bound to lay that dust; you must take the oath and submit yourself to cross-examination." A more exacting onus lies upon the Crown: to establish guilt beyond reasonable doubt. If they are incapable of doing that unassisted, the prisoner will be well advised to hold his peace.

As matters stood, had the Crown discharged this onus on the trial of Mrs. Thompson? Their case against her was based solely on her letters. Suppose Curtis Bennett had adopted a bold line; suppose he had called no evidence, addressed the jury, pointed to Mrs. Thompson's bent for vivid storytelling, and challenged them to convict her on the letters by themselves. Would they have dared?

Curtis Bennett's dilemma has been that of many advocates since the Criminal Evidence Act was passed in 1898. Until then no prisoner could give sworn evidence in his own behalf. That often placed him at a disadvantage—a disadvantage that the Act was intended to remove. But in removing one, it introduced another. In theory, the prisoner now enjoys an option; he gives evidence or not, exactly as he likes. But in practice, his election to keep out of the box will generally result in adverse comment by the judge and an assumption by the jury that he has got something to hide.

All this had to be weighed. If the final decision had been wholly Curtis Bennett's, if his client had placed herself entirely in his hands,

one is disposed to guess that she would never have been called. But
heavy pressure was brought to bear upon his judgment.

Mrs. Thompson herself had decided to give evidence. She would
hear no advice and brook no denial.

Mrs. Thompson's appearance in the box did her irreparable harm.

It was not that she offended in style or personality; nothing could
divest her of her native distinction. It was not that she brought forward any new and dreadful fact; hardly once during her testimony
did she break onto fresh ground. She certainly did not succumb to the
acumen of Inskip; his cross-examination, although long, was uninspired.

The cause of Mrs. Thompson's failure as a witness must be sought
in some sphere less obvious than these. I myself think that, despite
the seeming paradox, it was due to the acuteness and the strength of
her perceptions.

One may follow the thought process that set her on her course. The
jury must be made to see the motive for the letters. She knew the
motive best, so it was best that she should tell them. Looking on each
day from the seclusion of the dock, or brooding at night in the fastness
of her cell, she felt certain—*certain*—she could make them understand. But once face to face with the unforthcoming twelve, hope
drained suddenly like blood out of her heart. It is my belief she realised, in the moment of essaying it, the utter futility of her self-
appointed task. She learned the last agony afflicting those on trial—
knowing it is impossible to get oneself believed.

How could she put it? How could she find words? How could she
convince them that those letters to her lover consisted in part of sheer
escapist fiction, invented and written to compensate a little for the
drab dull existence to which the twelve belonged?

She perceived this and she faltered. Her mind refused to act. She
pathetically took refuge in the barest of denials.

"Did you ever put anything in your husband's tea?"

"No."

"Did he ever complain that his tea tasted bitter?"

"No."

"Did you ever intend to use an electric light bulb?"

"No."

"Did you ever use one?"

"Never."

But why write and say you had? That was the point, and it was
never really dealt with. Vaguely and feebly, when pressed upon the

matter, Mrs. Thompson talked of "holding Bywaters' affection." This does not convey to me the ring of authenticity, and doubtless it appeared even more inadequate at the time. It sounds hollow and would leave the jury still demanding, why? Why the *fantasy?* Why the *make-believe?*

Mrs. Thompson could not tell them—she who knew so well.

Responsibility lay heavy on Sir Henry Curtis Bennett. Four days of prim sententiousness and virtuous moralising could not fail to magnify that attitude of censoriousness so readily adopted by humans in the mass. It was on the whole an unfavourable atmosphere in which Mrs. Thompson's counsel began his final speech.

He made an admirable and sustained attempt to dissipate this atmosphere, to rescue his client from the dead hand of the law. He projected Mrs. Thompson as she could not project herself.

"Am I right or wrong," he asked, "in saying that this woman is one of the most extraordinary personalities that you or I have ever met? Bywaters truly described her, did he not, as a woman who lived a sort of life I don't suppose any of you live—an extraordinary life of make-believe in an atmosphere created by something which has made an impression on her brain. She reads a book and she imagines herself one of the characters. She is always leading an extraordinary life of novels."

At last the real Mrs. Thompson was being put before the jury. With unpretentious force Curtis Bennett drew a portrait of a woman whose mental horizon did not end at Chancery Lane. He took the letters themselves as the best corroboration of this reading of her mind.

"Have you ever heard more beautiful language of love? Such things have been very seldom put by pen upon paper. *This* is the woman you have to deal with, not some ordinary woman. She is one of those striking personalities that stand out."

Tactfully the defender endeavoured to diminish the whipped-up prejudice of moral disapproval.

"Thank God," he cried, "this is not a court of morals, because if everybody immoral was brought here I would never be out of it, nor would you. . . . We are men and women of the world."

When Mrs. Thompson had stepped down from the box, the darkness of doom enwrapped her like a mantle. Now it was growing lighter with every passing minute. As Curtis Bennett developed and enlarged upon his theme, his words always homely, his voice always sonorous, his burly figure like a tower of strength incarnate four-square to the world, he produced an immense and discernible impression on the throng of spectators crammed into the court.

The jury's response was more difficult to gauge, because juries, in the limelight's glare, try to be impassive. But at the afternoon's end, when he broke off his speech upon the bidding of the clock, Curtis Bennett had good cause for self-congratulation. There was reason to think he had made substantial headway. It was a Saturday, and all through the weekend recess it would be his words that were ringing in the jury's ears. He had done much to reverse the drift towards disaster, and he could confidently look forward to resuming on the Monday in a court altogether more cordially inclined.

It seems that this transformation had also struck the Bench, and that the Bench did not look upon the change with satisfaction. For, as counsel and solicitors were tying up their papers and the crowd was shuffling in readiness to move, Mr. Justice Shearman delivered a last word.

It is not uncommon for a judge to warn the jury against jumping to conclusions before hearing both sides. It is very uncommon—one would have liked to say, unheard of—for a judge to interject antagonistic comment in the middle of a closing speech by counsel for the prisoner.

Mrs. Thompson's evil star accorded her that judge.

"Members of the jury," said his lordship, "before the court rises for the day I wish to offer you this advice. Of course, you will not make up your minds until you have heard the whole case." (In fact, the evidence had long since been completed; all that remained before the jury's verdict was the Crown's reply and the judge's summing-up. If this piece of "advice" meant anything at all, it meant "Don't decide about Sir Henry's plea until you have heard Sir Thomas Inskip and me.") "The only other thing is, having regard to the surroundings for so many days, by all means look at the atmosphere and try to understand what the letters mean, but you should not forget that you are in a court of justice trying *a vulgar and common crime*."

In describing this amazing case as vulgar and common, Mr. Justice Shearman spoke for the profession he adorned. Curtis Bennett and those like him are rich and rare exceptions; rich in their humanity, rare in their comprehension. The representative lawyers, seeing no further than their notebooks, one after the other expressed agreement with the judge. "I ask you," said Inskip in his last speech to the jury, "to treat this as an *ordinary case*." "It is squalid and indecent," said the Lord Chief Justice later, presiding in the Court of Criminal Appeal. "It is essentially a *commonplace* and unedifying case."

These inane pronouncements, uttered in all solemnity by grown men, are a measure of the lawyers' incapacity to fathom the depths beneath the surface that they skim. They had missed or ignored the vital feature of the case—that it was highly unusual and possibly unique because of the character of the feminine protagonist. But the whole affair provoked their sour displeasure; it didn't fit inside a legal frame; it raised vast questions of sex and of psychology foreign to their experience and repugnant to their tastes. Because it was beyond them, they took refuge in aloofness; they branded it contemptuously as "ordinary" and "common."

Lawyers react thus to every manifestation of imaginative artistry or passionate desire. It is their sole defence. You can hear them crying "commonplace" after Beatrice and Dante, and stigmatising Héloïse as a vulgar little slut.

These legalistic preconceptions were painfully apparent in Mr. Justice Shearman's long and ill-phrased summing-up. He was bitterly hostile to Mrs. Thompson from the start. He dismissed her letters breezily as "gush," though if his own command of language had been comparable with hers he would not have dropped so often into slipshod imprecision. But his drift was plain enough. "It's a common or ordinary charge," he told the jury, "of a wife and an adulterer murdering her husband. . . . You are told that this is a case of a great love. Take one of the letters as a test." He took one and pointed out this solitary sentence: "He has the right by law to all that you have a right to by nature and by love." This had excited the judge's indignation. "If that means anything," he said, "it means that the love of a husband for his wife is something improper because marriage is acknowledged by the law and that the love of a woman for her lover, illicit and clandestine, is something great and noble."

That, needless to say, is not what it means at all. Mrs. Thompson was not *generalising* about love and marriage; she was writing particularly and solely of herself. In *her* life the only love that mattered was unlawful, but where does she suggest this is a universal rule?

Even fellow lawyers might be loath to defend this singular specimen of Mr. Justice Shearman's logic. But its author had no qualms, and the full force of his moral reprobation was visited on Mrs. Thompson's head. "I am certain," he said to the jury, "that you, like any other right-minded persons, will be filled with disgust at such a notion. Let us get rid of all that atmosphere and try this case in an ordinary, commonsense way."

Calls for "common sense," "plain common sense," "common sense principles," and "commonsense considerations" were repeated at intervals like ritualistic incantations. No one of course objects to common sense, but the judge's application of it was frequently bewildering. It was apparently common sense that made him warn the jury against Curtis Bennett's "flights of imagination" when imagination on the part of others was so sorely needed and so sadly lacking. It was apparently common sense that enabled him to see why "two people agreeing to murder don't make that agreement when anybody is listening," but prevented him from seeing the parallel presumption that they don't put their agreement into writing either. It was apparently common sense that made him speak of "this silly, but at the same time wicked, affection"; wicked possibly, but was silly the apt term for a passion so compelling that it drove a man to kill?

In any event, and contrary to popular belief, it is not every problem that common sense can solve. Some require uncommon sense, and Mrs. Thompson's case was essentially one of these. The jury should have received an impartial direction, free from irrelevant lectures upon ethics, and emphasising that their primary concern was to grasp the tendencies of Mrs. Thompson's mind. Instead they were fobbed off with a good many opinions that had been better unexpressed, a string of pious platitudes on sexual behaviour, and a total disregard of the question of psychology.

The result could be foreseen.

It may be said: you blame Inskip, who was subject to the judge; you blame the judge, who was subject to appeal; why not blame the jury, which was not subject to anything?

I do, but to a much smaller degree, for reasons which involve a short excursus upon juries. . . .

The twelve average people who occupy a jury box are, almost always, twelve frightened people too. They are little folk, leading little lives, scared of policemen and respectful to solicitors, who are suddenly called to responsibility and power. They are generally one-quarter proud, three-quarters apprehensive, and desperately anxious for guidance from the Law.

To them the Law is embodied in the judge. Counsel, with their wigs and gowns and sprucely starched white bands, inevitably take rank as superior beings, but they are identified with the fortunes of a side.

His lordship has a pure and godlike quality; placed physically and spiritually above the sordid strife, his lightest word reverberates around Mount Sinai.

It follows that, in the overwhelming majority of cases, juries follow the judge when he gives a definite lead. There are exceptions. Occasionally a judge will overdo it; he will espouse one party's cause so heatedly and fiercely that the jury find against him because they don't think it fair play. Even this happens only with a panel of strong jurors —or one strong juror who dominates the rest. For the most part judges get the verdicts that they want.

It is all the easier for a jury to accept the judge's promptings if these coincide with their own spontaneous instinct. And instinct in a jury is generally clear cut; it urges them to vindicate their corporate rectitude. They like to distribute penalties and rewards, and to uphold good morals as a by-product of verdicts.

There is one further element in the average jury's make-up; a propensity to condemn what they cannot understand. An unseen handicap rests upon a prisoner who in life or mind or habit appeals alien to themselves. They are more at home, and therefore more forebearing, with bookmakers and licensees than with prophets or with poets. . . .

It will be seen that Mrs. Thompson had the worst of every deal. The judge was against her; she was technically dissolute; her own counsel had described her as living "a sort of life I don't suppose any of you live." What chance had she against this combination of misfortunes?

For two hours and ten minutes the jury remained out, striving to do justice according to their lights.

Even when she cried out, "Oh God, I am not guilty," even when the judge assumed the black cap of her novels, even when she found herself receiving the sad privileges imposed on the condemned, Mrs. Thompson cannot have believed that she would die. Nor did a host of others. She had struck no blow; she had played no part; the intention of her letters was in strenuous dispute. A petition raised on her behalf was signed by many thousands and most people confidently expected a reprieve.

It never came. The legal system and its affiliated offices continued to react with a species of cold frenzy at Mrs. Thompson's name. No yielding to clamour; an example must be made.

And so it came about that the British Home Secretary, whose forerunners and successors have restored to society so many brutalised and violent murderers, turned a deaf ear to the plea of Edith Thompson and permitted her to hang for the glory of the law.

"We ourselves die and live in the books we read while we are reading them and then when we have finished, the books die and we live . . . until when . . . ? Who knows . . . ? We are not the shapers of our destinies."

The Thompson verdict is now recognised as bad, and the trial from which it sprang stands out as an example of the evils that may flow from an attitude of mind.

There was no failure of law; there was no failure of procedure; there was no failure to observe and abide by all the rules. It was from first to last a failure in human understanding; a failure to grasp and comprehend a personality not envisaged in the standard legal textbooks and driven by forces more powerful and eternal than those that are studied at the Inns of Court.

2

Steinie Morrison

WHAT should defending counsel do when he believes his
client is guilty?

Of all the problems that arise to plague a barrister, this one is surely
the most familiar. It is constantly debated by all kinds of people, just
as if Johnson hadn't settled it two centuries ago.

"What do you think," Boswell had asked him, "of supporting a cause
you know to be bad?"

"Sir," Johnson answered, "you do not know it is good or bad till the
judge determines it. It is his business to judge; and you are not to be
confident in your opinion that a cause is bad, but to say all you can
for your client and then hear the judge's opinion."

Read "jury" for "judge" in this admirable analysis and it can usefully
be extended to cover criminal trials. Let the advocate follow Johnson's
wise advice and the famous question is rapidly disposed of.

There is another problem, though, much knottier than this, which
is far less often made the subject of discussion. Suppose defending
counsel is convinced of his client's *innocence*. Suppose that, none the
less, he sees great risk of being found guilty. What should he do *then?*

The temptation is apparent: to depart from the beaten track of advocacy in frantic endeavour to procure means of escape. Such de-
partures are conceived in a spirit of self-sacrifice and counsel often
suffer for them grievously. Dr. Kenealy was formally disbarred for his
fanatical defence of the Tichborne Claimant. Marshall Hall's practice
was seriously damaged by the bluntness of his language when he
thought a judge unfair. And Edward Abinger, a lesser man than these
but able and sincere, raised up against himself a whirlwind of criticism
by his unorthodox defence of Steinie Morrison.

Steinie Morrison was brought up at the Old Bailey in March, 1911, and there charged with murdering Leon Beron, whose body, stripped of money and valuables, had been found on Clapham Common early on New Year's Day. He had been killed by a series of blows upon the head, and after death had been stabbed and cut about the face. A doctor who saw his body at nine o'clock that morning formed the view that Beron had then been dead six hours.

Legend soon grows around a classic crime, and Beron has been spoken of as rich and old. He was not old; he was forty-eight. He was not rich; his yearly income was but five and twenty pounds, derived from some small property. But notwithstanding this he always carried money on him; often there would be thirty sovereigns in his purse. He also sported a massive watch and chain which it was one of his foibles to show off to acquaintances.

Neither chain nor watch nor money was found upon his corpse.

Beron did not live near Clapham Common nor has it ever been discovered what induced him to go out there. He lodged with his brother near the Mile End Road and spent most of his time in a cheap Whitechapel eating-house. This place, the Warsaw Restaurant, forms an exceptionally outlandish patch in the fantastic background to the crime.

The Warsaw Restaurant served as a kind of club for the curious foreign colony to which Beron belonged. They came there early and they stayed there late; they ate, talked, sat about, dozed, meditated, quarrelled and then ate again. They may have gone to bed elsewhere, but for many of them the Warsaw Restaurant was home. Beron not least; for years it had been his habit to settle there each day at two o'clock and remain till about twelve.

In the last few weeks of 1910 one Steinie Morrison joined the corps of "regulars"; that is, he would call at the Warsaw nearly every day, though he limited his visits to more rational proportions. This Steinie was a striking, even fascinating figure; well-spoken, handsome and magnificently built. He must have looked out of his element in that bizarre assembly, as if Apollo at a fairground had strayed among the freaks.

What could there be in common between this dashing newcomer and the short, stumpy, eccentric little Beron? Perhaps opposites attracted or secret interests coalesced. At any rate the couple spent a lot of time together and they were often observed deep in private conversation during the last days of the dying year.

Beron, faithful to his custom, sat on at the Warsaw right through

New Year's Eve. He left only a few minutes before the bells rang in a year which was to grant him so short a breathing space.

He left, it was alleged, with Steinie Morrison. Some three hours later he was cruelly clubbed to death.

The results achieved by following this pointer provided the quintessence of the prosecution's charge.

Steinie's case sprang into instant notoriety as the "Riddle of the Scarlet S." This tag owed its origin to two of the slashes on the dead man's face which were spoken of as "S-shaped" by a doctor at the inquest. Many people took this rough description literally and indulged in the most wild and fanciful conjectures. Some thought they were the symbol of an anarchist society; some thought they stood for "spic," the Russian word for spy; some—and these were the most gullible of all—believed that the assassin had recorded his initial.

None of these theories was shared by Scotland Yard, nor did they cut much ice at the Old Bailey. "Anyone," said the presiding judge, "who sees the letter S in either of these scratches has either better eyes than I, or a more vivid imagination."

But there was no need of a scarlet S to make Steinie's trial dramatic. No case in the whole history of crime has worked up more feverish, uncontrolled excitement. Outside the court, in London's foreign quarter, witnesses were coaxed, threatened, drilled and even beaten by partisan groups owing warped allegiance either to Beron's family or the prisoner. At the Old Bailey itself, as day succeeded day, angry scene succeeded angry scene—between counsel and witness, between counsel and judge, between counsel and counsel. The tension, beginning at a morbid pitch, contrived uncannily to rise with every hour until at the end it grew almost beyond bearing. Wholly beyond bearing for one interested party. During Abinger's impassioned closing speech, Leon Beron's brother went clean out of his mind. Raving and gibbering, he hurled himself at counsel; he was dragged off, pinioned and taken from the court to permanent lodgment in a madhouse cell.

Such a shocking and sensational occurrence would have completely overshadowed any other case. In the trial of Steinie Morrison it was a passing incident.

On Monday, March 6th, the trial began. Mr. Justice Darling took his seat upon the bench; Steinie was put up in the dock. When asked to plead, he said, "My lord, if I were standing before the Almighty, I could give but one answer. I am not guilty."

The theatrical note was struck at once, and the curtain forthwith rose on a tumultuous drama that was to play to crowded houses for nine eventful days.

The two chief forensic actors were Abinger himself and Richard Muir. They fitted the popular conception of their rôles. Abinger, defending, was impulsive and emotional; Muir, for the Crown, was longheaded and case-hardened. A tough rock of a man who never spared himself or others, he had powers of endurance that seemed almost inexhaustible. He did not greatly care for kid-glove methods, and the case against Morrison was mercilessly pressed to the uttermost limits permitted by the law.

Muir's opening speech was characteristically thorough. It consisted in the main of solid narrative, occasionally seasoned with a comment strictly practical. He told how Steinie had become a friend of Beron's; how he had been seen examining Beron's watch; how on New Year's Eve he had turned up at the Warsaw with a long paper parcel which he said contained a flute; how a waiter who handled it thought it felt like an iron bar; how Steinie was familiar with the Clapham Common district; how straight after the murder he had deserted his old haunts; how he never again set foot inside the Warsaw; how he forsook his lodging in Newark Street, nearby, and went to share the room of a prostitute in Lambeth; how till the moment of the murder he had been hard up; how henceforward he was flush; how at a station cloakroom on New Year's morning he deposited a package containing a revolver ("anticipating arrest?" Muir slyly enquired); how exactly a week later, when Steinie *was* arrested, slight human bloodstains were detected on his shirt.

Thus was woven a fine web of suspicion. But all was subsidiary to Muir's main contention—that from midnight Steinie had been Beron's sole companion and was with him at Clapham Common shortly before three. The prosecutor was emphatic here; slowly and impressively he dealt his strongest cards. It would be proved, he said, that from midnight onwards the pair had walked together in the streets of the East End. It would be proved that at two o'clock they took a cab to Clapham, alighting by the Common about twenty to three. It would be proved that at three fifteen a cab was hailed at Clapham by a man who gave the driver the vague direction "Kennington." That man, Muir said, was Steinie, and he was alone.

This time-table was the real crux of the case. It depended on two separate groups of witnesses. The first consisted of Whitechapel inhabitants who had previously known Beron, or Morrison, or both. The second consisted of the cab drivers concerned, whose fares were naturally unknown to them at the time, but who claimed to have subsequently identified Steinie when given the opportunity at a police station parade.

These witnesses were bound to be of paramount importance. If their evidence in the box lived up to Muir's opening, Steinie's chances would look very slim indeed.

The formal and semi-formal witnesses had departed; the plans had been produced and the photographs received; now the Crown called for Solomon Beron and the temperature embarked on its uninterrupted rise.

The dead man's brother typified those unassimilated aliens for whom the Warsaw Restaurant was the centre of the world. He might almost have been peering out from that esoteric spot; puzzled, hostile, infinitely suspicious. He didn't like the methods of this damfool country; they let Steinie kill his brother and then allowed him a defence.

Solomon's mental instability was immediately apparent. Prosecuting counsel found him difficult to manage while he gave some simple evidence about his brother's habits. When Abinger got up to cross-examine, the witness did not trouble to conceal his rage.

"Did you describe yourself," he was asked, "as an independent gentleman?"

"Yes."

"Are you living in a Rowton House at sevenpence a night?"

Beron went up in smoke.

"What has that to do with the case?" Anger made his foreign accent even more pronounced. "What has that to do with the crime? If you ask me impudent questions I will not answer you."

"Did anybody help the deceased man with his rent?"

"You go and ask him. I cannot tell you. If you ask me silly questions I will give you no answer."

Abinger ran his eye over the independent gentleman who lived at Rowton House. Solomon Beron was tidy, almost smart, in a big dark overcoat with a velvet collar.

"You look very nicely dressed. Where did those clothes come from?"

In studying these questions, it is not easy to perceive what useful object Abinger had in view. Solomon Beron's evidence did not implicate the prisoner and there was little to be gained by an attack upon his credit.

If it was meant merely to goad him, it succeeded. The witness was now almost beside himself with fury.

"Very well," he shouted. "You want to know where these clothes came from? I am not going to tell you." Then as Mr. Justice Darling stirred slightly, he added, "If the judge asks me I will tell you."

"You must answer the question," said the judge quietly.

Beron bowed to this ruling, but he would not deal with Abinger. He addressed himself directly to the judge.

"If I must answer the question you may tell him that I have brought over to London about one hundred pounds that I have saved in Paris from my business."

Mr. Justice Darling preserved impassive silence. Abinger continued. He had one important point that it was necessary to put—and which might, with profit, have been put earlier. It was to be part of the defence that the witnesses from the Warsaw, prompted by a kind of tribal loyalty to Beron, had in concert shaped their evidence to ensure he was avenged.

This suggestion received the usual warm reception.

"I do not take any interest in it," Solomon Beron stormed. "It has nothing to do with this case. Do not put me so many questions or I will go out from here."

But Abinger persisted.

"How many hours each day do you pass at the Warsaw?"

"All the time I got."

"What time do you get there?"

"About one o'clock. I do not spend all the time."

"Where else do you spend your time?"

"I go nowhere else."

"Nowhere else?"

"Only to my business."

"What business?"

This pressure upon his rocking mind was more than Solomon Beron could endure.

"I go to my solicitors," he yelled. "What are you laughing at? I cannot see the joke. What are you laughing at?"

The veins bulged from his forehead; frenzy was consuming him like fire. When presently he stumbled from the box, the temper of the trial had been irrevocably set.

Let us pause a moment and take stock of the position as the defence would see it at the end of the first day.

In a long trial—as Steinie's was clearly bound to be—this is often the crucial moment for planning defence strategy. The Crown case has been revealed. Its strength and weakness can be approximately assessed. With tolerable certitude, the prisoner's advocate can chart his future course.

Abinger had thrown himself into the fight for Steinie with all the ardour of his generous nature. That first evening, one may be absolutely sure, he spent many hours in hard and anxious thought.

His main task stood out. If he was to have any chance of gaining an acquittal, he must smash the Crown's story of Steinie's New Year's night. He must break that chain of evidence which linked his client so damningly with the time, the place and the victim of the murder. In other words, he must satisfy the jury that some or all those witnesses ought not to be believed.

Under the strict but beneficent rules of British legal practice there is more than one method of inducing disbelief. You may seek to show mistake; this was the obvious way of handling the cab drivers who claimed to recognise a stranger they had only once set eyes on, and that in the doubtful darkness of the night. You may seek to show lying; something of that kind had already been foreshadowed in the questions put by Abinger to Beron. And you may seek to establish the witness's bad character; to show that he is a person of such dubious morality that his sworn statement is unworthy of belief. Any jury will think again and yet again before convicting on the word of a blackmailer or thief.

The attack upon character, appropriately used, gives the defender an invaluable weapon. But it is a weapon capable of boomerang effect. If it is used by the defence against a witness for the Crown, it may be used by the Crown against the prisoner himself. The latter thus forfeits his right to be protected against any mention of his "record" or his "past."

Of course, if you have neither a "record" nor a "past," this is of no consequence; you may make attacks on character with comparative impunity. But Abinger's client was not in that happy position.

The handsome Steinie, impressing all beholders by his dignity of bearing, was a convict by status and a burglar by trade.

To attack or not?

Here was a grave decision, perhaps the gravest in the case, and it must be made that night. For Abinger had reason to suppose that the Crown was not invulnerable on the score of character, and that the chance of proving this would be offered him next day. But if he took that chance, if he made character an issue, he would make Steinie liable to similar attack.

It is easy to criticise in subsequent detachment, far from the arena's dust and heat. None the less, one cannot help expressing the opinion that in Steinie's case it was unwise to take the risk.

Abinger thought differently. He had already discussed the matter with his client, who had approved, maybe even instigated, the adoption of bold tactics. But counsel of experience advise their clients; they are not advised by them. Abinger would have been the last to deny that in the ultimate resort the decision was his own.

He decided to attack.

Next morning the first witness was Joe Mintz. He was the waiter from the Warsaw Restaurant who had thought Steinie's parcel much too heavy for a flute.

"Have you ever tried to hang yourself?" Abinger asked him.

"That has nothing to do with the case," the witness snapped. (Frequenters of the Warsaw seemed curiously prone to *ex cathedra* pronouncements upon relevance.)

"But is it true?"

"It is true, but it has got nothing to do with the case."

"And did you afterwards go to Colney Hatch Asylum?"

"Yes, I have been there."

At this point Mr. Justice Darling intervened.

"I suppose you realise, Mr. Abinger, that suicide is a felony and that you are asking this man whether he attempted a felony?"

"If you lordship thinks I should not pursue this—" Abinger began.

The judge was quick with a correction.

"I am not saying you should not pursue it, Mr. Abinger. I did not quite know whether you knew what it might lead to."

Darling was in fact making absolutely sure that Abinger did not expose his client to unnecessary danger through mere forgetfulness or misreading of the rules. In effect, the judge was offering a reminder: if you attack character, you in turn will be attacked.

Whether these questions to Mintz really constituted an attack on character in the strictly legal sense is a question that will always be open to debate. The judge apparently considered that they did. But Abinger maintained, with some plausibility, that he was not seeking to impute an offence but to establish that Mintz was mentally deranged.

The point, to say the least of it, was arguable. Before the end of the day, though, it had become academic. An attack by Abinger upon one Mrs. Deitch put the Mintz affair completely in the shade.

Mrs. Deitch's evidence was awkward for the prisoner. She swore she had seen him in Whitechapel with Beron on New Year's morning between one and two o'clock. That came uncomfortably close to the time when they were supposed to have set off for Clapham in a cab.

Mrs. Deitch had had a rough passage at the police court. Rightly anticipating a similar ordeal, she had worked herself up into a fine state of resentment. If Abinger was lying in wait for her, Mrs. Deitch was equally lying in wait for him.

There were no preliminaries; no smooth approaches, no subtle skirting round. Both parties got to grips at once like a pair of fighting cocks.

"What is your husband?" was Abinger's first question.

"He is a gas-fitter."

"And what are you?"

The path to insolence lay wide open. Mrs. Deitch was in no mood to reject it.

"What am I? I am a woman of course."

"I can see that," said Abinger, "but what is your occupation?"

"That is a fine question to ask me," Mrs. Deitch exclaimed, with what must have seemed, at that moment, excessive sensitivity. "I am at home in the house, looking after my children."

"Do you know a woman named Lizzie Holmes?"

"No."

"You pledge your oath she did not live in your house?"

"I have never had any girls living in my house."

"Didn't Lizzie Holmes have a room with you for which she paid you three shillings a week?"

"No."

Then they came—the questions intended to encompass the rout of Mrs. Deitch, but which carried in their train the destruction of another.

"Used she to take men in?"

"No such thing."

"Did they not sleep with her, or stay a short time?"

"Never."

"Did she not pay you three shillings for every man that stopped all night?"

"That is an untruth."

"And a shilling for every man that stopped a short time?"

"I never heard of such a thing."

"Where did you get that fur from?"

"That is my business."

"Tell us, please."

Mrs. Deitch now gave way to that uninhibited rage which was the sign manual of actors in this extraordinary trial.

"Why should I tell you?" She spat the words at Abinger. "You insulted me last time, but you will not insult me today. You asked me last time where I got my fur from. My husband bought it, what he worked for. I do not ask you where your wife got her fur from."

Abinger prudently ignored this impudent ripost. He continued, however, to press for information about this Lizzie Holmes. Hadn't she followed Mrs. Deitch from one house to another? Hadn't Mrs. Deitch sent for her? Wasn't there a specific occasion in March of last year when Lizzie had "gone with a man" and Mrs. Deitch had got ten shillings? All of which gave rise to further vehement denials.

When the string of questions at last came to an end, the judge enquired if Lizzie Holmes was present. She was not.

"I expect her here tomorrow," said Mr. Justice Darling, "and this witness shall be here also."

Abinger did better than had been desired. When the court resumed next day, not only Lizzie Holmes but four other harlots lined up before the box. Each in turn confronted Mrs. Deitch; each in turn was flatly disavowed. The girls shouted "Liar," Mrs. Deitch shouted back, and the episode was suspended on this inconclusive note.

So far the comic element was uppermost. But the seeds of tragedy had been already sowed.

The jury's view of Mrs. Deitch can only be conjectured. They may have thought she was a back-street procuress; they may have thought she was a lady wickedly traduced. But from Steinie's standpoint, the sole test was this: were they now any less likely to believe that she had seen him with Beron where and when she said? It was the breaking of the Crown's time-table that mattered, not whether people kept a stew or tried to hang themselves.

Unhappily the uproar raised over the latter tended to obscure Abinger's march towards the former. In between the angry scenes, all through the second day, he had been quietly displacing various props of Muir's case.

Mrs. Deitch herself had conceded a point which, unlike her morals, was of primary concern. She still insisted she had seen Leon Beron with the prisoner, but, under Abinger's cross-examination, was given to declare she had been mistaken in the time. She fixed it now at two fifteen; a quarter of an hour after—on the prosecution's showing—Steinie and Beron left for Clapham in the cab.

This was a very valuable advance and gained without running any countervailing risk.

Then there was Weissberg, who swore he had seen Steinie walking with Beron at about twelve forty-five. Abinger ascertained that this witness had had supper at the Warsaw, that he had left there shortly after eight in company with one Zaltsman, and that they were still together shortly before one. Asked to recount their movements in the interval, Weissberg could only say that they had "walked about."

"You must have been getting rather weary," Abinger suggested.

"I met a girl friend," replied Weissberg, as though this had kept him going, "and I had a conversation with her."

"So the three of you walked about—you and Zaltsman and the girl?"

"The girl left us about eleven."

"Then did you and Zaltsman go on walking until a quarter to one?"

"Yes."

"Where?"

"Backwards and forwards, from Aldgate to Mile End."

"How many times?"

"Five or six or more."

"You would then be getting *very* tired," remarked Abinger with sarcasm.

"Yes, we got very tired," said the witness innocently.

Weissberg's story now sounded ludicrous. But Abinger's full triumph was only consummated when Zaltsman followed his friend into the box. As witnesses were kept out of court until they gave their testimony, Zaltsman of course knew nothing of what had just transpired.

He repeated the tale of the protracted, pointless walk, and then once again it was Abinger's turn.

"Did you meet anybody," he asked, "besides Morrison and Beron?"

"No."

"Think carefully whether you did not meet someone else and walk with someone else."

Did the witness then half guess and did he try a sporting shot? At any rate he permitted his memory to be jogged.

"Oh, yes, someone else walked with us, but I do not know *him* by name."

Abinger was expressionless.

"Anybody else besides that *man?*"

"Nobody else spoke to us besides that man."

Abinger sat down. When Muir, re-examining, put a leading question ("Did you have any conversation with a *woman?*") Abinger objected, and the judge rightly forbade this attempt to reconstitute a broken-down position. Messrs. Weissberg and Zaltsman had been settled for good by the invisible girl friend and the five-hour promenade.

The first part of the time-table was looking somewhat shaky. It had seemed far more convincing on the lips of Mr. Muir.

If this had been a normal case, conventionally conducted, the deciding factor would have been the evidence of the cabmen. Even amid the schoals of red herrings and the hysterical spasms that marked Steinie's trial, it was obvious that a great deal must depend on Abinger's handling of these key witnesses.

In a sense, of course, their evidence was only indirect. But indirect evidence can be powerfully persuasive. If the jury took these men at their face value; if they thought them neither dishonest nor mistaken; if they believed in the drives to and from Clapham and that Beron and Steinie were the passengers concerned—then one would surely plead with them in vain to look upon it all as pure coincidence. Juries are seldom scholastic logicians; they deal in probabilities, not absolutes.

In one respect, the cabmen lay wide open to attack. Recognising someone at the time is one thing; *identifying* someone subsequently is another, especially when a substantial period had elapsed. If you say "I saw so-and-so whom I *know*," the room for error there is infinitesimally small. If you say, "This is a stranger whom I saw on one occasion," the room for error there is almost without limit. And this was what, in sum, the cab drivers were saying when they picked out Steinie at the police station parade.

The whole technique of parades has been justly criticised, though it is hard to see what method could be adopted in its stead. It certainly offers opportunities for abuse; the long halt, the lifted eyebrow, the hand-picked crowd from which the wretched suspect unwillingly stands out. But deliberate rigging is exceptional; as a rule, no doubt, every effort is made to be fair. There are, however, certain defects which are inherent in the system. The more distinguished-looking your suspect, the less easy to place him with men reasonably alike. The less contrasted your full line-up, the more encouragement to guesswork. And—worst of all—if a case has already had considerable publicity, the witness may no longer be identifying a *person;* he may merely identify the source of a description or the original of a photograph.

Abinger seized upon this latter point when he came to cross-examine Hayman. Hayman was the first of the Crown's cab drivers and, in lawyers' jargon, he came right up to proof. On New Year's night he had been in Mile End with his hansom; he had been hailed and engaged by two men; he had set them down, on their request, at Clapham; one of the men was short—not more than five foot five; the other he had since picked out as the accused.

"And when did you first go to the police?" Abinger asked.

"About a week afterwards—either the 9th or 10th."

"Before you went to the police, did you see the *Evening News* of the 9th, with a description of Morrison?"

"No."

"If you didn't see it, why had you not been to the police on the 2nd, 3rd, 4th, 5th, 6th, 7th or 8th?"

"Well, I went to the station as soon as I could."

"Why did you not go before the 9th?"

"I don't know."

Abinger held up a police notice.

"This is dated the 6th January. Did you see it?"

"It was down in the cab yard."

"Then if you saw this police notice, offering a reward to cabmen, why did you not go to the station till the 9th or 10th?"

"I went when I thought proper."

"Why did you not go before?"

Hayman was now at the end of his excuses.

"I can't give you a reason," he said.

"When were you taken to identify the man?"

"On the 17th."

"Had you seen portraits of the accused in the newspapers before you went to identify him?"

"Yes."

This was an unqualified success for the defence. It seemed possible, if not probable, that Hayman had relied less on a genuine recollection of this fare than on what he had seen in the press and on posters.

The second cabman, Stephens, made a similar admission; he had seen a portrait before going to the police. But this fact was overshadowed by a further, new development, which Abinger exploited with admirable skill.

For the Crown to gain its purpose, the cabmen's times must dove-
tail, as they had done so perfectly in Muir's opening speech. Hayman
in the witness box had spoken, as forecast, of leaving Mile End at two
and reaching Clapham at two forty. Stephens now took up the tale:
he had been with his cab at Clapham Cross, where he was hired by
the supposed Steinie at twelve minutes past three. This conveniently
ear-marked half an hour for carrying out the murder and any accessories thereto.

Abinger had a document passed up to this witness. Stephens looked
at it without enthusiasm.

"Is that the statement you made to the police on January 10th?"

"Yes."

"I am going to read it."

The first few sentences were merely introductory; Abinger rattled
them off as one in duty bound. Soon, though, he went slower, glancing
up at times, giving each word due emphasis and weight.

" 'I remained on the rank until just before *half past two*, when a
man alone came from the direction of the Old Town, Clapham. He
said "Kennington" and then got in the cab. I have seen a photograph
of Steinie Morrison and identify him as being that man.' "

Abinger laid the paper down deliberately.

"So you told the police that you picked this man up at half past
two?"

"I told the police I was not sure of the time, but it was about one
hour after the last tram. The police asked me the time of the last tram
and I said it was about half past one."

"You know, don't you, that if your statement is true, that you picked
up the man at half past two, Hayman's evidence cannot be true, because according to that he would be in Hayman's cab at that
time?"

The form of this question left out of account the possibility that they
had carried two entirely different men. But here Abinger was tactically
justified; in dealing with juries, one point at a time.

"According to Hayman, at half past two the man would be in Hayman's cab, wouldn't he?"

"I don't know."

Certainly a strange picture was evolving—a picture of Steinie, in
one case accompanied, in the other case alone, travelling simultane-
ously in opposite directions.

Abinger now had Stephens with his back to the wall. The final blows
were swiftly delivered.

"Do you tell the jury that you do not know that Hayman has sworn that Morrison was in his cab at half past two?"

"I do not know."

"Have you spoken to Hayman?"

"Yes."

"I suggest that you altered your time to twelve minutes past three because that fits in with Hayman's time?"

"If it had been true," said Stephens, "I should have stuck to my time. I went to the tramway company and made enquiries about the last tram and on their statement I went to the police and altered the time."

What prompted Stephens to make these enquiries never came to light. He was suffered to withdraw, greatly the worse for wear. His story was not disproved, but, in the strictest sense, discredited. People often try to fix times by events and afterwards discover themselves wrong. But in Stephens's case the adjustment was a shade too providential for a jury to rely on when a man's life was at stake.

By theatrical canons, here should end the chronicle of the cabmen. But for the record, one must perforce make mention of a third, who thought he had picked Steinie up at half past three in Kennington, and driven him with another man to Seven Sisters Road. He was examined and cross-examined with as much care and solemnity as if nothing had gone wrong with this integrated sequence.

The courts, which so often produce orgasms of drama, are not concerned to avoid an occasional anti-climax.

The feeling of deflation, however, was short-lived. Battle was joined again on a harmless-looking matter: the evidence of the prisoner's capture and arrest.

Steinie was arrested by Inspector Frederick Wensley, who was destined to scale the topmost peak of his profession and become the first Chief Constable of Britain's C.I.D. He was a square, stern man with a burning sense of mission; as a Templar fought the Saracens so he fought the world of crime. He had fallen upon Steinie on January 8th at a coffee-house in Fieldgate Street as the latter sat at breakfast. "I said: 'I want you, Steinie,'" Wensley told the court. "I told him he would be detained, but I did not charge him with murder. I did not mention Beron or the murder in his hearing." Needless to say, the Inspector was corroborated *in toto* by every officer who had been personally involved. Nor, it was affirmed, either *en route* or at the station, had any other person enlightened the accused. He was apparently left to infer, if he so chose, that he was being taken in as a convict upon licence who had failed to notify a change in his address.

The significance of this presently unfolded. Shortly after Steinie had been shut up in his cell, he asked to see Wensley so that he might make a statement. "You have accused me of murder—" Steinie began. "No," Wensley interrupted, "I have done nothing of the kind."

Muir attached great importance to this matter as tending to reveal the prisoner's guilty knowledge. When Wensley himself came into the box, Abinger challenged his account of the arrest, suggesting that he had really said, "I want you *for murder*." Wensley insisted that his version was correct.

A lively exchange followed.

"Do you pledge your oath that you did not arrest him on suspicion of having committed murder?"

"Certainly."

"On the date of Morrison's arrest had the police received no statement or information connecting him with this murder?"

"No."

"When did Mrs. Deitch make her statement?"

"I think it was on January 2nd."

"Do you say that Mrs. Deitch's statement does not connect Morrison with this murder?"

"Not beyond the description."

"When did Castlin [the third cab driver] make his statement?"

"On January 4th."

"After Castlin's statement did you not connect Morrison with this murder?"

"I did not connect him with the murder till he was identified."

"Let me show you a copy of the *Daily Graphic* of January 9th. Do you see a photograph of the restaurant where Morrison was arrested?"

"I do."

"If you did not mention at that restaurant that you were arresting Morrison for murder, how could that photograph have got into the paper the next day?"

It was a very, very awkward question. Wensley had no decisive answer.

"I don't know," he said. "It might have got there by many means."

This passage shows Abinger at his best: acute, tenacious, rigorously germane, equally in command of the situation and himself. Nobody hearing it could possibly feel confident that, somehow or somewhere, the word "murder" wasn't used.

At this stage neither side could carry the point further. It was to flare up again several days later in the shape of an unlooked for and last-minute sensation.

Halfway through the fourth day the Crown case was closed and Abinger opened Steinie Morrison's defence.

The official halfway mark and turning point is sometimes followed by a change in atmosphere that puzzles and disturbs the lay observer. So far, he argues, we have heard what can be said *against* this man; now we are going to hear what can be said *for* him. So any change henceforth should operate, not to the prisoner's hurt, but in his favour.

This reasoning ignores two cognate factors: the power disposed by cross-examination and the pattern traced by every English trial. The Crown evidence offers defence counsel an Aunt Sally, and rare is the case where he does not in some degree diminish the effect of the prosecutor's opening. During this phase, indeed, it is the defender who attacks and the prosecutor who defends.

But with the transfer of the bidding, the position is reversed. It is the defence's evidence that offers an Aunt Sally. It is the prisoner and his witnesses who come under raking fire. It is the prosecutor who gets the opportunity to whittle away the fabric set up by his opponent.

The more substantive and positive the defence's case, the greater the risk of undoing and disaster.

No defence could be more substantive than an alibi. It was in part upon an alibi that Abinger relied. Departing from the usual order of events, he called the witnesses on this issue before Morrison himself.

The first two were a Mr. and Mrs. Zimmerman, with whom Steinie had been lodging in Newark Street, Mile End. Both swore that on New Year's Eve he had come home about midnight, taken the key of his own room and then retired to bed. Both swore that he was in the house when they got up next morning and the woman said his bed appeared to have been slept in. Both swore that the street door had been bolted for the night, that the bolt was stiff and exceptionally noisy, that they slept lightly and would have heard if the bolt had been withdrawn.

The Zimmermans were not without material support: a reputable surveyor said the bolt "shrieked terrifically," and a next door neighbour spoke of seeing Steinie arrive home.

Muir questioned these people without notable success. The surveyor's evidence was virtually unchallengeable, and there seemed no ground for disbelieving the assertions of the others that they had seen Steinie Morrison as and when they said. But the inference that he stayed home all night depended on two assumptions: (1) that otherwise he must have opened the street door, (2) that the bolt was an infallible alarm. Perhaps Steinie (who had a ground floor room) made a doorway of his window. Perhaps Mr. and Mrs. Zimmerman slept sounder than they knew.

What may conveniently be called the Zimmerman evidence was not, therefore, conclusive. So far as it went, though, it assisted Steinie's case; nothing was lost by calling it and perhaps a little gained. The same cannot be said of the evidence of the Brodskys.

One wonders why Abinger ever called these two young sisters. They had nothing to say that was really to the point. They claimed to have gone on New Year's Eve to a show at the Shoreditch Empire, where they saw Steinie Morrison sitting near them in the stalls. They did not speak to him, as at that time they only just knew him by sight.

Supposing they were believed, what then? Would Steinie's cause be in any way advanced? They would have fixed his whereabouts from nine until eleven—four hours before the murder was committed. They would have made liars of the habitués from the Warsaw who said that Steinie spent the evening in their midst. They would have confirmed a part—an inessential part—of the story that Steinie was presently to tell. But what bearing could the Shoreditch Empire have upon the vital hours after twelve?

If, on the other hand, the girls were *not* believed, better by far that they had never come to court. A false witness—who is for this purpose one so deemed by the jury—blackens the prisoner on whose behalf he speaks.

Even a genuine alibi is difficult to prove, and often provides a field day for a clever cross-examiner. Muir had had an unexpected rebuff with the Zimmermans, but he was soon making headway with the Misses Brodsky.

A single devastating question and reply wiped the elder sister completely off the map.

"Can you tell me," Muir enquired, "any single item in the programme which you saw?"

"No," Miss Brodsky said.

But Muir's real duel was with the younger sister, Jane. She was only sixteen, but mature for her years and she stood up for herself with energy and spirit. She expressed her "certainty" that Steinie was the man who had sat in the same row at the show on New Year's Eve. She did something to repair her sister's swift collapse by recalling in detail at least one turn on the bill ("Harry Champion; he was the favourite; he comes on with a ginger wig and sings 'Ginger, you're barmy'"). She spoke with indignation of the attentions of the police ("They fetched me to the station four or five times; I've signed three different statements on three different occasions").

When Muir began to cross-examine Jane, he used this as the basis for a neat counter-attack.

"Did you ever at any of these interviews," he asked, "tell the police you had seen Morrison in the Shoreditch Empire on New Year's Eve?"

"No."

"Why not?"

"Because I was angry at the time and would not answer any questions."

"What were you angry about?"

"The people in the street were talking of policemen coming to my door. I asked them several times not to, but they went on doing it."

"You told the police that you had seen Morrison on January 2nd."

"Yes."

"Also at the Shoreditch Empire?"

"Yes."

"Why did you keep back from them that you had seen him sitting in the same row of stalls on New Year's Eve?"

"They did not ask me the question, and I did not answer them."

Jane was hitting back, but she was now on the defensive. Muir, moreover, had reserves of ammunition. Piece by piece he used it to draw damaging admissions—that Jane had lately become closely linked with Steinie, that she had frequently visited him in Brixton Prison, that he had asked her to marry him, that she had told him she "would see." It could hardly be maintained in face of this that Jane was altogether free from partiality.

To deliver his *coup de grâce*, Muir had both the girls recalled for questioning "on a point on which I have just received information."

They had sworn that they had paid a shilling each for seats. They swore it again and would not be dissuaded.

"I suggest," Muir said to Jane, "that on New Year's Eve the price for stalls was raised to one and six."

"I do not know that."

"And that well before nine o'clock, when you say that you arrived, there were people standing and there were no seats in the house?"

"People may have been standing," Jane responded doughtily, "but I got two vacant seats."

In due course Muir produced the theatre manager, who confirmed upon oath that his suggestions were well founded.

The Brodskys, it may be taken, did not impress the jury. It is absolutely certain that they did not impress the judge. After counsel had finished, Mr. Justice Darling questioned Jane, and he made a scathing reference to them in his summing-up. "You may come to the conclusion that this is a fabricated alibi, sworn to falsely by the Brodskys." He added, though, this caution. "The fact that a man calls a false alibi does not by a long way prove that he is guilty. Is it not very common among people of certain classes and certain nationalities if they have got a good case not to rest on that good case? If you have ever talked to anybody who has administered justice in India, you will know that. If you come to the conclusion that this alibi is false, you should not judge it as strictly against the prisoner as if it had been produced by an Englishman."

Despite the overtones of sententious insularity, the warning was a wise and fair one. It is questionable, though, whether the jury paid regard once they had heard the words "fabricated alibi." . . .

If the Shoreditch Empire alibi had been successfully established, its effect upon the case would have been comparatively small. Since it had ignominiously broken down, its effect on the case was likely to be great.

This kind of paradox is familiar in the courts.

In the late afternoon of the fifth day of his trial, Steinie Morrison went into the box. He remained there the rest of that day, the whole of the day after, and most of the morning of the day after that. For more than half of this time he was being cross-examined with a severity rare among twentieth-century prosecutors.

First, however, Steinie placed on record his own story. During December, he said, he had been travelling in jewellery, mostly around the Jewish area of Whitechapel. He made a number of sales which brought him a small return, and during the same period had profited by two windfalls: £20 from his mother in Russia, and £35 from a lucky faro game. So far as he was "flush" at all, here was the reason why—and the flush condition dated back some weeks before New Year.

As to the 31st December, that was simple. He had called in at the

Warsaw about eight o'clock that night and left a flute that he had bought during the day. From the Warsaw he went on to the Shoreditch Empire, where he sat—just as the Brodskys said—in the stalls, alone. After the performance he returned to the Warsaw, where he collected his flute and had some refreshment. He left there before twelve, and on his way home saw Beron standing with a tall man in the street. Beron had called out to him in greeting: Steinie had responded. Then he had made tracks for his lodging and his bed.

Next day? Oh yes—why should he deny it?—Steinie had suddenly uprooted his home. It was an *affaire de cœur,* if you care to call it so; more crudely, an arrangement with a woman of the town. It was to go to her he left the sympathetic Zimmermans. It was to spare her feelings he got rid of the revolver. (The woman herself had already been called to substantiate at least the first of these assertions.)

And the days following? Steinie strongly contested the charge that he had flown. He had gone about his business every day in the East End; he had eaten at restaurants in his usual neighbourhood; why, Wensley had arrested him a stone's throw from the Warsaw. True, he had given the latter place the go-by, but that was because on New Year's Eve he had had words with Joe Mintz. ("Are you trying to hang yourself again?" Steinie had shouted, and Mintz had darkly threatened "to get it out of him." "I believe," Steinie said, "he is getting it out of me now.")

In Steinie's story, certain things were hard to swallow. The flute (even though one was produced in court); the money (even though there was some play with receipts); the revolver (even though his tenderness with women was established). It all *might* have been true, but it had an unreal air—like Stephens' excuse for altering the time.

A tradition has gradually grown up in England—where persons are held innocent until guilt is proved—that a prisoner, especially on a capital charge, should not be browbeaten or harried in the box. This need not make his cross-examination ineffective. Sir Patrick Hastings, in his questioning of Vaquier, showed how a great advocate can be a deadly prosecutor without aping the methods of a petty sessions despot.

No one should underrate Muir's array of gifts: his shrewdness, his integrity, his mastery of detail. But he belonged, by legal upbringing and nature, to what is now affectionately termed "the old school." Defending or prosecuting, it made no difference to Muir; he went all out for the triumph of his side. Steinie's case, with its partisan setting and its personal antagonisms, can only have served to accentuate this tendency.

When they faced each other in the crowded court, the burglar with the clean-cut profile and the lawyer with the granite face and heavy jowls, there was no hint of quarter being given or received. It was to be, in the dreadful literal sense, a battle to the death.

Muir did not play at once the ace that Abinger had thrust into his hand. He began instead with an enquiry, grim, harsh and undisguisedly hostile, into the sources from which Steinie's money came. What date was the game of faro? December 1st. Had Steinie ever been to that gaming-house before? Yes, once. Had he any witness who would say he won that money? Yes, the croupier. Had he any witness?

"I can give you the name of the croupier," Steinie said.

"Have you any witness?"

This was the third time of asking, as the tone implied.

"I tell you," Steinie repeated, "I can give you the name of the croupier."

"Answer my question," Muir rapped out sharply.

"He is trying to answer it," Mr. Justice Darling said. "He says he can give you the name of the croupier."

It is happily seldom that judges have to protect a prisoner in this fashion.

Muir went on with his research into Morrison's finances. Had he the letter that accompanied the money from his mother? It had been destroyed. How much had he made each week selling jewellery? £2 or £2 10s. Might Muir call his attention to the large sum he had spent on personal purchases on one particular day?

The implications were still half veiled, but growing clearer every moment. The crisis was at hand.

Abinger stood up.

"May I ask my friend to what issue this cross-examination is directed?"

"Yes," said Muir, "to the issue whether he was, on January 1st, in possession of the proceeds of the robbery of Beron."

"Ah!" Abinger exclaimed. "Then that is directed to the credit of the witness and I object to it."

The judge was patently—and understandably—surprised.

"You object, Mr. Abinger? On what ground?"

"On the ground that such questions can only be put to a prisoner if the prisoner or his advocate have brought themselves within the provisions of Section One of the Criminal Evidence Act 1898. May I remind your lordship of those provisions?"

"I know them quite well," Mr. Justice Darling said. "Have you forgotten your cross-examination of Mrs. Deitch?"

"I have forgotten nothing," said Abinger stubbornly.

"But did you not impute to Mrs. Deitch that she kept a brothel?"

"Will your lordship allow me to deal with this in order? It is a most serious matter. I respectfully call your lordship's attention to the language of the Section." Abinger began to read it while the judge waited with what patience he could muster. " 'The prisoner shall not be asked any questions tending to show that he has committed any offence other than that wherewith he is charged or that he has a bad character *unless* the conduct of the defence is such as to involve imputations on the character of witnesses for the prosecution.' "

"Well?" Mr. Justice Darling said.

Abinger now developed an extraordinary argument. At the police court two persons who had given evidence for the Crown later withdrew their statements and said they were untrue. Neither was called by Muir at the Old Bailey. This was a proper and fruitful theme for comment, but Abinger went further; he tried to make it the basis for a justification of his attack on Mrs. Deitch. "When a man is being tried for his life," he said, "and it has been established that two witnesses who have given deadly evidence against him have stated that which is untrue, is his counsel to stand mute when a woman who may be of immoral character gives evidence against him?"

"No, he is not bound to stand mute," Mr. Justice Darling said, "but if he puts questions that come within the Criminal Evidence Act, he takes the consequences."

Abinger was labouring under considerable stress. The all-important battle was being lost; gathering round Steinie were the lowering shades of doom. "It would be barbaric cruelty," Abinger cried, "if a man on trial for his life is to have to stand mute by his counsel while a person of the most infamous character gives evidence against him, and if his counsel dares—"

The judge cut into his outburst.

"Please do not address me, Mr. Abinger, in such rhetorical terms. I am bound by the Act of Parliament, and I am not to consider whether it is barbaric or otherwise. If it is within the Act, I shall allow the cross-examination. If it is outside the Act, I shall reject it."

This logic was unanswerable. Abinger struggled on a little longer.

He urged the judge to "exercise a discretion" (for which the Act does not provide) and talked vaguely about the prisoner "having his whole life ransacked." Then, in some distress, he resumed his seat.

The judge did not call on Muir to argue. He briefly summarised the law, and said that there could be no graver imputation on a woman than that which Abinger had made on Mrs. Deitch. "Therefore it seems to me that the conduct of the defence has been such as to involve imputations on the character, certainly of Mrs. Deitch, and I think also of Mintz—but I give the go-by to that: I found my decision on the imputation on the character of Mrs. Deitch. The consequence is that the prisoner may be cross-examined like any other witness. His privileged position has been lost; the matter is now at large."

The floodgates were opened; the questions poured through.

"Were you first convicted for felony in December, 1898?"

"That may be so."

"Was it for stealing?"

"I was charged with that."

"Did you get a month's hard labour?"

"I did."

"Were you sentenced to six months' hard labour for burglary in August, 1899?"

"Yes."

"Were you arrested in April, 1900 for being in possession of the proceeds of a burglary?"

"Yes, and I got fifteen months' imprisonment for a crime I had nothing to do with."

"Were you sentenced to five years' penal servitude for burglary in September, 1901?"

"Yes."

"Did you plead guilty?"

"I believe I did."

"In August, 1905 were you released on licence?"

"Yes."

"In January, 1906 were you arrested on the charge of being a suspected person?"

"Yes."

"When you were arrested had you a brace and bit in your possession?"

"Yes."

"And the proceeds of three burglaries?"

"Yes."

There was much else besides, but this was what really mattered. Steinie, who had left the dock an ordinary citizen, returned a desperado with a dossier of crime.

In theory, disclosure of a prisoner's bad character should have no influence on the outcome of his trial. In practice, it almost invariably has. Why otherwise, as Abinger pertinently asked, did Muir insist on raking up the past of Steinie?

The effect made on the jury was probably twofold. First, as the judge observed when he addressed them later, they were now liable to misinterpret all the prisoner's acts. "It is almost impossible," said Mr. Justice Darling, "to put as good a construction upon the most innocent thing that man may have done as it was when you believed him to be unconvicted."

Second, the jury might be betrayed into assuming a special relationship between the prisoner and society. Here was a burglar, a worthless individual, a man who if set free would be a constant malefactor. Why then split legal hairs and balance fine distinctions if we *feel* that he is guilty—feel it in our bones . . . ?

This was the result of introducing "character." This was the price paid for asking Mrs. Deitch whether her house was a resorting place of drabs.

The strain imposed on defending counsel by a long trial for murder has few, if any, parallels. One can think only of the surgeon who, in the operating theatre, holds the life of his charge in the skill of his two hands. But the surgeon's burden lasts only hours; the barrister's lasts for days, sometimes for weeks, during which the trial absorbs his every waking moment. It does not admit of limited endeavour; it cannot be put aside at a fixed time. An idea conceived in the solitude of chambers may be the precious instrument of acquittal, just as an indiscreet utterance in court may set the seal upon an adverse verdict.

Such continuous and anxious concentration tests the nervous stamina of the strongest. This test is twenty times as great when things are going badly, when counsel senses that the tide of events is running inexorably against his client.

Abinger had been conscious from the start that his was an uphill and ungrateful task. He had tried to compensate for this by daring tactics and sheer force of will, but these, so far from rendering him aid, had merely served to make his prospects worse. Steinie's chance of freedom dwindled daily, and with it Abinger's poise and self-control. As the trial wore on his touchiness increased, involving him in scenes that grew more frequent and more violent. In particular it brought him into conflict with the judge.

Judges are not always right, nor always patient; the blame may rest with either side when Bench falls out with Bar. But here there can be little doubt where provocation lay. It was Abinger, by his curious conduct of the case, who often forced the judge against his will to intervene. It was Abinger who, by the warmth of his reaction, made these interventions so bitter and prolonged. It was Abinger who tried to make the jury act as arbitrators, and who transformed arguments on cold points of law into passionate tirades and emotional appeals.

The friction that resulted reached its unwelcome zenith in the last phase of the trial.

Abinger began his final speech late on the seventh day and did not finish until the next mid-afternoon. He had many points to make and made them forcibly, but ever and anon returned to one—the issue of character and his grounds for introducing it. He said he was glad that the jury now knew Steinie's history (a statement hard to reconcile with his fight to keep it from them). He reiterated his views about Joe Mintz and Mrs. Deitch. He spoke at great length of Eva Flitterman and Rosen, the witnesses from the police court whom Muir had failed to call. "There is a woman," he declared, referring to the former, "who can be found to come to court and invoke the name of the Almighty and swear a lie—and in a murder trial! It is appalling! You have consciences; we have consciences; has that woman?"

The vigour of this was more apparent than its point. The judge, one thinks, was genuinely perplexed.

"Mr. Abinger, what *do* you want? Do you want the prosecution to call Flitterman or not?"

"No, my lord, it would be a terrible spectacle. May I respectfully tell your lordship *what* I want?"

"Do, certainly," said Darling, who doubtless longed to know.

"I want that woman to be brought into court so that the jury may see the class of woman that she is."

The judge responded temperately to this singular request.

"But you have got it established that what she says is not true. What is the use of looking at one liar more or less?"

Deliberately Abinger swung round to face the jury.

"Gentlemen, I pass from that," he said, ignoring the judge as though he were some petty official. "I pass from that. But you won't. What my lord meant by saying one liar more or less is easy enough to guess. My lord must have been thinking of Rosen."

"I was not thinking of Rosen," said Mr. Justice Darling quietly. "I was thinking of King David."

This scriptural allusion excited Abinger's scorn.

"Gentlemen," he cried, "I wish I had the remarkable abilities of my lord, who is able to allow his mind the luxury of dwelling upon King David when we are discussing this sordid case."

A more offensive observation can seldom have been made in open court by counsel about judge. It speaks volumes for Mr. Justice Darling's magnanimity that Abinger was permitted to proceed without rebuke.

Without rebuke, but not without much further interruption, for which the fiery advocate had himself to thank. The judge would not descend to *quarrel*, but neither would he tolerate distortions of the evidence or transgressions of the rules. As Abinger's speech pursued its turbulent course; as far-fetched theories were outlined, Cabinet Ministers criticised, and alternative murderers suggested *ex hypothesi*, so Darling insisted, in cool, firm tones, on conformity with the normal practice of the courts. Abinger contested each objection to the last, and long before the end his speech had ceased to be a solo; it was more like a duet between barrister and judge.

When Muir followed Abinger, the duet became a trio. Muir spoke; Abinger protested; Darling mediated—and occasionally the trio turned into a quartet when Steinie interjected something from the dock.

Heat always begets heat. Excitement breeds excitement. Hysteria's harvest was now being fully reaped.

The whole of the eighth day had been spent on speeches. In the evening, when the court adjourned, Muir, Abinger, Darling and Steinie were about halfway through Muir's. . . .

The end of the trial was now in sight. The moment of decision could not be long delayed. But, in an assembly almost jaded with sensations, one last surprise had yet to come.

Next morning, when Mr. Justice Darling sat, it was Abinger, not Muir, who stood up in his place. Looking tired and drawn (he had been busy half the night), he applied for leave to call some further evidence. The judge gave his assent and, amidst a rustling of whispered speculations, Police Constable Greaves made his way towards the box.

Who was he? Where did he come from? What had he got to say?

The mystery was soon solved. Greaves had been on duty in the charge room at the station when the detectives brought the prisoner in. He had heard Steinie ask "What am I brought here for?" and he had also heard one of the officers reply: "I told you before; you are on suspicion of *murder*." Immediately after, they took Steinie to the cells.

At the time Greaves attached no importance to this incident. He only felt himself compelled to take action when he read in the paper an account of Steinie's trial. He then wrote a letter direct to Mr. Abinger, stating what he knew, expressing reluctance to give evidence, but affirming his concern for "the interests of justice." As a result, last night he was summoned from his duty to the station, where he was interviewed by Abinger and the head of the C.I.D.

If Greaves was telling the truth about the charge-room conversation —or, to be crudely practical, if the jury thought he was—here finally collapsed one of Muir's most cherished points. No matter now whether Wensley mentioned "murder" on arrest. Steinie, said Greaves, had heard the word before going to the cells, and it was only in the cells that he had mentioned it himself.

Muir swooped down on this supernumerary witness with the relish of a gourmand for an unexpected meal. A policeman, too, was he? A traitor to his side. This made the proffered feast the sweeter.

"When did you first speak of this conversation?" Muir asked.

"Two or three days ago."

"To whom?"

"Some officers."

"Who are they?"

"I can't say with certainty," Greaves answered, "but I think one of them was 299H—Police Constable Heiler."

"Let Heiler be telephoned for," said Mr. Justice Darling, "and not be informed by anyone what this witness is saying."

While Heiler was sought out and fetched, Muir went on cross-examining in the fashion that had become part and parcel of the case. Had Greaves frequently been transferred from Division to Division? Yes. Had he corresponded with an ex-Inspector Syme? Yes. Had Syme accused the police of perjury and corruption? Yes. Had Greaves on one occasion been suspended from the Force? Yes. Was that for making a false accusation against a superior officer? Well, not exactly. He was suspended for making accusations he was not able to prove. . . .

Meanwhile Heiler had arrived at the Old Bailey and an element of lottery crept into the proceedings. Not even counsel knew what he was going to say. Abinger put him in the box, asked his name and rank, then cannily sat down again and left the rest to Muir.

Muir must have found the sequel irritating. All Heiler's answers favoured the defence. So far as it lay with him he confirmed Greaves absolutely. They had met on the beat, he said, a couple of nights ago, and Greaves had described what took place in the charge room. His story, as repeated by Heiler upon oath, corresponded with the story that Greaves had told in court.

Heiler's record was exemplary; Muir could do nothing with him. He passed from the box unshaken and unsullied—a rare event in this pageant of detraction.

Little now remained of Muir's hard-run theory that the murder charge was conjured up in Steinie's guilty mind. But it was the judge's lance that despatched the dying monster. "This point," he said, "which has been represented to you as though it were the critical and crucial point of the whole case, is to my mind one of the smallest points in it. It would not seem to me at all unnatural that a man arrested where he was, within a few days of the notorious Clapham Common murder, should assume, even with nothing said, that he was arrested for murder."

Envious, perhaps, of the universal loquacity, the foreman of the jury attempted to reply.

"May I say—" he began.

"No, no." Mr. Justice Darling stopped him instantly. "Don't you say a word. Juries should never express any opinion, except by their verdict."

Nothing now stood between the prisoner and that verdict save only Mr. Justice Darling's summing-up.

This was not the kind of case in which his lordship felt at home. Some judges—not so many—would have taken it in their stride: Avory, for instance, with his impersonal logic, and Travers Humphreys, with his hardy worldliness. But Darling—Darling was the exquisite of the Bench; the wit, the beau, the laughing cavalier. His delight was to preside over a Special Jury suit, in which the stake was merely money which both parties could afford, and wherein he was frequently presented with the chance of bandying epigrams with fashionable counsel. The raw inelegance of Steinie's trial can only have induced in him a nausea of distaste.

None the less, within the limits of his personality and reputation,

Darling tried the Morrison case well. If he could not prevent others losing their equanimity, at least he carefully preserved his own. If he could not exclude scenes tinged with macabre humour, he refrained from embellishing them with ironic jest. If he could not stop a reference to "my lord's literary talents," he did nothing to earn the mockery with which Abinger invested it. If there were moments in the trial when everyone, judge included, seemed to be bobbing about like corks on an unpredictable sea, in perspective it is plain that Darling kept a clear sense of direction and strove gallantly to impress it on the rest.

The summing-up fittingly crowned his long effort. Into a court still rocking with the clash of factions and echoing with the sound of voices raised in anger, the judge's even accents flowed like a solvent. Whatever could be done to lay the dust, he did.

It was a closely-knit review, analytical and balanced, which deftly disentangled the true issues from the false. Essentials were exhibited and stressed; irrelevancies were branded and dismissed. The case against the prisoner was put afresh, shorn of vindictiveness and rancour. The case in his favour was equally examined and cleansed of prejudice, implanted or ingrained.

Above all, Darling placed the facts in due proportion. No one could tell, no one can tell now—what had influenced the jury most in those nine days of frenzy. But despite the mass of detail which distracted and confused, Darling tried to keep their minds fixed on the point that mattered. "Are you satisfied," he asked them, "beyond reasonable doubt that that is the man who was in Hayman's cab, in Stephens's cab, in Castlin's cab that night? . . . Think for yourselves. With what certainty could you swear to a man whom you saw on a night like that, by the kind of light there was at those places? Can you feel certain that a man would not be mistaken? . . . Let us assume they were honest. Even then, are you so sure that they really took notice enough, that they had opportunity enough, to be able some days afterwards to swear with certainty to the man that they had driven?"

Was Steinie identified beyond reasonable doubt? This Darling called "the deciding point of the case." If the jury did not share that view by the time the judge had finished, it probably lay beyond the power of mortals to convince them.

The jury retired at eight o'clock that night. It was far from being an ideal time for grave deliberations. Weariness of the body promotes impatience of the mind; instincts and emotions usurp the place of judgment. . . .

Thirty-five minutes later they trooped back into their box.

The judge passed the only sentence sanctioned by the law. As he ended with the traditional words of solemn benediction, "And may the Lord have mercy on your soul," Morrison's anguish found dramatic outlet. "I decline such mercy," he cried out in despair, "I do not believe there is a God in heaven either."

So the curtain fell on the trial of Steinie Morrison—fell, as it had risen, with the chief character declamatory in the centre of the stage, but renouncing the God he had formerly acknowledged.

There was to be an epilogue, however.

The authorities needed no prodding from the public to reconsider Steinie Morrison's fate. The verdict had been indirectly disapproved by all the trained intellects qualified to judge. Mr. Justice Darling, on receiving it, had conspicuously abstained from expressing agreement and had recommended the accused to be guided by his lawyers "as to anything you may have to say hereafter." The Court of Criminal Appeal, to which Steinie had recourse, cast its decision in a most significant form: "*Bearing in mind that we are not entitled to put ourselves in the position of the jury*, we can only come to the conclusion that the appeal must be dismissed."

To many, therefore, it did not come as a surprise when Mr. Churchill, who then occupied the office of Home Secretary, advised the King to grant Steinie a reprieve. This was done; the usual course was followed; the death sentence was commuted to penal servitude for life.

It was merciful, if death be the greatest of all evils. But Steinie, behind prison bars, wished desperately to die. He was persistently violent, apparently in the hope that if he made himself intolerable the reprieve would be annulled. While his solicitors without were pressing for his release, the prisoner within was petitioning to be hanged. Finally, by long and drastic fasting he undermined his strength and died in Parkhurst prison at the age of thirty-nine.

Did Steinie die in the consciousness of innocence, the tortured victim of a terrible mistake? Or did he take the knowledge of his guilt, unconfessed and unrepented, to the grave?

In his admirable life of Mr. Justice Darling, Derek Walker-Smith reveals the judge's own opinion. "I had no doubt myself," he remarked to his biographer, "that Morrison was guilty. But the view I took was that, had I been a juryman, the evidence that I had heard was not sufficient to prove to me beyond all reasonable doubt that he had committed murder."

The verdict upon Steinie was doubtful, not outrageous. It was open to dispute, and will remain so for all time, because it failed to give the prisoner the benefit of a doubt, and was rooted in a trial that gave scant cause for satisfaction.

3

Neill Cream

For the prostitute, murder is an occupational risk. There are two major and distinguishable reasons, both of which spring from the nature of her trade. Because it is her frank object to capitalise male lust and her inescapable lot to symbolise male degradation, she tends to stimulate passions that readily generate violence even among the mildest of those whose appetites she serves.

Because her daily life is without roots and without moorings, because her associations are promiscuous and many, the murder of a prostitute has less chance of solution than the murder of someone more regular in conduct—a fact that affords a strong temptation to the habitual murderer; the one who does not murder as the result of another passion, but whose passion—for whatever reason—is murder in itself.

Into this latter group fall Jack the Ripper and Neill Cream.

The medical profession cannot wholly disclaim either, although their respective links with it are not of equal strength. The slaughter of streetwalkers in Whitechapel in 1888–89 has never been conclusively brought home to anyone; it can therefore only be a matter of inference, based upon his technique in mutilation, that the so-called Ripper possessed a surgeon's skill.

But the slaughter of streetwalkers in Lambeth in 1891–92 has been conclusively brought home to Neill Cream; and it is a matter of certainty that he was a qualified doctor, holding both Canadian and Edinburgh degrees, and that he used his knowledge and advantages as such in contriving the destruction of his prey.

Cream did not begin his career of crime in Lambeth, nor anywhere in the British Isles at all. The Glasgow-born son of highly respectable parents, he emigrated with them to Canada as a child; grew up in comfortable and prosperous surroundings, studied medicine at a famous school in Montreal; distinguished himself on gaining his diploma as MD—and then, disregarding the prospects of legitimate practice, swiftly established himself as a specialist in abortion.

No external pressure, economic or financial, can be blamed for setting Neill Cream upon this path. It was simply the first clear manifestation of a bent for wickedness that continually grew, both in scope and in degree. Like the visible fragment of an iceberg, Cream's known misdeeds in America constituted but a modest fraction of those that lay and still do lie—concealed. But even his public record speaks plainly enough.

In 1879 the death of a girl "patient" created such a scandal that he was forced to leave Canada for the United States. In 1880, at Chicago, he was acquitted only by a hair-breadth on a murder charge arising out of an illegal operation. In 1881 he stood trial there again for murdering by poison the husband of his mistress; this time he was found guilty in the second degree, and he spent 10 years in an Illinois jail.

It is an odd, but a true, reflection that this sentence sealed the fate of several girls who at the time when it was passed, were playing tig or hopscotch 3000 miles away. For Cream came out of prison with a fixed determination to shake the dust of America off his feet.

Fortified in pocket by a timely legacy, sharpened in vicious inclinations by an enforced restraint, within a very few weeks of his release he sailed for England. He reached London on October 5, 1891, and on the 7th, notwithstanding the ample means at his disposal, moved into a single room in the Lambeth Palace Road. Almost at once terror began to stalk among the tatty and pathetic harlots that thronged the squalid neighborhood that abuts on Waterloo.

On October 13 a girl named Ellen Donworth died in an abrupt attack of agonising convulsions. A post-mortem disclosed that she had taken a fatal dose of strychnine.

On October 20 a girl named Matilda Clover died in an abrupt attack of agonising convulsions. Those were negligently ascribed to delirium tremens: only on exhumation of her body six months later did it transpire that she, too, had taken a fatal dose of strychnine. But coming so soon after the Ripper outrages the two deaths were closely interlinked by local gossip, and Lambeth waited on events with bated breath.

As it turned out, there was a considerable pause before the next blow fell. Private affairs necessitated Cream's return to Canada and

Lambeth's ladies of the town passed safely through the winter months.

Cream returned to London on March 24. On the 12th of April two girls named Alice Marsh and Emma Shrivell died in abrupt attacks of agonising convulsions. Post-mortems disclosed that each had taken a fatal dose of strychnine.

These murders had not been very difficult to accomplish. The Lambeth prostitutes were neither choosey nor expensive; they went home with any man, provided he would pay them a paltry recompense which they usually rushed forthwith to spend in the nearest public-house. Why should they have rebuffed the well-dressed, well-spoken, 40-year-old stranger, even if he had cross-eyes and a peculiar glance? And if he proclaimed himself to be a doctor, why should they have disbelieved what was, after all, the truth?

And if he offered them capsules to cure whatever they suffered from, whether it was pimples or whether it was pregnancy, why should they not have availed themselves of this gratuitous treatment?

And when they had died in torment through the agency of the strychnine that Cream's medical status enabled him to obtain, who was to trace and identify the evil-doer among the motley jumble of their clients?

Who, indeed? Cream might have continued indefinitely on his homicidal course, enjoying the same immunity as the Ripper did before him, had he not betrayed himself by his own fantastic rashness.

After each of his murders, with punctilious regularity, he wrote and despatched a letter to some prominent person bluntly accusing him of being the murderer. All these letters, naturally, were signed with a false name, and were therefore unlikely to cause Cream any harm unless and until through other means he fell under suspicion. That, though, is exactly what did happen in the end.

Perhaps it goes too far to say he was suspected; the police had merely got a little curious about him; interested enough to make a few inquiries, interested enough to know what his handwriting looked like. The day came when they compared it with one of the accusing letters, and from that day the mystery was a mystery no more.

For not only were the accusing letters written in Cream's hand—as, in the last resort, he himself conceded, they might easily have been the production of a crackpot, prompted by cases of which he had heard or read. But on occasion Cream's letters made references to facts which had *subsequently* proved to be correct, but which, at the time of writing, *only the murderer could have known.*

Notably so in the case of Matilda Clover. When there had been no whisper, no hint of poisoning; when her doctor had certified that she died from alcoholism; when she had been consigned to the grave without autopsy—at this period Cream could write in his accusing letter: *"Miss Clover died last month from being poisoned with strychnine."*

It was on the Clover charge that Cream was ultimately tried, but the Crown tendered, and the judge quite properly admitted, evidence on the other charges as corroboration. The cumulative effect was only comparable to that similarly produced at the trial of Brides-in-the-Bath Smith.

It took a jury less than a quarter of an hour to find Cream guilty. . . .

The motives that actuated Cream are still debated. At the trial it was suggested by the prosecution that the real key might repose in the false charges; that the murders were solely designed to furnish Cream with a convenient instrument for blackmail. But while it is true that he made demands for money in his letters, he never seems to have exerted any pressure when those demands failed to evoke response.

I think myself that blackmail can safely be dismissed as his original and principal objective; it takes rank as a by-product or an afterthought. It is far more probable and consistent with the facts that Cream was a pervert—and one whose pleasure mounted with the agony involved.

The species is fortunately rare, but it exists. What distinguishes Cream from other monsters of this kind is that he did not witness the outcome of his act; long before the poison took effect he disappeared; he could apparently gratify his sadistic impulses merely by *imagining* the transports of torture endured by his victims out of his sight and hearing.

All he needed was his scientific knowledge—and a watch.

4

Travers vs. Wilde

A DOCTOR is in perpetual hazard with his female patients. His relationship with them is, of necessity, much more intimate and personal and private than that which a woman ordinarily maintains with any man except a lover or a husband.

It offers allurement to the frustrated woman, and opportunity to the designing one—as many honest and honourable practitioners have discovered, greatly to their cost.

But there are also doctors—though infinitely fewer—who exploit the relationship instead of being exploited by it; who use their professional contacts with women to place themselves on terms of wholly unprofessional familiarity.

That was the allegation made against Sir William Wilde at the very peak of his illustrious career.

Sir William Wilde ranked among the most distinguished citizens of Dublin. He was the leading eye specialist in Ireland, with a reputation as a healer that reached other lands. In addition to receiving the honour of a knighthood, he had been appointed Surgeon Oculist-in-Ordinary to the Queen.

Sir William and his wife—a poetess of note—lived in lavish and hospitable style, and were universally recognised as leaders in the intellectual and artistic life of the Irish capital.

A personage so prominently in the public eye cannot hope that his indiscretions will escape attention, especially in a town as gossipy as Dublin.

It was well known—it had been well known for years—that Sir William yielded the palm to none in his pursuit of women: and that, despite his squat and simian appearance, women as a rule responded readily to him. Fame often exerts a magnetism of its own.

Certainly the tally of his intrigues and his bastards had long since grown beyond general computation. If Dubliners viewed the matter tolerantly, doubtless they took into account his services to suffering humanity. Even so, there were those who shook their heads. If he doesn't watch out, he'll get his dues, they said in their own idiom.

The instrument through which Sir William ultimately got his dues was a young woman by the name of Mary Travers.

At the age of 19 Miss Travers had come to him as a patient. Thereafter she had returned for further consultations frequently over a period of years. It is significant that, on her own subsequent admission, she never either paid, or even offered, any fee.

A time came eventually, however, when the free medical advice was discontinued. Miss Travers ceased to see Sir William, and apparently the parting had not been cordial. For Miss Travers wrote and printed and distributed a pamphlet in which, without any real concealment of the fact that the characters concerned were Sir William and herself, she related the story of a doctor violating a female patient in his surgery.

Sir William would have ignored it. Lady Wilde did not. She had become indifferent to her husband's amorous adventures, but not to direct attacks on his professional integrity.

She therefore wrote to Miss Traver's father—himself a practising doctor—deploring his daughter's "disreputable conduct" and attributing to her "the hope of extorting money."

Miss Travers sued for libel.

The ensuing action worked all Dublin up to fever pitch. No one cared much whether Lady Wilde had libelled Mary Travers. A far more important question was involved: Had Sir William sexually assaulted a woman who had reposed her confidence in him as a doctor?

The celebrated surgeon was as assuredly on trial as if he had been literally standing in a dock; and when Miss Travers went into the box she appeared as not only plaintiff, but accuser.

Treading with exquisite verbal delicacy so as not to shock the audience which had assembled to be shocked, her counsel drew from Miss Travers's own lips an account of the occurrence on which she had based her pamphlet.

How one day when Sir William was examining her she fainted; how she recovered consciousness to find she had been "ruined"! how she declared that his behaviour was "an outrage"; how he begged her not to tell anyone what had happened; how he persuaded her to renew her visits; how he pressed gifts upon her.

Through this recital she preserved an air of pained reluctance. But when Serjeant Sullivan got up to cross-examine, it was as if she had suddenly been confronted with Sir William Wilde in person.

Malice and hostility visibly possessed her.

"Now as I understand you," Serjeant Sullivan began, "and as your counsel told the jury when he opened, this one—ah—transaction between you and Sir William occurred in the October of 1862, and nothing of the sort occurred before or after?"

"Not before."

"Nor after?"

"I consider—"

Serjeant Sullivan, who had thought he was merely clearing the ground, cut in impatiently.

"Did anything occur after—yes or no?"

"I can't say yes or no."

"Can't say yes or no?" The Serjeant's surprise was shared by the murmuring spectators.

"No, I can't." Miss Travers hesitated. So he was asking for it, was he? Very well; here goes. "I can't answer yes or no, because I consider it was attempted."

"The same thing was attempted again?"

"Yes."

"When?"

"In the next July—the July of 1863."

So she's changing her tale in midstream. The Serjeant could hardly credit his good fortune.

"Why did you not say a word about this just now, when you were examined?"

"Because I wasn't asked."

"Not asked? But didn't you draw out all the instructions for this case yourself?"

"I did."

"With your own hand?"

"Yes."

"Every line of them?"

"Yes."

Serjeant Sullivan drew a deep breath of satisfaction.

"Did you hear your counsel mention one—ah—transaction against Sir William, and no more?"

"I did."

"And you now say there was a second attempt upon you in July?"

"I consider there was."

Serjeant Sullivan fished hopefully.

"Was there another after that, now?"

"No."

"Or in the interval?"

Miss Travers could not reject the bait twice running. "I don't know," she said, and the murmuring was renewed.

"You don't know?" Serjeant Sullivan repeated scornfully. "Do you mean to tell me that's your answer? Were there or were there not attempts made to violate you?"

But Miss Travers did not fancy getting into deeper waters.

"There was rudeness and roughness leading to it," she at last pronounced.

"How often?"

"Two or three times."

Sergeant Sullivan now had more than sufficient for his purpose.

He simply threw Miss Travers's earlier evidence in her teeth.

"Though this was the kind of conduct offered you, you went back time after time to him?"

Miss Travers had no option but to answer, "Yes."

"And you took his money?"

"Yes."

"You got tickets for a ball from him?"

"Yes."

"Did you ask for those tickets from the man who violated you?"

"Yes."

"Did you buy a dress for the ball?"

"Yes."

"And did you put it on you?"

"Yes."

"Whose was the money that bought it?"

"His."

The Serjeant smiled sarcastically.

"All that going on with these repeated attempts at violation?"

"Yes," said Miss Travers, malignantly defiant to the last.

She had forfeited all confidence, though, in her unsupported word. It only needed Sir William to give her the lie on oath, and her case would surely crumble in the dust.

But Sir William did not go into the box.

Perhaps he did not fancy the whole truth coming out—that for years

Miss Travers had been his acquiescent mistress, and that this was a discarded woman's effort at revenge.

Perhaps he felt it safer to leave things as they were.

The jury, however, neatly resolved the situation. They found for the plaintiff; damages, one farthing.

Thereby they set on lasting record their opinion that Sir William was a goat—and that Miss Travers had not minded.

5

William Herbert Wallace

*The Wallace case was a highly professional affair. It was
planned with extreme care and extraordinary imagination. Either the
murderer was Wallace or it wasn't. If it wasn't, then here at last is the
perfect murder. If it was, then here is a murder so nearly perfect that
the Court of Criminal Appeal, after examining the evidence, decided
to quash Wallace's conviction.—James Agate in* Ego 6.

Agate was fascinated by the Wallace case. He made it one of his
constant bedside books. He wrote on it from time to time in his famous
published diary. And if he ever felt depressed or bored he would
telephone and say: "Come over, my dear boy; let's have a good talk
about Wallace."

Those good talks about Wallace were spirited but exhausting. I
have often sat up with him half the night probing the mystery of
Menlove Gardens East. . . .

Agate's interest in Wallace was not at all surprising. It was a case
to delight that hard and lucid brain which had allied itself so oddly
to a subtle sense of art. The latter had become the instrument of his
profession; the former he made the foundation of his hobby, and he
loved to dedicate his scanty leisure hours to exercising a prodigious
gift of logic. He doted on detective problems of the higher type; he
could meditate for hours over a cunning move in chess; he was in fact
a devotee of scientific puzzles.

And Wallace is the perfect scientific puzzle. Perfect because it
hasn't a solution—and, so far as anything in this world can be certain,
never will have now. Other crimes have other qualities in far greater
abundance; more psychological interest, wider human appeal, greater
social significance. But, as a mental exercise, as a challenge to one's

powers of deduction and analysis, the Wallace murder is in a class by itself. It has all the maddening, frustrating fascination of a chess problem that ends in perpetual check.

At the time of the tragedy that broke up his home and ruined his life, William Herbert Wallace was fifty-two years old. A placid, good-tempered, gentle individual, he incurred no enmities if he attracted few close friends. Integrity and stability were the distinguishing marks of his modest and respectable career. For sixteen years he had been a valued whole-time agent of a famous insurance company—the Prudential. For sixteen years he had rented the same small house in Liverpool, one of a dull and featureless row in a dull and featureless district. For more than eighteen years he had shared married life with a woman as unassuming as himself. His business accounts were always in good order; his rent was always punctually paid; he and his wife enjoyed a relationship of uninterrupted concord and affection. "A very loving couple," said their next-door neighbour, and this judgment has never been challenged or gainsaid.

In one respect only Wallace sharply differed from the average worthy man of provincial middle class. He was remarkably studious and intellectual in his tastes. He enjoyed a wide range of cultivated interests which his wife either encouraged or participated in. There was chess, which he played regularly at the Liverpool Central Chess Club. There was chemistry, which he practised in an amateur laboratory he had rigged up for himself in the back part of his house. And there was music; Mrs. Wallace was accomplished at the piano, Wallace had taken lessons on the violin, and they often entertained themselves by performing duets in the comfort and privacy of their sitting room.

It was this harmonious and inoffensive couple that became involved in "the perfect murder case"; she as the victim, he as the accused. For of all men in the world, Wallace, the mild, peaceable, easy-going Wallace, was to face a charge of murdering his wife. Murder—if it were done by him—not in sudden heat or rage but by cold and brilliant calculated plan; murder not committed with the minimum of violence, but with vicious, wasteful and horrible brutality; murder not prompted by some clear and powerful motive but without the slightest purpose and without the slightest gain.

The first overt move in the deep-laid plot to murder Julia Wallace was taken almost exactly twenty-four hours before she died. A telephone call, which at the time appeared commonplace, is seen in retrospect to have presaged her end.

It was Monday, January 19th, 1931. There was a match that evening at the Liverpool Central Chess Club, and Wallace was among the members scheduled to take part. Shortly after seven o'clock, when the players were assembling but before Wallace had arrived, someone telephoned the club and left a message with the captain. Would Mr. Wallace go out at 7.30 the next night and visit Mr. Qualtrough—Mr. R. M. Qualtrough of 25, Menlove Gardens East? "It is something," said the caller, "in the nature of his business."

If we knew for certain who this caller was, the Wallace puzzle would be solved at once. For whoever left that message did it for the purpose of advancing a murderous design.

When Wallace arrived, about half an hour later, he seemed somewhat puzzled by this telephoned request. "Qualtrough, Qualtrough, who is Qualtrough?" he said. "I don't know the chap. And where is Menlove Gardens East?" None of the club members were absolutely sure, but they all—Wallace included—knew of Menlove Avenue. Menlove Gardens East, they thought, must be in the same neighbourhood, and Wallace accepted this plausible supposition. "After all, I've got a tongue in my head," he said. "I can ask when I get in the vicinity."

The Wallaces had no children and no servants. They were very seldom visited by relatives or friends. So if Wallace went out at night, almost certainly Mrs. Wallace would be in the house alone. The case turns on this fact.

On the evening that followed the chess match and the message Wallace returned home from work at about six. At half past, or thereabouts, a milk boy called, and Mrs. Wallace responded to his knock. Very soon after seven Wallace was on a tramcar, travelling in the direction of Menlove Avenue, which was a distance of three or four miles from his home. A few minutes later he had reached "the vicinity" and began asking for directions to Menlove Gardens East.

In Liverpool there is a Menlove Gardens South; there is a Menlove Gardens North; there is a Menlove Gardens West. There is no Menlove Gardens East. And the Mr. R. M. Qualtrough who should have lived at Number 25 and who ought to have been waiting to discuss insurance business has never been discovered to this day.

Wallace undoubtedly made numerous enquiries and roamed round the neighbourhood for the best part of an hour. At last he gave up and, without visible recompense for his errand, quitted "the vicinity" and started off for home.

At about a quarter to nine it so happened that his neighbours came out of their back door. In the alley they saw Wallace who, they thought, looked "anxious," and who asked them whether they had heard anything "unusual." He couldn't get into his house, he said; both the front door and the back were locked against him. At their suggestion he tried the back door again. "It opens now," he called, and they waited, neighbour-like, while he went inside to look around.

A minute or two later he came out to them again. "Come and see," he said. "She's been killed."

Horrified, they followed him through the house to the front parlour. Mrs. Wallace lay there, stretched across the floor. Her brains had been dashed out and her blood was spattered everywhere.

There was no sign that the murderer had broken in by force. There seemed to be nothing missing except, so Wallace said, four pounds in cash from a box kept in the kitchen. One bedroom, it is true, was found in some disorder, but, to the expert eye of a Detective Superintendent, it did not look as though a thief had been searching round for valuables. The Superintendent formed an exactly contrary opinion: that the place had been deliberately upset in order to mislead.

Robbery, then, could be virtually excluded. It was not a crime of sex. What feasible hypotheses remained? Who could have nourished such malignant hatred against this amiable and harmless lady that he painstakingly evolved a plot the aim of which was to bring about her death? For the murder was unquestionably linked with the phone call to the chess club on the evening before.

But linked in what respect? Either—and this was the obvious conclusion—someone had wanted to get Wallace out of the way; or—this was a more circuitous approach—*Wallace himself* wanted people to *think* that someone had wanted to get him out of the way.

After diligent enquiries, spread over a wide area and lasting many days, the police threw their weight behind the second of these alternatives. They believed that Wallace had made the telephone call himself. They believed that on the following night, shortly after half past six, he had murdered his wife in the front room of their home. They believed that he had then gone out and conspicuously engaged in an elaborate search for a place that he knew did not exist in order to equip himself with a strong and well-knit alibi.

On February 2nd Wallace was arrested. The detectives stood ready to take down any statement. But "What can I say," asked Wallace, "to a charge of which I am absolutely innocent?"

The trial at St. George's Hall was presided over by Mr. Justice (afterwards Lord) Wright, one of the greatest of contemporary judges, and fought out by two redoubtable King's Counsel, E. G. Hemmerde and Roland Oliver.

Roland Oliver had played a minor part in two of the cases already examined in these pages. At the trial of Steinie Morrison he had been second junior to Abinger; at the trial of Mrs. Thompson he had been second junior to Inskip. By the time of the Wallace case, where he led for the defence, Oliver was in the front rank of English advocates. He was an all-round man, equally effective and constantly briefed in "fashionable" jury suits, "society" divorces, and so-called "heavy" crime.

Hemmerde was something of a stormy petrel. At the fiercely competitive Liverpool Bar of the early nineteen hundreds he had established himself with such rapidity and brilliance that there were those who predicted an even greater future for him than for his dashing colleague, F. E. Smith. He took silk early, entered politics, and for a while his youthful promise looked certain of fulfilment. But in later years his career went awry. Private transactions, ill-judged or unlucky, did him grave and permanent disservice; irrepressible combativeness and an outspoken tongue involved him in injurious dissensions; an honourable but unbending pride did nothing to win back those he had estranged. His practice suffered, and though he always could command a fair volume of work upon the Northern Circuit, there is not the faintest doubt that in the twenties and the thirties his status did not equal his professional capacity.

It is important to bear this in mind when studying the trial. Both through technical skill and sheer personal dominance, Hemmerde's impact on a jury was immense. He was a remarkably handsome and imposing-looking man, to whom ripening age had lent an additional authority. If he believed—and he usually did quite genuinely believe —that the side he represented was the side of right and truth, he threw into a case his very heart and soul. He conducted this prosecution with his customary fairness, but in a trial there are imponderables to take into account. In the Wallace case, one of them is the effect that would be produced by this able, forceful and convincing personality presenting a charge that he himself felt sure was true.

Hemmerde opened his case characteristically "high"; that is, he spoke as though all his witnesses would come right up to proof, and none would retreat or qualify under cross-examination.

Opening "high" has one serious disadvantage. If your opponent has any real success, he may induce a violent swing in his direction merely because the Crown case has been patently over-stated. What remains may be discounted because of what has gone.

But there is also a corresponding advantage in the method. At the very outset the jury get the Crown version in one solid and coherent piece. Its destruction can only be accomplished in distinct and maybe widely separated stages. The first impression, if deep enough, may be difficult to dislodge.

In the Wallace trial, which depended more than most upon the accumulation and interpretation of a mass of tiny details, opening "high" was likely to pay dividends. This is not to say that Hemmerde acted on design. Given the circumstances and his temperament, a "high" opening was inevitable.

Certainly the Crown case never afterwards appeared quite so formidable as it did at the end of Hemmerde's opening speech.

"The evidence for the Crown," said Hemmerde, slowly and emphatically, "will not show you any motive. Nevertheless I suggest it will carry you almost irresistibly to the conclusion that, in spite of all the happiness of that little household, in spite of everything that one knows about the relations of these people, this woman was murdered by her husband."

Almost irresistibly. The keynote had been struck in the first minute, and thereafter Hemmerde held the court enthralled while he gave chapter and verse in a masterly oration.

He plunged into the story with the telephone call, and straight away created a sensation. "We know where the call came from," he asserted. "In the ordinary way, it would not be possible to tell, but in this particular case difficulty was experienced." In fact, there had been some hitch in the automatic machinery and the operator had had to intervene. "As a result, we can trace the call to a call-box four hundred yards from Wallace's house—the nearest call-box to his house there is." Hemmerde paused for a moment. "You may think it curious that a total stranger to the prisoner speaking from a place four hundred yards from his home—where, according to him, he actually was—should have rung up the chess club. . . . It is a club that does not advertise; a club the meetings of which are known only to its few members.

. . . There he leaves a message that Wallace is expected to call next night on someone he does not know at an address which does not exist." The ground was prepared for Hanging Point Number One. "You will have to consider whether this was part of a cunningly laid scheme to create an alibi for the next night."

After a reference to Wallace's insistence at the club that he did not know either Qualtrough or Menlove Gardens East ("You may think that this ignorance was assumed to draw attention to the fact that next night at half past seven he was going some miles from his house"), Hemmerde passed to Hanging Point Two: Wallace's conduct that next night as he went upon that journey. He had made much of this, and legitimately so, for everything that Wallace did seemed perfectly consistent with the prosecution's theory that he was out procuring witnesses. "Does this car go to Menlove Gardens East?" he asks one tram conductor. "No," says the man, "but you can get on and I can give you a penny ticket or a transfer." "I am a stranger in the district," Wallace volunteers, "and I have important business." ("You will remember," Hemmerde commented acidly, but not altogether justly, "that he did not know Qualtrough or what his business was.") Presently the conductor goes upstairs to collect fares. "You won't forget," Wallace calls after him, "I want to get to Menlove Gardens East."

He changes cars; there is another conductor; Wallace goes through the self-same hoops. He asks to be put off at Menlove Gardens East; the conductor does his best and puts him off at Menlove Gardens West; Wallace says "Thank you, I am a complete stranger round here." "You may think," observed Hemmerde, with significant inflection, "that these conversations with the conductors are natural—or unnatural."

But this was only the beginning; there was more, much more, to come.

From twenty past seven until after eight that night Wallace is busy in the Menlove Gardens region. He starts by enquiring of a passer-by, who tells him flatly "There is no Menlove Gardens East." He rings the bell of 25, Menlove Gardens West and asks the lady who answers it if Mr. Qualtrough lives there. He gets into conversation with a policeman, who, having added his official reassurance that Menlove Gardens East is non-existent, receives in return an account of the whole episode—how Wallace is an insurance clerk, how a Mr. Qualtrough had rung up his club, how a message had been taken for him by his colleague. Then Wallace pulls out his watch. "It isn't eight o'clock yet," he remarks, "it's just a quarter to." The policeman inspects his own watch and confirms. "You may think," said Hemmerde, "all this is perfectly natural—or you may think it over-elaborated. The taking out of the watch, so that the policeman should know exactly when he was there, you may think is of some importance." (The harmless, non-committal "you may think" can shoot like deadly poison from a rhetorician's tongue.)

Even this was not the end of Wallace's researches. He goes into a newsagent's and asks for a directory. It is given to him; he looks through it; and then— "Note this," Hemmerde interjected sharply— "he says to the manageress, 'Do you know what I am looking for?' 'No,' she not unnaturally replies. 'I am looking,' says Wallace, 'for Menlove Gardens East.'"

The gathering power of this narration could not fail to impress even a neutral and impartial jury. It is to be doubted, though, whether the ten men and two women appointed to sit in judgment upon Wallace qualified for this commendatory description. All provincial towns smack of the parish pump, and Liverpool had hardly changed since the days of Mrs. Maybrick. The buzz of voices and the clack of tongues were never stilled in the weeks before the trial, and Wallace had been prematurely tried in every local shop and public house. The verdict of these crude tribunals was seldom in his favour.

One may surmise that not all the jurors were unenthusiastic as Hemmerde developed his indictment.

He followed his stirring and tendentious curtain-raiser with a devastating commentary on Wallace's return.

"The next we know of him is at 8.35, when he is seen just outside his house, at the back." Hemmerde recounted Wallace's talk with his neighbours and his statement that the doors were "locked against him." "Now supposing you came to the conclusion"—oh, the guilelessness of counsel with their decorous "supposings" and forbearing "you may think"—"supposing you came to the conclusion that the doors were never shut against him, and that you then find a man who could get in if he wanted to, pretending that he couldn't. There he is"—it's axiomatic now—"there he is, able to get in when he is there alone— but the neighbours are not there."

So it was settled, wasn't it? Wallace could have gone straight in. There was nothing to stop him. The whole business was a fake. Hanging Point Three.

The flood mounted and quickened. "He goes in and the neighbours follow his course. If you went into a house like that, where would you go? You have left your wife downstairs; would you have looked in the downstairs room, or would you have gone upstairs? . . . First of all, *he* goes upstairs, then comes down into the *kitchen,* and *then* goes into the front sitting room. Then—then—he finds his wife lying dead."

And his demeanour when confronted with this shocking tragedy? Hemmerde was rising to the heights. "You might have expected a cry of agony, bitter sorrow—but what happens?" Well, *what* happens? Wallace, says the Crown, is calm, cool, collected, realistic. Too calm and cool for a man in his position.

From calmness it is but a step to callousness, which slips into its place as Hanging Point Number Four.

Hanging Point Number Five depended on the mackintosh—one of the most bizarre and puzzling clues that ever stepped outside detective fiction.

When Mrs. Wallace's body was discovered, she was lying in a twisted position on the rug. Pressed close against her, rolled up and half hidden, was a blood-drenched mackintosh that had been partially burnt. It was Wallace's mackintosh, as he did not deny.

"Now," said Hemmerde, with a glance at the jury which could and did speak volumes, "Just let me draw your attention to this. The mackintosh is found there after some attempt has been made, if it was not an accident, to burn it. Just consider. Who had an interest in burning that mackintosh? Assuming that someone had broken into the house—there is no trace that anyone did—such a person might have taken down the raincoat and put it on to prevent the blood getting on his clothes. But having done so, why should a stranger want to destroy it? Why should he want to destroy *someone else's* mackintosh?"

It was a persuasive argument, at its most deadly in reverse—the mackintosh's owner, by the same token, *would* want to destroy it. Having placed this implication in every juror's mind, Hemmerde offered a most ingenious reconstruction of the crime.

Mrs. Wallace, he stressed, was lying in a pool of blood. Blood had spurted on to the furniture and walls. But although the murderer had gone upstairs directly afterwards, there was not a trace of blood detected on his route. With one tiny exception, irrelevant for this purpose, the only blood found anywhere outside the room of death was a single clot in the water-closet pan which stood by the side of an ordinary wash bowl. "One of the most famous criminal trials," Hemmerde said, "was of a man who committed a crime when he was naked. A man might perfectly well commit a crime wearing a raincoat, as one might wear a dressing gown, and come down when he is just going to do this with nothing on upon which blood could fasten; and with anything like care he could get away, leaving the raincoat there, and go and perform the necessary washing."

A jury, like an audience of children, always responds to a really vivid picture. Here was conjured up an entire series of pictures, each with its own hard outline and effect. Wallace upstairs, coolly putting on his mackintosh; Wallace descending, step by step, to his unsuspecting victim; the fierce and bloody act of swift annihilation; Wallace slipping off the saturated mackintosh as a boxer in a floodlit ring might shed his dressing gown (how apt and telling was Hemmerde's simple phrase); Wallace trying to burn the mackintosh and finding his carefully plotted time-table in arrear; Wallace doing the best he could and bundling the mackintosh underneath the inanimate body of his wife; Wallace stepping out of his house into the street—wicked, triumphant, satisfied, and free.

Wallace; always Wallace. For who else—who else—could have wanted to destroy that mackintosh?

In order of chronology this was Hanging Point Five. In order of effectiveness, it may have been Number One.

The biggest shots had now been fired; Hemmerde followed with a fusillade of shrapnel.

There was "an iron sort of poker thing" which had lain by the parlour gas stove from time immemorial, according to a woman who came in to do the cleaning. It had been there on her last visit; after the murder it was missing. It was, said Hemmerde, a weapon "amply sufficient to have done this deed," and moreover one which could be disposed of without trouble. . . .

There were some treasury notes in a vase upon the bedroom mantelpiece, one of which, rather curiously, was marked or smeared with blood. This showed, said Hemmerde, that it had been handled by the murderer, and therefore the idea of theft could be utterly ruled out. "And if you eliminate money," counsel added, "what are you left with? . . ."

There had been a talk in the street on January 22nd between Wallace and the chess captain who had taken "Qualtrough's" message. "Can you tell me," Wallace asked him, "at what time you received it?" About seven o'clock or thereabouts, the captain thought. "Can't you get nearer to it than that?" said Wallace. "It is of great importance to me." Now

why, demanded Hemmerde, why was it of great importance to him?
The police at that time had certainly not told him that they thought
that *he* was the person who had phoned. . . .

These, however, were secondary items, and Hemmerde was far too
sensitive an artist to conclude such a bravura effort on a diminuendo.
He had made a memorable speech and he meant to wind it up in
memorable style.

He laid down the heavy black notebook which, according to his
habit, he had used throughout both as symbol and mnemonic. Confronting the jury squarely, hands unencumbered for the comminatory
gesture, he moved with a master's ease to his finale—a dazzling sum-
mary of the case he had presented.

The telephone call from the nearby box, the ostentatious and persistent quest for Menlove Gardens East, the trouble with the doors that
"evaporated" so opportunely, the prisoner's "cold, collected air," the
mackintosh—all these weapons, so industriously assembled, were
hurled upon the target in shattering succession.

The peroration was not uncharacteristic, nor unworthy. "If you think
that the case is fairly proved against this man, that brutally and wan-
tonly he sent this unfortunate woman to her account, it will be your
duty to call him to his account."

During this long and gripping tour de force, Roland Oliver of necessity sat silent as his client. There was nothing he could do except
possess his soul in patience. Now Hammerde had finished; the evidence
was beginning; henceforward the defender would come into his own.

But there was not to be a sudden and spectacular transformation.
The procedure of the English courts did not admit of that. Whittling
down the Crown case in cross-examination must precede any attempt
to supplant it by your own, and in the Wallace trial, with its multiplicity
of points, the whittling-down process was bound to be prolonged.

The first consequential steps in this direction were taken when the
chess captain came into the box.

This innocent instrument of a diabolical scheme had just been in-
terrogated by Hemmerde for the Crown. He was not invited to give a
direct account of his telephone talk with "Qualtrough"; in the lack of
proof positive that "Qualtrough" was really Wallace (proof that would
have determined the issue at one stroke) this would have infringed
the hearsay rule. His evidence on the matter had had to be confined to
the message he had passed to Wallace later on.

Oliver, though, representing the prisoner, could, if he thought it expedient, waive the rule's protection. This he proceeded to do with immediate advantage.

"I am interested," he said to the witness, "in the voice that addressed you on the telephone. Could you reproduce the conversation for us, do you think?"

"I can give you an idea of it."

"The part I am interested in particularly," said Oliver, "is the part in which the voice told you about the business, whatever it was. Can you remember that?"

"Oh, yes." The chess captain, unfamiliar with the rules that govern moves on the forensic board, may have been wondering why nobody had asked him this before. Willingly he got it off his chest. "I told him that Mr. Wallace was coming to the club that night; would he ring up again? He said, 'No, I am too busy; I have got my girl's twenty-first birthday on, and I want to see Mr. Wallace on a matter of business; it is something in the nature of his business.' "

"Something in the nature of his business, coupled with a reference to his daughter?"

"Yes."

The sting had been fully drawn from one of Hemmerde's sharpest strictures—that Wallace on the tram had talked about "important business" when nobody had told him what "Qualtrough's" business was.

Having made this neat score on a minor matter, Oliver passed to a much more vital point.

"You had altogether quite a conversation with the voice?"

"Yes."

"You said it was a strong, gruff voice?"

"Yes."

"And a confident one?"

"Yes; sure of himself."

Then followed five of the most momentous questions ever asked and answered in a court of law.

"Was it a natural voice?"

"That is difficult to judge."

"I know it is. But did it occur to you that it was not a natural voice at the time?"

"No, I had no reason for thinking that."

"Do you know Mr. Wallace's voice well?"

"Yes."

"Did it occur to you that it was anything like his voice?"

"Certainly not."

The definiteness of this reply carried extra weight because the witness had shown himself exceptionally scrupulous and disinclined to dogmatic assertion.

"Does it occur to you now that it was anything like his voice?"

The witness cogitated with a chess player's deliberation.

"It would be a great stretch of the imagination for me to say anything like that," he said.

The reporters scribbled madly. The spectators raised their eyebrows. One or two found themselves impelled to glance at Hemmerde who looked straight ahead with majestic unconcern.

The whittling-down operations had got well into their stride.

They continued all through that day and the next. The regiment of witnesses—there were no less than twenty-six—called to make good that overwhelming opening undid in sum as much as they established. One Crown weapon after another that had seemed so mortal as it sped from Hemmerde's hand crumpled like paper and fell harmlessly away.

The second day ran specially well for the defence. It produced two witnesses of paramount importance—Mrs. Florence Johnston and Professor John MacFall.

Mrs. Johnston and her husband were Wallace's next-door neighbours. Circumstances had imposed on them not one but two ordeals: after the horror in the house that night came the undesired publicity and nerve rack of the trial. They stood up gallantly to both. Between them they drew a picture, unstudiedly graphic and palpably veracious, of the supposed murderer's arrival home.

Mr. Johnston gave his evidence first. He was lucid, objective, manifestly unbiased. He covered the ground so thoroughly—and so fairly —when examined by the Crown that Roland Oliver had few questions to put. But one useful point emerged in cross-examination: that Wallace, *with the Johnstons looking on*, had not fumbled nor pushed at the lock of his back door. If, as Hemmerde so strenuously suggested, he could have got in at any time, but was waiting for an audience, one might have expected some pretence of awkwardness to lend a little colour to his bogus protestations.

Mrs. Johnston's tone was as sterling as her husband's, and her evidence-in-chief closely followed the lines of his. Oliver, though, detained her rather longer in the box. Maybe he had sensed what proved to be the fact—that she had the woman's observant eye for *people* as her husband had the male's observant eye for *things*.

Oliver asked her at once about Wallace's demeanour, which Hemmerde had termed "extremely cold."

"Before your husband left to fetch the police, did Mr. Wallace appear to be suffering from shock?"

"Yes," said Mrs. Johnston, "to an extent."

"It is very difficult, isn't it, to judge what is passing in other minds?"

"Manners are so different, are they not?" replied the witness, thereby showing both sensibility and sense.

"But while you were with him did he break down?"

"Yes, twice; he put his hands to his head and sobbed."

"That was before the police arrived?"

"Yes. If we were left alone he appeared as if he would break down, and he appeared to pull himself together when a great many were knocking about."

"When the police came?"

"Yes."

"He made an effort to control himself?"

"Yes."

"Did you think," Oliver asked boldly, "that there was anything suspicious about his manner from beginning to end?"

"No," said Mrs. Johnston firmly. "I did not."

That was at once concise and comprehensive. Good advocates do not stop to paint lilies at the wayside, and Roland Oliver immediately pressed on. He ascertained that, just before leaving her own home, Mrs. Johnston had heard knocking on Wallace's back door—further support, this, for the defence's contention that Wallace was genuinely unable to get in. He ascertained too that Wallace, when asked in her presence by the police about the mackintosh, frankly and promptly declared it was his own—a valuable statement to have upon the record, as the police were now asserting that Wallace had been evasive.

Oliver then turned to this strange business of the mackintosh, and its singular position in relation to the body.

"Do you think it possible," he asked, "that Mrs. Wallace might have thrown it round her shoulders to go and open the front door?"

"That was my idea," said Mrs. Johnston.

"You had the idea, too?"

"It just flashed across my mind because it was a peculiar thing, a mackintosh."

"I quite agree. Do you know that in fact Mrs. Wallace had a cold?"

"Yes."

"Did you know that she had seen the doctor for bronchitis?"

"No, but I knew she had been very poorly."

These questions foreshadowed Oliver's theory of the crime; an alternative reconstruction to set up beside Hemmerde's and to pit against the surmises of Professor John MacFall.

Macfall was a very great expert. He instructed the students of Liverpool University in forensic medicine. He examined the students of four other universities in medical jurisprudence. He had been on the scene of the crime within an hour of its discovery; scientifically he had acquired the necessary data; now, facing the jury as he so often faced his class, he prepared to demonstrate exactly what had happened.

He had examined the body at ten past ten that night and observed the progress made by *rigor mortis;* from that he could deduce that death had taken place at least four hours before. (This, as a matter of fact, was a little awkward for the Crown, as they had already called the milk boy, who swore to seeing Mrs. Wallace alive at half past six. But MacFall was unmoved; perhaps he placed more faith in *rigor mortis* than in milk boys. He stuck to his view, making only this concession —that there was a margin of error in *rigor mortis* calculations, which he fixed in this instance at an hour either way.) He had examined the blood marks on the furniture and on the walls; from them he could deduce that, at the moment of attack, Mrs. Wallace had been sitting in an armchair by the fireplace, head inclined a little forward "as if talking to somebody." He had examined the bloodstains that were "all over" the mackintosh; from them he could deduce that blood had "spurted" on to the garment from *in front.* He had examined the blood clot in the water-closet pan; from that he could deduce that it had been spilt at the same time as the blood clot by the body. He had examined the position of the blows upon the head; from them he could deduce the murderer's mental state. "I know it was not an ordinary case of assault or serious injury. It was a case of frenzy."

Here was an exercise in the deductive faculty that would not have been scorned by Dupin or Sherlock Holmes. Much of it was highly detrimental to the prisoner. If MacFall was right, the murder had disrupted a quiet, homely talk with someone Mrs. Wallace knew. If MacFall was right, the idea that Mrs. Wallace wore the mackintosh was wrong. If MacFall was right, the blood clot reinforced Hemmerde's theory that the murderer had gone upstairs to wash.

It was a critical moment for his client when Roland Oliver got up to start a cross-examination which must rank among the best and most adroit of recent times.

He first took the witness's categorical assertion that the murderer, whoever he was, had acted in a frenzy. There was obvious capital to be derived from this.

"If this is the work of a maniac, and he is a sane man, he didn't do it. Is that right?"

MacFall knew, as Oliver did, that Wallace had been under the usual observation, and that the experts held him to be of perfectly sound mind. He gave a canny answer.

"He may be sane now," he said.

"It is a rash suggestion, is it not?" Oliver said sternly.

"Not in the slightest."

"The fact that a man has been sane for fifty-two years, and has been sane while in custody for the last three months, would rather tend to prove that he has *always* been sane, would it not?"

The sarcasm was evident and justified. MacFall's response was the equivalent of a boxer covering up.

"Not necessarily," he said.

"Not necessarily?"

"We know very little about the private lives of people or their thoughts."

Oliver might have asked what sort of frenzy it would be that began at least twenty-four hours before it reached fruition. But he saved this for later comment; there were other, more vital, matters calling for attention.

The police had found three characteristic burn marks on Mrs. Wallace's skirt, corresponding with the gas fire in the room. From that common ground, Oliver launched his attack upon MacFall's reconstruction.

"Those burn marks would indicate that the gas fire had been alight, would they not?"

"Yes."

"The handle to the gas fire is on the right-hand side of it?"

"Yes."

"And just above it is a gas light?"

"Yes."

"Suppose a woman went into that room, lit the gas, and lit the fire, she would have to stoop down, wouldn't she?"

"Presumably."

"If she did this with her back towards the doorway and someone was on her right-hand side, he would be in a position to strike her as she rose?"

"He would."

"And her head might very well be in the position in which you have put it?"

"Exactly."

In six questions the defence theory had been erected on MacFall's own foundation. It seemed as valid as his own. And it evoked, of course, an entirely different picture—that of a caller being admitted and brought into the parlour, perhaps on the pretext that he wished to leave a note. Such a request would not be startling to the wife of an insurance agent.

At this point Oliver reintroduced the mackintosh.

"If she had had it round her, and the gas fire was alight, and she fell when she was struck, so as to burn her skirt in the lit fire, don't you think it is quite possible that the mackintosh swung round on to the fireplace and caught fire?"

"No," said MacFall, "because there is no evidence of it being on her right or left arm."

"Suppose it was round her shoulders, and she collapsed, do you not see the possibility of the bottom of the mackintosh falling into the fire and getting burnt too?"

"There is the possibility," MacFall conceded.

"Her hair was pulled away from her head, all up?"

"Yes."

"And the pad which had been under her hair was away from the body?"

"Yes, some inches."

"Do you not see the possibility of someone having grasped her by the hair to pull her from the fire?"

"Yes."

This again was completely successful. But while giving all credit to the advocate, one should not withhold it from the witness. MacFall was a theorist, but a fair-minded theorist; present him with a logical proposition and he would accept it without quibble.

Having established his own position, Oliver proceeded to advance upon MacFall's. The Professor had backed up, at least by implication, Hemmerde's postulate that Wallace wore the mackintosh.

"Whether clothed or whether naked," Oliver asked, "it would be necessary, would it not, that many splashes of blood would fall on the assailant?"

"Yes," MacFall said, "I should expect to find them."

"The last blows being probably struck with the head on the ground, there would be blood upon his feet and the lower part of his legs?"

"I should expect that."

"And the mackintosh would not come down below the knees, which would leave the legs from the knees downward exposed to the blood?"

"Yes."

"And there would be blood on his face?"

"Yes."

"And his hair?"

"Yes."

"Would you agree that if blood gets below the finger nails it is difficult to get away?"

"It is difficult."

"Would you agree it would be almost certain that the assailant would have blood under the finger nails?"

MacFall jibbed at this and cautiously covered up again.

"Not necessarily," he said.

But Oliver held the initiative and declined to be put off.

"Supposing the mackintosh were placed under the body, the assailant would have had to lift the shoulder and the head to do it?"

"He would."

"That would have involved getting himself heavily dabbled in blood, would it not?"

"Dabbled in blood," MacFall agreed, "but not heavily."

The qualification, however fitting, hardly mattered. Oliver had achieved an advantageous situation. He had struck at MacFall's strongest points and carried them in triumph. Now he could strike at points where MacFall seemed weak.

"With regard to the time of death," he said: "When did you first think it was important?"

"Immediately I saw the body."

"And you made a series of observations, first as to *rigor mortis*, and second, as to the condition of the exuded blood?"

"The blood is a help," MacFall said, "but it is not so definite as *rigor mortis*."

"You put *rigor mortis* first. How many notes," Oliver asked offhandedly, "did you make with regard to *rigor mortis*?"

"Practically none."

"Can you show me one?" Oliver said pleasantly.

"No," said MacFall, "I do not think I can."

"So you, being intent from the start on the importance of *rigor mortis* as to the time of death, have not made one note with regard to *rigor mortis?*"

This, of course, was no more than a debating point. The real issue over *rigor mortis* was joined with the next question.

"*Rigor* is a very fallible test as to the time of death?"

"Not in the present case of an ordinary person dying in health."

"I suggest it is a very fallible factor even in healthy people."

"Well," said MacFall, "it is, just a little."

"And a powerful, muscular body will be affected much more slowly than a frail, feeble body?"

"Yes."

"Was this not a frail, feeble body?"

"She was feeble."

"Was she not frail?"

"She was a weak woman."

"Frail?" Oliver insisted.

MacFall surrendered.

"Yes," he said, "she was frail."

"Bearing in mind that this frail, feeble woman would be more likely to be affected by *rigor*, are you going to swear that she was killed more than *three* hours before you saw her?"

(Three hours before ten past ten, be it remembered, Wallace was already on the tramcar, chattering to the conductor about Menlove Gardens East.)

"No, I am not going to swear," MacFall replied punctiliously. "I am going to give an opinion, and I swear that the opinion shall be an honest one."

It was a good answer; both honourable and engaging.

"Then what *is* your opinion?" the judge interpolated.

"My opinion was formed at the time that the woman had been dead about four hours."

The witness could now be likened to a sitting bird.

"If she was alive at half past six," said Oliver agreeably, "your opinion is wrong."

"Yes," MacFall admitted. He could do no other.

The duel was nearly over now, with counsel unquestionably gathering the honours. Only the blood clot still remained to be considered.

Oliver suggested that it must have dropped upon the pan at least an hour after the woman met her death. MacFall thought not.

"Didn't it occur to you that someone who came in after nine might have dropped that clot of blood upon the pan?"

"The possibility did occur to me."

"Didn't you think that there was a chance that the police had carried it there?"

"Yes," MacFall said candidly.

Oliver sat down. He had realised the dream of every cross-examiner. He had turned the chief expert for the Crown into a witness for the defence.

Wallace is not one of the tidy cases. It has no single theme round which the evidence revolves. It is a compound of many parts, contributed from many sources, which build up an effect not by unity but by mass. Frith's *Derby Day* is perhaps its parallel in art. . . .

As the long line of prosecution witnesses passed in turn through the harsh test of the box, Oliver was repeatedly picking up small gains, which, in the aggregate, greatly changed the picture. There was the Prudential Superintendent, Wallace's immediate superior, who said the normal accounting day was Wednesday, and that anyone who knew Wallace's habits or employment might expect him to have the bulk of his cash at home on Tuesday night. There was a police officer, the first upon the scene, who agreed that he saw Wallace fingering the treasury notes, one of which was smeared with blood—and this of course was after he had touched the bespattered body. There was a locksmith who had inspected the locks on both the doors; the back, he said, was rusty and opened upon pressure; the front was defective, with a worn and slipping latch. There was the City Analyst, who agreed with Roland Oliver that the burnt part of the mackintosh lay in *front* of the gas fire.

And, finally, there was the Detective Superintendent, whose cross-examination reached a climax in this fashion.

"You don't doubt, do you," Oliver asked him, "from your knowledge of this type of house, that the back kitchen was the sitting room?"

"Yes, it was."

"And the parlour was kept for visitors?"

"Yes."

"When a visitor comes in at the front door he is shown into the parlour, is he not?"

"I suppose so."

"And the gas lit and the fire lit; that is the usual thing?"

"Yes."

"What I am putting to you is that everything in that room was consistent with a knock at the front door, and the admission of someone, and the visitor being taken into the parlour."

"It is quite possible," the Superintendent agreed.

When the Crown evidence ended, early on the third day, the trial had assumed the shape that renders it unique. Any set of circumstances that is extracted from it will readily support two incompatible hypotheses; they will be equally consistent with innocence and guilt.

It is pre-eminently the case where everything is cancelled out by something else.

One small episode in the Crown case, deliberately excluded from our general scrutiny, must now be treated—as is appropriate—*in vacuo*. It was an episode without point, without bearing, without force; it defies connection with reasoning and logic; it detracts by its almost imbecile irrelevance from the dignity with which the trial was otherwise invested.

A constable was called to say he had seen Wallace, looking "very distressed," on the day of the murder at 3.30 *p.m.*—that is, at least three hours, on the Crown's own showing, before Mrs. Wallace was savagely done to death. Asked what signs of distress he had observed, the constable replied that Wallace was dabbing his eye with his coat sleeve and appeared to him as though he had been crying.

"I wonder," Oliver said, "if it occurred to you that your eyes could water with the cold?"

The constable assented.

"And you might rub them?"

"Quite possible."

"I suggest that you are mistaken in thinking that the signs you saw were signs of distress occasioned by committing a crime."

"He gave me the impression," said the constable, "that he had suffered some bereavement."

"If I were to call about twenty-five people who saw him that afternoon round about that time and they said he was just as usual, would you say they had made a mistake?"

The deepest of police instincts were aroused.

"I should stick to my opinion," the constable said stubbornly. . . .

Put aside the possibility that the constable was mistaken. Put aside the possibility that he misconstrued what he saw. Consider the time element alone. If this evidence was accepted, together with the inference the prosecution drew, Wallace went about the streets of Liverpool that day weeping over a crime that he was *going* to commit!

The notion is farcical, and I doubt whether Hemmerde relished the job of presenting such a witness. He was never afraid to criticise police follies, and one can imagine the blistering comment he would have made if this particular episode had occurred in a case which he had been trying in his capacity as Recorder of the city.

Oliver had abundance of material when he rose to introduce the prisoner's case. The Hanging Points had been blunted one by one. The telephone call, the trouble with the doors, the accused's demeanour, the riddle of the mackintosh—each had either assumed a different colour or shown itself open to a new and harmless inference. The garrulous quest for Menlove Gardens East alone retained its full initial force; but Oliver was to argue trenchantly that Wallace's enquiries, though prosy and persistent, came naturally from a man out in pursuit of business who did not want to return without profit or reward. If the jury would recognise that this possibility at least could not be excluded, by any rational assessment of the evidence the Crown's five Hanging Points had lost the power to hang.

But Oliver did not rest upon a negative defence. He counter-attacked with vigour, concentrating particularly on the limits set by time. If Wallace was indeed the murderer of his wife, he had a great deal to do that night before leaving the house. He had to make himself clean —hands, face, nails, hair—after a filthy and polluting deed. He had either to dispose of his blood-splashed, blood-smeared clothes, or— adopting Hemmerde's hypothesis—take off the mackintosh, go upstairs and dress. He had, presumably, to disarrange the bedroom. He had to wipe, secrete, and smuggle out the weapon. All this, together with the crime itself, must have been done in less than twenty minutes. No one disputed that, it was the Crown's case that Wallace had left home at ten to seven. It was the Crown's case that Mrs. Wallace was alive at half past six.

Less than twenty minutes; even if the first blow fell with the milk boy's cans still clattering outside. Most improbable, Oliver said; most improbable that any man in so short a time could have accomplished so much with such thoroughness and success. Not a mark on his body. Not a stain on his clothes. Not a trace of a weapon anywhere.

If it was improbable in twenty minutes, it was clearly impossible in five or even ten. Oliver sought to narrow down the gap. As a preparatory step he put in the box the Professor of Pathology at Liverpool University, who drew from the evidence of *rigor* the conclusion that death might well have taken place after seven o'clock. Having justly pointed out that the Crown based the time of Mrs. Wallace's last appearance on the word and recollection of a fourteen-year-old boy, Oliver proceeded to call three similar boys himself. One said that he actually saw the milk boy standing on the step in front of Wallace's house; this was two minutes after he had looked at a church clock and noted that the time was twenty-five to seven. The other two both swore that, on the night after the murder, the milk boy—by then no doubt the hero of the neighbourhood—remarked, in the course of conversation in the street, that he had seen Mrs. Wallace at a quarter to seven.

Which of these lads was telling the truth? Who could decide? And unless it could be decided, definitely and clearly, in favour of the milk boy and against his companions, could a verdict of guilty properly be found? On *ten* minutes? On *five?*

Hemmerde, in his otherwise exhaustive final speech, skated lightly and swiftly over this question of the time factor. He had already displayed power; now he displayed discretion.

In the last resort a prisoner is always his own chief witness. His influence on events cannot be gathered from the record. The jury try to mark, not only what he says, but what he *is*. They form an impression of the man himself which, whether true or false, may move them more than logic.

In the witness box Wallace lived up to all the descriptions given of his nature. He was quiet, gentle, unflustered and precise. His nerves were throughout under an absolute command which, independently of innocence or guilt, appeared remarkable for one in his position. Perhaps it was stoicism; perhaps it was callousness; perhaps it derived from ineradicable grief that made him await his fate without concern.

"Is there anyone in the world," Oliver asked him, "who could take the place of your wife in your life?"

"No," said Wallace, "there is not."

"Have you got anyone to live with now?"

"No."

"Or to live for?"

"No."

In the days immediately following the crime Wallace made numerous statements to the police. They were lengthy, they were detailed, and there was nothing in them he desired to change. "I need not have called him," declared Oliver rhetorically, and in the strict sense this was true. But expedience and policy could not be disregarded, and besides, there were several minor points that only Wallace himself could satisfactorily clear up.

They were put to him, these points, one after another. Why, if his usual accounting day was Wednesday, had there been so little money in the house that Tuesday night? "I did not collect on the Saturday," he said, "because I was laid up with influenza. . . . I paid ten guineas out in sickness benefit out of what I had collected up to then." Why, if he was not trying to fabricate an alibi, did he take out his watch when talking to the policeman and call the latter's attention to the time? "The policeman told me I could get a directory at the post-office up the road. . . . I realised that if it was a local post-office it was probably a mixed sort of shop, and if I left it till after eight it would be closed, so I looked to see what time I had to spare." Why, unless prompted by consciousness of guilt, did he tell the chess captain, two days after the crime, that the exact time of the telephone call was of great importance to him? "I had just come from the police station. Superintendent Thomas had given me the information that they had been able to trace the call to a call-box near my home. . . . I felt that if I had left home at a quarter past seven, and the telephone call had been made at seven o'clock, and that the police up to then had believed all my statements to be true (and I had no reason to think otherwise), then that automatically cleared me of having sent the message."

You believed—or you did not believe. You trusted—or suspected. But at least you did not have to search the void for explanations. Each item in the Crown case was meticulously met.

Hemmerde's questioning of Wallace was rigorous and close. He did not bully or harass him, as Muir had bullied and harassed Steinie Morrison, but the pressure he exerted can be fairly called relentless. It became apparent that nothing in the course of the hearing had shaken Hemmerde's conviction that Wallace was the culprit.

The cross-examination attained a rare level of technical accomplishment. Much of it was not designed to extract new information, but rather to restate and recapitulate the alleged improbabilities in the defendant's case. The telephone call, for instance; in a series of questions Hemmerde scoffed at the idea that the caller could have been anyone but the prisoner himself. The alternative, it appeared, was positively absurd.

"Of course," he remarked, " 'Mr. Qualtrough' had no means of knowing whether you would receive the message that night, because no one knew for certain you were going to be at the club?"

"Yes," said Wallace. "That is so."

"Then without knowing you would even get the message, and without knowing you would ever go to Menlove Gardens East, he was waiting for your departure the next night?"

"It would look like it."

"Did it ever occur to you that he would have to watch both doors, front and back?"

"No," said Wallace simply. "It did not."

"You're a man of business instincts; you could hardly be a Prudential agent if you were not?"

"That is so."

"You must have realised that he had not the slightest idea whether you got his message?"

"Yes, I did."

"And in spite of that," said Hemmerde incredulously, "you go off to Menlove Gardens East?"

"Yes."

"Not only could he not know that you would go, but he couldn't have known that you wouldn't look up a directory and find there was no such place?"

"No."

"He would have to risk all that?"

"Yes."

"And of course, you *could* have found out at once, if you *had* looked it up in the directory, where Menlove Gardens East was—or was not?"

"Yes," said Wallace. "I could have done."

Hemmerde's share in this dialogue was manifestly brilliant. But one should not pass over the part played by the prisoner. The form of the questions must have tempted him to *argue*, to show that the medal looked quite different in reverse. He never once succumbed to the temptation. He answered always with the utmost candour and made no attempt at self-justification. The facts, he implied, would have to speak for themselves.

Occasionally Hemmerde seemed to catch him out. There was a dramatic moment early in the long interrogation when Wallace said he had never observed any blood upon his hands. "Then," said the prosecutor in pardonable triumph, "no blood from your hands could have got on to those notes in the vase on the mantelpiece?" There were times when Wallace's evidence did not wholly correspond with one or other of his many written statements. There were "discrepancies," too, in these statements themselves, but the judge was to put this in correct perspective. "I have read through them very carefully," he said, "and I think it is wonderful that they are as lucid, accurate and consistent as they are."

The scope of this comment might not improperly be extended to cover the prisoner's testimony on oath.

The fourth day of the trial was well advanced when, after hearing two impressive final speeches, Mr. Justice Wright began his summing up.

Some judges, taciturn and unaspiring, here make their first real impact on the jury. Others, persistently voluble and assertive, merely pass from conversation into monologue. Wright could be placed in neither category. He intervened seldom in a well-conducted case; he made no effort to impose himself; but by the majesty of his mind and presence he occupied always an ascendant place.

There was nothing in Wright's career at the Bar to prepare him for the tasks of a Red Judge on assize. He had been a gifted specialist in commercial work, engaged on recondite disputes of admiralty and contract. His merits as a lawyer were admittedly outstanding, and he was now paying a brief call on the King's Bench Division in the course of a swift journey upwards to the House of Lords. His fame and his achievement were in the domain of pure intellect, and one might have supposed that the run of criminal trials, which demand from a judge other and broader virtues—imagination, worldly sense and human understanding—belonged to a sphere in which he would not excel. But the contrary was the fact. Wright was that infrequent and superlative phenomenon: a great lawyer who was also a great man.

The judge *directs* the jury on the law, and they are bound to comply with his direction. He does not direct the jury on the facts; he may, and often does, express his own opinion, but they have the legal right to disregard it. This is as it should be; if the jury is to be nothing more than the judge's rubber stamp there is no valid reason why it should be convoked. One could find it possible to wish that, in a great many cases, juries would show more independence than they do. But indictments for murder are in a class apart. The jury may entertain a personal belief that the prisoner is guilty on a capital charge. But should they not feel there *must* be reasonable doubt if a judge of massive and renowned ability indicates his view that the case is not made out?

Time and time again this theme recurred in Wright's incisive, luminous address.

He started with a solemn caution against prejudice. "Members of of the jury, you, I believe, are living more or less in this neighbourhood. I come here as a stranger, and know nothing about the case until I come into court or look at the depositions, and I need not warn you that *you must approach this matter without any preconceived notions at all.* Your business here is to listen to the evidence, and to consider the evidence and nothing else." He followed this by reminding them that the evidence against Wallace was purely circumstantial, and explained in simple terms the test to be adopted. "Circumstantial evidence may vary in value almost infinitely. Some is as good and conclusive as the evidence of actual witnesses. In other cases, the only circumstantial evidence which anyone can present still leaves loopholes and doubts. . . . The real test of the value of circumstantial evidence is this: *does it exclude other theories or possibilities?* If you cannot put the evidence against the accused beyond a probability; if it is a probability which is not inconsistent with there being other reasonable possibilities; then it is impossible for a jury to say, 'We are satisfied beyond a reasonable doubt that the charge is made out.'" By this, the correct test, the charge against Wallace failed, as Mr. Justice Wright repeatedly implied.

He discussed the telephone call and asked: "What is the reasonably certain evidence, substantially excluding other possibilities, that it was the prisoner who rang up that night?" Such data as they had, indeed, pointed the other way. "*It is difficult to imagine that a man like the chess captain, in a conversation so prolonged, would not, even if the voice had been disguised, recognise the prisoner's voice if it was the prisoner.*" He referred to the conversation between Wallace and the chess captain two days after the crime had been committed: "*It would be very dangerous to draw from that any inference seriously adverse to the prisoner.*" He advised them to dismiss the blood clot from their minds: "*It is difficult to see how it has any connection with the murder.*"

As the judge approached the major issues, he was equally penetrating and forthright. "If the prisoner was the murderer, what time had he available? That is the most vital part of the whole case. You will have to consider whether the narrow limits allowed, possibly of not more than ten minutes, would be sufficient. . . . There was a lot to do, and twenty minutes afterwards he was found, apparently completely dressed and apparently without any signs of discomposure, on a tramcar twenty minutes' journey from his home. . . . It does not follow that he did not do it, *but you have to be satisfied that he did do it.*" Again: "How did he get rid of the weapon in the time open to him? The only possible place where he could have dropped it on his way, an open space between the house and the tram, has been combed, and the drains have been searched, but no trace can be found of it. . . . I do not say it is impossible for a murderer under these circumstances to have disposed of a weapon, but *when you are considering whether it is brought home to the prisoner, you must carefully consider all these aspects.*" Again: "If he was going quite honestly to search for Mr. Qualtrough in Menlove Gardens East in the hope of getting a useful commission, then no doubt he would have probed the matter to the bottom. . . . *It is no use applying tests to evidence if none of them really excludes the possibility of the prisoner being innocent.*" And again: "*It is not at all impossible that he might have been so upset at the moment as to have had a difficulty in overcoming the friction of the two locks.*"

The regular frequenters of the court—solicitors, officials, lawyers' clerks and pressmen—nodded knowingly to each other as the judge's charge progressed. No mincing matters; no beating about the bush. His lordship clearly thought it would be improper to convict, and he was telling the jury so in terse and pithy terms.

"However you regard the matter, the whole crime was so skilfully devised and executed, and *there is such an absence of any trace to incriminate anybody as to make it very difficult to say*—although this is a matter entirely for you—*that it can be brought home to any one in particular.*"

Judicial guidance was never more explicit. The news seeped out and spread along the corridors; Wallace'll get off; he's summing up for an acquittal. . . .

The jury remained out for just over an hour. One marvels that they dared return to court at all. But their fathers had perversely convicted Mrs. Maybrick, and now these representatives of a more enlightened epoch jealously preserved the Liverpool tradition.

Wallace in 1931 possessed a remedy denied to Mrs. Maybrick in 1889. There was the Court of Criminal Appeal.

The Court of Criminal Appeal—which generally consists of three King's Bench judges—exercises only defined and limited powers. It does not re-try cases. It does not, as a rule, examine any evidence unless already tendered in the lower court. It does not put itself in the position of a jury; it is not enough for the three judges to say:

"Had we been asked, we would have found a different verdict." (In effect the Court said that about the trial of Steinie Morrison; Steinie's appeal was nevertheless dismissed.) The Court is a court of law rather than of fact; it will quash a conviction on a purely legal point (inadmissibility of evidence, misdirection by the judge), but it will not otherwise interfere with a verdict unless it is unreasonable and against the weight of evidence.

Since its inception in the year 1907 the Court has allowed hundreds of appeals on the ground that a verdict was against the rules of law. It has allowed appeals but seldom on the ground that a verdict was against the weight of fact, and until 1931, in a case of murder, never. Wallace was to create that precedent. After a two days' hearing, in which Oliver fought magnificently to save his client's life, the Court delivered judgment with dispassionate formality. "Section Four of the Criminal Appeal Act of 1907 provides that the Court of Criminal Appeal shall allow the appeal if they think that the verdict of the jury should be set aside on the ground that it cannot be supported having regard to the evidence. The conclusion at which we have arrived is that the case against the appellant, which we have carefully and anxiously considered and discussed, was not proved with that certainty which is necessary in order to justify a verdict of guilty, and therefore it is our duty to take the course indicated by the Section of the Statute to which I have referred. The result is that this appeal will be allowed and the conviction quashed."

And so William Herbert Wallace was set free—free to return to Liverpool, where he was ostracised and hounded; free to resume his employment, where he was mercifully transferred to inside work; free to retire for refuge to the country, where two years later he died, solitary, broken, a victim of despair.

"The great fascination of Wallace," said Agate, "is that the case of both sides is unanswerable."

"And, therefore," I said, "you would agree with the Court of Criminal Appeal?"

"Certainly."

"And the likelihood of Wallace being guilty is no less, but also no greater, than that of his being innocent?"

"Of course."

"Very well," I said, "let us adopt—as we ought to adopt—the theory of his innocence. Somebody else, then, did this dreadful thing. Somebody else invented Mr. Qualtrough; somebody else invented Menlove

Gardens East. And this somebody else has got away with it completely. He killed that woman in her own house, in a populous district, with her neighbours at home next door—and vanished into space. Possibly, probably, he is still alive. What sort of a person, now, do you think he'd be? A clerk? A writer? A civil servant? A priest?"

"A genius," said Agate flatly. "A brutal, bloody fiend—and a genius."

"I wonder if he reads the stuff that's written on the crime," I said, "and sometimes talks about the case among his friends."

"That," said Agate sombrely, "is the most shocking thought of all."

6

Norman Thorne

OF ALL the verdicts examined in this book, the least disputable, admittedly, is that on Norman Thorne. His trial was a model of dignity and fairness; he was finely defended by a notable defender; the issues and the evidence were handled by the judge in a manner that drew praise from the Court of Criminal Appeal. And indeed it is highly probable that, in convicting Thorne of murder, the jury did no more than register the truth. But a high degree of probability is not to be equated with sufficient legal proof, and study of this case makes one inclined to wonder whether the Crown did not fall a fraction short of discharging the heavy onus that rightly lies upon it.

On Friday, December 5th, 1924, Elsie Cameron, a young London typist living with her parents, set off for Crowborough to see her sweetheart, Norman Thorne. She bought her ticket, passed through the barrier, found a seat in a third-class carriage, put her cheap little attaché case on the rack above her head, and settled herself down for the short journey, mercifully unaware that it was the last she would make on earth.

The expedition was not prompted by romantic passion, though Elsie Cameron was very much in love. At the moment practical matters occupied her mind. She and Thorne had been engaged since 1922; for more than a year there had been signs that he was cooling; lately he had even written of another girl. Now Elsie Cameron believed that she was pregnant by him, a state of affairs which would not brook vacillation or delay. She was going to Crowborough to claim her rights, to insist that her fiancé should marry her at once. It was an anxious, overwrought, but above all determined girl that drummed her fingers on the rough upholstery and watched the bleak winter landscape rolling by. . . .

Several days passed. Elsie Cameron did not come home, neither did she write. Her family's surprise soon turned to deep concern, and on the following Wednesday her father wired to Thorne. "ELSIE LEFT FRIDAY. HAVE HEARD NO NEWS. REPLY." Thorne wired back at once. "NOT HERE. OPEN LETTERS. CAN'T UNDERSTAND."

The letters in question were duly opened. There were two of them, each written by Thorne, each posted in Crowborough, each addressed to Elsie at her London home.

"Well," asked the first, "where did you get to yesterday? I went to Groombridge and you did not turn up."

"I was expecting a letter today," said the second, in mild but perceptible accents of reproach, "especially after not seeing you and not hearing from you."

The dates upon these letters confirmed the distracted parents in their fears. Thorne, it appeared, had written them to Elsie days after they had supposed that she was with him.

In yet a further letter, following up his telegram, Thorne shattered their last lingering hope of some misunderstanding. As it sets forth the substance of a story and conveys the essence of an attitude both of which he maintained during the subsequent six weeks, this letter merits quotation in full.

DEAR MRS. CAMERON [it ran,]

I have re-read the telegram over and over again and it has given me quite a shock. I presume from that that Elsie left home on Friday. She wrote to me asking me to meet her at Groombridge on Saturday morning. I went but she did not turn up and I take it something had prevented her at the last moment.

I have been expecting a letter from her all the week and wondering why I did not hear. Apparently she has been gone six days now, and no delay must be made in making enquiries.

Send particulars of how she was dressed. I will try and get what information I can locally. It is an awful position and I fear the worst. What time did she leave and by what train? Why did she not write and say she was coming?

I cannot write any more, as needless to say I am very worried and upset.

> With love to all,
> Yours truly,
> Norman

There was hardly a word of truth in this document. The telegram had not come as a shock to Norman Thorne. He had no need to deduce the day when Elsie left her home, or surmise why she did not present herself on Saturday. He *knew* the reason for her unaccustomed silence. He *knew* how many days—how many hours—she had been "gone." And as for her garments, he had had ample opportunity to study them in detail when he burnt them in his grate. . . .

But all this was a secret locked in his own breast, where he intended that it should remain. The Camerons, left without a clue to guide them in the mystery, reported the disappearance of their daughter to the police.

Investigation into the whereabouts of a missing person is seldom restricted to the immediate physical facts. Character, background and personal relations point out the paths where enquiry should prove fruitful. What was in the missing person's mind? Where would he want to go? What would he want to do? The answer, which may be critically important, can only be sought in the individual's history.

The history of Elsie Cameron was slowly pieced together. Bit by bit, the whole sad, tawdry business came to light: the courtship, the betrothal, the tentative attempts by Thorne to wriggle free, the girl's inflexible resolve to hold her man.

They had met, this hapless couple, under pious auspices, where the cold flame of Wesley casts its light on Kensal Green. Elsie was plain, fragile, inclined to introspection; Thorne was strong, healthy, good-looking in his way. What drew them together is not subject to analysis; one can only set on record that the formula did its work and held them in bond for a short, uneasy space.

Bad luck dogged them from the very start. In the slump Thorne lost his job as engineer; debilitated nerves kept Elsie unemployed. Throughout their engagement they were woefully short of cash.

Thorne's reaction at least showed enterprise. He turned his back upon the engineering trade and, with a small sum borrowed from his father, took a plot of land at Crowborough and began a chicken farm. But the farm failed to prosper. He lived there by himself in a hut twelve feet by seven: primitive, cramped, squalid beyond thought. Even so, Elsie refused to be discouraged. "We can manage in a hut like yours," she wrote, and urged the hesitating bachelor to marry. At every stage, it is clear, the girl had made the pace and the man had, in any given circumstance, recoiled. They were, in fact, a fundamentally ill-assorted pair, possessing nothing in common except a habit of chapel-going and the prospect of privation.

The Other Girl's appearance on the scene was an overt symptom of this underlying trouble. If no Other Girl had ever materialised, if the path of love had technically run smooth, the match would still have ended up in tragedy. It might have been a tragedy of the gradual, wearing sort: resentful husband and disillusioned wife unable or afraid to break their irksome ties. As it was, it turned into a tragedy of violence, where the pressure would not yield without the sacrifice of life.

Thorne had met The Other Girl about six months before. She lived near by. Elsie Cameron had seen her once when she was staying at Crowborough but does not appear to have regarded her as a potential rival. Such confidence was misplaced. Affection soon matured between The Other Girl and Thorne. Presently she took to visiting him at night and local gossip had it that "there was something going on."

Elsie remained in blissful ignorance of this and might so have continued but for Thorne himself. He deliberately chose to reveal his double-dealing, but, one may be sure, not at conscience's dictate. His confession was significantly timed. It was fired back as a counter to reports of Elsie's pregnancy, and was manifestly meant to stave off the immediate marriage for which his fiancée now more than ever pressed. Thus he had written to her on November 25:

> You seem to be taking everything for granted. . . . There are one or two things I haven't told you for more reasons than one. It concerns someone else as well. . . . I am afraid I am between two fires.

Perhaps Elsie's attention was fixed on other things; perhaps she closed her eyes to what she did not want to see. Her reply, which was by return, had expressed merely bewilderment.

> Really Norman, your letter puzzles me, I can't make it out. Why are there one or two things you haven't told me and in what way does it concern someone else? . . . What do you mean by you are afraid you are between two fires. Oh I don't understand things at all.

Dismissing her lover's cryptic utterances, she had reverted to the theme that monopolised and obsessed her.

> Well, Norman, please arrange about getting married as soon as possible. I feel sick every day and things will soon be noticeable to everybody and I want to be married before Christmas and Christmas Day is only a month from tomorrow. . . . Please do get married quickly.

Wilfully or guilelessly, she had not construed his meaning. He must make it plainer—so plain, so simple and so unequivocal that there would be no room for misinterpretation.

On the 27th he had written to her again.

> What I haven't told you is that on certain occasions a girl has been here late at night, I am not going to mention her name, nobody knows. When you gave in to your nerves again and refused to take interest in life I gave up hope in you and let myself go; this is the result. I didn't know last week what I know now. . . . I must have time to think, she thinks I am going to marry her of course, and I have a strong feeling for her, or I shouldn't have done what I have.

Now was *that* straight enough? Not an ambiguous sentence in it except "I didn't know last week what I know now," and surely even Elsie would grasp the drift of that.

She had grasped it, fully. Her next letter, again by return of post, was a genuine cry of anguish.

> You have absolutely broken my heart [she had written], I never thought you were capable of such deception. . . . So I am to take it that you have got this other girl into the same condition which you have got me?

But if Thorne had expected her outraged feelings to turn her from the project upon which she was set, he was doomed to disappointment. She reiterated her demand with emphasis.

> Your duty is to marry me. I have first claim on you. . . . I expect you to marry me and finish with the other girl as soon as possible. My baby must have a name, and another thing I love you in spite of all.

It is an ironical feature of this correspondence that neither allegation of pregnancy was true. Elsie Cameron's was honest but mistaken; Thorne's was a calculated lie. But that had not been known to Elsie Cameron when she started off to Crowborough and vanished into space. She saw herself confronting a desperate situation: a baby on the way, another girl in the same plight, Thorne torn between the two, and her rival being on the spot holding the advantage. Was it not natural, was it not inevitable, that this girl, who had at all times been clamouring for marriage, should hurry to the man by whom her fate was being decided . . . ?

The more the police found out, and the more they thought about it, the more they were driven to work from this conclusion: that nothing bar a catastrophe of the greatest magnitude would have sufficed to divert Elsie Cameron from her goal.

But Thorne stood in the way of this hypothesis. He steadfastly affirmed that she had not come to the farm, that he had not set eyes on her, that he did not know where she was. He behaved, too, exactly as a person should behave who is innocently suffering the torments of suspense. He wandered restlessly about with a troubled, harassed air, appearing to seek comfort in discussion with his neighbours. He canvassed the opinion of everyone he met, while frequently expressing his own melancholy forebodings. He was touchingly eager to assist with the enquiry and bombarded the police with little scraps of information. All in all, observing it in retrospect, his acting through this period was consummately skilled.

One thing robbed his bravura of its full effect. Two nurserymen came forward, one of whom at least knew Elsie Cameron by sight. They had been passing Thorne's gate, they said, on the evening of the 5th, and had seen Elsie Cameron going towards the farm.

It seemed very odd and they might both be mistaken, but of course the police could not afford to disregard this hint. Thorne was asked if he objected to an inspection of his farm, and at once spoke to the contrary with something like enthusiasm. "I'm glad you're coming," he said, "to clear the matter up."

A Superintendent and an Inspector went over the farm, looked into the huts, and found no trace of the girl. Before they left they took a statement from the owner. "She did not come here," Thorne again assured them, "and I have not seen or heard from her."

It was tempting to discount the nurserymen; it was tempting to accept the word of Norman Thorne. Who could be better entitled to belief? His character was unblemished, his record clear; he taught at Sunday School, worked for Temperance societies and spoke on occasion for the Band of Hope; no one could breathe a word to his discredit. Besides, if Thorne was wrong and the nurserymen were right, *where was Elsie Cameron now . . . ?*

Come to think of it, that was the very thing they didn't know.

Meanwhile the public had grown intensely interested in Elsie Cameron's fate. It was almost a matter of principle. You could vanish without trace, no doubt, in the Sahara Desert or the Australian Bush or the upper reaches of the Amazon. But not between Kensal Green and Crowborough. Not in the close-knit network of communities that was southern England. Not where a highly trained, expensive staff of police guarded the safety of the humblest citizen.

It might be good news or bad, it might be life or death, it might be fair play or foul—but don't tell us that the woman can't be *found.*

So Britain grumbled and police efforts redoubled; a crack inspector from Scotland Yard went down to help the Sussex force; but December passed and January began its chilly cycle and still they had made no appreciable advance. Already Elsie Cameron was like some figure in a myth; her name was familiar, her story known, but her existence half forgotten. The case was approaching the edge of that abyss below which lies the limbo of mysteries unsolved.

Then, on January 1st, came the turning point.

Like so many turning points, in other fields besides detection, it did not appear outstandingly important in itself. It was merely that a Crowborough lady—who, one must conclude, saw newspapers but seldom —read for the first time a full account of Elsie's disappearance. She meditated on this singular event, so closely linked with local folk and places. Thorne's farm—she'd passed it more times than she could count. Whenever she went to visit Mrs. Tester, she walked along that road right by his gate. She had been to Mrs. Tester's, too, somewhere about the time they said this girl had vanished. Early in December it was, wasn't it? On a Friday afternoon. The first Friday afternoon . . . the first. . . .

And it all came back to her. Of course; on her way home that evening shortly after five, she had seen a young woman entering Thorne's farm. An ordinary young woman; nothing to distinguish her. One thing, though; she was carrying an attaché case. . . .

It was, in a sense, only the shadow of a story. She couldn't describe the person she had seen. She couldn't say she answered to Elsie Cameron's description. Being absolutely honest she couldn't say more than that she had seen *a* girl, in that place, at that time. But the police now had *three* people all of whom were saying that they had seen *a* girl, in that place, at that time. Sunday School and Band of Hope and Temperance notwithstanding, Thorne must be subjected to a further, final test.

No one could complain that this test was not rigourous—nor that, in the event, the rigour was unjustified. At half past three in the afternoon of January 14th, Chief Inspector Gillan of the Yard, together with other officers, arrived at the farm, where he found Thorne in his hut. Gillan explained in time-honoured phrases that he was making enquiries into Elsie Cameron's disappearance on December 5th, and that he had reason to believe she had been seen alive there on the evening of that day. Thorne was unshaken. "I have heard remarks to that effect," he said, "but I don't believe them." Gillan told him that he proposed to search; Thorne offered his assistance. Gillan asked him whether he would make a further statement; Thorne readily agreed. Gillan then suggested that, as accommodation was lacking in the hut, they might adjourn to the station, and take the statement there.

It might be thought that, however scanty its facilities, the living hut was at least equipped to fulfil this simple function. There were writing materials, there was a table, there were chairs. But perhaps Gillan was right. For this was to be a colossus, a mammoth, a marathon among statements. They began on it at eight o'clock that night: Thorne talking, a Sergeant writing, Gillan breaking off and coming back as other work allowed. When they finished, it was half past three next morning, and a tired Chief Inspector gazed on the fruit of their joint labours —an amplified re-echo of what Thorne had said before.

But meanwhile the new search was getting under way. Once again a squad of police descended on the farm, pledged to explore every inch for Elsie Cameron.

This time they carried spades.

At four minutes past eight on the morning of January 15th one of the policemen digging at the farm turned up an attaché case which had been buried near the gate. Inside it were a jumper, some shoes, and a broken pair of spectacles.

The part which Thorne had so far played with flawless plausibility was exposed in that instant as a fake and a sham. The gathering storm now broke over his head and it raged with unremitting fury till it had destroyed him.

In the station cell where he was now confined, Thorne spent the day pondering his next step. When Gillan had told him he would be detained and probably charged with Elsie Cameron's murder, he had held his peace and uttered not a word. But Thorne was no fool; he must have known that his game of wide-eyed innocence was up.

What could he put in place of all those lies that had served to shield him for so many weeks? A different fiction? Or the naked truth?

Which of the two he chose will never be known certainly. But by the evening he had made up his mind. He asked to see Gillan and, when that officer appeared, announced: "I want to tell you the truth of what took place." (The words are no criterion; they are common form when a suspect changes tune.)

And so another statement, the last and most important, made its laborious way towards the prisoner's file. Again Thorne talked; again the Sergeant wrote; again the Chief Inspector watchfully presided. But they no longer spoke and wrote and listened to soothing words of virtuous denial. Instead there was unfolded a tale so grisly that it sent a thrill of horror pulsating through the land.

Elsie Cameron, said Thorne, had indeed come to the farm on December 5th. She had walked into his living hut at tea time, taking him completely by surprise. She told him she intended sleeping in the hut and, moreover, staying till she was married. An argument had opened up at once; it continued on and off for several hours, till the last London train had gone and Elsie's persistence had temporarily prevailed.

Thorne was then in an uncomfortable dilemma. Earlier on, before Elsie's sudden advent, he had made an appointment to meet The Other Girl. At half past nine, as the hour was drawing near, he told Elsie this and made ready to go. She protested, he insisted, and on this occasion the advantage lay with him. He kept his appointment, leaving her behind him in the hut.

He was away about two hours. In simple, shocking words, he depicted his return.

"When I opened the hut door I saw Miss Cameron hanging from a beam that supports the roof, by a piece of cord as used for the washing line. I cut the cord and laid her on the bed. She was dead. I then put out the lights. She had her frock off and her hair was down. I lay across the table for about an hour. I was about to go to Dr. Turle and knock up someone to go for the police and *I realised the position I was in,* and decided not to do so. I then went down to the workshop . . . I got my hacksaw and some sacks and took them back to the hut. I took off Miss Cameron's clothes and burned them in the fireplace in the hut. I then laid the sacks on the floor, put Miss Cameron (who was then naked) on the floor and sawed off her legs and the head by the glow of the fire. I put them in sacks, intending to carry them away, but my nerve failed me and I took them down to the workshop and I left them there. I went back to the hut and sat in the chair all night. Next morning, just as it got light, I buried the sacks and a tin containing the remains in a chicken run. It is the Leghorn chicken run, the first pen from the gate."

The Sergeant laid down his pen. The statement was read out. Coolly Thorne affixed his signature.

Chief Inspector Gillan's face was grim. He had solved one problem, only to raise another. The case of Elsie Cameron was over; the case of Norman Thorne had just begun.

Important trials are usually held in important places—in London, or in one of the large provincial cities. But there are occasional exceptions. Several small towns still enjoy, by ancient heritage, the periodic pomp and pageantry of Assize. And now and again high drama visits one of these quiet spots in the shape of a trial that sets all England by the ears.

It happened in 1921 at Carmarthen when they tried Harold Greenwood, and crowds lined the streets to watch counsel going to court. It happened in 1922 at Hereford when they tried Herbert Armstrong, and those who failed to get into the building patiently waited in the snow outside. It happened in 1924 at Guildford when they tried the volatile, spade-bearded Vaquier. It happened in 1925 at Lewes when they tried Norman Thorne.

Throughout the five days of the battle for Thorne's life, Lewes was in a ferment of unwholesome curiosity. It is hardly fair, though, to blame the town itself for that. Norman Thorne was the talk of the whole country, and people flocked from near and far as to some prize entertainment. After all, even if you weren't one of the lucky ones who gained a seat in court, there were several fascinating ways of filling time: celebrity spotting, slandering the witnesses, gaping and goggling at the broken-hearted parents, and—most agreeable diversion of them all—booing and gibing at The Other Girl.

This lamentable atmosphere encompassing the courthouse was never permitted to penetrate within. That was assured from the outset by the character of the lawyers in whose hands the conduct of proceedings mainly lay. There was to be neither the weakness on the Bench that prejudiced the famous Mrs. Maybrick's trial, nor the disorder at the Bar that so disfigured Steinie's. Mr. Justice Finlay was as clear-headed and capable as he was self-effacing. Sir Henry Curtis Bennett, chief prosecuting counsel, was as impartial in this rôle as he could be fervent when defender. And J. D. Cassels, who had accepted the brief for Thorne, was almost the prototype of modern criminal advocates: economy and point were his watchwords; verbiage and barnstorming he alike eschewed.

The lines of Cassels' plea were predetermined. Thorne's last statement did not admit of an alternative. "When I opened the hut door I saw Miss Cameron hanging"; those were the words that governed the defence. They pointed not to murder, but to suicide—or at the very least, to death from shock in the attempt. And if that was once accepted, all the rest could be explained. The concealment, the lies, and even the dissection could then be attributed to overwhelming fear —a fear not unnatural in a man who quickly realised that appearances were against him and that he was likely to be blamed. "I thought of the letters I had written. I remembered I had been telling people that I wanted to break the engagement. I remembered that it was known that another girl had been coming down to me and I had been walking out with her. In view of these things, I became afraid." These were Thorne's words when he went into the box and one cannot deny them considerable force.

So the real battle in the trial of Norman Thorne was a battle to discover *how* Elsie Cameron died. If, as the defence was to maintain, she had died from shock while trying to hang herself, Thorne, whatever his conduct afterwards, was not guilty of murder and entitled to go free.

If, on the contrary, she had in fact been murdered, the jury could have no doubt who her murderer was.

Suicide isn't everybody's exploit. The majority of people go through the world without ever seriously contemplating self-destruction. Human capacity for suffering is immense, even more so in the female than the male. Pangs of jealousy, faithlessness of lovers, the prospect of social dishonour and disgrace—such agonising tortures are endured (and survived) by millions of young women in every generation. Only the neurotic prove unequal to the strain.

That Elsie Cameron was neurotic had been evident to her intimates; it was Cassels' task to make it evident to the jury. Much of his work on the first day of the trial was directed to this end. Scores of questions, skilfully placed and timed, ultimately united to compose a telling picture: a picture of Elsie at home, at work, at Crowborough; often depressed, sometimes hysterical, always plagued and harried by her "nerves." Her father, who was the first witness of substance, agreed that she had left employment because of "nerve trouble," that on one occasion office colleagues accompanied her home because her "nerves" were bad, that she had been treated by doctors, both in London and Crowborough, for "nerves."

"Did it ever come to your knowledge," Cassels asked him, "that she had been brought from Crowborough to Victoria Station by the prisoner?"

"Yes," Mr. Cameron said.

"Did your other daughter meet her?"

"Yes."

"Did your other daughter make any communication to you about a message she had had from the prisoner?"

"Yes."

"Was the communication that your daughter Elsie had threatened to throw herself out of the train?"

"Something to that effect," Mr. Cameron admitted.

Presently Cassels handed up a letter and the witness identified the writing as his wife's.

"I put that letter in, my lord," Cassels said, and the letter, thus formally introduced in evidence, was read out to the jury by the Clerk of Assize. Dated December 16th, it was addressed to Norman Thorne. "The suspense is terrible," it said, ". . . we get no rest night or day. *If it had been a week or two ago I should have thought she might have done something rash, poor girl.*"

That, then, was how Elsie had appeared to her own parents. Acquaintances in Crowborough had formed similar opinions. One, with whom she had lodged from time to time, spoke of her being "nervy" and "brooding over things"; another had remarked, soon after her disappearance, "that there was no telling what might happen to a person who got so low."

Cassels' cross-examination brought all these things to light. That first evening when the court adjourned and each man went his way, the barristers to their Mess, the judge to the stately solitude of his lodging, the prisoner to his cell—that evening saw Thorne's chances reach their highest mark. On the record up to December 5th he was not a likely murderer. Elsie Cameron was a not unlikely suicide.

This in itself did not constitute a case; it merely laid the foundations of a case. Suicide was possible, yes—but had it really happened?

The second day's hearing was largely taken up by the Crown's attempts to show that it had not; to dispose of any theories that might tend to show it had; and to prove, beyond that reasonable doubt which every prisoner lawfully invokes, that Elsie Cameron had lost her life under the violence of another's hand.

The method used was necessarily oblique. Of that dark and angry evening in the hut, Thorne was the sole survivor. The only eye-witness beside himself had been carefully buried underneath his farm. But the remains of that poor girl (divided and stowed away exactly as Thorne said) had been dug up, scrutinised, analysed, interred, dug up, scrutinised and analysed again. The tale that Elsie Cameron did not live to tell pathologists sought to read upon her decomposing flesh.

Speaking broadly, there are three kinds of evidence: direct, circumstantial and expert. It is direct evidence when one man says he saw a second plunge a dagger into the vitals of a third. It is circumstantial evidence when the knife of a lover is found, stained with blood, by the stabbed corpse of his mistress. But when test-tubes are mobilised and microscopes unleashed, when crimes are reconstructed and assaults revisualised, when the testimony of onlookers is scornfully swept aside by reference to a shred of skin or a dented metal bar—then the Experts have descended on the scene.

Each kind of evidence in turn can be disparaged. Eye-witnesses may lie. Circumstances may deceive. Experts may lack learning, err in observation, be faulty in logic or dogmatic in conclusions. Occasionally an expert has contrived to be all four.

Genuine experts, though, make few mistakes of fact. Disputes between them are generally confined to the interpretation that acknowledged facts should bear. In other words, they differ in opinion.

The experts in the Thorne case differed in opinion. A distinguished corps assembled at Lewes for the trial, and it was they who were to be the principal protagonists.

The real expert evidence, which was wholly scientific, followed semiexpert evidence on the subject of the beams.

There were two beams straddling the little living hut. If Thorne's story were true Elsie Cameron must have hanged herself with a piece of washing line secured to one of these. Her physique, of course, was slight—she weighed only eight stone—but the suspension, and still more, the jerk, might well have left a mark or nick on the beam that took the strain.

Three days after Norman Thorne's arrest, Gillan accompanied by an aide from Scotland Yard had been to the hut with this idea in mind. They observed no mark on either of the beams. Then they conducted two experiments with an eight-stone weight fastened to the beams by a length of washing line. First the weight was slowly raised and swung. Next, it was placed upon a chair which was kicked away to cause a sudden jerk. Both these experiments were said to have caused marks, which Gillan pointed out when the beams were exhibited in court.

No marks before the tests; marks as a result of the tests. The deduction invited was dangerously simple—that no comparable weight could have swung from there before.

There was some disagreement about the marks themselves, about the character of the cord, about the possible effect of a knot in the wood. But the defence's sharpest impact upon this part of the case was packed into two questions which Cassels put to Gillan.

"Was anyone present representing the defence when your experiments took place?"

"No," the Chief Inspector said.

"Had the defence any notice of the fact that you were making the experiments?"

"No," the Chief Inspector said.

The effect of this admission ought to have been great. Experiments of the kind described depend on tiny details: the balancing of the weight, the adjustment of the cord, the direction in which the chair is kicked away. Exclusion of the defence from even passive participation was a considerable police error, conducing to offend a sagacious jury's sense of right and fitness.

But how far did the Thorne jury merit this description? That is impossible to say. A jury, that must perforce sit silent till passing judgment with a simple yea or nay, preserves its secrets as no prisoner can. The latter faces a two-fold exposure—by the willing tongues of others and by the loosening of his own. He cannot hope to pass wholly unscathed; some part, at least, of his soul will be stripped bare. But a jury—every jury—is protected and remote, and remains a complete enigma for all time.

It would be foolish, then, to set at naught the evidence of the beams, since we cannot be sure that the jury did likewise. But one may justifiably guess that it very soon sank into the background of their thoughts. The beams were no more than a penny-whistle overture, soon to be drowned in the crashing chords of the mighty one-man orchestra on which the Crown relied.

That orchestra dispensed a dance of death, scored and conducted with diabolic brilliance.

In almost every big trial there is a moment of transcendent crisis; a moment, as in Priestley's *Dangerous Corner*, that determines by remote control all the events to follow. It may come early or late; it may burst unheralded or have been long foreseen.

The crisis in the trial of Norman Thorne occurred on the second afternoon and it took the shape unanimously expected. Everyone in court and millions elsewhere had been waiting breathlessly upon the time when Sir Bernard Spilsbury would get up from his place and walk with calm assurance to the box.

Spilsbury was the Crown's sole expert witness. The defence had four or five, at least three of whom could boast qualifications on a par with Spilsbury's own. They agreed between themselves and disagreed with him, so that the defence enjoyed an easy lead on a mere counting of heads. How then did Spilsbury's evidence acquire such vast importance? Why was it being said by those conversant with the courts that, unless he were completely smashed in cross-examination, Spilsbury's opinion was certain to prevail?

The answer is simple. Juries are formed from members of the public, and the British public believed Spilsbury infallible.

Spilsbury had indeed done what few can hope to do; he had become a legend in his own lifetime. To the man in the street he stood for pathology as Hobbs stood for cricket or Dempsey for boxing or Capablanca for chess. By the middle twenties he had achieved a status merited by none—not even by himself. His pronouncements were invested with the force of dogma, and it was blasphemy to hint he might conceivably be wrong.

This situation was not of Spilsbury's seeking. It arose partly because, as Home Office pathologist, he was constantly appearing in the most sensational cases; partly because his qualities were genuinely outstanding. Even so, it was a situation fraught with danger. As Cassels was to say in his final speech for Thorne: "We can all admire attainment, take off our hats to ability, acknowledge the high position that a man has won in his sphere. But it is a long way to go if you have to say that, when that man says something, there can be no room for error."

It *is* a long way to go; far beyond the territories of reason. But many a jury had gone that way before, and none knew better than Cassels himself how grave was the danger they would go that way again.

Spilsbury answered Curtis Bennett's questions in his own easy but authoritative style. Always matter of fact and unemotional, he spoke not as a champion of a cause but rather as an objective scientist announcing his conclusions. His courtesy, though, did not obscure the fact that he regarded these conclusions as indisputable.

Spilsbury's evidence-in-chief was damning against Thorne. He had examined the remains of Elsie Cameron; taken measurements, made slides, peered at them through magnifiers. He told the jury what he had observed: eight bruises on the head, face, arms and legs, *all of them inflicted shortly before death,* and one—on the temple—caused by "a crushing blow." ("One of those might have done it," Spilsbury said, referring to a pair of Indian clubs that the police had picked up outside Thorne's living hut.)

Spilsbury also told the jury things he had noted by their absence: signs of asphyxiation and scars or grooving in the neck ("such as I should be certain to find if the woman had been hanged").

How then, in his view, did Elsie Cameron die? From shock; shock due to the combined effect of all the bruises. "I found nothing else to account for death," said the Crown expert oracularly—and if Sir Bernard could find nothing else, what else could there be?

The effect of this was clear. There had been no hanging and no suicide. Somebody had attacked the girl and injured her so badly that she died.

Such an assumption would be fatal for the defence. Cassels could not afford to let it stand; Spilsbury did not make a habit of retraction. So the famous advocate and the famous expert prepared to cross sharp swords while Thorne, who knew the truth, sat quiet as a spectator.

Cross-examining a man like Spilsbury calls for special gifts. He is not only an expert in the technique of pathology; he is also an expert in the technique of giving evidence. He is not only a professional lecturer and theorist; he is also a professional cross-examinee. He is as used as any counsel to the atmosphere of courts; as trained in the rules, as familiar with the tricks. The Bar thus forfeits its customary advantage and joins battle with him on strictly level terms.

Half the art of cross-examination resides in knowing what not to ask. Cassels' questioning of Spilsbury was in this respect a model. Seldom did the pathologist get a chance to enlarge, expand, or re-emphasise his views. There was no direct attack on a broad front. With infinite delicacy Cassels moved one small step at a time, sometimes at this point, sometimes at that, consolidating instantly after an advance, covering up and switching in face of a repulse. It was not showy; the sensation seekers in the gallery may even have found it dull; but those who care for true forensic skill could seek no sounder exercise in craftsmanship.

The first major issue raised was that of the bruises.

"In no case," Cassels asked, "did you find a breaking of the skin?"

"No."

"Would you think it possible that a heavy club like that"—Cassels made play with one of the Indian clubs—"could produce bruises and yet not break the skin?"

"Oh, certainly," said Spilsbury. "It depends upon the part of the body, of course."

"Take the bruise on the temple. Do you think it possible for that bruise to have been produced with that instrument upon that part of the face?"

"May I show you?" Spilsbury said. The club was handed to him. "Used *this* way, and striking *that*, it would produce the bruise without breaking the skin." He demonstrated from the box.

The Indian club swished murderously. The sound of words was momentarily replaced by the sight of action. Such moments in a courtroom have the vivid glare of lightning and Cassels made full use of the impression thus produced.

"For the purpose of that answer are you assuming a blow with force?"

"Certainly."

"Was the bone unbroken?"

"Yes."

"With such an article as that, the weight alone is sufficient, is it not, to break the skin?"

"Certainly not."

"If it were to drop, say, three feet on to wood, wouldn't it produce a considerable dent?"

"It would."

"And yet you think it might produce that bruise on the human face without breaking either the skin or the bone?"

"Only on certain parts of the face, of course."

It will be noted that, though Spilsbury had given nothing away, Cassels had none the less improved his position. The questions had been framed to bring out the inconsistencies—apparent or real—in Spilsbury's hypothesis.

Cassels now foreshadowed his alternative. The defence would contend—and their experts would affirm—that the bruises on the body were consistent with a fall. *Their* hypothesis was that Thorne returned to the hut just before Elsie died and that she sustained the bruises as he cut her down.

No conceivable expenditure of time or energy would ever make Spilsbury subscribe to this. It would mean utterly repudiating all that he had said. But minor reconciliations might be effected between the contradictory points of view. Treading warily as ever, Cassels sounded out the ground.

"The bruise which you found under the left eye—is that as consistent with a fall as with a blow?"

"Yes," Spilsbury conceded, "it might possibly have been caused by a fall."

"And the one at the back of the head?"

"That is much more likely to be the injury produced by a fall."

Cassels had taken the two safest examples. He prudently refrained from putting further specific instances and instead asked a portmanteau question shrewdly designed to capitalise his gains.

"So several of the bruises might have been caused by falling and striking a hard surface?"

There was but one answer to this. Spilsbury said yes.

Cassels crept a little further forward.

"The fall that produced the bruise under the left eye—would it be a heavy fall?"

"It must have been."

"The fall that produced the bruise at the back of the head—would that be a heavy fall?"

"Yes."

It was modest progress, but not unsatisfactory. Many able counsel grappling with Spilsbury have found themselves forced back behind their starting place.

"You found no injuries to the hands?"

"No."

"Nor the forearms?"

"No."

Another scoring point. Its virtue is apparent if one pictures how a woman would instinctively defend herself.

To have pressed Spilsbury harder, though, on the subject of the bruises would have been to incur an unwarrantable risk. The other half of the art of cross-examination resides in knowing exactly when to stop.

In any event, Cassels' hardest task still lay ahead. While both sides agreed upon shock as the cause of death, they did not agree upon the cause of shock. The defence case rested on an attempt at hanging—a supposition that Spilsbury had pooh-poohed. Once again, there could be no thought of converting the Crown expert; only of inducing him to qualify his assertions. Using every resource of experience and talent, Cassels embarked on this unhopeful venture.

"You found the cause of death, shock?"

Spilsbury assented, quickly adding "Shock due to injuries."

"Did you find anything to *demonstrate* the cause of death as shock?

Or did you arrive at that conclusion because you could find no other cause?"

"It *is* conclusion," said Spilsbury pontifically. "It must be so."

This was not one of his most ingratiating replies. Cassels followed up.

"Finding no other cause of death on the post-mortem examination, the conclusion which you arrived at—I am not contesting it—is that death was due to shock?"

"Yes," Spilsbury said. These, he knew, were preliminary passes; he was all vigilance for the thrust itself.

"Can you get death from shock in an attempt at hanging?"

This time the approach was naked and direct.

"No," Spilsbury answered, "I do not think you can."

"Why not?"

"Because the attempt at hanging is an asphyxial condition and death occurs from that."

Deliberately or otherwise, this begged the question. Cassels, smoothly polite, declined to be put off.

"That is when death occurs from hanging?"

"Yes."

"I'm asking you to deal with death occurring from shock due to an *attempt* at hanging."

Spilsbury closed with the problem.

"I don't believe death could occur instantly from an attempt at hanging."

"You get pressure on the neck, don't you?"

"Yes."

"A very delicate part of the human frame?"

"Yes."

"Containing the means whereby the communications pass from the brain to the rest of the body?"

"Yes."

"Have you considered the effect of such circumstances upon a neurotic?"

"I have."

"Do you still exclude the possibility of death by shock brought about by an attempt at hanging?"

"Certainly. If she died immediately after the cutting down, the death would be due, not to shock, but to asphyxia from hanging."

Spilsbury had offered one of his rare openings. Cassels was not the man to miss it.

"You are *pre-supposing*, aren't you, that in all cases of hanging death *must* be due to the hanging?"

There can be little doubt that Spilsbury would have liked to recast his previous answer. But what he had said, he had said; he never shuffled; as he granted no favours, so he asked for none.

"Yes," he replied.

A scientist might conceivably endorse his attitude, but the average man intuitively dislikes "pre-suppositions." . . .

The cross-examination neared its end without the slightest falling off in tension. The closing passages, fought out in the last minutes of the long spring afternoon, revolved around a point that bid fair to prove decisive.

Were there signs of injury visible on the neck, such as one would expect from the tight grip of a cord? Spilsbury gave an unhesitating no.

"On January 17th, when you performed your post-mortem, did you examine *microscopically* any part of the neck?"

"No."

"Why not?"

"Because it was quite unnecessary. I made a thorough examination of the neck and found no marks."

"Because *externally* you found no mark, you did not examine further?"

"Oh yes," said Spilsbury, "very much further."

"But did you examine *microscopically?*"

"No. I deeply probed the tissues."

"By the naked eye?" Cassels insisted.

"Yes."

"Very well. On February 24th you were present at a further post-mortem conducted by two doctors who will be called for the defence?"

"Yes."

"Was a section taken of the neck on this occasion?"

"Yes."

"Did you have a part of that section for the purpose of microscopic examination?"

"I did."

"And a part was retained by the other doctors?"

"Yes."

"Slides would have to be made of them?"

"Yes."

The defence doctors, sitting close to counsel and following every word, framed the next question in their minds before it had been asked.

"Did not microscopic examination definitely show extravasation of blood, consistent only with pressure?"

"No." Spilsbury spoke in uncompromising terms. There was no extravasation to be seen, he said; indeed water had by then so soaked the tissues that all the elements of blood had been destroyed.

Here the very heart of the matter had been reached. If Spilsbury was cocksure, the rest were cocksure too; they believed they could see extravasation in their slides and were waiting their turn to say so upon oath.

The duel between Spilsbury and Cassels ended with honours even. Gains and losses on either side were small. Conflict remained on every major point, and in some cases was sharpened, but Cassels at least had cleared and mapped the ground for the group of doctors he was going to call.

They were eminent men, these doctors; rich in distinctions and respected by their colleagues. One was Director of the pathological department at Great Ormond Street Hospital; another, formerly professor at Glasgow University, was a medical legal examiner for the Crown; a third, as Crown Analyst for the government in Dublin, had been for many years the Spilsbury of Ireland. All of them were practising pathologists; all of them were adept in the use of slides. They were as definite in saying that there *was* extravasation as Spilsbury was definite in saying that there was not. Nor did a consultation held outside court hours, at which the rival experts met and examined each others' slides, shake them any more in their opinion than it shook Sir Bernard Spilsbury in his.

Count the three as one, and you still had a stalemate. But trials, unlike chess, are not determined mathematically. There was one name in the four the jury knew; to them the rest were as remote and strange as Einstein would be to a Hottentot. Spilsbury had spoken, and the idol, though at times hard pressed, had not been dethroned. Long before the defence experts were heard, even as Spilsbury stepped down from the box, the sensitive in court could tell which way the wind was blowing.

But there was still a chance for Thorne to be his own salvation. A prisoner in the box has curious powers which some times cancel out all other evidence. Let him but seem a worthy, decent man; let him appear "a chap just like ourselves"; and, whatever the evidence on the charge preferred, a jury will be glad to wipe the record clean.

Thorne was in the box almost the whole of the third day. By academic tests, he was an admirable witness. He wooed the jury with the common touch; he challenged them with unexpected frankness. "I absolutely lost my head and became frantic. . . . I was trembling from head to foot and broke into a cold perspiration. . . . I flung myself on the bed and cried like a baby." And again: "I was trying to build up evidence. . . . I was trying to assume a rôle of knowing nothing about it. . . . I did not go for help as I should have done and consequently I had to go forward as I did." One says he wooed them and he challenged them, but neither was necessarily the result of conscious art. It might— it *might*—have been the overwhelming impact of the truth.

Thorne laboured, however, under two great disadvantages which were inherent in the substance of his case. He was forced to proclaim himself a fluent, brazen liar, who could act and live as well as speak his lies. He was forced to recite a fearful inventory of horrors which would arouse more repugnance than homicide itself.

These were matters that refused to be forgotten. Thorne himself was their unwilling memorial. As they heard him tell his story with a host of vivid touches, the simplest would recall a different, earlier tale: equally credible and equally embellished with plausible minutiæ—such as letters to the dead. As they watched him in the witness box, so suave and almost gentle, the stolidest would conjure up a different, earlier scene: the darkened hut, the active crouching man, the body of the girl stretched out stark naked on the floor, the hacksaw flashing over neck and limbs, the whole ghastly tableau lit to a dim red by the glow and flicker of the tiny fire.

If a man had told such clever lies before, could he not tell such clever lies again? If a man was capable of dismembering his sweetheart, was there anything, *anything*, from which he would recoil?

Whatever chance Thorne had was lost in cross-examination.

Curtis Bennett stood out as a master of this art. Without bluster, bullying or other resort of the third-rate, he exerted a singular authority and power. He relied on the one legitimate weapon of a cross-examiner: the form and arrangement of the questions that he put. Because his skill in this respect fell not far short of genius, he secured his objects with the minimum of words.

The first four questions he addressed to Thorne were typical of his method and his gifts.

Curtis Bennett's aim was to elicit an admission that, by the day of Elsie Cameron's death, Thorne had transferred his affections to The Other Girl. It was not a matter of concrete fact, readily ascertainable, but a delicate enquiry into a state of mind. If the question had been baldly put without due preparation, Thorne would have been free to answer as he pleased.

Now consider the technique that Curtis Bennett used, not to trap him into falsehood, but to force him into truth.

"On the morning of December 5th were you still in love with Elsie Cameron?"

To answer "No" would be to furnish forthwith superabundant evidence of motive. Thorne answered "Yes."

"On the morning of December 5th were you in love with the other girl?"

This was more tricky. To answer "No" would be immediately expedient but there was his first statement to Gillan lying convenient to Sir Henry's hand. "Almost every night from the middle of November she came to my hut . . . we had during this time gradually fallen in love."

It was no use flying in the face of that. Again Thorne answered "Yes."

"On that morning which of these two girls that you were in love with did you desire to marry?"

"I do not know I was particularly desirous of marrying any just at that time."

The evasion served to gain only a few seconds. Curtis Bennett's next question slammed and locked the door.

"Which did you intend to marry in the future?"

Which did he intend to marry in the future? If he said Elsie, there were his letters registering reluctance ("you seem to take everything for granted"). If he said neither, he would convict himself at once of double-dyed and callous caddishness in inducing both girls on to terms of intimacy without intending to play fair with either.

"Well," he said, "of the two, I suppose I thought more of the other girl."

Four questions only, and each of them as compact as it was clear. A less accomplished cross-examiner might have asked four hundred without obtaining such a definite result.

The rest of this truly searching cross-examination bore the same hallmark of precise economy. There was, for example, the so-called "Piper incident." A Mrs. Piper, of Crowborough, with whom Elsie had often lodged, had been called as a witness for the Crown. She had told Cassels how one night Elsie refused to go to bed and, appearing "stupefied . . . not normal," insisted on going back to Thorne from whose farm she had just returned after being there all day.

The defence dilated on the Piper incident to support their contention that Elsie was neurotic. Curtis Bennett sought to alter the motif from mental instability to passionate affection. It took him barely a dozen questions.

"Certainly after you were engaged," he said to Thorne, "Elsie Cameron was deeply in love with you, wasn't she?"

"Yes."

"And being deeply in love with you, she was anxious to be with you as much as she could?"

"Yes."

"And may I take it that you were very pleased to see her too at that time?"

"Oh yes," Thorne answered promptly.

So often the form of Curtis Bennett's questions practically determined the reply.

"This incident when she was staying with Mrs. Piper—at that time was she deeply in love with you?"

"Yes, passionately."

"Upon that particular day she had spent the day with you?"

"Yes."

"And you had been very happy together?"

"Oh yes."

"She had then been engaged to you for about nine or ten months?"

"Yes."

"She left you about half past ten at night; you took her back to Mrs. Piper, and then she insisted on coming back to you to spend the night?"

"Yes."

"Prior to that you had been intimate, had you not?"

"Oh yes."

The purpose of this questioning was not to ferret out new facts but to create a new *atmosphere* round facts that had already been established. Curtis Bennett did this again, with certain variants, when he came to enquire about the reasons for dismemberment.

"When you made up your mind to dismember the body, was it because you were afraid that somebody might think that you had murdered her?"

"Not necessarily so."

Used in such a context, the word "necessarily" implied some hidden reservation.

"I want to know," Curtis Bennett said. "It must have been some very strong impulse which would make you, there and then, dismember the body. What was it?"

"I cannot really explain," Thorne said. "My desire was to hide it, not to dismember it."

"You had got nothing to be ashamed of?"

"No."

"What was it that made you do it?"

"I suppose, as I've already explained, realising the position I was in, I was desirous of hiding her body lest I should be blamed for having caused her death by any means."

The last phrase showed that Thorne still hoped to steer clear of full surrender.

"I do not want there to be any misunderstanding," said Curtis Bennett calmly. " 'For having caused her death'—you mean for having murdered her?"

"Through any means." Thorne clung to his straw stubbornly.

Again a key question fell neatly into place.

"Did you want to hide the fact that she had committed suicide?"

"No," Thorne answered. "I thought they would perhaps think that she had not committed suicide."

"Then it was because you thought they might imagine you had murdered her?"

"Yes," said Thorne reluctantly.

It had taken a little time to get round to it. But they were there now.

The cross-examination was over, but before he returned to the immunity of the dock, there was still one last ordeal in store for Thorne. Mr. Justice Finlay, biting his pen abstractedly and puckering his face, detained the prisoner a moment longer in the box.

"Just one or two questions, Thorne."

There is room for a monograph on the one or two questions that judges have, from time to time, asked in similar circumstances, and which, coming with the weight of intervention from above, exercise immeasurable influence. Any such monograph would naturally begin with Darling's interrogation of the poisoner Armstrong, and perhaps follow up with Avory's inquisition of Frederick Guy Browne.

Finlay resembled neither of these judges; he had not Darling's hard and lacquered surface, nor Avory's reserve of cold remorselessness. He was a genial, kindly, unaffected man who spoke in a mild and almost diffident way. But his questioning of Thorne could hardly have been more deadly.

"When you came back to the hut, Thorne, your first act was to cut Miss Cameron down?"

"Yes, my lord."

"Did you make any attempt to resuscitate her?"

"No. I thought she was dead."

"Did you ever think of going to fetch a doctor?"

"Not until after I got up from the table."

"That was about an hour later?"

"I should think it was about an hour."

Then came three short, sharp and paralysing blows.

"You never thought of fetching a doctor *at once,* on the *chance* of her being revived?"

"No, I thought at once she was dead."

"You have heard, I suppose, that people who are apparently dead are sometimes revived?"

"Yes, I have heard of such things."

"But you never thought of getting a doctor, and you did not get one?"

"No."

The judge bit his pen again and nodded a dismissal.

There was an eloquent closing speech by Cassels, a massive reply by Curtis Bennett, a careful, thorough summing up by Finlay—perfectly fair, but not disguising his own belief that the Crown case had been proved.

At twelve minutes past five on the fifth day the jury withdrew, and at twenty minutes to six returned to pronounce the prisoner guilty.

Many murder appeals are devoid of substance; few have any real hope of success. But Norman Thorne's application for leave to appeal at least raised a novel and interesting point.

The Criminal Appeal Act of 1907 (which, among other things, founded the Court of Criminal Appeal) provides that where any question arising on appeal involves scientific investigation or expert knowledge either it may be referred to a Special Commissioner for enquiry and report, or else a skilled assessor may be appointed to assist the court. Although the best part of two decades had passed, these powers had never previously been invoked. It was the defence's argument on appeal that they precisely fitted a case like Norman Thorne's. The bruises, the neck marks, the state of Elsie Cameron's nerves and mind, were all put forward as proper subjects for the special procedure which the Act envisaged.

There was much to be said for the defence's proposition. The whole trial may have turned on the interpretation of a slide showing a fragment of the skin of a person three months dead. Expert One looks at his slide and says he can see nothing. Expert Two looks at his and says he can see something—and the something he can see is extravasation of blood. Expert One looks at the slide of Expert Two and says, ah yes, he sees what the other means; there *is* something there, but it is not extravasation; it is the degenerated remains of some sebaceous glands.

Is any layman competent to judge between them? Should any man's life be at the mercy of such a judgment? If there could ever be a case for a Commissioner or assessor, was it not the case that now occupied the Court?

How a Commissioner would have reported, or an assessor advised, is a point which can only offer material for conjecture. They were never given an opportunity to show. The appeal court of three judges—two of whom were not among the ablest—dismissed the application without calling on the Crown. The usual petition was presented and refused, and in due course, like his jilted love, Thorne died a violent death.

No one now will ever know what happened in Thorne's living hut that winter evening many years ago. Did he, as the jury evidently believed, wilfully murder Elsie Cameron to avoid the unwelcome necessity of marriage and free himself for pursuit of a new passion? Or was there a struggle when he tried to leave the hut, with this dreadful but unpremeditated consequence? Or—and this is the most terrible alternative—did Thorne in the last resort speak nothing but the truth?

One thing alone is certain. However Elsie Cameron died, it was Thorne who slashed and hacked her corpse and cunningly concealed the severed fragments. Assuming that this had never been found out, one is tempted to speculate on what he meant to do. Perhaps, after a decent lapse of time, he would have gone abroad and lost his identity in some far-off land. Perhaps he would have wed the other girl and moved from his farm to less evocative surroundings. Perhaps he would have stayed on where he was, feeding his chickens, attending Sunday school, and sleeping sound and dreamlessly at night while Elsie mouldered in the quiet earth.

Any and every course would have required a heart of marble and a nerve of steel. Both these attributes were possessed by Thorne, as he had proved in the weeks before arrest. It is this inhuman streak in the man's character that bedevils assessment of the evidence and makes him one of most baffling of all convicted murderers.

7

Frederick Seddon

I ADMIT I've never counted them, but my guess is there are about thirty murder trials—British murder trials—which are really entitled to be described as classic—classic because they not only created a big stir at the time, but their fame—or, if you like, their notoriety—it's lasted; each generation discusses them afresh. And these classic trials split roughly into two kinds: there are those where doubt is expressed about the verdict, and there are those where the verdict's been generally approved of—sized up as satisfactory, correct.

The Seddon trial—a poison charge it was, and a number one sensation back in 1912—that's nearly always reckoned nowadays in the satisfactory class. Whatever may have been said and thought and written there and then, looking back upon it now across the years, the verdict seems to have been inevitable, gives no ground for complaint. Nobody now—so far as is known to me at any rate—no one feels at all uneasy about the fate of Seddon, as many of us do about—well, say Edith Thompson. Seddon was guilty, as the jury found; we take it quite for granted, just as we take for granted the guilt of Ruxton or of Rouse. And yet, you know, if you push beyond this vague general impression, if you go right up and look at it close to, the case against Seddon was very thin indeed. In fact, when the prosecution witnesses had finished, Marshall Hall, who was defending, submitted that he hadn't got anything to answer, that he hadn't any need to open his defence at all. And he wasn't so far from getting away with it, at that.

How did it come about, then, that Seddon was convicted? Well, you could almost say he died by his own hand. He hanged himself when he went into the box, and Rufus Isaacs—one of the greatest counsel of them all—Isaacs got him under cross-examination. But it didn't happen in the way that you perhaps imagine. What settled

Seddon's hash was not that Rufus Isaacs tore him into shreds, but that Isaacs, for all his skill, he *failed* to tear him into shreds.

If you aren't familiar with the background to the Seddon case, it'll sound as though I'm talking—*must* be talking—utter nonsense. But let me begin the story right at the beginning, and you'll see.

The beginning—it lies not in a date, but in a character—the character and spirit of this Frederick Henry Seddon. On the surface, on his record, it could hardly have been better. He was a perfect pillar of respectability—everything a middle-class citizen should be. Starting from scratch, he had got on by ability and drive and loyalty to the insurance corporation that employed him. As a district superintendent, handling large sums, he was scrupulously honest and remarkably efficient. As a Freemason—a Mason of some standing in the craft—he fully discharged his duty to his brethren. Seddon was the sort of man looked up to by his neighbours; the sort of man whose advice is sought after and valued; the sort of man parents pick out as an example. When you grow up, they said, I hope you'll do as well as Mr. Seddon.

His intimates, however, his real intimates, they knew a different side, a foul side, of Seddon. In his office, his subordinates knew him for a bully. In his home, his wife and family knew him for a tyrant. And both home and office knew—and so did some with whom he had transacted *private* business—they knew he was a greedy and ruthless money-grubber, that avarice was the ruling passion of his life.

This characteristic—it's the key to Seddon and his story, so I think we ought to get its nature absolutely clear. You see, it wasn't only that he wanted to be rich. It wasn't only that he loved the feel of money, though he did; talk about running coins through your fingers —he was as bad as any miser in a fairy tale. But there was something else—something else besides. Seddon loved the hard bargain for the bargain's sake, quite apart from—in addition to—the profit that it made. He prized his business skill and toughness as an end; he expressed himself through it, just as an actor expresses himself through acting, a musician expresses himself through playing or composing. If he could squeeze an extra threepenny bit where another person couldn't —or where Seddon *thought* another person couldn't—he felt complete fulfilment. His day, as they say, was made.

It wasn't a very agreeable form of self-expression, this. And in the long run it proved to be a fatal one. It led to Seddon's interest being aroused by Eliza Mary Barrow, and to a sequence of events which ended with him on the drop.

Miss Eliza Mary Barrow has one claim to distinction, other than being the victim in a famous murder case. She was an even less lovable personality than Seddon. Everything about her, it seemed almost as if it were intended to repel. She had an appalling temper, unpredictable, and when she lost it, which was frequently, she spat in people's faces. She wasn't over-fussy about keeping herself clean. She was as greedy and as grasping and as on the make as Seddon, but without a hundredth fraction of his cuteness and his brains. Brains weren't really Miss Barrow's strongest suit. She was what is politely termed eccentric.

Miss Barrow first met Seddon over some insurance. Quick, snap of the fingers, there was mutual attraction—though not what they mean by that in the women's magazines. She was fifty, he was forty, and they'd better things to think of. What Miss Barrow found attractive about Seddon was his smartness, his cunning, his will to outwit the world. What Seddon found attractive in Miss Barrow was her wealth; not wealth as millionaires account it, certainly, but the lease of a shop and a public house, a good many hundred pounds in safe and solid stock, and a good many golden sovereigns which she didn't put in a bank but stowed away and carted around with her in a box. Oh yes, this was it, this was a soul-mates' meeting; but how could they get the best advantage from each other?

It was Seddon, of course, who thought of it. Hadn't Miss Barrow quarrelled with her relatives—no wonder—so that she was looking for another place to live? Hadn't *he* got his house there in North London, a bit crammed with the family, but still not so crammed that room couldn't be made?

Why shouldn't Miss Barrow come to lodge with Seddon?

No reason at all. In the July of 1910, she came.

She had the top floor to herself, she paid twelve and six a week, and Seddon's wife did her housework and her cooking. I'm afraid I forgot to say anything before about his wife, but that's just how it would be; easiest thing in the world, forgetting Mrs. Seddon. She, poor woman, was a cypher and a drudge, frightened of her husband, never daring to question him or argue, like an obedient animal, doing what she was told. You forget her, as I say, at every stage in the affair; you forget she was as much mixed up in Miss Barrow's death as Seddon; you forget she too had to face a charge of murder and she stood side by side with Seddon in the dock; you forget she was acquitted at the time he was convicted—although as it appears to me, there was just as much—and just as little—evidence against her. I'd like to say another word about this later on.

During Miss Barrow's stay at Seddon's house, a great change was made in her finances. She now had what she wanted—one of the reasons she had moved for—that is, regular access to Seddon's wise advice. In the result, she had parted with all her property—the lease of the shop and the public house, the safe and solid stock—parted with it to Seddon upon his undertaking to pay her a fixed sum every week for the remainder of her life. Seddon paid her, as long as she was there to pay it to. You'll realise, of course, that with an arrangement of this kind, the merits of the bargain, for Seddon, would depend entirely on how long Miss Barrow lived.

She only lasted in fact about a year. In the September of 1911 she fell sick; vomiting, internal pains, acute diarrhœa. She's treated by the doctor, bismuth mixtures, what-not; none of it seems to do her any good. The illness drags on, with Mrs. Seddon doing the nursing, plus such help from Seddon as he thought fit to give.

The doctor last saw Miss Barrow on a Wednesday, about noon. On the Thursday morning, early, Seddon came round to his house. "She's dead, doctor," he said. "We've been up with her all night; thought it was just another bout—she's had so many, but she went sort of unconscious and at six o'clock she died."

"Dear me," the doctor said; "oh well, I'll give you a certificate." He wrote it on the spot, entering as the cause of death epidemic diarrhœa.

There are always a lot of "ifs" in any case of crime. I've been stressing my opinion—and it isn't mine alone—that if Seddon had been less *good* a witness, he would not have hanged. Now here's another "if," still more firmly founded. If Seddon had dealt differently with the funeral of Miss Barrow, never mind being hanged—he wouldn't even have been charged.

For see what he does, this cold-blooded man of business. He goes to an undertaker on the morning of the death, and he tells him that an old girl has popped off at his house, and that the doctor's bill and the funeral will both have to be met out of four pounds ten—all she had in the world. The undertaker says that that means the cheapest kind of funeral, burial in a common grave, for which he quotes four pounds. Seddon agrees to the common grave but he jibs at paying four pounds, and so—this has no bearing on the question of his guilt, but goodness it does show up the nature of the man—he insists on the price being knocked down by twelve and six—as his commission for introducing business!

Then he has the funeral carried out without a single relative of Miss Barrow's being present. True, they'd fallen out. True, Seddon swore he did send them a letter—a letter which the relatives swore they never got. But the letter, on Seddon's showing, didn't mention the common grave, and with the relatives living some four hundred yards away, it might have been worth while going round to see if they wished to contribute.

The Crown was to make a lot of this behaviour at the trial—wasn't it evident, they asked, that he wanted to get Miss Barrow safely underground before any investigation could be made? If that *was* Seddon's intention he defeated his own purpose. Had the relatives been informed at once, it might never have occurred to them that something might be wrong. But getting to know, as they did, by chance, when everything was over—straight away, of course, they were resentful and suspicious. They got no change, need I say, out of an interview with Seddon. So they bring in the police; the police dig up the body; and there, sure as eggs, they discover arsenic—a fatal dose of arsenic, according to the experts, which Miss Barrow must have taken *within two days of her death*.

You can see at once how that put both the Seddons in a spot. There was a check to make sure that the doctor hadn't included any arsenic in his medicines. There was an inquest, at which both Seddon and his wife testified. Then, first one, and then the other, they were both arrested, and in due time they were put up to stand their trial.

Now what can Sir Rufus Isaacs—who's then Attorney-General, and as such he's in charge of the Seddon's prosecution—what can Sir Rufus lay at *Frederick* Seddon's door? Motive, yes; there was motive and to spare, seeing that while Miss Barrow lived she cost him so much a week. But you can't convict people of murder merely because they stand to profit from a death; otherwise you'd have to hang the British Government every time someone died who'd held a Post Office annuity. Then there's opportunity; well, yes, certainly he had the opportunity; but that again, it could hardly be conclusive. Motive and opportunity show he *might* have done it; but what have the Crown got, what do they claim really *proves* he did it?

For one thing, they've got this, which the Attorney-General says is of considerable importance. The Seddons' daughter, a youngster of sixteen, is supposed to have bought flypapers from a chemist's shop three or four days before Miss Barrow's last illness began. Each flypaper—I should perhaps make it clear that they *were* labelled poison— they each contained enough arsenic to kill a grown-up person, and you could extract the poison by boiling them in water.

The Seddons deny they ever sent the girl for flypapers. The girl denies that she was sent or that she ever bought them. The only evidence that she did is the evidence of the chemist. He didn't know her personally, didn't know her name, hadn't any note, any record of the sale. He picked her out at an identity parade on February the 2nd as a girl who had bought flypapers on August 26th. The whole flypaper episode depended upon that.

Now identification is a delicate thing to deal with, especially when the witness isn't wilfully dishonest. Cross-examining the chemist in the box at the Old Bailey, Marshall Hall was at his very best.

"What sort of a day," he asks, "was the 26th of August?"

"A Saturday."

"Was it a hot day, or a cloudy day, or a fine day, or a wet day or what?"

"It was a hot day."

"It was a very hot summer, wasn't it?"

"Yes."

"Was August 26th a hot day like the rest of the hot summer?"

"Yes."

Marshall Hall looks at him hard.

"Do you know there was only one hour's sunshine on that day?"

The chemist wavers a bit.

"No," he says.

"It was the exceptional day of that summer, with very little sunshine, but you remember it as a day like the other days. Tell me, who was the customer you served before you served this girl?"

"I don't remember."

"Who was the one that you served after?"

"I . . . don't remember."

So he doesn't remember the weather or his other customers. Why should he only remember this one girl?

Marshall Hall suggests an explanation.

"Isn't the Seddon girl a friend of your own daughter's?"

"She's known to her."

"On two occasions she's called to see your daughter, hasn't she, and you have opened the door—the private door?"

"She didn't come in."

"But this girl you identified as the person who came to your shop and bought flypapers is a girl who's been to your home to see your daughter?"

"Yes."

"I suggest you made a mistake—that you really identified the girl who came to see your daughter?"

"I've seen her in the shop," maintains the chemist.

He's stubborn in his belief, all right, but he's quickly losing ground. And Marshall Hall hasn't finished with him yet.

"Have you ever seen a picture of the Seddon girl in the papers?"

"Yes."

"*Before* you went to identify her?"

"Yes."

"So you're taken by the police to identify a girl whose picture you had seen?"

"Yes."

"Of course the moment you saw her the face was familiar to you?"

"Yes."

That blows the flypapers out of the story, don't you think? After that, who could be sure he'd sold them to the Seddon girl?

Very well; what *else* has the Crown got against Frederick Seddon? This argument—that as Miss Barrow was too ill to go out and nobody except the doctor came to visit her, she must—*must* have been—poisoned by someone in the house.

That leaves out of account the unlikely possibility that Miss Barrow took the arsenic herself. All right, let's—let's leave it out of account. Even so, the point about it being someone in the house, it's just as strong a point against Mrs. Seddon too. And that's what I was saying, the case against the one is the case against the other. Mrs. Seddon, too, had motive; she had opportunity; if the daughter did buy flypapers they might have been for her. And yet the case which is held sufficient proof to convict one, it isn't held sufficient proof to convict the other.

Very illogical, it seems, but one must face the fact that juries are swayed as much by emotion and instinct as by reason. You'll know exactly why they came to the conclusion that they did, if we watch Seddon for a little in the box.

Marshall Hall hadn't wanted him to go into the box, had urged him and pleaded with him to stay out. The experienced defender had a pretty good idea of the impression his client was likely to create. But in a matter of this kind the accused has the last word, and Seddon overruled his counsel; he insisted. I'm sure he thought, quite genuinely, it would advance his cause. But there's no doubt, too, that the dominating trait in him asserted itself again, even at this moment of agony and crisis. So he was a great counsel, Rufus Isaacs, was he? A deadly cross-examiner? Been in all the big cases, had he? Earned tremendous fees? Even great financiers quailed before him, did they? All right—let him match his wits with Frederick Seddon; let 'em haggle, let 'em bargain, we'll see who comes out best.

For a second or so they take stock of one another: the handsome advocate with the beautiful voice and the polished courtesy; and the man of business, tough, arrogant, ready for hard trading, brain with brain.

Isaacs begins. It's a beginning that has never yet been bettered.

"Did Miss Barrow live with you," he asks, "from July, 1910 till September, 1911?"

"Yes," Seddon replies.

"Did you like her?"

Did you like her? It's very nearly a knock-out. Answer yes—well, knowing all we do know now about Miss Barrow, he'll write himself down at once as a lying hypocrite. Answer no, I didn't like her—if possible, that's worse.

It almost shakes Seddon—and that's saying something; it's the first and last time, though he's to be questioned for six hours.

"Did I like her?"

He's gaining time to think.

"Yes," says Isaacs, "that is the question."

Seddon's found an answer now; he's used the breathing-space he won to good advantage.

"She wasn't a woman you could be in love with," he says, "but I sympathised with her deeply."

A really astute answer; fair match for the astuteness of the question. And as it has started, so it goes on, this duel, right to the end.

Isaacs enquires into Seddon's financial arrangements with Miss Barrow.

"She had some leasehold property?"

"Yes."

"And some investments?"

"Yes."

"And you say you arrived at an agreement with her for the transfer of them all to you in exchange for an annuity?"

"What she wanted."

"You were advising her."

"I was *agreeing* with her."

See that; there isn't a shade of meaning that escapes him.

"Had you ever done an annuity transaction before?"

"Never."

"This one," says Isaacs, "has turned out a remarkably profitable investment from the monetary point of view?"

Seddon looks deliberately round the court; at his wife in the dock, at the chaplain sitting up beside the judge.

"*Only* from that point of view," he says.

"When she came to you, Miss Barrow had a cash box with some money in it?"

"Yes."

"When she died, according to you, all that was left was four pounds ten?"

"That was all I found."

"While she was at your house, she was living well within her income, was she not?"

"I couldn't say."

"Have you any reason to doubt it?"

"I was the superintendent of an insurance company," says Seddon. "I was not the housekeeper."

"Your office assistants have sworn you counted out two hundred pounds in gold the afternoon she died."

Seddon flies off the handle—just for once.

"You make me out an inhuman monster, to commit such a vile crime, and then bring her money down and count it in front of my assistants. Flaunting it like that. It's a scandalous suggestion."

This outburst, this display of human feeling, this hint that he wasn't just a calculating machine—it might have done Seddon quite a power of good. But he spoils it instantly, before Isaacs has time to ask another question.

"I would have had all day to count the money," he says.

And then everyone can see the real point of his anger. It's not "Do you take me for a monster?" but "Do you take me for a fool?"

The more debating points he scores, the worse his plight becomes. The jury—any jury—has a preconceived idea about the sort of man who might commit a crime like this. Seddon is proving his fitness for the rôle.

There is his smugness, his pride, his delight in pulling a fast one even at the expense of the helpless and the weak.

"After it had been transferred to you," Isaacs asks, "did you sell Miss Barrow's stock?"

"I did, for a better investment."

"For fourteen houses?"

"Yes, for fourteen houses." Seddon speaks in triumph. "Brought me four pounds a week against her one—four against her one."

There is his callousness, his indifference to the death, which comes out when he's being questioned about his early morning visit to the doctor.

"Didn't you ask him to come and see her?"

"No. It's not for me to teach a doctor his duty."

"But didn't you want, for your own satisfaction, to make sure she was dead?"

Seddon shrugs his shoulders.

"I had no desire."

And above all, of course, there is that hideous avarice that knows no limits and no shame. He is not at all abashed when Isaacs refers to the twelve and sixpence rake-off he got out of the funeral.

"A business commission," Seddon says.

"But you had it?"

"Of course I had it. An agent for a sewing machine gets a commission if he buys one for himself."

On and on it went. He had an answer for every question, a retort to every argument. When at long last it was over, he could truthfully boast that the great Rufus Isaacs couldn't break him down.

But it was a hollow victory for Seddon. Meanwhile the jury, they'd been assessing *him*—not the evidence, but *him*—and it resolved all doubt for them, they could make up their minds. *This* was the villain— not the timid, shrinking woman, no—but this one: the heartless brute, the money-mad man, the clever devil who could stand up to Rufus Isaacs. This was the murderer—the one who killed Miss Barrow.

I agree with them to this extent. It is, I think, a *moral* certainty that Seddon did it. But was that proved by evidence such as the English law requires? You may say, what does it matter? But it does, you know, it does. Our legal system is designed to shield the innocent; start making exceptions and the shield turns into straw.

Mind you, I can't pretend I ever worry about the Seddon case. But at the same time I feel there's something wrong with me for not doing so.

8

Lizzie Borden

I'M SURE you know as well as I that murderers don't necessarily all resemble the classic pictures of Bill Sikes. Crippen, for example, was a meek-faced little man; Patrick Mahon—remember him? Mahon and his gruesome bungalow on The Crumbles?—he was a handsome chap, with a load of social charm; and quite lately, there's been Haigh— Haigh of the acid baths—dapper, trim, extremely debonair. No, you shouldn't put too much faith in looks and personality to give you a line on whether somebody might kill. But even bearing that in mind, could you believe *this?* That a modest, reserved and well-bred . . . gentle-woman—I can think of no better word; she *was* a gentlewoman—could you believe that such a person would attack her stepmother in the family home with such devilish ferocity that her head was smashed to pulp; that she would then quite coolly wait more than an hour for her father, filling in the time by ironing handkerchiefs; that she would then attack *him* with even greater violence, crushing and mangling his face so horribly that hardened doctors shuddered when they looked upon his corpse?

Could you believe a gentlewoman could commit such crimes?

Well, that's what the jury were asked to believe in the case of Lizzie Borden, and it helped to make her trial—which took place in America around sixty years ago—it helped to make her trial just about as sensa-tional as any that's been recorded.

First though, let me tell you a little about the Borden family, and their domestic life. There were four of them, living in Fall River, Massa-chusetts; an old Yankee town, that, about the size of Bath. The Bor-dens were by way of being local aristocrats, and they occupied a fair-sized house in a pleasant neighbourhood. Andrew Borden, the head of the family, was a wealthy banker; tight-fisted, domineering, not a very attractive type. His wife—his second wife it was—she was a pleasant, docile woman; rather a doormat, I suspect, where her husband was concerned. Emma and Lizzie Borden were Andrew's daughters by his first wife who had died; to all appearance, typical ladies of their kind. In 1892, when the story really opens, Andrew was nearly seventy; his wife was sixty-four; Miss Emma forty-one; Miss Lizzie thirty-two.

They were not a very united, a very harmonious quartet, though by now they had all shared a roof for twenty-seven years. But the daughters and the stepmother, they didn't hit it off—hit it off less and less as every year went by, until it got to the stage when Miss Lizzie never said "Mother" but always "Mrs. Borden." There was a variety of causes: traditional antipathy, personal dislike, there were disputes over property and who was to have what. In most of this, I'd say, the daughters were to blame. But whoever was to blame—no matter—that was how it was; the old pair and the younger pair were . . . not at daggers drawn, perhaps, but, let's say, at arms' length.

The summer of 1892 was uncomfortably hot, and Fall River being an inland town, it positively sweltered. By the end of July, Miss Emma had had enough of it, and off she went to the seaside for a holiday with friends. Miss Lizzie stayed at home; nobody there but the two old folks and the servant, Bridget, and Miss Lizzie appeared to get rather low, rather morbid and depressed. One evening she confided in a friend: she feared some terrible misfortune was impending. "My father," she said, "has so much trouble with his men," and she told her friend that strangers came lurking round their house, obviously bent upon some evil purpose. "Yes," Miss Lizzie said, "I'm afraid *someone* will do *something*."

Perhaps the heat had got her down. Perhaps there really *were* such men lurking round the house. Or perhaps . . . Well, there is one other possible alternative, one that we shall come to in its proper place and time—that is, in the courtroom, when Miss Lizzie's on her trial.

But whatever the correct construction to be placed upon them, Miss Lizzie's forebodings were amply justified. *Someone* did do *something* —and someone did it soon. It was on the 3rd of August that Miss Lizzie met her friend. By midday on the 4th, the Borden home had been turned into a shambles, and both Andrew Borden and his wife had been sent to their account.

It had started as a perfectly ordinary day—this day that was to stand out in the history of crime. The old people got up early, as was usual; Bridget served their breakfast just after seven o'clock. Miss Lizzie didn't appear till nine, as was also usual; she just had a cup of coffee, wasn't hungry, didn't eat. By that time Mrs. Borden—and this was usual, too—Mrs. Borden had got busy dusting round the house.

At a quarter past nine—I'm giving you all the times now because, from this point on, every minute's of importance—at quarter past Andrew Borden went out on his business round, visiting various places with which he was connected. At *half*-past nine Bridget went out through the side door; she gossiped for a while with a friend over the fence; then she began to clean the windows of the lower floor. Miss Lizzie and her stepmother remained—somewhere—inside.

At half-past ten Bridget went back in through the side door, carefully slipping the hook on it behind her. There was nobody downstairs. Bridget listened; the house was very quiet; not a rustle, not a murmur to suggest a living soul. They're taking it easy, sure enough, Bridget grumbled to herself. She started on the ground floor windows from inside.

At a quarter to eleven Andrew Borden came back from his round. When she heard him, Bridget ran out into the hall. She then saw Miss Lizzie coming down the stairs, eyes fixed on her father immediately below.

"Mrs. Borden has gone out," Miss Lizzie said. "She had a note from someone who is sick."

This was news to Bridget. Mr. Borden made no comment. He was tired after walking in the heat. He went straight into the sitting-room and lay down on the couch, and in next to no time he had fallen fast asleep.

Bridget resumed her cleaning, this time in the dining-room. Presently Miss Lizzie, plus ironing board, plus handkerchiefs, joined her there as if for company.

"You going down town?" Miss Lizzie asked, after a while.

Um—Bridget might be and she mightn't.

"There's a sale, you know—a sale of dress goods on," remarked Miss Lizzie.

But Bridget didn't fancy any more of the fierce sun. Much pleasanter to have a rest—yes, that's what she would do. "I won't be long, Miss Lizzie; just for a half hour or so, I'll lay down on the bed."

As Bridget reached her attic room a church clock struck eleven.

She had been there—how long? Ten minutes? Or fifteen?—when she heard Miss Lizzie's voice float up through the house.

"Bridget! Come down quick! Father's dead; someone came in and killed him!"

That touches it off. The Borden drama has begun.

The scenes that follow—they're the characteristic stuff of nightmare. Police and other officials racing from all sides; great crowds of onlookers collecting round the house; friends and neighbours, who've somehow been admitted, craning to get a horrified glimpse into that sitting-room where the doctors, shocked and helpless, talk in whispers; people comforting Miss Lizzie; people wiring for Miss Emma; people planning how to break it to the wife when she returns.

No such plans need have been made. They found Mrs. Borden soon enough—found her in the house; stretched out she was, on the floor of the guest bedroom, her shattered head almost adrift in a pool of blood. Most spine-chilling point of all, perhaps, in this spine-chilling affair, she'd been dead at the very least an hour longer than her husband—that's to say she must have been murdered while Bridget was outside, and she must have been lying there on the guest room floor at a quarter to eleven when Miss Lizzie came downstairs.

The mere revelation of these two appalling crimes was enough to throw the State of Massachusetts into ferment. When a search of the Borden home discovered, in the cellar, an axe, or rather a hatchet, with a three and a half inch blade—the exact length of the larger wounds on Andrew Borden's head—the ferment rose and overflowed the Continent. And when finally, after seven days of close investigation, none other than Miss Lizzie was placed under arrest, an excited discussion opened up throughout the world—a discussion that's far from being concluded even now, but which reached its peak, of course, during the fortnight of her trial.

Anyone dispassionately considering the matter—if it were humanly possible to do so at that time—anyone could have foreseen that the charge against Miss Lizzie of committing both the murders—a charge so incredible upon the face of it—it would never have been made, would never have come to court, if the prosecution hadn't been extremely firmly based. And so it proved to be. The reporters from Boston and Chicago and New York, the artists who were sketching Miss Lizzie in the dock, the privileged spectators crammed along the public seats—they heard a most formidable case put up against her.

There is evidence of opportunity, said the prosecution; she was there—all the time—there, about the house. There is evidence of motive, said the prosecution; she hated her stepmother, she didn't like her father, she would benefit financially by removing one or both. There is evidence, too, of premeditation, of design; what about her talk, the night before, of lurking men—wasn't that a smart contrivance to divert suspicion? There were contradictions, too, in statements she made afterwards; wasn't this another sign of guilt?

All these things, granted, they don't amount to *proof*. But they were only minor points in the case against Miss Lizzie. The prosecution had three major points which they claimed to be cast-iron—and not, I think, without a substantial show of reason.

First: not only did Miss Lizzie have ample opportunity to carry out both murders, but did anyone else have any opportunity at all? You could rule out any other members of the household: Miss Emma, who was at the sea, some fifteen miles away; Bridget, who at the time of the second murder was upstairs. An intruder, then? Well, but how square that with this—that there'd been no entry by force, that nothing had been disturbed, that no one had been seen to enter or been seen to leave.

Next point: three days after the murders had been done, a few hours after the police had told her she was now under suspicion, Miss Lizzie had burned one of her dresses in the kitchen stove. It had got stained with paint—that was her explanation. But it was an odd time to choose to burn a paint-stained dress. Might there not have been some more pressing reason? One of Miss Lizzie's strongest cards was that nobody ever saw any blood on herself or her attire. But suppose that, after each murder, she had washed and changed. She would then have had to dispose somehow of the discarded clothes. And after the second murder, there'd be very little time—probably only enough to hide them until later.

Third and last: there was that note from someone who was sick. Miss Lizzie had told her father it was because of such a note that Mrs. Borden had gone out; it wasn't only Bridget's word they had for that: Miss Lizzie herself admitted it when she was examined at the inquest. But though the very skies were ringing with the Borden case, and in Fall River itself no other topic raised its head, the note and the sick person were never, never found. "Her statement," said prosecuting counsel, "was a lie. No note came; no note was written; nobody brought a note; nobody was sick. Mrs. Borden had not had a note. I will stake the case on your belief in the truth of that proposition."

With such a case to meet, Miss Lizzie stood in need of an experienced and resourceful and ingenious defender. She got him all right in Governor Robinson.

Governor Robinson—he was really an *ex*-Governor of the State, but most people still called him by his former title—Robinson was the right man in the right place at the right time. He was a shrewd, worldly chap, but with a very simple style; his thoughts might be as crafty and as subtle as they come, but his language—that was always home-spun and direct. He knew the State of Massachusetts through and through—the way it lived, the way it felt, the way its mind worked. Give him a jury of his own folk and a bit of elbow room, and ten to one he'd make them eat out of his hand.

Robinson scored success after success for Lizzie Borden. He blunted and deflected the weapons ranged against her by every device in a defender's repertoire.

She might have done it, might she, just because she was in the house? "But," the Governor said, "after all it's her own home! I don't know where I'd want my daughter to be, except at home, attending to her ordinary duties!" And her talk about lurking men, that showed premeditation, did it? Well, the jury knew now that when she said these things, Miss Lizzie was suffering from a female disability, "and we know"—said Governor Robinson—"that many a woman at such a time is unbalanced, unsettled. Everything is out of sorts and out of joint." There were contradictions in her statements, were there? The Governor poured ridicule on the officers who'd taken them—and prudently refrained from putting Miss Lizzie in the box. The dress was burned because of bloodstains, was it? Governor Robinson had Miss Emma Borden there to swear that the dress had been stained with paint as long ago as May and that she herself prompted Miss Lizzie to destroy it. And Governor Robinson, if he didn't seem quite so happy trying to explain away the note from someone who was sick—well one can only say he skated over this as delicately and as gracefully as human wit allowed.

Oh, yes, he was on the ball, was Governor Robinson. Just watch him at one of the critical moments in the trial: his cross-examination of the Borden's servant, Bridget.

Just let's think a minute what he wanted from this girl. First of all, she'd been the only independent witness of the state of affairs that had obtained inside the Borden home. It was the prosecution's case that ill-feeling ran so deep, it furnished sufficient motive for the taking of two lives. Now if the Governor could get Bridget to paint a different picture, the motive would diminish or even disappear—and if the jury thought Miss Lizzie hadn't any motive, the notion of her guilt would be still more incredible.

That, then, that point is the one from which he starts. Mind, he's no idea what Bridget's going to say on this, and he's got to be on guard, he's got to frame his questions with the greatest skill and care,

because of the risk her answers may do more harm than good. She's
a tough little nut, too; quite cool, quite self-assured. And Governor
Robinson, he's only got just one hard fact to work from. Bridget had
been with the Bordens for three years. That settles the form of the
first key question he puts as they face each other across the crowded
court.

"Did *you* have any trouble there?" he asks.

It sounds pretty dangerous, but it isn't really so. By wording it that
way, by putting the stress on whether Bridget *herself* had any trouble,
the Governor's made it as safe as circumstances will permit. You see,
if she *should* answer "Yes, I did have trouble," Governor Robinson is
absolutely ready with his comeback. "But you stayed three years,
didn't you?" he'll say, with an air of triumph; and then he'll accept the
warning light and go on to something else.

He doesn't have to, though.

"*I* have trouble?" Bridget says. "No sir, I did not."

Governor Robinson advances a few inches.

"A pleasant *place* to live?"

"Yes, sir."

"A pleasant *family* to be in?"

"I don't know how the family was, sir. I got along all right."

Hm, this is tricky. Very gentle, very cautious, Governor Robinson
probes.

"You never saw anything . . . out of the way?" he asks.

Out of the way—he's hit the phrase exactly. Decent, respectable girls
—and that's just what Bridget is—they don't stay three years in places
where there's anything "out of the way." Robinson has sized up the
witness; he's shaped the question for her—shaped it so he can be
almost certain how she'll answer it; and the answer's going to take him
a great leap towards his goal. There may not seem much in it to the
ordinary spectator, but this is the very heart and soul of cross-examination.

Of course, it's as he guessed; certainly not, sir, Bridget never saw
anything out of the way.

The Governor's getting close now. He only wants to make the position rather more clear-cut.

"You never saw any conflict in the family?"

Conflict—well, that would have been something out of the way, and
Bridget has already said she saw nothing out of the way.

"No, sir; no conflict."

Almost home, the Governor is.

"Never saw any quarrelling or anything of that kind?"

"No, sir, I did not."

Starting from scratch, the Governor's done it in six questions. The family may or may not have been affectionate. But the jury isn't likely to think of it any more as a house of passionate hatreds and potential violence.

So far Governor Robinson has got on well with Bridget. It has suited him to do so. But now a new matter is raised and things take a different turn.

It was an essential element in Robinson's defence that an intruder had got into the house. As there'd been no breaking in and the front door was kept locked, the *side* door was the vital factor in the situation. Bridget agreed she left it off the hook while she cleaned the windows, and that part of the time it would be hidden from her view.

That was something. But Robinson intended to get more.

Bridget had been out through the side door earlier that morning; when she came in again, did she hook it up or no? Months back, at the inquest, she had said she couldn't remember. Now, at the trial, she was asserting that she did. "Yes," she said flatly. "I put it on the hook."

Robinson wasn't going to let her get away with this. His client's very life might depend on that side door.

As he picks up some papers from the desk in front of him—it was a transcript of what Bridget said at the inquest, word for word—the expression on his face is still quite genial, quite friendly. The tone of his voice, though—that, perhaps, is not quite what it was.

"Do you think you have told us today just as you told us before?"

Bridget decides to stall.

"I've told all I know," she says, and looks at him defiantly. She can be rather a cheeky little baggage when she likes.

"I don't ask you that." He isn't at all friendly, not at all genial now. "What I want to know is whether you've told it *today* just as you did *before?*"

The court is hushed by Governor Robinson's displeasure. Bridget's shaken, you can see it, but she's the pugnacious kind, and she's going to fight it out.

"Well, I think I did," she says.

"What did you do as to the side door when you came in from the yard?"

"I hooked it."

"Did you say so before at the other examination?"

"I think so."

"Do you *know* so?"

Bridget's got her eye on the papers in his hand. She's cute enough to have a good idea what they are.

"Do you *know* so?"

"I'm not sure," she says.

"Let me see if you said this." The Governor reads aloud. " 'Question: When you came in from the yard, did you hook the side door? Answer: I don't know whether I did or not.' " He puts the papers down again, very deliberately. "Did you say that?"

"Well," Bridget says, "I *must* have hooked it because—"

"That isn't it. Was that the way you testified?"

"I testified the truth, sir."

"I don't imply that you didn't." Of course he wasn't doing so. It was Robinson's whole point that she did—that she had told the truth at the inquest but wasn't telling it now. "I merely want to know if you recall saying that—that you couldn't tell whether you hooked the door or not."

"It's *likely* I did hook it, for it was *always* kept hooked."

She's done it; Robinson's got her now; he's only to press his advantage home.

"Do you positively recollect one way or the other?"

"I *generally* hook the side door—"

"That isn't what I asked. Did you hook it or did you not?"

"I *must* have hooked it for I always—"

"That isn't it. Did you hook the door or did you not?"

The position's hopeless. Bridget throws in the sponge.

"I don't know," she says. "I don't know whether I did or not."

So the side door may have been open much longer than they said. Governor Robinson becomes quite genial again.

You know there are actors who are called actors' actors because they're more admired by their colleagues than the public. If Governor Robinson hadn't enjoyed such popular success, I'd have been tempted to call him an advocate's advocate, because his gifts were of the kind that fellow professionals can best appreciate. Nothing could have been more characteristic of the man than the close of his final speech for the defence. No stirring peroration, no high-flown appeals. He gazes at the jury for a moment without speaking; then he extends his arm and points towards his client. "To find her guilty," he says, "you must believe she is a fiend. *Gentlemen, does she look it?*"

They looked, and they saw Miss Lizzie, seated in the dock; the features refined; the hair modestly groomed; the clothes severe and simple; and the hands—the long, slim, white, delicate hands. A lady, if ever there was one. "Gentlemen, does she look it?"

Oh yes, there are a lot of questions left unanswered. How and where did this hypothetical intruder hide himself in the house all the while between the crimes? Why was a dress that had been stained with paint in May not considered ripe for destruction until August? And again and again and again, the note from someone who was sick. But—gentlemen, does she look it? That was the way to leave it to a country jury, and reward was duly reaped in the shape of an acquittal.

Do you want me to say what I personally think about the case? About the verdict, I mean. Whether justice was or wasn't done in setting Miss Lizzie free?

If you don't, please switch off now, with my grateful thanks to you for listening. If you're still there, here it is. I don't say that if I'd been on the Borden jury, I'd have kept them up all night trying to persuade them to convict. I won't even say that I think Miss Lizzie did it—which after all is quite a different thing. I'll only go as far as this—and it doesn't commit me one way or the other—I do think she had the devil's own good luck to get away.

9

Richard Pigott

CROSS-EXAMINATION—it *is* one of those words; for most people
it conjures up a phantasy which almost has no connection with the
humdrum daily facts. For, after all, what is this thing called cross-
examination? Nine times out of ten—no, 99 times in a 100—at best, it's
some efficient legal hack asking the stock questions about who was and
who wasn't on the wrong side of the road. I put it to you that your off-
side wheels were over the white line. No, they weren't. My client will
say they were more than a yard over. Not true. I put it to you that when
you approached the corner—oh dear, and so it goes on, one case after
another. There are six people at the back of the court and three of them
are asleep. Talk about excitement—you can get more at a good Council
meeting any day.

And yet if I suddenly said to you—cross-examination; what would
you think of—think of, so to speak, before you'd time to think? I know
my own reaction—I've had it too long not to; years of studying cross-
examination, even years of doing it myself—nothing's ever cured me.
Say the word, and I think at once of the masters of the art, and think
of them on the very biggest of their big occasions. A packed and breathless court; the nation waiting on each word; the dramatic and ruthless
unmasking of a rogue, who rushes from the box and promptly shoots
himself.

Piling it on a bit, you think, even for the masters? Well, I'll admit,
even with them, a situation just like that, it doesn't happen often. But it
can happen—it can; it *did* happen at least once, in a setting more theatrical than you'd dare put on a stage. The greatest counsel of the time.
The most burning issue of the day. And the biggest scamp who ever
fancied he'd got away with it.

What I'm talking about, it happened back in 1889—the exposure of the forger Pigott by Sir Charles Russell when Pigott was a witness before the Parnell Commission.

Parnell, the Irish Land League, Home Rule and all that—the rights and wrongs of it are no concern of mine. What interests me—what I hope may interest you—is Pigott's crime, his shocking crime, and its sequel in the court. So forgive me if I don't go into the politics of the thing—indeed if I hardly mention politics at all, except to give you three preliminary facts.

It is a fact that, in the 'eighties, the Irish question dominated British politics. It is a fact that the Irish Party in the House of Commons was led by Charles Stewart Parnell in its battle for Home Rule. It is a fact that THE TIMES newspaper published several articles charging the Irish Party with lawlessness and violence and with being mixed up in various outrages; and, in particular, they printed, in photographic reproduction, a letter signed Charles S. Parnell—what seemed to be a private letter written by his hand—a letter expressing approval of the murder in Dublin of a British Government representative—a letter, clearly, which could do enormous damage both to Parnell and his party.

Now that—if you don't mind—that's all, or it's nearly all the politics. For when Parnell disclaimed the letter, said it wasn't his, and demanded that the Government should set up an enquiry, a Commission was appointed consisting of three judges. So this charge against Parnell, it's taken out of the partisan political arena and it's handed over for investigation by the law. From now on, it becomes a Case, like any other. Instead of delivering speeches and writing articles, the parties in this row are going to give evidence on oath, and when they've given their evidence, they're going to be cross-examined. And with cross-examination, in come the cross-examiners, including one whose gifts have never been surpassed. Charles Russell is appearing for Parnell.

In every way Russell was the fitting choice. He was Irish-born himself and, as a leading figure in the English Liberal Party, he'd been staunch and active in support of Home Rule. But far more important in the present circumstances, he was the commanding figure at the Bar—certainly the most commanding figure of his time, maybe the most commanding that the Bar has ever known. And commanding is exactly what I mean. I wouldn't say there's never been a more *persuasive* advocate—persuasive in the sense of ingratiating charm. My goodness, Russell wasn't the ingratiating sort; being charming wasn't in his line. His quality was power—almost irresistible power—a power through which he dominated others without effort. That went for judges nearly as much as juries, but most of all of course for witnesses on the other side. To be cross-examined by Russell if you'd anything to hide, if you weren't being absolutely straight and above board—it was a fate you'd think twice about wishing your worst enemy. A will of iron, a mind as quick as light, utterly remorseless in dragging out the truth—in any branch of advocacy Russell was a giant, but in cross-examination he was a giant among the giants.

No, you may be sure, Parnell could not have chosen better. If it was a forgery, that letter in THE TIMES—and after all, that was the one substantial point, that was what the enquiry was about—if it was a forgery, there was no man on earth more likely to compel the fact into the light of day.

Now, before the three judges sat to open the enquiry, it wasn't known where THE TIMES had got this letter from. It wasn't addressed to anyone by name—it just began "Dear Sir"—and there was nothing in the contents of it to suggest a source. But now this was something that had to be disclosed; something that their Lordships very much required to know. So THE TIMES people told what *they* knew of the transaction. They had bought the letter—together with several others of a similar kind—bought it from a gentleman named Houston, an official of an Irish body hostile to Parnell. Yes, but where had Mr. Houston got them from? Mr. Houston had bought them from a gentleman named Pigott. Yes, but where had Mr. Pigott got them from? Ah —that was where the mystery began.

It was obvious that at some stage Mr. Pigott must be called, and it was equally obvious that the subsequent exchanges between himself and Russell would probably be the crucial passage in the case.

Let me tell you what ammunition Russell had for Pigott, so you can appreciate that moment when it comes.

First, a misspelt word. The Irish Party, the supporters of Parnell, from the very start they had suspected Pigott, a man of Irish origin who had had a sticky career and was now known to be completely on the rocks. They were put on to him by the fact that in THE TIMES' letter the word "hesitancy" was misspelt—*"hesitency"* instead of *"hesitancy"*—and one member of the party who knew Pigott of old said he was sure that that was how he always spelt the word. But they hadn't any writing of Pigott's to confirm it, and to say someone *remembered* one of his misspellings—especially when that someone was an interested party—it was hardly enough to establish him a forger. Of course, in the box he could be asked to write the word, but imagine how wary, how much on guard, he'd be. If you simply say, "Mr. Pigott, please write 'hesitancy,'" he'll think over very carefully why you want him to, and although he may misspell it when he writes in haste, he may very well correct it when he's being ultra-canny. So even assuming that Irish member's right, that this is one of Pigott's habitual misspellings, whether it can be driven home for everyone to see—that depends entirely on Russell's art and skill.

Second, there was a letter—not, unfortunately, containing the word "hesitancy"—a letter Pigott himself had written to the Archbishop of Dublin, Dr. Walsh, who was a strong supporter of Parnell. The date of this letter is of some importance—4th March, 1887—that is, three days before the first anti-Parnell article came out in THE TIMES. In his letter Pigott was warning Dr. Walsh that there was a design afoot to try to ruin the influence of Parnell and his party by identifying them with criminal outrages in Ireland, and he said that he, Pigott, was able to point out how this design might be combated and defeated. Dr. Walsh handed the letter to the Parnell group and Russell now had it in his possession. Considering that Pigott had supplied the Parnell letters —or rather, the *alleged* Parnell letters—to THE TIMES, this little *billet-doux* to Dr. Walsh was a pretty good piece of out and out two-timing. Certainly it could be used to show that Pigott was willing to run with either side, or both sides at the same time, if it would bring him any personal advantage; that he hadn't any political conscience or morality. But could it be used for any more than that?

Presently we'll see what use a master made of it.

It was a Wednesday afternoon when Pigott went into the box. He looked very cool, very serene, very sure of himself—not at all like a man with a guilty secret locked up in his breast. In fact, at this stage while Pigott was answering questions put by counsel for THE TIMES, Russell, fidgeting and fretting in his place—Russell appeared the more uneasy of the two. He was always highly-strung, like every great performer, but he had *never* felt more conscious of responsibility. Parnell, the Irish Party, almost, you might say, the future of Home Rule itself —all seemed to cast their weight upon his shoulders.

For the rest of that day and for the whole of the next morning, Pigott was still replying to counsel for THE TIMES. He didn't mince matters. He'd been employed, he said, by the Irish Loyal and Patriotic Union— that's the body I mentioned that was hostile to Parnell—he'd been employed by them to search for any documents that might incriminate the Irish Party leader. He'd bought the letter that had created such a stir—bought it in Paris—bought it from someone who thought less about loyalty than cash.

You mightn't think much of this activity of Pigott's—being hired to grub around to see what mud there was to sling—but politics, it's often said, is a pretty dirty game, and it's a far cry from grubbing around to committing forgery. What was there to suggest that this letter, in the writing so exactly like Parnell's—what *was* there to suggest that the letter had been forged?

On the Thursday morning, when counsel for THE TIMES concluded his examination, it was already after 1 o'clock and the court adjourned for lunch. As it drew near the time that had been fixed for the resumption, the atmosphere became most electrical and tense. Everyone knew that the climax was at hand, but very few foresaw the kind of climax it would be.

The three judges take their place upon the Bench. Pigott is called back into the witness-box; he looks as confident as ever, even jaunty, you might say; he rests his hands on the ledge, he gazes down at Russell, and he smiles slightly, like a man expecting a good time.

Russell rises. There isn't a trace of anxiety or nerves about him now; his whole bearing speaks authority. He faces Pigott, and he smiles a little too, though somehow or other, it is a different sort of smile.

"Mr. Pigott, would you be good enough, with my lords' permission, to write some words on that sheet of paper for me?"

The usher hands Pigott the sheet of paper. Pigott seems a bit puzzled, a little bit unsure. Russell doesn't miss it.

"Would you like to sit down, Mr. Pigott?"

"Oh, no, thanks."

"Well," says the presiding judge, "I think it's better you should. Come here and sit down at this table, and you can write it in the ordinary way, just as you always do."

Pigott goes to the table and sits down, pen in hand, and waits.

"Will you write the word 'livelihood'?"

Pigott writes.

"Just leave a space now. Then will you write the word 'likelihood'?"

Pigott writes.

"Will you write your own name?"

Pigott writes.

"Will you write the word 'proselytism' . . . Done that? And finally— I think I'll not trouble you with any more at present—finally will you write 'Patrick Egan' and 'P. Egan'? 'Patrick Egan' and 'P. Egan.'"

Once more Pigott writes.

"Thank you; that'll do . . . oh, yes, there is one word I had forgotten. Lower down, please, *leaving spaces*, write the word 'hesitancy.'"

Then just as Pigott's hand was poised to do it—

"With a small 'h,' Mr. Pigott, with a *small* 'h.'"

Pigott wrinkled his brow—what's the catch in the small 'h'?—then he wrote again and laid aside his pen.

"Will you kindly give me the sheet?"

It was duly handed back. Russell gave it the merest glance. His expression never altered, but he knew he was already half-way home. For there it was, the last word on the sheet—"hesit*ency*"—spelt, and wrongly spelt, as in the letter signed Parnell.

It's an object lesson, that, in the art of cross-examination. By his emphasis on "Patrick Egan" and "P. Egan"—which didn't matter a hoot—and on leaving spaces—which didn't matter a hoot either—and on the small "h"—which had nothing to do with it at all—by all these devices Russell first occupied Pigott's mind with what was not important, and finally got him to write the key word "hesitancy" without realising that the point at issue was the spelling. "With a small 'h,' Mr. Pigott"—it was a stroke of genius.

For the present Russell says nothing of his prize. He goes on to ask Pigott a number of different questions upon different matters. As these early questions aren't particularly contentious and Pigott feels he did all right with the small "h" and "P. Egan," he is sailing along with Russell very happily indeed. Doesn't expect to be kept much longer in the box; looks forward to his dinner tonight, with all his worries over.

Then suddenly—suddenly—the balloon goes up.

"The first publication of THE TIMES' articles," says Russell, "was that on the 7th of March 1887?"

"I don't know the date," says Pigott.

"Well," says Russell, "you may assume that is the date."

"I suppose so," says Pigott. Sounds as though he couldn't care less, as though he were getting bored.

"And you were aware," says Russell, "of the intended publication of the incriminatory letters?"

"No." That wakes Pigott up. "No, I was not aware of it at all."

"*What?*"

"No, certainly not."

"Were you not aware there were grave charges to be made against Mr. Parnell and the leading members of the Irish Land League?"

"No, I was not aware of that until publication actually commenced."

"*What?*"

"I was not aware of it till publication actually commenced."

There's two of us can get tough—that's Pigott's attitude.

"Do you swear that?" says Russell.

"I do."

"Very good. Then there is no mistake about it, is there?"

Russell puts a hand among his papers. He draws out a letter and has it passed to Pigott.

"Is that your letter?"

Pigott looks at it closely.

"Do not trouble to read it. Just tell me, is that your letter?"

"Yes, I think it is."

"Have you any doubt of it?"

"No."

"Then let me have it back. My lords, this is a letter addressed to Archbishop Walsh. The date is the 4th of March, 1887, three days *before* the first of THE TIMES' articles. Follow me, will you Mr. Pigott, while I read how it begins. 'I have been made aware of the details of certain proceedings that are in preparation with the object of destroying the influence of the Parnellite Party in Parliament.'" Russell stops reading. "*What* were the certain proceedings that were in preparation?"

All the bounce has gone right out of Pigott.

"I don't recollect," he says.

"Turn to my lords and repeat that answer."

"I don't recollect."

"You say that, writing on the 4th of March, less than two years ago?"

"I do."

"You don't know what that referred to?"

"I don't, really."

"Doesn't it refer, among other things, to the incriminatory letters?"

Pigott ploughed into the quicksands.

"The letters, they hadn't been obtained, had they, at that date?"

"I don't want to confuse you, Mr. Pigott." Russell's amiability is sinister. "This is the 4th of March, less than two years ago."

"Oh, yes," says Pigott, "some of the letters, yes, they had been obtained before that date."

"Then didn't the passage I've read refer, among other things, to the letters?"

Pigott's groping desperately, anywhere, for escape.

"No," he says, "I rather fancy it referred to the forthcoming article."

"I thought you said you didn't know anything about the forthcoming articles?"

Pigott's confusion is getting worse—and more apparent every minute.

"I find I'm mistaken—I must, I think, I must have heard something about them."

"Try not to make the same mistake again." Russell goes back to the letter and reads some more of it aloud. " 'The proceedings consist in the publication of certain statements purporting to prove the complicity of Mr. Parnell and his supporters with murders and outrages in Ireland.' " Russell looks up at Pigott. "Who told you that?"

"I've no idea."

"Doesn't it refer among other things to the incriminatory letters?"

"I don't recollect it did."

"D'you *swear* it didn't?"

"I won't swear it didn't."

"D'you *think* it did?"

"No, I don't."

"D'you think that those letters, if genuine, would prove or would not prove Mr. Parnell's complicity in crime?"

"I think they'd be very likely to prove it."

"Now, reminding you of that opinion, I ask you again, whether you did not intend to refer among other things to those letters?"

Pigott surrenders.

"I may have had them in me mind," he says.

But there's no respite for him now, and there's never going to be.

"You believe those letters to be genuine?" asks Russell.

"I do."

"And did so at that time?"

"I did."

Again Russell reads from the letter to Dr. Walsh. " 'I am able to point out how these designs may be successfully combated and finally defeated.' " Pigott stares helplessly, seeing what is coming. "Assuming the letters to be genuine," says Russell, "*what* were the means you could point out for defeating the designs?"

"I can't conceive."

"Oh, try. You must really try."

"I can't."

"Try."

"I can't."

"Try."

"It's no use," says Pigott.

"Is your answer then that you can't give an explanation?"

"I really can't."

There is murmuring in court.

"Look how your letter goes on." Russell reads again. " 'I could furnish details, exhibit proofs and suggest how the coming blow may be effectually met.' What *was* the coming blow?"

"I suppose the coming publication."

"How was it to be effectually met?"

"I haven't the slightest idea."

"Assuming the letters to be genuine, does it even now occur to your mind how it could be effectually met?"

"No, Sir Charles, it doesn't."

The witness is transformed. You wouldn't recognise him as the man of half an hour ago. And still the pitiless Russell drives him back and forth.

"You procured and paid for a number of letters?"

"Yes."

"Which, if genuine, would gravely implicate the parties from whom they were supposed to have come?"

"Yes."

"A serious charge?"

"Yes."

"Did you believe that charge to be true?"

"I believed it to be true."

"In your letter to Archbishop Walsh, this is what you say. 'I need hardly add that, did I consider the parties really guilty of the things charged against them, I shouldn't dream of suggesting that your Grace should take part in an effort to shield them.'" Russell deliberately pauses. "Well, Mr. Pigott, what do you say to that?"

"I say nothing, except that I'm sure I didn't have the letters in my mind when I wrote that. I must have had something else—some other charges in my mind."

"What charges?"

"I don't know."

"What charges?"

"It must have been something far more serious."

"What was it?"

"I cannot tell you. I've no idea."

The wretched man is standing there in the box, the sweat rolling off him, quite unable even to parry the rain of blows, knowing that he's finished, knowing that he's beyond his own or anyone else's aid.

"It must have been something," Russell says, "far more *serious* than the letters?"

"Far more serious," Pigott says. He's almost punch drunk now.

"Can you give my lords any *clue* as to what it was?"

"I can't."

"Or from whom you heard it?"

"No."

"Or *when* you heard it?"

"No."

"Or *where* you heard it?"

"No."

Russell steps back and surveys the reeling figure, as a boxer might before he moves in for the knock-out.

"Have you ever mentioned this *fearful* matter—whatever it is—to anyone?"

But Pigott is insensible to stinging sarcasm.

"No."

"Still locked up, is it?" says Russell, "hermetically sealed in your own bosom?"

"No," Pigott says stupidly, "because it has gone out of my bosom, whatever it was."

A great burst of contemptuous laughter fills the court. Russell permits himself the shadow of a smile, and he sits down. It's over, and everybody knows it; it is over; Pigott is smashed, beyond hope of repair.

There is another day of it, but it doesn't really count—a day when Russell flogged at will a pulverised opponent. And there was another day after that—a day when Pigott's name was called, but Pigott didn't answer.

"If there is any delay in his appearance," Russell said, "I shall ask your lordships to issue a warrant for his apprehension."

But it was no good issuing any warrant for Pigott's apprehension. First there came an admission of his guilt, posted from Paris; "I said I had discovered the letters," Pigott wrote, "but I grieve to confess that I fabricated them, using genuine letters in copying words and phrases and the character of the writing."

After this, no alternative was left for anyone. THE TIMES withdrew the much-debated "Parnell" letter; the Special Commission of Enquiry branded it as forged; the police had a warrant out for Pigott—on a perjury charge. But before they could catch up with him, he had settled with himself—blown his own brains out in an hotel room in Madrid.

That's how it finishes—this story of a crime that, just for once in these talks of mine, wasn't the crime of murder. But if it wasn't a murder there was still an execution. That hour or so of Russell's cross-examination—it terminated Pigott's life as clearly and as surely as any early morning date at Armley or the Scrubs.

10

The Brothers Staunton

THE progress of time and of morbid anatomy alike demand a thorough re-appraisal of the Staunton case.

Too long it has been cited as a glaring instance of heated emotions mastering cold reason; of prejudice displacing evidence; of public anger, crystallised and reflected in a jury, swamping infallible conclusions reached by science. According to this interpretation of events, the conviction of the Stauntons for murder was unjust.

But at least the two male members in that gang of four were guilty; I make that categorical assertion. The whitewash on the Staunton brothers—zealously applied by Government departments, leading newspapers, established authors, medical "authorities"—has been wearing thin to the critical eye for half a century.

Its removal is overdue.

The key to murder generally lies in the nature of the murderer. Heath was going to find his girls, Rouse was going to find his tramp, Burke and Hare were going to find their "subjects," come what may. Occasionally, though, the position is reversed, and the key to murder lies in the nature of the person murdered. So it was with the dreadful crime committed by the Stauntons; their murderous conspiracy could never have succeeded but for the victim's curious blend of childish docility and childish stubbornness.

Childish is indeed the aptest word for Harriet. Although she had married and had become a mother before she died at the age of thirty-six, in knowledge and capacity she was no more than a child. A pathetic and yet a rather unattractive child; for what is fresh simplicity in one of tender years becomes mere vacant silliness in one who is adult. There is a photograph of her that survives—a photograph taken in full physical maturity—from which her mental make-up may readily be deduced. The heavy, drooping lids; the eyes, expressionless; the slightly scared and yet complacent simper—Harriet, in the significant vernacular, was wanting. Not insane, nor even imbecile, but of immature mind and arrested intellect. "She had never been able to avail herself of much education," said her mother, testifying at the trial that followed Harriet's death. "My daughter was a very simple-minded girl." You look again at the photograph; it is ample confirmation.

Harriet was of gentle birth and decent upbringing. She was also comfortably endowed; in possession and reversion, she had three thousand pounds. Her infancy and youth were serenely commonplace, marked only by the unescapable vexations of being the backward child in a family of four. Temperamentally passive as a rule, she was subject to occasional outbursts of irrational wilfulness that characterise the truly childish mind at any age. As she progressed into and through her twenties, these outbursts naturally became more and more difficult for others to restrain.

In 1874 Harriet was thirty-three. Still single and lacking any eligible suitors, she had probably almost abandoned hope of marriage. Her mother, on the other hand, having lost her first husband had acquired a second, and this may have altered the domestic atmosphere. Presently Harriet embarked on a series of protracted visits to relations, and through one of these she got to know an impecunious auctioneer's clerk named Louis Staunton.

Louis Staunton would have fitted best into the world of Dickens. Balzac or Dostoevsky, with their acute awareness of the infinite gradations that stretch between the absolutes of Evil and of Good, would have found Louis's starkness disconcerting and unreal; they would have humanised him, they would have watered him down. Only Dickens's fierce genius for caricature could have painted Louis as black as he deserved. One would be tempted to say that there has never been as big a villain—if one hadn't to introduce his brother Patrick later on.

At this early stage in a life that was unwarrantably extended, the depths of Louis's wickedness were yet to be revealed. On the surface, he was no more than a cold-hearted vulgarian, much preoccupied by money and by women, and always rapacious in pursuit of each. But, none the less, at twenty-three he was possessed of neither, and his warped mind began to canvass new expedients.

Harriet's appearance on the scene was providential. Her attractions, of course, were strictly limited. She had no claims to beauty, although —sad irony in light of subsequent events—she was always fresh and neat and had excellent taste in clothes. She was ten years Louis's senior. She was mentally deficient. But she had the wherewithal; and by the law of that day, in the absence of a settlement, it would all pass to her husband if she married. The situation was exceptionally auspicious, and Louis began to favour Harriet with his attentions. It is not to be supposed that at this stage in the matter he looked much beyond his immediate objective. Let him only get his hands on Harriet's little fortune; then he could decide how to deal with Harriet herself.

Harriet's mother, who had always considered her disqualified for matrimony, was not reconciled to the notion of her marriage by the personality of the prospective groom. She sized him up as a cheap adventurer, and was shocked when Harriet, highly gratified by a younger man's devotion, accepted his proposal and bestowed on him her hand. But could anything be done? Harriet was of age; entreaty or advice to break off the engagement were met with her own individual obstinacy —the intractable and violent obstinacy of a child. The despairing mother then adopted drastic action. She sought to place Harriet under the protection of the Court of Chancery as a lunatic. Dreadful as it sounds, dreadful as it is, none the less it would have been a better fate than that to which Harriet was irrevocably heading. The mother's application, however, was refused, and its sole result was to aggravate Harriet's anger and resentment.

Every effort had been made, and all had failed. On 16th June, 1875, Harriet married Louis, and both her fortune and her life passed into his keeping.

Harriet's mother had not been present at the wedding. Hurt feelings on both sides were too strong. But reflecting on the situation in the days that followed, she felt it would be foolish to perpetuate the estrangement. She distrusted and heartily disliked her son-in-law; but she still loved her daughter, was anxious for her welfare and wished to keep in touch. It was no good, she concluded, nursing grievances; what was done was done, and she must make the best of it.

One day in July, she presented herself at the front door of the house which the couple occupied in Loughbrough Park Road, Brixton, and which had been furnished out of Harriet's private purse.

On the whole, the encounter passed off fairly well. Harriet opened the door, immediately asked her mother in, and called out to her husband—"Louis, mama is here." In the sitting-room the three of them then talked amicably enough, and on Louis's suggestion Harriet showed her mother round the house. When the latter left, they both walked with her to the station. There was no dissension, there were no high words. The sole remaining indication of some coolness was the brevity of the visit—ten minutes in all.

Certainly there was nothing to prepare Harriet's mother for the two letters she received next day—one from Louis, in offensive and insulting terms, telling her he would not have her in the house again; the other from Harriet, more moderately couched, but saying that, as Louis objected to her mother calling, she had better not come, to prevent any disturbance.

This affront was final; no more gestures of goodwill or of forgiveness were forthcoming. That visit from her mother in the first weeks of her marriage was Harriet's last real contact with the world she had always known—a world which had not exploited her defects but, on the contrary, had treated her with sympathy and kindness.

Henceforth her mother fades right out of Harriet's life, and the remainder of the Staunton gang gradually fade in.

Patrick Staunton was Louis's brother, and his peer in infamy. They differed, however, in kind, if not in degree. Louis was sly, underhand, treacherous, reptilian; Patrick was a savage brute, evil-tempered and foul-tongued. Scratching together some kind of a living as an artist, he occupied a secluded house in a desolate part of Kent. This house was to be the *mise-en-scène* of Harriet's martyrdom.

Patrick's wife, Elizabeth, is the most difficult of the Staunton quartet to assess. There is no evidence to suggest she was by nature depraved and vicious like the brothers. When one has to find an explanation of her conduct, it is possible and forbearing to assume that, living in so remote a spot, cut off from neutral friends, with a husband who often struck and beat both her and their two children, she felt herself unable to offer a successful resistance to his will.

Elizabeth's younger sister, Alice Rhodes, completes the Staunton four. Though strictly, of course, a Staunton neither by birth nor even by marriage, as she very soon became the paramour of Louis she might be proclaimed a Staunton by adultery. Alice was a good-looking, unimaginative girl, selfish and rather callous in her quest of a good time. Her illicit affair with Louis was already under way in the spring of 1876 when Harriet gave birth to a boy.

During that summer the whole of Harriet's household was uprooted and moved, each member separately, towards Patrick's house in Kent. The baby went in May, when it was only a few weeks old; Elizabeth had undertaken to look after it. Harriet went in August; Louis had arranged to pay Patrick a pound a week for "taking care of her." In November Louis himself, drawing on what remained of Harriet's depleted fortune, set up in a farm nearby with Alice Rhodes, and the curious migration was complete.

Harriet meekly acquiesced in these unnatural measures. She may have been deceived into thinking they were temporary. ("I have been here a month on Saturday," she wrote to Louis in one of her misspelt and semi-literate letters. "It is time I should be at home.") Not that there was really any need for such deceit. Once again Harriet's childish nature furthered Louis's game. As she had shown her mother unwavering resistance, she showed her husband unquestioning compliance. Harriet never dreamed of disobeying Louis. His was the master's rôle, hers the supine slave's; he issued decrees, she accepted and obeyed them. Even if they meant a separation from her child; even if they meant a separation from her husband.

On 23rd October, 1876, Louis took Harriet up to London for the day; he had sold, for spot cash, one of her reversionary interests, and her formal consent and signature were required. The solicitor concerned had known Harriet some time and observed her, as always, with compassionate interest. She was no different from usual; rather flustered and bewildered and uncertain what to do, but physically robust and plainly in good health. When the business was concluded she shook hands and said goodbye and prepared to accompany her husband back to Kent.

That was Harriet's last appearance for six months. Henceforward she saw none outside the Staunton circle, and moved nowhere except within the walls of Patrick's house.

The veil that shrouded her was so impenetrable that even calling tradesmen did not know that she was there.

Having regard to the disagreeable nature of the last communication she had received from Harriet, her mother was not at first disquieted by her silence. She became uneasy through a report that reached her ears in the new year—a report of the liaison between Louis and Alice Rhodes. This uneasiness was not at all allayed by an accidental meeting with Alice Rhodes herself.

Harriet's mother had known both Alice and Elizabeth in days past; they were indeed her distant relatives by marriage. When she came upon Alice at London Bridge one day in February, she accosted her at once and, while wisely refrained from direct impeachment, demanded information and news of Harriet.

"Where is she living now?"

Alice Rhodes, taken unawares, stammered, blushed, and said she didn't know.

"You *must* know where she is."

"Upon my word, I don't."

"You *do* know, Alice," said Harriet's mother quietly.

Alice was but nineteen; the older woman overawed her. She changed the initial lie for one easier to sustain.

"Harriet's at Brighton, with her husband and child," she said.

"What's her address?"

"Sorry, I don't know."

"Is she well?"

"She has been ill," said Alice Rhodes, "but she is better now; I believe she's better now."

It seemed nothing further could be got out of the girl. Harriet's mother was about to turn away when something caught her eye.

"Alice, you have got my daughter's brooch," she said.

Alice coloured again, took off the brooch, and put it in the other's hand.

"You can have it if you like."

"Oh no, not if my daughter has given it to you." The brooch was firmly handed back. "But I can't *understand* her giving it you; it was her *favorite* brooch."

"I must go," said Alice Rhodes, and forthwith dashed away. . . .

The more Harriet's mother thought about the brooch, the sharper grew her fears for Harriet. Determined to track her down and resolve her own uncertainty, she pursued inquiries in any quarter that offered the least hope. At last she reaped the fruits of perseverance. Someone hinted that she might profitably make investigations in a certain rural part of Kent, and so on the 5th March she travelled down by train to Cudham.

Someone in the village directed her to Louis Staunton's farm. When she knocked on the door, Elizabeth Staunton answered.

"What do *you* want?" she said.

"I want to see my daughter."

Before Elizabeth could reply, Louis came upon the scene. His face was contorted and his voice shook with rage.

"You shan't see her," he shouted. "Clear off, you damned old bitch, clear off. Mind your own bloody business."

There could be no more touching evidence of the mother's anguish than that even under these insults she did not retaliate.

"If you will only let me hear her voice," she pleaded, "if you will let me see her hand on the banister, I shall go away content."

Louis's response was to advance upon her with a knife. Even Elizabeth was shocked.

"Don't, don't," she begged.

"I appeal to you." Harriet's mother turned now to the woman. "You have children of your own whom you may want to see some day."

But Elizabeth was not as tender-hearted as all that.

"Your daughter is well cared for," she retorted, "and that's enough for you to know."

The door was slammed. The veil over Harriet remained opaque and undisturbed.

It was shortly to be lifted, but only after a grim sequence of premonitory events.

On the 8th April, Patrick Staunton and his wife left a sad little bundle at a hospital in London. It was Harriet's child, a forlorn and wizened goblin, who had known scant comfort in his tiny span on earth. "The mother can't take care of it," they said as they departed. That night the infant died—*died of sheer starvation.*

On the 10th April, Louis, giving his name as Harris, arranged with an undertaker for the burial. He strongly emphasised that it should not be expensive "because the father of the child is away."

On the 12th April, Louis and Elizabeth went to Penge, on London's south-east outskirts, a dozen miles or so from their establishments at Cudham. They called at an apartment house at 34 Forbes Road and booked accommodation there—a sitting-room and bedroom—for "an invalid lady living in the country." "Her doctor," Louis vouchsafed, "doesn't understand her case." "We want to bring her here," Elizabeth added, "so as to be nearer London for advice." Meanwhile, though, they asked about the local doctors, and on being given the name of a surgeon, Mr. Dean Longrigg, they immediately went to call on him. They repeated what they had said at the apartment house, adding that the invalid was feeble-minded and paralysed down one side. Mr. Longrigg asked the name of the patient's present doctor. After some hesitation they purported to inform him—"Dr. Creasey of Brastead"—but it was a lie; neither the doctor they named nor any other had been attending the invalid lady who was living in the country.

Mr. Longrigg agreed to call next day at 34 Forbes Road, and Louis and Elizabeth hastened back to Cudham.

That evening all four Stauntons combined strength. Shortly before

dusk, from Patrick Staunton's house they brought forth all that was left
of the luckless Harriet. Half conscious, half paralysed, unable to speak
or walk or stand, she was dragged from door to carriage, from carriage
to train, from train again to carriage, and finally up the steps of the
apartment house in Penge. *It was not thought necessary to bring any
of her clothes.*

They were in a different district. Medical men, police, coroners would
not know them. All was now in order. Harriet might be allowed to die.

Their timing could hardly have been neater. The very next day
Harriet obliged.

Mr. Longrigg had seen her first at ten o'clock that morning (attempts
to secure his presence on the previous night had failed). Both Elizabeth
and Alice Rhodes were in the room. By then Harriet was quite insensible and also, he noted, emaciated and dirty. Her arms were rigid, her
breathing stertorous, her eyeballs shrunken, her pulse rapid and weak;
without any question, she was past a doctor's aid. None the less, it is
difficult to deny that Mr. Longrigg acted in a rather casual style; he
did not make any minute examination, but simply pronounced that she
would not survive. At the request of the two women, he sent in a trained
nurse.

When the latter arrived, Harriet was appreciably worse, and the
nurse insisted on the doctor being fetched again. It was apparent to
him at a glance that Harriet now was dying. There was nothing he
could do; he said a few consolatory words and went away.

Harriet did in fact die within an hour. Mr. Longrigg gave a certificate
of death—causes: "cerebral disease and apoplexy"—based more on
what he had heard than on what he had observed.

The Stauntons swiftly made arrangements for the funeral. They asked
the nurse meanwhile to take charge of the corpse. Then, all their business in Penge having been concluded, they took themselves off home
again that very afternoon.

It really looked as though they were going to get away with it.

That they did not do so—at any rate, completely—was due to one
of those remarkable coincidences which happen in real life but which
no novelist dare invent.

Close by the apartment house in Forbes Road, Penge, there was a
sub-post office which formed part of a shop. It was a natural place for
strangers in the district to inquire where they should register a death.
On the very day that Harriet died, a customer in the shop overheard

someone make precisely that inquiry; there had been a death at 34, the postmaster was told—a lady normally domiciled at Cudham.

Now the customer in the shop—and it is this that almost strains the limits of fortuity—happened to be the husband of one of Harriet's sisters. Of Harriet he knew little but he did at least know this: that she had last been heard of in the neighborhood of Cudham, and that her family suspected she was being harshly used.

He decided to report the circumstances to the police.

From the police to 34 Forbes Road; from 34 Forbes Road to Mr. Longrigg; from Mr. Longrigg to an inspection of the body. Her brother-in-law identified it as that of Harriet, and told the doctor something of her story.

The death certificate was revoked, the funeral postponed, the coroner informed. An inquest was formally opened and a post-mortem arranged.

The wheels of justice had started to revolve and there now could be no stopping them till they had run their course.

It is not unknown for pathologists to assert that an autopsy need not be disagreeable. The post-mortem examination of Harriet, however, revolted even the hardened professionals who performed it.

They found—as the nurse who laid her out had found before them—that the corpse was caked with filth and quick with lice. The feet were horny, as if she had long walked barefoot. Some false hair that she wore had become so matted and entangled with her own that it could only be detached from the scalp by the use of forceps.

There was not a single particle of fat upon the body. There was not a single trace of fat in any of the organs. Her weight was five stone four —against a height of five foot five. The state of emaciation, in medical opinion, must have taken at least three months to bring about.

There were "slight" tubercular deposits on the brain but these appeared to them as of subsidiary importance. Certain symptoms—principally congestion of the organs—suggested that some irritant poison might have been introduced. Analysis, however, disclosed that none was present.

In its absence, the examining doctors had no doubt. They found no indication of a death-dealing disease. The woman had died, they said, from prolonged starvation and neglect.

The arrest of the Stauntons came after an inquest that lasted, upon its resumption, for six days, during which public wrath continuously mounted as part at least of the real facts was disclosed. Nor did the effort of the Stauntons in the box to counteract the clear impression made by other witnesses meet with any conspicuous success. As was pointed out by Mr. J. B. Atlay, who edited the transcript of the trial and was certainly not unduly prepossessed against the Stauntons, the story that they told had been "evidently concerted." More than that, some of it was manifestly false; as when Louis—loyally supported by the others—declared that he and Harriet had agreed to separate because of her persistent insobriety. And yet, said the specialist who had analysed the organs, "there was no evidence whatsoever of excessive drinking; the liver had not the slightest appearance of habits of intoxication." Nor could Louis himself, when invited so to do, name one person who had ever seen Harriet worse for drink.

The crowds gathered around the coroner's court grew larger and more threatening with each successive session, and there is little doubt that, if the Stauntons had come into their hands, they would have been lucky to come out again alive. However comprehensible in the special circumstances, such mass demonstrations are to be deplored. If the emotion they engender does not lead to the same conclusion as the evidence, the jury may respond less to the evidence than to the emotion and hence arrive at an erroneous verdict. If the emotion and the evidence *do* lead to the same conclusion, the mere existence of the emotion tends to cast a slur on a verdict fairly based upon the evidence.

Even at that early stage in the celebrated Penge case, there were pundits ready enough to make this last mistake. Concession to clamour, they said, with contemptuous assurance, when the coroner's jury imputed the crime of murder to all four.

It was just as well, from every point of view, that the High Court granted an application made by the defendants to transfer the trial from the seething territory of Kent to the more remote and impartial atmosphere of the Old Bailey.

Certain points in the Stauntons' trial, though nominally disputed, were universally recognised from the start as fact. During the last few months, at any rate, of her stay with Patrick Staunton, Harriet was virtually a prisoner in the house. Her physical disintegration—whatever the cause—was slow, could not have been unnoticed by those with whom she lived, but did not prompt them to procure medical aid. Her bedroom, to which she was progressively confined, had been squalid, dirty, and inadequately furnished. Whether she was actually manhandled is less certain; at the trial the Stauntons' little servant girl alleged that Patrick had struck Harriet on more than one occasion, but the girl had said nothing of this nature at the inquest, and one cannot accept her word without due reservation.

But the issue of violence was hardly relevant. Nobody suggested Harriet had died from violence. And in so far as evidence of violence was adduced, it was merely incidental to the Crown's prevailing theme.

That theme was propounded through three alternatives.

One: that Harriet had been deliberately starved with the intention and design that she should die. In that event, whoever did it or combined to do it, and whoever knowingly aided and abetted those who did, would be properly convicted on the major charge of murder.

Two: that she had been starved through negligence and inattention. In that event, all those who had an obligation—voluntarily assumed by contract or imposed by law—to feed this helpless creature who was kept under duress would be properly convicted on the lesser charge of manslaughter.

Three: that she was removed from Cudham to Penge in such condition that her death was thereby caused or accelerated. In that event, if those who so removed her knew that this was probable, they would be guilty of murder; if not, and yet they were reckless or grossly negligent, of manslaughter.

The medical evidence at the trial (and not only that which was tended by the Crown) proved overwhelming upon this third contention —that the removal did at least accelerate Harriet's death. It therefore seemed hardly conceivable that any of the four—all of whom took an active part in that removal—could ever have expected or hoped to go scot-free. Each was guilty at least of manslaughter on this ground alone, though there were great variations in degree of culpability which might have been marked by the judge in passing sentence. But it is, in my view, exceedingly improbable that a murder verdict would have been returned upon this issue; that a jury would assume a suddenly formed plan to exploit a condition not purposely provoked. "Look, Harriet's ill; here's a great chance to get rid of her; let's move her somewhere else— she'll never stand the journey." It is not *impossible*, but it sounds far-fetched; nor did the circumstances point in that direction.

So a verdict of murder against any of the Stauntons depended, in practice as distinct from theory, on the jury holding that starvation was deliberate. And on this score—indeed, on the whole issue of starvation, in direct contrast to the issue of removal—no valid case was made out against Alice Rhodes. There was no sufficient evidence that she, unrelated and living somewhere else, took part in any plot concocted against Harriet; just as she should not have been held negligent in feeding her when she was under no duty to supply Harriet with food.

But what of Louis, of Patrick, of Elizabeth?

Louis, the husband, spending his wife's money and enjoying Alice's embraces (in gaol she had a child by him which was so registered); Patrick, in receipt of a stipend from his brother for "taking care of Harriet"—whatever that might mean; Elizabeth, the housewife, who might have seen to it that Harriet had sufficient food. The deductions were altogether unavoidable. If it were proved that Harriet had died of starvation, then—to quote Mr. Atlay once again—"there was no possibility of acquittal for her husband, her brother-in-law, and her brother-in-law's wife."

But *was* Harriet's death the outcome of starvation? The Crown doctors said yes; the defence doctors said no. And thus, as in the trial of Norman Thorne, the great question in the Staunton case was this: *how* did the woman die?

Apart from the Stauntons themselves, no one could know *at first hand* whether Harriet had starved—save for the little servant girl whose veracity was in question. At the trial—departing once again from her inquest evidence—she swore that Harriet had been deprived of food deliberately; but no one would or should accept that statement without satisfactory confirmation from elsewhere.

All turned, therefore, on medical observations and inferences therefrom.

Mr. Dean Longrigg was the first and most important medical witness for the Crown.

He was the last doctor to see Harriet alive; the only one to see her at all after the move to Cudham; one of several who conducted the post-mortem. He had consequently had the chance of surveying Harriet's case more directly and more often than any other doctor. This is perhaps worth remembering in view of the counter evidence brought by the defence. Undeniably the physicians whom they called were more experienced, more distinguished, better known than Mr. Longrigg, but they laboured under one practical disadvantage. They had never set eyes on Harriet, neither alive nor dead. . . .

In reply to the Attorney-General (Sir John Holker), Mr. Longrigg said he had known on sight that Harriet would die. He had given a certificate in the form he did because he had been told that she had

had a fit. He had not ascertained whether she was paralysed in fact; the patient was so near death, he did not go into it. At the post-mortem he had noticed the presence of tubercles on the brain, but these, in his belief, were not connected with the death. Having been informed there was no poison in the body, he had at once concluded that the death was from starvation.

"Did you give that as your opinion before the coroner?"

"I did."

"Do you still adhere to that opinion now?"

"I do."

Mr. Longrigg could not have been more sure and definite. But now he was open to attack in cross-examination.

Counsel defending Louis (Montagu Williams), Elizabeth (Douglas Straight), and Alice (Percy Gye) had agreed among themselves that the medical aspect of the case in its entirety should be left in the hands of Edward Clarke, who was defending Patrick. This was a highly sensible decision. Clarke's three colleagues were skillful advocates—Williams, indeed, achieved real brilliance in a criminal court—but Clarke himself was destined to join that tiny band of giants who stand out like massive towers in the history of the Bar. Although at the time of the Stauntons' trial he was only thirty-six—that trial, above all others, confirmed his growing fame—Clarke's powers had matured early, and his conduct of this difficult and delicate defence does not suffer by comparison with his many later triumphs. Moreover, he had a special flair for cross-examining doctors—a flair he reinforced by most industrious research. The brief for Patrick Staunton was delivered to him in July; the hearing did not begin until the 19th September. Meanwhile "I gave up the greater part of my holiday," wrote Clarke, "to working hard at the study of works upon tuberculosis, and upon the post-mortem appearances which could be expected where death had taken place from starvation."

He did not, however, have to rely upon his reading only. Clarke was personally acquainted with Dr. J. S. Bristowe, an eminent London physician of the day with a special and enviable reputation as an expert on morbid anatomy. Having read the press reports of the preliminary proceedings, Dr. Bristowe formed the opinion that the doctors who had made the post-mortem upon Harriet had misinterpreted the indications there revealed; they pointed, not to starvation, but to tubercular disease. He sent Clarke a letter signifying as much; the defender called him forthwith into consultation and invited him to amplify and justify his view.

The influence of this unexpected ally is manifest in Clarke's protracted duel with Mr. Longrigg. The deftness of the cross-examination was, of course, Clarke's own, but for the medical thesis on which much of it was based the credit or otherwise must go to his adviser.

Clarke led up to this thesis by well-proportioned steps. The architectonics of his advocacy were always beautiful.

"When you gave your certificate," he said, "you had no reason, had you, to suspect anything?"

"No."

"You gave it in good faith?"

"Yes."

"You had no idea at the time that there was any starvation?"

"No."

"The symptoms did not indicate starvation?"

"No."

Henceforth, in sustaining the theory of starvation, Mr. Longrigg would be exclusively confined to the post-mortem. Clarke now turned his fire in that direction, extracting maximum value from the doctors' discarded hypothesis of poison.

"You thought at one time that poisoning caused the death?"

"I was suspicious of it."

"Suspicious? Did you not *conclude* that it was so?"

"No."

"Was it not because of this that the organs were sent for analysis?"

"We could not find enough disease to account for death."

Clarke faced the witness squarely.

"Will you undertake to say that the word 'starvation' was so much as mentioned during the post-mortem?"

"Yes, I will."

"By you?"

"Yes, by me."

"In what context?"

"I mentioned starvation as one of the causes of death."

"*One* of the causes?"

"Possible causes. We all thought it was poison *or* starvation, and that analysis would determine which."

Clarke picked up a copy of the depositions.

"Did you give evidence on this point before the magistrates?"

"I believe I did."

"Do you remember what you said?"

"Not exactly." Mr. Longrigg was a trifle disconcerted. "It is three or four months ago; I cannot recollect."

Clarke still held the depositions; he looked at them as he spoke.

"If you said before the magistrates that you had *expected* the analysis to show sufficient poison to cause death, would that be true?"

"If I said it, it is true."

The answer seems an odd one, apparently implying that the test of its truth was whether it had been said before the magistrates. But one fact had been positively established; that, until the results of the analysis were known, Mr. Longrigg had favoured the theory of poisoning at least as much, and probably more, than the theory of starvation.

Clarke ostentatiously laid the depositions down.

"You yourself cut open the stomach?"

"Yes."

"And observed it carefully?"

"Yes."

"And you have already told us all that you observed?"

"So far as I am aware."

"Then we can take it, can we, that the stomach was of ordinary thickness?"

"No." Mr. Longrigg's brows were puckered. "No, it was rather thinner than in nature; the coats of the stomach were thin."

"So the coats of the stomach were thin!" Clarke repeated the witness's words with stinging sarcasm. "How many times in the course of this case have you been examined?"

"Two or three," Mr. Longrigg said uncomfortably.

"Before the coroner?"

"Yes."

"Before the magistrates?"

"Yes."

"And here to-day before my lord?"

"Yes."

"Until *I* put the question to you, have you ever—*ever*—mentioned that the coats of the stomach were thin?"

In a very hushed court, Mr. Longrigg took his time.

"No," he said at last. "I do not think I have."

"The thinning of the coats of the stomach would be a strong indication of starvation?"

"It would."

"One of the most natural and obvious signs?"

"Yes."

"And you have never mentioned it till now."

It certainly confirms one's earlier impression that Mr. Longrigg was inclined to be slapdash, and Clarke had rightly turned this factor to account.

"Let us consider the condition of the brain. You told us, did you not, that it was firm and healthy?"

"Yes."

"Not wasted, therefore?"

"No."

"Nor pale?"

"No."

"In the case of starvation, would it not be both?"

"Not wasted."

"Pale?"

Mr. Longrigg was in difficulties again.

"I should expect to find it pale," he said.

Clarke next raised in quick succession the possibility of Harriet's death having been caused by phthisis, diabetes or Addison's disease. But these were introduced rather to elicit defects in the post-mortem than to discharge the function of plausible alternative. The latter point, and the full development of Dr. Bristowe's thesis, is only reached at the climax of the cross-examination.

"You spoke earlier, Mr. Longrigg, of the tubercles on the brain?"

"Yes."

"Doesn't the presence of tubercles on the brain constitute the disease known as tubercular meningitis?"

"Yes."

"A fatal disease?"

"Yes. But it wouldn't account for the symptoms in this case. Tubercular disease wasn't sufficiently established—there wasn't enough of it— to produce the symptoms that I saw."

"Assume," Clarke says, "a stronger, a more advanced, condition of the disease. Will you tell me any symptom of this case that it could not have produced?"

Mr. Longrigg does not answer. The seconds tick away.

"*Any* symptom?" Clarke repeats.

Mr. Longrigg takes a deep breath.

"The rigidity of the muscles," he says. "The rigidity of the muscles of the upper extremities."

Clarke confidently pounces.

"Do you say there is no rigidity in death from tubercular disease?"

"I have never seen it," Mr. Longrigg says defensively.

"Do you say it can't exist?"

Mr. Longrigg's uncertainty can be read in his expression. These are deeper waters than those to which he is accustomed.

"I can't say that positively. I can only say that *I* have never seen it."

"You can't say positively that it could not exist in cases of tuberculosis. And there is no other symptom that you can point out?"

Mr. Longrigg looks thoroughly unhappy.

"That is so," he says. "But may I repeat—in this case the disease wasn't sufficiently advanced; I can be absolutely positive of that. The amount of tubercle was very, very slight."

Clarke has held his trump card suspended for this moment.

"Did you examine the brain with a microscope?"

"No."

"Would you agree," says Clarke suavely, "that the microscope is a great advantage to diagnosis?"

"Oh yes." There can't be any quibbling over that. "But it wouldn't have told me more than I knew—that tubercle was there. You could see the amount quite well with the naked eye."

But the advocate adroitly drives home his advantage.

"Can you speak as positively as you could have done had you used the microscope?"

The question is phrased to admit only one reply.

"Well, no," says Mr. Longrigg.

"You can see more with the microscope than with the naked eye?"

"Well, yes," say Mr. Longrigg.

"So what the microscope would have shown you in fact you did not see?"

"Well, no," says Mr. Longrigg.

Of course it was a brilliant cross-examination. It had placed Mr. Longrigg in the poorest possible light; he seemed slipshod in method, defective in memory, unstable in diagnosis. But Mr. Longrigg was not alone and unsupported. The other doctors who had helped in the postmortem similarly rejected outright the suggestion that the tubercles they had seen indicated death from meningitis ("They did not fulfil the description of the symptoms"). And although the microscope might be preferable to the naked eye, the naked eye in turn is vastly preferable to inspection made at second or third hand.

Dr. Bristowe was not the first doctor to appear when the defence's turn came to substantiate the theory which Clarke had adumbrated in his cross-examination. Priority of place was reserved for Dr. Payne, an anatomist and pathologist of comparable rank. Possibly the order had been so arranged because Dr. Payne possessed one great advantage over Dr. Bristowe; he had at least read the depositions and had heard the Crown's medical witnesses give their evidence at the trial, whereas Dr. Bristowe's knowledge of that evidence wholly derived from the columns of the newspapers. Both, however, were forced to rely in forming their opinion on the facts as affirmed by the Crown's doctors—one, at least, of whom the defence was representing as an unreliable observer.

So in expressing his view that Harriet had died from tubercular meningitis, Dr. Payne was very careful to point out that this was entirely based on the assumption that the post-mortem appearances had been accurately described. "I am not responsible," he said, "for the description."

"When you speak of tubercular meningitis," the Attorney-General asked him, "you mean the acute disease?"

"I mean an acute disease."

"How long, do you think, had this acute disease been going on?"

"The post-mortem appearances don't supply the information."

"But isn't the acute disease generally fatal very quickly?"

"Yes," admitted Dr. Payne. "The acute stage could not have been more than a few days."

"And disease is more likely to appear in a person of enfeebled bodily condition than in a person in good health?"

"There is no doubt of that."

"What, in your opinion, caused the emaciation?"

Dr. Payne was having none of this. He would not commit himself.

"I cannot tell," he said, "without consideration of the history of the case."

"I need hardly ask you," the Attorney-General said, "whether, if a woman was given insufficient food, she would probably become emaciated?"

"Oh yes; undoubtedly she would."

Dr. Bristowe followed. In cases of death from tubercular meningitis, he said, it is a frequent thing to find rigidity. Emaciation in one of the recognized features of tuberculosis—in its acute form, often the only sign. The tubercles are frequently so minute as to defy detection without a microscope.

"You have read the evidence?" the Attorney-General asked him.

"Yes."

"Read it in the newspapers?"

"Yes."

"That is all the knowledge you have of it?"

"Yes."

"You read that there wasn't a particle of fat upon the body?"

"Yes."

The Attorney-General put the question he had put to Dr. Payne.

"What, in your opinion, caused the emaciation?"

Dr. Bristowe gave the answer that Dr. Payne had given.

"I cannot attribute it to anything without knowing more of the case."

"Is it consistent with starvation?"

"Yes, it may be."

"Is it consistent with tuberculosis?" Clarke interpolated.

"Yes, it is consistent with tuberculosis."

The judge had been listening with unconcealed impatience to the academic theorising of the two physicians. In the end he could not refrain from comment.

"To my mind," he said, "this is a most unsatisfactory sort of evidence."

Mr. Justice Hawkins himself has been the subject of so much bitter and protracted controversy arising from his handling of the Stauntons' trial that it may be useful to consider the kind of man he was before considering what he said and did.

Hawkins's notable and long career as counsel ended upon the threshold of the Bar's Golden Age; the age which opened with Clarke and Russell at their peak, and which—through social changes affecting legal practice—after Hastings and Birkett irrevocably closed. Whether, had he been born a little later, Hawkins would have ranked with the greatest of that age—with Carson, Isaacs, Smith and Simon in addition to the four already named—is a question that lawyers may endlessly debate. In my opinion he fell short of that supreme eminence, belonging rather to the group immediately below, wherein are to be found men of such majestic talent as Henry Duke and Douglas Hogg. In some respects, Hawkins could hold his own with any: as cross-examiner, as expositor, as forceful personality. But he had one serious failing: an insensitivity and indifference to atmosphere which sometimes marred performances that otherwise were perfect. This failing was not cured by his accession to the bench.

The Staunton case—which he tried in his first year as a judge—

earned him admiration and criticism in almost equal measure. No one could fail to acknowledge the mental grasp and theatrical virtuosity displayed throughout his lengthy summing-up. "As an exhibition," wrote Clarke, "of tenacious and exact memory, it was wonderful. The narrative was complete and perfectly arranged. But," he went on to say, "of the judicial fairness that should characterise a summing-up, especially in so grave a case, there was not the slightest trace." Clarke, indeed, could never forgive Hawkins for what he deemed his scandalous conduct in the Staunton case. Writing forty years afterwards, he termed him "a wicked judge"; noted that after the trial "Hawkins continued his career of public disservice"; and dwelt with patently continuing satisfaction on the fact that when the judge retired in 1898, he himself wrote to warn the Attorney-General that, if there were eulogistic tributes paid at a formal leave-taking, he would respond by making public protest.

What, specifically, were Clarke's allegations against Hawkins?

Out of a general indictment that "there was constant emphasis on the facts which told against the prisoners," and that "every point which had been made in their favour was answered or turned aside as being of no importance," three particular causes of Clarke's discontent emerged. One: The judge did not warn the jury that the case against Alice Rhodes was of the slightest possible kind. Two: His summing-up, of almost eleven hours' duration, was packed into the compass of a single day, and broken only by two short intervals totalling in all three quarters of an hour. Three: He virtually ignored the medical evidence for the defence.

Under the first and second heads, there is much to justify Clarke's contentions. It was wrong of Hawkins to press an insufficient case, as he did against Alice Rhodes upon the murder count. It was wrong of Hawkins to send the jury out to find a verdict late at night when they may have been impatient and they must have been exhausted. Even in regard to Louis and to Patrick, the verdicts upon whom were unexceptionable, this latter fault cannot be retrospectively excused. Justice must not only be done, it must also be seen to have been done, and the endurance test which Hawkins imposed upon the jury tended to make their judgment suspect even when correct.

But neither of these factors would have led to the case of all four Stauntons being reopened, after each had been convicted of murder and condemned to die. What brought this about was Clarke's third head of complaint: the judge's treatment of the defence's doctors. It gave rise to what Clarke himself described as "the remarkable protest which subsequently caused the setting aside of the death sentence."

The trial ended on the 26th September, 1877. On the 6th October, *The Lancet*—then as now a representative medical journal—devoted its leading article to comment on the case. It expressed the view that the evidence of criminal *neglect* was overwhelming. But "the judge left the case to the jury on the allegation of murder by starvation. . . . It must obviously be impossible to prove *murder* by starvation without first showing *death* by starvation. . . . The post-mortem appearances were not consistent with the hypothesis of death from the cause assigned; they afford irresistible evidence of other causes at work."

The Lancet was thus placing its full weight behind the theories of the doctors called by the defence. Nor was it content with a purely passive rôle. "The issue raised is so serious," the leading article concluded, "that we venture to think the medical profession should mark its sense of the emergency by a combined expression of opinion. Again we protest that this view of the situation is not in the least degree suggested by sympathy with the prisoners or a low estimate of their crime—that of gross neglect. . . . What we desire to place on record is a strong belief that the indications offered by a dead body imperfectly examined have been misinterpreted, and an inference drawn which the facts do not warrant, but which, on the contrary, they controvert. The interests of science no less than justice call for an assertion which shall make this apparent. We have therefore to ask those members of our profession who share this conviction to send us their names, to be affixed to a memorial printed in another column, and which we will undertake to place before the Secretary of State for Home Affairs."

There was almost a stampede in response to this appeal. The profession, especially its upper group, had been seriously offended by the contemptuous indifference of Hawkins to opinions so esteemed as those of Payne and Bristowe; and some seven hundred doctors, with the great Sir William Jenner at their head, hastened to signify that they did "share this conviction"—i.e., that the morbid appearances observed at Harriet's post-mortem, together with the symptoms recorded during life, denoted death from cerebral disease, and, conversely, did *not* denote death from starvation.

"With the presentation of this memorial," wrote Clarke, "it became clear that the death sentence could not be inflicted." It is certainly true that any Home Secretary would find it difficult to resist such highly organised and clamorous mass pressure by those one must presume to be most expert on the subject. A swift reaction followed from the Minister concerned. On the 14th October, the four Stauntons were reprieved.

The Lancet of that day was doubtless satisfied that "the interests of

science no less than justice" had been served. But the unsoundness of
this belief was later demonstrated by one who—our contemporary
Lancet would maintain—possessed a knowledge of morbid anatomy in
all its varied aspects with which Doctors Payne and Bristowe could not
venture to compete.

As one of the very few who have dared to suggest in print that Sir
Bernard Spilsbury may sometimes have been wrong, I have been
roughly handled by his biographers. They misconstrued me, but perhaps it was my fault. All that I have said of Spilsbury is this: that,
through accident of circumstances and no fault of his own, public
opinion deemed he was infallible; whereas, like every other mortal,
howsoever gifted, he was liable to occasional misconception or mistake.
Unless one is prepared to assume that he was superhuman, I should
have thought that statement indisputable.

At the same time, no one acquainted with Spilsbury's career could
deny that the occasions when he erred were few and far between. And
there is not the slightest reason to suppose that his conclusion from the
Staunton evidence ranks with those occasions.

His interest in the case was keen and his study of it close. He had
read every word in the transcript of the trial—he was therefore considerably better briefed than Dr. Bristowe—and had meditated long
upon its implications before presenting his considered judgement to the
Medico-Legal Society in 1921.

What he said there has been summarised in the biography referred
to.* Spilsbury pointed out that morbid anatomy was in its infancy in
1877. The doctors concerned knew less about the subject than present-
day students. *The findings of the post-mortem, he said, were "overwhelmingly in favour of starvation being the cause of death, as against
tubercular meningitis."*

The jury and the local practitioners had been right.

Once starvation is firmly established as the cause of death, it is not
difficult to reconstruct the pattern of the crime. No purely fanciful conjectures are required. One need only examine such facts as were proved
beyond dispute in the light of what we know about the characters involved.

Louis, having possessed himself of all Harriet's money and conceived an ardent passion for young Alice Rhodes, pondered how to rid
himself of both wife and child. He had no qualms of conscience about

* *Bernard Spilsbury* by Douglas G. Browne and E. V. Tullet, London, 1951.

the means adopted; only qualms of physical squeamishness. For Louis (despite his histrionics with the knife when Harriet's mother called on him at Cudham) was not the type to commit grave crimes of injury and violence, though he would not in the least object to such crimes being committed out of his presence but on his behalf. Patrick, on the other hand, was a sadistic ruffian, as his own family had ample cause to know. There is a significant parallel between the Staunton pair and the fictional pair in *Oliver Twist*, Fagin and Bill Sikes. Each man, for a certain evil purpose, complements the other.

It seems to me highly improbable that the conspiracy—which, I am satisfied, did exist between them—was ever formulated in a clear-cut fashion. One does not visualise them with their heads together, using words like "death" and "kill" and "murder," and agreeing on a precise division of the loot. The conspiracy may indeed have been a tacit one, but each thoroughly understood the part he was to play. Louis had been—and would continue to be—generous in handling the spoils derived from Harriet; and Patrick—by no means to his dissatisfaction—acquired two helpless victims whom he could methodically ill-treat in the knowledge that every hurt and every deprivation conduced towards the end which the conspirators desired.

Once this semi-silent bargain had been struck, Louis left to Patrick the dark work of dispatch. He had put the job in safe hands and he wanted to see none of it. In the words of a half-forgotten novelist, Charles Reade, who appointed himself unofficial spokesman for the Stauntons, Louis and Alice in their nearby farm were "self-indulgent adulterers absorbed in adultery." Certainly both, though they often went to Patrick's house, saw little of Harriet and did not want to see her. But Louis knew—had instigated—what was going on. Alice may not have known, preferring ignorance.

The same could not possible be pleaded for Elizabeth. She was at the heart and centre of offence; she watched every move in the game of slow destruction. It would not be fair to say that she did nothing to prevent it; only that, over many months, she did nothing effective. A legal submission that, because she was Patrick's wife, it ought to be assumed she acted under his coercion and therefore could not be held separately liable, suffered rejection by the judge, and I think rightly so. It is not, however, paradoxical to add that Elizabeth would never have so acted of her own accord, that she felt horrified and shocked when she guessed what was afoot, and that she even tried at times to check Patrick's worst barbarities. Tried, but not hard or frequently enough to escape altogether from responsibility. Elizabeth should have been convicted of manslaughter—not, like Alice, solely because of her share in the removal, but also because of her share in the starvation.

As the months went by and Patrick's cruel campaign produced its terrible effect, all four began to take for granted Harriet's decline. The abrupt realisation that she might be near to death created an atmosphere bordering on panic. The dash to Penge was not part of a preconcerted plan, but a frantic improvisation born of sudden fear—the fear felt by three, if not by four, of the associates that exposure and retribution hovered perilously close.

A good deal can reasonably be said for both the women, and in the result they received roughly their deserts—Alice her immediate release (which possibly was justified) consequent upon a free pardon (which probably was not), Elizabeth a period of several years' imprisonment (more, but not greatly more, than befitted her offence).

There is nothing whatever to be said for either of the men. That they escaped the scaffold they so rightly merited (Louis surviving to be set free when barely middle-aged) not only travesties the appropriate instruments of justice; it also attracts the mind to an insidious alternative. For though one knows that lynch law is always wrong in principle and almost always horribly unjust in actual practice, it is possible to wish that, in this particular case, the Staunton brothers had been left to the mercy of the mob.

11

Barney Blitz

Race gangs?

Organised bands of ruffians ready to carve and slash and stab for the privilege of levying toll on bookmakers? Men who make their living by violence or the threat of violence practised on the vulnerable betting industry?

Do such things exist except in novels and in films?

Impossible, they like to think in the dormitory suburbs, where betting means a ten bob wager on the telephone. Impossible, they like to think in decent working homes, where betting means a slip of paper and a coin passed in the pub. Impossible, they like to think in glossy Club Enclosures, where betting is as elegant as at Deauville casino.

Every now and again, though, all get a rude reminder that in racing there is perpetually present an evil underswell.

One such came last year, when extensively reported court proceedings followed the encounter of Messrs. Spot and Dimes in Soho. One such came in the year 1924, when extensively reported court proceedings followed the encounter of Messrs. Blitz and Solomon at the Eden Social Club. The degree to which they parallel each other has significance; in a fluctuating world at least evil is a constant.

The Eden Social Club was neither so idyllic nor so convivial as its name suggests. Tucked away in a back street close to Euston Road, it provided, as an Old Bailey jury were subsequently informed, "a resort for the lower circles of the racing world." In plainer words, it was a sink for scum.

The event that conferred upon this club a fame temporarily eclipsing that of any in St. James's occurred late one night when forty or fifty men were assembled in its squalid premises. Among these was a bookie's hanger-on named Barney Blitz, who had lately faced a charge as a "suspected person." Blitz felt certain he had been shopped by a rival named Emmanuel, with whom he had had a feud over what counsel delicately termed "Bookmakers' lists." Drink was flowing freely at the Eden Social Club that night, so all ingredients were gathered for a blazing row when Emmanuel, accompanied by a friend named Solomon, appeared there about midnight and walked up to the bar.

"Here's the copper," constituted Blitz's greeting. Emmanuel swore at him, and Blitz swore back with interest. Tempers rose fast, and presently Emmanuel—perhaps emboldened by Solomon's presence—flung beer in Blitz's face. Blitz picked up a glass and, suddenly advancing, cut a deep wound in Emmanuel's forehead with the open end.

Solomon was not the man to stand by and see his friend served in such a fashion. If Blitz could be tough, Solomon could be tougher; belonging as he did to the Sabini gang, he was used to razor fights against their chief competitors, the gang of Brummagem Boys. As the blood spurted and streamed down Emmanuel's face, Solomon seized a carving knife from a nearby table and drove it into Barney Blitz's head behind the ear.

Somehow or other, Blitz managed to stumble down the stairs and into the street, where he immediately collapsed.

There followed a mass exodus of members from the club. Leaving their hats and coats behind them in their haste, they fled heedlessly past their fellow hoodlum as he lay prostrate and dying in the road. No one wanted to be in any way involved, and next day, when the police sought witnesses, barely one in ten of those who had been present admitted seeing anything that had taken place.

Employees of the club, however, were less unforthcoming, and Solomon was duly charged with murdering Barney Blitz. "What I have done, I have done in self-defence," he said, and this remained the plea relied on at his trial.

Marshall Hall, who represented Solomon—a fund had been raised by the latter's chums to cover the legal fees—thus faced two separate but interlinking tasks. He must show that Solomon, in going to his friend's aid, had reasonable cause to apprehend an attack upon himself. He must show that the attack threatened was of such a nature that it could reasonably be countered with the weapon Solomon used.

"Was Blitz a boxer?" Marshall Hall asked Emmanuel (doubtless a very unwilling witness for the Crown).

"Yes."

"Not particular about using only his fists?"

"No."

"A dangerous man in a scrap?"

"Yes."

The value of this evidence might be in part discounted by Emmanuel's natural desire to help the friend on whom he had unwittingly brought such trouble. But Marshall Hall immensely reinforced it when the Detective Inspector in the case agreed with him that Blitz had been convicted several years before of hitting someone in the face with a glass bottle.

This instructive exploration of the dead man's history could hardly fail to satisfy the least perceptive juror that Blitz might savagely manhandle *anyone* who crossed him—as would be well-known to those acquainted with his temper. But twelve average citizens, happily unfamiliar with the *improvised* techniques of doing violence, were still likely to jib at a knife being employed against an ordinary domestic drinking glass. It would look to them rather like a soldier drawing his sword because his wife is going for him with the rolling pin.

How to dislodge this misconception from their minds? How to drive home, with compelling vividness, that, in the hand of a practised desperado, the glass might be even more deadly than the knife?

Marshall Hall was a master of visual demonstration, especially of provocative behaviour with weapons. Give him a pistol, and he would point it at the jury, moving it a little from one side to the other, so that every one of them experienced at first hand the sensation of gazing directly down the barrel. Give him a dagger, and he would hold it poised menacingly an inch or two above a colleague's jugular, so that sensitive spectators turned away as people turn away from seeing somebody run over. No actor ever surpassed his power of making these scenes live.

Pistols and daggers, though, are recognized instruments of offence. An ordinary drinking glass called for something different.

Marshall Hall rose to the challenge. He surpassed himself.

On the desk before him, while he made his closing speech, stood a glass of water which his clerk had brought. An ordinary glass. A domestic drinking glass. Exactly the sort of glass with which Barney Blitz had armed himself, and that had brought upon him such retaliation that he died.

As Marshall Hall reviewed the various incidents that led up to that brief but fatal fight, the jury's eyes were often resting on the glass. Sometimes he sipped from it. Sometimes he moved it to a more convenient spot. Once or twice he held it in his hand for quite a minute, meanwhile continuing to address them earnestly. Over and over again they were reminded how harmless is a glass devoted to its proper purpose.

Until, as Marshall Hall approached the climax of the story, as he spoke of Blitz picking the glass up in the Club, he gripped his own glass, turned it upside down, and crashed it against the desk with electrifying force.

For a moment no one moved, and the water dripping to the floor was the only sound in court.

Then Marshall Hall lifted up the broken glass and held it with the jagged end towards the jury, so that they faced a gleaming ring of wicked spikes that could penetrate an artery or slit a human throat.

The startling impact of this superb performance—and one does not use that expression deprecatingly—must have substantially influenced the outcome: a manslaughter, and not a murder, verdict. . . .

The promised parallels with Spot and Dimes will have been noted. The feud over a contested monopoly on the racecourse; the part played by a knife in pursuance of the feud; the open fight before a crowd which the crowd did not observe—it fits as well with old Compton Street in 1955 as with the Eden Social Club in 1924.

Only in the final sequel do their paths diverge. Solomon got three years, and thereby the law acknowledged that a crime had been committed and that someone was to blame.

12

Chapman vs. Stewards

In 1930 Don Pat, trained by Charles Chapman, won the Bedfont Plate High Weight Handicap at Kempton Park.

Subsequently a Statement concerning this event was issued by the Stewards of the Jockey Club. It reported that, after the race, the acting Stewards of the Kempton meeting had given orders for an examination of the horse. On receiving the result of the examination they had referred the case to the Stewards of the Jockey Club.

"After further investigation," this Statement continued, "the Stewards of the Jockey Club satisfied themselves that a drug had been administered to the horse for the purpose of the race in question. They disqualified the horse for this race and all future races under their rules, and they warned C. Chapman, the trainer of the horse, off Newmarket Heath."

You are an ordinary member of the public. You are interested in racing, bet once or twice a week, study the press tipsters, have theories about form. But you don't know a thing about the racing hierarchy, or how it operates, or its self-appointed rules.

What, then, would you have inferred from that official Statement—published, not only in the Racing Calendar, but also in a number of national newspapers? Could it mean anything other than that Mr. Chapman had been warned off for administering dope to the horse Don Pat himself? Or, at the very least, for being mixed up in the business?

I confess that would certainly have been my own conclusion. But it would have got me nowhere near the truth.

That Don Pat was doped lay established beyond question by the usual veterinary tests. No one, though, ever suggested for a moment that Mr. Chapman, a young man of highest character, doped the horse or had prior knowledge of the doping. He—in the outcome, more than anybody else—was the hapless victim of another's roguery.

But among the rules, or practices, of the Jockey Club—by which all who seek a living out of racehorses are constrained, willy-nilly, to abide—there is one, affecting trainers, which the Stewards applied rigorously to the doping of Don Pat. Because it is difficult to detect the perpetrators of doping, and because an essential element in it is access to the horse, the Stewards hold the trainer absolutely liable unless he can *prove* that he is not to blame.

This rule reverses the general rule of law that a person's *guilt* must be proved, and not his innocence. It may be expedient; it may even be necessary; but the effects of it on innocent parties are bound to be severe, and one might expect every measure to be taken by the Stewards which would at least reduce this to a minimum.

But if Mr. Chapman entertained such expectations, they were shattered.

Not only was he warned off. Not only was he refused an adjournment of the Stewards' Inquiry so that he might further pursue inquiries of his own. Not only was that elliptical and misleading Statement published. The Stewards flatly declined to explain or qualify it even when Mr. Chapman, finding the Statement widely construed to mean he was a rogue, begged them to make clear to the world what they had really meant.

No appeal lies against a decision of the Stewards to warn a trainer off. But even the Jockey Club is not above the laws of defamation, and therefore—lacking any other means to clear his name—Mr. Chapman brought an action in the High Court, alleging that their Statement constituted libel.

It was an action studded with famous and distinguished names. Among the defendants were my lords Harewood, Rosebery and Ellesmere (sued as Stewards of the Jockey Club), and no less notable a journal than THE TIMES (unluckily involved through automatically printing the Statement in good faith). Among counsel engaged were Patrick Hastings (for the Plaintiff) and Norman Birkett (for the Jockey Club), the two brightest stars of the Special Jury courts and old opponents truly worthy of each other's steel.

The major battle of the trial centred round one question: What did the words of the Statement mean in their *ordinary, natural sense?*

Did they mean, as the plaintiff said, that he had been a party to the doping of Don Pat? Or did they merely mean, as the Stewards still maintained, that he was warned off because he had failed to *prevent* Don Pat being doped?

It devolved upon the Earl of Rosebery, as the senior Steward, to act as chief witness in support of his contention and to bear the main brunt of Hastings's cross-examination.

"Do you realise," it began, "that the decisions of the Stewards of the Jockey Club may bear the gravest consequences?"

"Yes," Lord Rosebery said.

"A trainer who is warned off will be ruined, socially and profession-ally?"

"Yes," Lord Rosebery said.

"In a case like this," said Hastings, "where a trainer has had nothing to do with the doping of a horse, you convict him of carelessness?"

Lord Rosebery demurred.

"I think it is more than carelessness. I should call it a grave derelic-tion of duty."

Hastings accepted the amendment.

"Do you realise that, in the eyes of fair-minded persons, there must be all the difference in the world between a man who has doped a horse and a young trainer at the beginning of his career who is guilty of dereliction of duty?"

"Yes," Lord Rosebery said.

"If the wording of the notice sent out by the Stewards conveyed to ordinary people that Mr. Chapman had been warned off the Turf for doping, a grave injustice would have been done him, would it not?"

"It would be an injustice."

Hastings did not take kindly to the omission of his adjective.

"The answer is Yes?" he said sharply.

"The answer is Yes."

"It would have been a simple matter for the Stewards of the Jockey Club to have stated in the notice that Mr. Chapman had been found guilty, not of doping, but of dereliction of duty as a trainer?"

"Yes."

"Why did they not do it?"

"I think we did."

Hastings flourished the document that was the cause of all the trouble.

"Is there a word in this notice that would convey to a man of or-dinary intelligence that the only thing Mr. Chapman had been found guilty of was not taking care of the horse?"

"Yes."

"Where?"

Lord Rosebery could only repeat the hotly disputed words.

"You say that conveys his sole fault was not taking care?"

"Yes."

Hastings let the Statement drop with manifest derision.

"Were you informed last summer by the Duke of Richmond that Mr. Chapman was anxious that it should be made public that he'd been warned off, not for doping, but for negligence?"

"Yes."

"Why didn't you make it public?"

"*I did not think it necessary,*" Lord Rosebery said, "*as the Stewards had never said that Mr. Chapman doped the horse.*"

This is the attitude I find so hard to fathom—why the Stewards so stubbornly resisted the addition to their Statement of a dozen words which, without remitting Mr. Chapman's punishment, would have defined in plain terms what he was punished for. I fancy the jury found it equally hard to fathom, and that they expressed their disapproval in the damages—£13,000 against the Jockey Club, £3,000 against the morally unoffending TIMES.

This sensational verdict, however, was not held.

The Court of Appeal pronounced that the Stewards were protected on the legal ground of privilege (a plea that had been rejected by the trial judge), and they were dismissed completely from the suit. THE TIMES, ironically, could not claim privilige, but the Court of Appeal, considering the damages excessive, ordered a new trial—a trial that never came to pass.

One is bound to think that Mr. Chapman suffered a raw deal. He restored his reputation as an honourable man, but was forced to pay for what should have been his right. The Stewards may have correctly interpreted *their* law, the Court of Appeal may have correctly interpreted *theirs;* but one is left with the uneasy feeling that this was a case where both private law and public law did something less than justice.

13

Smith vs. The Winning Post

WOULD you, sir, as a sedately married man of fifty, feel desperately aggrieved if you found reports being circulated that you had won the favours of a famous actress when you were a carefree bachelor of twenty-eight?

Would you, sir? Would you? Honestly?

Yet this is the complaint of the man now occupying the witness box and facing the jury in Mr. Justice Ridley's court. This is the "disgraceful conduct" which his counsel says was imputed to him by a "serious libel" in "The Winning Post."

"The Winning Post"—a saucy and characteristically Edwardian publication, dedicated to racing but not uninterested in sex—has been printing extracts from the memoirs of Helena Odilon, one of the best-known Austro-German actresses of her day. In these she describes how her liaison with a certain Herr Oehlschaeger was ruptured through his jealousy of a gentleman rider named Smith who came over from England to ride for Oehlschaeger in 1888. Smith stayed at their house, and one day, when he had been hurt in an accident, the actress visited his room to see how he was progressing.

"I was on the point of leaving," Miss Odilon wrote, "when Herr Oehlschaeger appeared. He stormed at me in rage. Not a word would he allow me to say in self-defence. I left the house without obtaining a chance of proving my innocence."

Later on, however—by her own account—Miss Odilon caught up with Herr Oehlschaeger's premature suspicions. The innocent pair consoled each other for the injustice done them, and she became in truth the mistress of the gentleman rider named Smith.

Now the man in the witness box bears the name of Smith. He is, or has been, a gentleman rider ("One of the best known on the Turf," according to his counsel). He did go out to Germany in 1888—and 1887, and 1889—to ride Oehlschaeger's horses. He did there meet Helena Odilon).

These facts, it is argued on Mr. Smith's behalf, would identify him in the eyes of anyone knowing him well as the English lover of whom Miss Odilon wrote. So now he seeks damages for a slur upon his chastity.

Because, as he repeatedly and indignantly insists, he has never been the lover of Miss Odilon at all.

It is no part of "The Winning Post's" defence to contradict him. Quite the reverse. They say that Smith was not even the lover's real name; that they deliberately conferred it on him as a pseudonym, just as they might have chosen Jones or Robinson or Brown; and that use of our commonest surname could not reasonably be held to single out the plaintiff from all the other Smiths.

This argument acquires piquancy through counsel for "The Winning Post" being a Smith himself—the redoubtable F.E., afterwards Lord Chancellor, and at present reaping the harvest of his brilliance at the Bar. It has almost the savour of a family dispute when the two Smiths confront one another.

"You don't suggest, do you," asks F.E., "that you have suffered any pecuniary damage?"

"I do," says the plaintiff.

"How?"

"When a copy of the paper was posted to me by a friend, I thought the safest thing to do would be to show it to my wife. When she read it, she got extremely angry."

"Of course you assured her that there was nothing in it?"

"Oh yes." The plaintiff nods. "But my wife said it wouldn't be in the paper if it were not true."

There is a laugh. The plaintiff shows no disposition to join in.

"How long have you been married?"

"Since 1891."

"Nearly twenty years," observes F.E. "No doubt your wife has learnt by experience to rely upon your word?"

"On this occasion," says the plaintiff, "I could not convince her."

"That is regrettable. But I am still waiting to hear how you have suffered pecuniary damage."

The plaintiff looks embarrassed and takes time before replying.

"You see, it's my wife who has most of the money," he explains.

"Did she cut down your allowance?" asks F.E., sarcastically.

"It's nothing to do with an allowance. She was going to buy me a new farm. Because of this, she wouldn't."

Such a loss is not ingratiating, though it may be real. But the issue of damages will be academic if the plaintiff fails to establish a recognisable likeness between himself and the picture drawn by Miss Odilon.

"After all," F.E. says, "I'm sure you've found out, as I have, that our name is often taken simply to label types?"

"Yes," agrees the plaintiff.

"Miss Odilon's story is that of a gentleman rider who spent several months in Germany during 1888?"

"Yes."

"She says it was some time before the love affair began?"

"Yes."

"And the gentleman rider remained in Germany till the affair concluded?"

"Yes."

"I suggest," says F.E., with sudden menace, "that you were not so well-known a gentleman rider as has been made out?"

"I was well known."

"Many were better known?"

"Some."

"Many?"

"Perhaps."

"A *great* many?"

The plaintiff concedes the point.

"Possibly," he says.

"I suggest, too," says F.E., pressing his advantage, "that during 1888 the amount of time you spent in Germany was very small indeed?"

"I rode there for Herr Oehlschaeger."

"Staying only a few days?"

"I didn't stay long."

"Staying only a few days?"

The plaintiff concedes the point.

"Possibly," he says.

So far the action has proceeded on a highly moral basis. It has been tacitly assumed that the allegation is defamatory, and that the plaintiff only need prove it points in his direction. No one has asked whether a pre-marital affair would be treated with profound concern outside a monastery.

The first intrusion of more realistic values is effected by a witness called to testify that when he read the story in "The Winning Post," he believed that Mr. Smith, the gentleman rider, was the plaintiff.

"Have you a good opinion of the plaintiff's character?" F.E. asks.

"Very good," says the witness.

"You would find great difficulty, then, in believing that he would get involved in an immoral intrigue with an actress?"

It is an ingenious move by counsel, but doesn't work out exactly as intended.

"Well," says the witness, with cheerful amorality, "we were all younger once than we are now."

Prim Mr. Justice Ridley gives him a disapproving glare. The judge and "The Winning Post" look on life from different angles. If he is out of sympathy with its readers, he is even more out of sympathy with its writers, as becomes manifest with startling clarity when the principal witness is called for the defence.

Yes, that witness translated Miss Odilon's memoirs. Yes, he edited them for "The Winning Post." Yes, he had changed the gentleman rider's name to Smith. Yes, he took it for granted that what Miss Odilon said was true.

"Did you not think," asks the plaintiff's counsel, "that it would interest a certain section of the public to know of a gentleman rider who had had such an intrigue?"

"That was certainly the most interesting part of it."

"Don't you think," counsel goes on, "that people would think the worse of the gentleman rider referred to?"

"Oh well," says the witness, with a cynical shrug, "everybody has had adventures of that sort."

The sentiment might pass muster at the offices of "The Winning Post." It is altogether too much, though, for Mr. Justice Ridley.

He turns upon the witness.

"I am sorry to hear you say such things. It rouses my wrath." The judge does indeed appear ablaze with fury. "I don't believe the whole of mankind is as bad as you say. If we are all to be classed in the same condemnation, I won't stand it."

The storm of applause that followed this outburst demonstrated how closely it echoed *public* thought—not *private* thought, maybe, but the thought men suppose it is their duty to think when they think en masse.

It could not affect the verdict, but it could affect the damages. And the jury, finding there was a libel on the plaintiff, awarded him no less than £550 to compensate him for the shame and odium of being credited with a prize he really hadn't won.

14

Adelaide Bartlett

ALL through that winter of 1886 London had resounded with the Bartlett case. At fashionable dinner parties, at humble public houses, at female tea fights in the remoter suburbs, at masculine strongholds in the heart of the West End; in cafés, in waiting rooms, in shops, on omnibuses—everywhere this topic commanded pride of place. Competition contemporaneously was keen. The Government fell; unemployment riots spread; on Parliament's table lay the dynamite of Home Rule. But to those attracted by a human drama—and how many in any age are not?—these became matters of secondary interest. The general public, right through from Submerged Tenth to Upper Ten, found Adelaide Bartlett a more fascinating theme.

There was much to excuse this apparent aberration. Here was no ordinary hackneyed murder case, no tedious repetition of a thousand former crimes. It was more like some baroque literary concoction—as if one had crossed the Decameron with Don Quixote and seasoned the mixture with the Book of Kings. It involved a young wife who had wed her older husband on terms that were almost exclusively platonic; a husband who "gave" his wife (whom he loved) to his friend (whom he loved also), enjoining them to marry after his own death; a clergyman, the donee of this unusual gift, who cherished for the wife a reciprocated passion; the husband's unexpected death in circumstances that perplexed and baffled the best scientific brains; the arrest of the wife, charged with her husband's murder, and of the clergyman, charged with being accessory thereto; the ugly and painful spectacle of the latter trying to save his skin at the expense of the former. Only the most exalted—or else the least perceptive—could have failed to gaze intently on this strange panorama as it gradually unfolded before coroner and bench.

When at last the hour of the full-dress trial drew near, popular excitement rose to fever pitch. One thing only remained to raise it even higher. Just as the most enthralling play calls for the glamour lent by a great actor, so the most absorbing capital trial calls for the presence of a great defender. Artistic instinct and desire for justice are equally insistent upon this.

For Adelaide Bartlett an advocate of the needful stature was forthcoming. Her solicitors, shrewd observers of the forensic scene, offered the leading brief to Edward Clarke. He accepted it, and in so doing assured her a defence that would rise to the challenge of an unparalleled occasion.

Edward Clarke was a perfect period piece. It is almost impossible to imagine him in any age except his own. He possessed to a degree that has never been surpassed the highest attributes of the noblest Victorians. So deep were his roots in that distinctive generation that he cannot be fitted, like most counsel of his eminence, into the prevailing dynasties of the Bar. Russell was the forerunner of Carson and of Hastings, Coleridge of Isaacs and of Simon. But Edward Clarke was the forerunner of nobody, just as he was nobody's successor. Like Gladstone and Millais in very different contexts, he was at once the product and the symbol of his time.

His prime characteristics were not of a description popularly associated with the pleader's craft. He neither had nor wished for what is commonly called worldliness; compared with most of his great rivals he was in some respects naïve. He had none of the arrogance or haughtiness of bearing that descends so readily upon successful advocates; his demeanour reflected a true modesty of the heart. His long and great career in a disillusioning profession never infected him with the slightest taint of cynicism; at the end he remained as he had been at the beginning, inviolate in his simple piety.

The chronicle of his life would have delighted Samuel Smiles. It tells of one who was born—to quote his own words—"in somewhat humble and difficult circumstances"; who was compelled by slender family finances to leave school early in his teens and become assistant at a little shop that was managed by his father; who occupied almost every leisure moment in reading hard or attending evening classes; who presently graduated from the little shop to the post of writer at East India House; who saved out of his salary till he had put aside enough to maintain him while he studied for the Bar; who embarked on that competitive vocation without resources or influential friends;

who established so rapid and so rare a reputation that fifteen years later he was wearing a silk gown (and winning election to the House of Commons); who in 1886 became Solicitor-General; who in 1897 declined to become Master of the Rolls; who in 1908 was appointed Privy Councillor; and who in 1914, after half a century of continuous practice, was entertained to dinner by the entire Bench and Bar—a tribute and an honour without precedent in history.

The unaffected book in which Clarke subsequently recorded this remarkable progression would have afforded Smiles additional satisfaction. "My chief reason for undertaking the task," he wrote, "is the wish that such a book may interest lads whose early lives are spent as mine was . . . and who may be encouraged by the story of my happy and successful life to be vigilant to find, and active to use, opportunities of self-improvement by study, by exercise of mind and body, by the habitual companionship of books, by the cultivation of worthy friendships." And then, with his unfeigned humility, he added: "As I write I am humbled by thinking how far my life has fallen short of my own ideals. Still I have not been consciously untrue to them; and perhaps the story of my life will help others to a fuller success."

Despite his extraordinary catalogue of achievement, Clarke's place in the hierarchy of advocates is not altogether easy to access. As a cross-examiner he certainly was not equal to Russell. As a lawyer he was not the peer of F. E. Smith. As a tactician a good many have eclipsed him. But then it was as none of these that he excelled. Clarke's endowment was persuasiveness, and his weapon was the speech—not the smooth persuasiveness of wheedling or blandishment, but that powerful persuasiveness that springs from deep sincerity; not the speech of conventional court rhetoric, but the speech informed with the passionate eloquence of genius.

In complex, abstruse, or tricky litigation Edward Clarke might not invariably shine. But when he was concerned as a principal participant with the terrible simplicities that govern life and death, he had it in him to exert an appeal that sometimes bordered on the irresistible. The Bartlett case presented him with such an opportunity.

Edward Clarke, like everybody else, had read newspaper reports of the preliminary proceedings. He was thus already acquainted with the salient features of the story. Although well accustomed to sensational cases (it was the trial of the Stauntons, nine years earlier, that had set the final seal upon his fame) Clarke did not find them pleasing or enjoyable. While some are fascinated by the scandalous, he was

sickened and repelled. But there was one element in the Bartlett
case which could not fail to attract his sympathy. Like Catherine
Ogilvie before her and Florence Maybrick after, Adelaide Bartlett
was a friendless woman, hounded by her husband's relatives, deserted
by her erstwhile confidants, and by strangers often condemned unheard. Such circumstances operated to excite all Clarke's essential
kindliness and compassion.

Having espoused Mrs. Bartlett's cause, Clarke acted with characteristic conscientiousness. He was now an extremely fashionable leader;
solicitors competed for his services; every term remunerative briefs
piled high upon the table in his chambers. He had in fact reached the
stage when it is not unknown for counsel to flit each day from court
to court; here arguing a point of law, there questioning a witness,
arriving elsewhere just in time to make a closing speech. And though
a murder case during its course exacts unremitting attention (especially from those engaged for the defence) busy barristers are often
deep in other work right up to the eve of an arduous capital trial.

Not so Edward Clarke, who had his own canons of conduct. The
defence of Mrs. Bartlett was an immense responsibility; the odds were
perilously poised and he could truly say that her life depended on her
counsel's skill. All other matters must make way. He postponed some
cases, returned the brief in others, and, free from all distraction, settled
down to prolonged and anxious study of his client's story.

When a wife is charged with murdering her husband the story
should begin not later than their marriage. Events, however violent,
are seldom totally detached; their roots are to be found, and they
themselves interpreted, by the light of personal history and relations.
Thus one may sometimes learn *why* murder was committed. Thus one
may sometimes learn *whether* murder was committed.

Adelaide Bartlett had married her husband Edwin, a prosperous
provision dealer, on the 9th of April, 1875. She was then less than
twenty years of age. The circumstances in which they met are not
altogether clear, nor are those surrounding Mrs. Bartlett's birth and
upbringing. It would appear, though, that she was born at Orleans,
the illegitimate child of a Frenchwoman and her English lover; that
she was taken to England at an early age; that her father, reputed to
have been a man of substance, provided liberally for all her needs;
that she brought to the marriage partnership an ample dowry that
was turned to good account by her husband in his business. In part
perhaps through this accession of capital, in part without doubt

through his own energy and exertions, Edwin Bartlett's enterprises steadily expanded during the ten years and nine months that composed his married life.

Mrs. Bartlett (it may not be wholly irrelevant to state that her full maiden name was Adelaide Blanche de la Tremoille) was too beautiful to be pretty, too pretty to be beautiful. In a language that does not lend itself to the finer distinctions in feminine attractiveness, possibly the half-French "piquant" comes closest to the mark. She had a slender, graceful figure, though somewhat lacking height; fine, very large and wide dark eyes; unusually heavy but trimly shaped black eyebrows; a pleasantly broad forehead; luxuriant hair that curled in upon the scalp; a strong straight nose with proudly arching nostrils; full lips over a smoothly rounded chin. A charming girl, to become a fascinating woman, baited with allurement for the hungry, youthful male.

At thirty, Edwin Bartlett could not be so described. Nor did the first phase of the union imply any undue extravagance of passion. Mr. Bartlett had an almost mystical reverence for formal education, and though his bride was not lacking in the recognised "accomplishments"—she played and sang and worked skilfully with her needle—he desired her to acquire at least the rudiments of scholarship. In acquiescent deference to his wishes, Mrs. Bartlett started married life with the status of a schoolgirl. First at an English boarding-school, then at a convent abroad, she developed her talents and improved her mind, only returning to her husband for the holidays. It was three years before this strange routine was ended and a conventional domestic establishment set up.

These protracted and unorthodox preliminaries had no apparent untoward effect upon the couple's happiness. Mrs. Bartlett was devoted to her husband; Mr. Bartlett idolised his wife. There is not the slightest evidence that this bond of affection appeared broken, or even loosened, so long as they both lived. The Crown did not suggest it at Mrs. Bartlett's trial. "They seem to have lived," said the Attorney-General, albeit somewhat grudgingly, "upon fairly good terms."

They were not, however, immune from stresses imposed on them by others. Trouble sprang early from a traditional source: the spite and animosity of relatives-in-law. Mr. Bartlett's father, a coarse-grained old curmudgeon, with many of the unpleasing characteristics of the sponger, took instant dislike to the wife of his son's choice—mainly, one may assume without unfairness, because of her competing claim upon that son's munificence. This did not prevent him from making his home with them when Edwin unwisely invited him to do so. He stayed for some years in their household at Herne Hill, never shrinking from abuse of this abundant hospitality and weathering at least one serious dissension occasioned by his vicious hatred of his daughter-in-law. In this dissension, to his credit, Edwin did not temporise; he made it plain that his loyalty as a husband must take precedence of his duty as a son. Fearful of losing his free and favoured place, old Bartlett abjectly climbed down. It was not till 1883, when they moved from Herne Hill to East Dulwich, that the married pair at long last shook him off.

They stepped unknowingly towards far deeper shadows. In 1884 they moved again, this time to Merton Abbey, an agreeable spot between Wimbledon and Mitcham. In Merton High Street was a tiny Wesleyan chapel and Mr. and Mrs. Bartlett often attended service. The minister was a young man by name of George Dyson; he had soft, dog-like eyes, a long drooping moustache, and a wounded expression like that of a spoilt child. He did not look like one who could stand unbowed in adversity, still less sacrifice himself to save or shield another.

The Reverend Dyson in due course called upon the Bartletts in their capacity as members of his congregation. Mr. Bartlett took to him at once; Mrs. Bartlett was not unfavourably impressed. The triangular acquaintance ripened rapidly into friendship—a friendship that grew ever more intimate and close until death or catastrophe had fallen on them all.

Whether Mrs. Bartlett ever became the Reverend Dyson's mistress it is impossible to say with anything like assurance. The balance of probability, in my view, points against it. But even if she did—and it could only have happened at a much later stage—it was certainly not she who encouraged him initially. Edwin Bartlett was the one who made the pace; who insisted on the Reverend Dyson's presence; who drew him within the tiny family orbit; who appointed him the constant companion of his wife. "I want you to be her guardian," he said. "I know you'll be a friend to her when I am dead."

Meanwhile Edwin Bartlett was very much alive, but he still had demands to make upon the Reverend Dyson's friendship. Who better than the latter to tutor Adelaide, to carry further forward still her cherished "education"? So it came about that presently two, three, four or even five times a week the Reverend Dyson would present himself at the Bartlett home and, while the master was absent at his business, instruct the master's lady in a variety of subjects. There were no children to interrupt their studies; Mrs. Bartlett had been once confined, in 1883, but after an agonising labour the baby was still-born. They therefore did their work in the style that pleased them best—in one instance at least, by the testimony of a servant, with Mrs. Bartlett sitting on the floor and resting her head on the Reverend Dyson's knee.

Mr. Bartlett knew how matters were developing; if not in detail, at any rate in substance. He did not object; on the contrary, he approved. "Would that I could find words," he wrote on one occasion, "to express my thankfulness to you for the loving letter you sent Adelaide today . . . I felt my heart going out to you. Who can help loving you?" And when the Reverend Dyson, tormented by the pangs of a tender Wesleyan conscience, told Edwin that he had conceived an affection for his wife, and asked whether it would not be best to terminate the friendship, Edwin Bartlett countered with an indignant "Why? I have confidence in you," he said to the harassed minister. "I shall be pleased if you will continue as friendly as before."

The Reverend Dyson continued as friendly as before and Mr. Bartlett loaded him with tokens of regard. He confided in him freely and often sought his counsel. He extended the scope of Dyson's future office from that of Mrs. Bartlett's "guardian" to that of second husband. He made a new will, naming Dyson as executor, and—as in his previous will—his wife as his sole heir. (It was said, but never strictly proved, that by this previous will Mrs. Bartlett only benefited if she did not remarry. No such condition cramped the later document, which was to be in solemn fact Edwin Bartlett's final testament.)

The Reverend Dyson was flattered by his friend's respect, solaced by his bounty, attracted by his wife. His mild protest had been overruled and now he offered no further resistance. Wherever the Bartletts went, at Edwin's behest the Reverend Dyson followed. Did they contemplate a trip or expedition, then he must plan his cure of souls to make himself available. Did they take a summer holiday by the sea, then he must travel down—at their expense—to stay with them. Did they change their London dwelling, and depart from Merton Abbey, then arrangements must be made and expedients devised whereby the connection could be maintained intact.

And so early in October of 1885 Edwin Bartlett, mindful as usual of his friend's slender resources, bought him a season ticket between Waterloo and Putney in order that he might, without hardship to himself, continue to visit them after they had moved to their new town apartments in a house in Claverton Street.

By an odd irony the owner of this house was a Registrar of Deaths.

If today you were to pass through Claverton Street—it runs from Lupus Street to Grosvenor Road—you would find it typical of the seedy neighbourhood that lies between Victoria Station and the river. It is a neighbourhood that novelists like to label "shabby-genteel," though in fact it is not nearly so genteel as it is shabby; a neighbourhood that once enjoyed distinction and prestige, but has given up the fight and surrendered to decay. Plaster peels, woodwork rots, broken fanlights are filled up with boards; overshadowing all, and making it seem meaner, is the mammoth modern mass of Dolphin Square.

It is sad because much of the fabric is unchanged; the buildings of Pimlico are still mostly those that saw the district in its pride and heyday years ago. The face is ravaged, but the bones remain.

In Claverton Street itself there is a gaping bomb site now, to commemorate our generation's intellectual progress. Otherwise the houses stand exactly as they stood when the Bartletts occupied their suite at Eighty-five. The house has been converted since into several separate flats but, wear and tear excepted, shows the same front to the world. The windows are the same, and the steps, and the street door; above is the balcony of the Bartletts' drawing room. As you stand and gaze on this ordinary house that became the mise-en-scène of an extraordinary drama, it is possible to feel that the years have slipped away; to grow deaf and blind to the nearby radio and the intrusive motor car; to imagine oneself standing in the self-same place, watching the Victorian tradesmen vanish down the area, watching Mrs. Bartlett peer impatiently from the window, watching the Reverend Dyson primly ring the bell, watching the doctors drive up in their sleek carriages.

Especially the doctors. Because a few weeks after they arrived at Claverton Street Edwin Bartlett started to be ill.

This was unusual enough to be disturbing. Mr. Bartlett had always been a very healthy man. Some years earlier an insurance doctor had pronounced him a first-class life; otherwise he had had little truck with the medical profession. Lately, however, he had been greatly overworked and had sometimes complained about a feeling of fatigue. On the 10th of December he suddenly got worse; he felt so unwell that he lay prostrate on the sofa and agreed with his wife that a doctor should be called. She selected Dr. Leach because his house was close at hand and it was obviously convenient to have a local man. Neither she nor Mr. Bartlett had heard of him before.

Dr. Leach was in no doubt about his patient's malady. It was mercurial poisoning.

This term need not be construed in its most melodramatic sense. It merely meant that Mr. Bartlett had somehow taken more mercury than his constitutional idiosyncrasies would tolerate. But how did he come to take mercury at all? This was the point that puzzled both the doctor and the patient. Mercury is an antidote to a pestilent disease, but that disease had not afflicted Mr. Bartlett. The only feasible solution lay in the latter's statement that recently, while feeling indisposed, he swallowed a large pill sent to him as a sample, without ascertaining what it was for or what ingredients it contained. A curious story, but the only one there was, and Dr. Leach had no alternative but to accept it. Nor has anything ever come to light to suggest that in so doing he was wrong.

Dr. Leach treated and prescribed for his new patient and the symptoms of poisoning rapidly cleared up. But the attack left distressing torments in its wake: weakness, depression, wearisome insomnia. A specially painful sequel related to the teeth; within fifteen days, at four separate sessions, Edwin Bartlett underwent eighteen extractions, and endured into the bargain bouts of toothache both violent and prolonged.

None the less, on an objective view, he gradually made progress and Dr. Leach was not dissatisfied. He had no reason to regard the case as intrinsically grave; it was now a matter of rest and care and building up. The idea of getting a second opinion never crossed his mind until it was raised by the Bartletts themselves in words that could not fail to make their mark upon his memory.

It was the doctor's fifth or sixth attendance at the house. He had examined Mr. Bartlett, found his state improved, and slightly varied one of the prescriptions. Preparatory to departure, he was exchanging general conversation with his patient when Mrs. Bartlett suddenly broke in.

"Doctor, will you excuse what I am about to say?"

The doctor turned courteously.

"Mr. Bartlett is very contented with your treatment," she went on, "but his friends have on more than one occasion requested him to let them send a doctor of their own choosing."

"Yes," Mr. Bartlett added quickly, "but we intend in future, doctor, to manage our own affairs and not to be interfered with by my friends and relations. I am sorry to say they are not kind to my wife."

"By all means have a consultation," said the doctor, who may have wished to stem the tide of family revelations. "As many consultations as you like."

"No," Mr. Bartlett said firmly. "I will not see anyone they send, but

I will see any gentleman you choose to bring to see me once. I do this for the protection of my wife."

If Dr. Leach was startled by this last remark he must have been dumbfounded by the next one.

"Doctor," said Mrs. Bartlett earnestly, "if Mr. Bartlett does not get out soon, his friends will accuse me of poisoning him."

The "friends" referred to existed only in the singular; it was cantankerous old Bartlett who had been round raising trouble, criticising the treatment, crying out for specialists. It was against him that Edwin sought to give his wife protection. It was he that Mrs. Bartlett feared would welcome an excuse for taxing her with poisoning her husband.

Her fears were to prove depressingly well founded. But meanwhile the appropriate protection was invoked. Dr. Leach invited to the house another physician, who duly confirmed his diagnosis and his remedies.

Any suspicions formed by Mr. Bartlett's "friends" seemed ludicrous when measured against Mrs. Bartlett's conduct. Throughout these trying weeks she nursed her husband with unfaltering devotion, herself discharging the most repulsive duties, and foregoing whatever sleep could not be snatched in a chair or on a sofa by his bed. She did not hesitate to hazard her own health until she reached the pitch of near exhaustion. Her concern was deep, her toil unremitting, her affection manifest.

Until, in the last days of the fading year, came a strange and sinister sequence of events.

They followed each other, these events, with that metronomic timing seldom found outside a well-constructed play; indeed they would fit better into the neat world of Sardou than into the untidiness of ordinary life.

On 27th December Mrs. Bartlett saw the Reverend Dyson (who was still paying his customary visits) and privately asked him if he could get her chloroform. On his enquiring for what purpose, she told him that her husband had an internal complaint which was shortening his life and which periodically occasioned him great pain; that he was sensitive about the matter, would not discuss it, and would not be treated by anyone but her; that during severe spasms she could only soothe him and enable him to sleep by the use of chloroform; that she usually obtained it from a nurse named Annie Walker, but Annie Walker was at that moment abroad; that she was accustomed to sprinkle the chloroform on a handkerchief, and as it was highly volatile required a large amount—as much as would fill a medicine draught bottle. "Can't you get it through the doctor?" the Reverend Dyson asked. "The doctor doesn't know I'm skilled in drugs," Mrs. Bartlett said.

On 29th December the Reverend Dyson handed Mrs. Bartlett a bottle of chloroform.

On 31st December Mr. Bartlett seemed in better appetite and spirits; he had oysters for lunch, jugged hare for dinner, more oysters and some palatable accessories for supper; then ordered his breakfast with meticulous care. "I shall get up an hour earlier," he said to the maid, "at the thought of having it."

Nobody, save Mrs. Bartlett, saw him again alive. Some time early on 1st January—or possibly late on 31st December—Edwin Bartlett died, in the presence of his wife, from a cause which the doctor could not ascertain. Mrs. Bartlett was unable to enlighten him. The bottle of chloroform had disappeared for good.

The mere chronology spoke out for itself.

There was to be much more, though, than mere chronology thrown into the scales which were already being set up and in which the fate of Mrs. Bartlett would be weighed.

Her own story was simple. She had fallen asleep, she said, in the chair by her husband's bed; she woke up in the middle of the night and found him lying on his face; she was shocked to find him stark cold, and tried to give him brandy; failing to bring him round, she roused the house and sent for Dr. Leach.

Thus far unchallengeable. But soon suspicions mount. The Registrar landlord, on entering the room, detects a smell resembling ether, as well as that of brandy, in a wineglass on the mantelshelf, and—collecting data with official zeal—deduces that the fire has lately been built up. The landlord's wife, casting her mind back, recalls a conversation on the previous evening when Mrs. Bartlett asked her if she had ever taken chloroform, and added that Mr. Bartlett took some sleeping drops. "Ten is a strong dose," Mrs. Bartlett said, "but I would not hesitate to give him twelve." Dr. Leach, arriving post-haste from a broken sleep, cannot conceal his deep perplexity; not only is there no apparent cause of death, but there had been no reason to suppose the man was going to die. "Can he have taken poison?" he enquires.

Only two points of light gleam through the cloud of doubts now gathering round the unhappy Mrs. Bartlett. The doctor observes a bottle of chlorodyne on the mantelshelf. "What is this doing here?" he asks. "Oh, that," says Mrs. Bartlett; "Edwin rinsed his mouth with it." "Rinsed his mouth!" exclaims the doctor. "Then he must have swallowed some." "No, no," says Mrs. Bartlett; "he only rubbed it on his gums." She will not accept this plausible solution, she will not grasp the proffered chance to clear herself. There are no poisons that her husband could have had; none he could have got at without her knowledge. And—the second gleam of light—when Dr. Leach bends over the corpse he notes the characteristic smell of brandy on the chest; on the chest, down which it would naturally trickle if feverishly pressed against the numb lips of the dead.

But none of this helped to solve the doctor's problem; reluctantly he refuses his certificate. "Must there be an inquest?" Mrs. Bartlett asks. "I *ought* to report to the coroner," says the doctor, "but as I have no suspicion of foul play, we will have a post-mortem, and then, if the pathological cause of death is found, I will give a certificate in due course. . . ."

The post-mortem took place on the following afternoon. It was directed by an eminent pathologist and performed by his assistant, in the presence of Dr. Leach and two other physicians. The first thing they noticed on opening the stomach was an overwhelming smell of chloroform—"almost as strong," said one, "as a freshly opened bottle."

For nearly two hours they probed and searched without finding anything to account for death. The vital organs were all healthy. No injury was manifest. They could find, in medical phrase, no pathological lethal cause. There was nothing more that they themselves could do, except carefully preserve the contents of the stomach and patiently wait for a chemical analysis.

"They think it's chloroform," Dr. Leach told Mrs. Bartlett. He was blissfully unaware of the dreadful implications. She, whether guilty or guiltless, knowing what she did, may well have been afraid.

There followed a period of tense, uneasy waiting—not for the public that were as yet hardly aware of the tremendous drama that was brewing, but for the principal actors in the piece, who were kept in a state of quivering uncertainty about the parts they would be called upon to play. After hearing only formal evidence, the Coroner adjourned his inquest for a month; various relics of the departed Edwin Bartlett were sent to the Home Office in packages and jars; the days went by, but no report was issued; and Adelaide Bartlett and the

Reverend Dyson, chafed by the increasing burden of suspense, entered upon a train of conversations that altered their relationship for good and all. It was no longer a question whether he would lead her to the altar; only whether he would send her to the drop.

The Reverend Dyson did not know at first of the suspicions that the doctors had formed at the post-mortem. Nevertheless he showed considerable apprehension. That very afternoon, as he escorted Mrs. Bartlett from the shrouded room in Claverton Street to the home of friends, he asked her pointedly if she had used the chloroform. "No," she said. "I have not had occasion. The bottle is there, just as you gave it to me." As the Reverend Dyson still exhibited disquiet, she told him to dismiss the matter from his mind.

Any chance of his doing so vanished a few days later after he had had a talk with Dr. Leach. The latter, acting of course in perfect innocence, freely disclosed to him the notes of the post-mortem. The reverend gentleman did not waste a minute. He hurried from the surgery straight to Mrs. Bartlett. "I have seen the doctor—I know everything," he cried. *"Now* will you tell me; what did you do with the chloroform?"

Mrs. Bartlett may have felt she had sufficient nervous strain without adding the catechisms of the Reverend Dyson. She certainly did not trouble to dissimulate her rage. She got up from her chair, stamped her foot on the floor, shouted "Damn the chloroform!" and fumed about the room. But the Reverend Dyson was too frightened to be intimidated. He began to load her with querulous reproaches. She had told him that Edwin had an internal complaint; there was nothing about this in the notes of the post-mortem; she had told him that Edwin's life would be a short one. "I did not," snapped Mrs. Bartlett. "Alas!" exclaimed the Reverend Dyson, *"I am a ruined man."*

In these five words may be found the key to the Reverend Dyson's subsequent conduct. Henceforward he had but a single thought: am I going to get mixed up in this, and, if so, how shall I stand in the opinion of the world? He spared not a moment's solicitude for the woman—the woman to whom he was admittedly attracted, the woman he had accepted as his wife to be, a woman who might well be free from any sin and yet was standing in the deadliest of perils. One might have expected even a less godly individual to be prompted by charity if not by affection. But no words of comfort or encouragement ever rose to the Reverend Dyson's lips. "I am a ruined man"; that was the scope and measure of his spiritual nobility. It is possible to doubt whether Adelaide Bartlett was a deeply wronged woman; it is not possible to doubt that the Reverend Dyson was an egotistical and sanctimonious man.

The workings of his mind at this juncture are transparent. If *she* is accused of killing him with chloroform, and they find out that she got the chloroform from *me*, and they are able to prove that there is anything between us, then everybody will at once assume the worst. What, then, must I do? Watch my step very carefully in future, try to erase any evidence of the past.

What other interpretation can be placed on his request, made in the midst of such a stormy interview, that Mrs. Bartlett should give him back his "poem"? A stanza from this powerful and inspiring work is quoted by Sir John Hall in his valuable preface to the transcript of the trial:

'Who is it that hath burst the door,
Unclosed the heart that shut before,
And set her queen-like on its throne,
And made its homage all her own?—
My Birdie.'

The Reverend Dyson had presented this poem to Mrs. Bartlett with all that its sentimental images implied. Mrs. Bartlett now returned it without delay or cavil, apparently unimpressed by his literary gifts. . . .

Having safely recovered the incriminating paper, the Reverend Dyson gave free rein to his nonconformist feelings. Later that day he again saw Mrs. Bartlett and told her he intended "to make a clean breast." "I wish," said Mrs. Bartlett, "you wouldn't mention the chloroform." "I shall," the Reverend Dyson said, "I am going to tell everything I know."

He proposed to make this "clean breast" at the inquest. But he was not called at the first hearing, nor at the second either, and meanwhile a new gravity had invested his intention.

Late in January the Home Office analyst completed his report. On the 26th Dr. Leach had just received it when Mrs. Bartlett called. "I have good news for you," he said, with genuine satisfaction. "Had it been one of the secret poisons which may be administered without the patient knowing, you would most certainly have been accused by some people of having poisoned him. But the government analyst says the cause of death was chloroform. That should set your mind at rest."

The Reverend Dyson was as good as his word. When at last his turn came, he made a clean breast at the Coroner's Court. Repeatedly stressing how he had been deceived, he told the story of the chloroform in detail. The effect on the jury, who had already heard the Home Office analyst, was naturally and inevitably immense. When Dyson stepped down, they proclaimed their opinion that Mrs. Bartlett (who, on the advice of her lawyer, had declined to give evidence) ought to be placed in custody forthwith.

A week later they met again and concluded their enquiry. A verdict of Wilful Murder against Mrs. Bartlett was foreseen. But the Reverend Dyson did not, at this stage, escape with the whitewashing he had hoped and worked for. A verdict was returned against him also; his pastorless sheep in suburban Merton Abbey heard with dismay that he had been arrested and charged as an accessory before the fact.

This sharp series of detonating shocks projected the Bartlett case into that notoriety which was henceforth to be one of its distinguishing concomitants. Public debate became continuous, and in social exchanges to venture no opinion on the innocence or otherwise of the two accused was to confess oneself completely out of touch. About Dyson's complicity there were opposing schools of thought. About Mrs. Bartlett there was a greater measure of agreement; on its first impact the clergyman's disclosure was to seem as decisive outside court as it had seemed within. Weighing what they knew as fairly as they could, before trial the majority were certain of her guilt.

Edward Clarke was now to form his own opinion. Having digested every detail of his brief, he pondered long upon their implication. In the austere surroundings of his chambers, or in the library of his house in Russell Square, he would pace to and fro with regular, slow tread; the fine brow furrowed, the firm lips set, the massive mind intent upon arriving at the truth.

Very deliberately he came to a conclusion. He believed that the popular judgment was at fault, and that he sustained upon his shoulders the burden of defending an innocent woman who bore every mark of guilt.

To the very end he never wavered in this view.

The defender was indeed faced with a formidable task. He could not challenge the findings of the analyst; he must fight on the footing that chloroform caused death. He could not challenge the substance of the Reverend Dyson's story because Mrs. Bartlett did not challenge it herself. And yet their conjunction would assuredly prove fatal unless fresh facts were introduced by way of explanation.

Those were days before a prisoner could give evidence at his trial, so Mrs. Bartlett herself could not be heard. She had, however, previously given an account—on 26th January when she visited Dr. Leach; and the doctor, a principal witness for the Crown, was obviously bound to repeat it in the box. This, though, did little to improve the prospect. It necessarily dictated the trend of the defence, and Mrs. Bartlett's explanation as it stood was much less likely to convince than to astonish.

It had astonished honest Dr. Leach, for whom the interview provided a surfeit of amazement. He was almost stupefied at the outset when he found that Mrs. Bartlett, instead of showing relief at the analyst's report, at once exhibited symptoms of distress and said: "Doctor, I wish anything but chloroform had been found." "Why?" cried the doctor. "What on earth do you mean?"

This brief question drew a very long reply. Mrs. Bartlett entered on a closely detailed statement going back to the beginning of her married life. She told Dr. Leach of a platonic relationship that was interrupted upon one occasion only; of the happiness she enjoyed with her husband none the less; of his wish that, if he died, she and the Reverend Dyson should be married, and of his "giving" her to Dyson with that object in view; of his subsequent and unexpected sexual overtures; of her reluctance to submit now she was "practically affianced"; of her procuring chloroform with the misguided idea of waving it in his face and sending him to sleep on any occasion when he might be importunate ("If you had put that plan in practice," Dr. Leach observed, "it would have been both dangerous and ineffectual"); of her uneasiness at having the chloroform in her possession ("I had never kept a secret from Edwin in my life") and bringing him the bottle on the night before he died, with a frank declaration of what had been her purpose; of his putting the bottle on the mantelshelf beside him; of them both going off to sleep; of her terrible awakening. Had she noticed whether much was missing from the bottle? "No," said Mrs. Bartlett, "I do not know." Who had got the chloroform for her? She did not answer, and, said Dr. Leach, "I saw it was a question to which no answer would be given."

This bizarre tale, verging on the unbelievable, formed the dubious base on which Edward Clarke erected one of the greatest defences in the history of our courts.

It was clearly a case in which the evidence of experts would play a large, perhaps a dominating, part. Though the cause of death had got to be accepted, much would depend on other scientific points: the effect of chloroform in different modes of application; its scope and limitations as an instrument of murder; the possibilities of administering it in sleep without the victim's knowledge and resistance.

Edward Clarke left nothing to chance. In the reading room of the British Museum he familiarised himself with the relevant literature, and when he had done, there were few in Harley Street whose knowledge of chloroform was greater than his own. Guy and Ferrier's *Forensic Medicine,* Alfred Taylor's *Medical Jurisprudence,* Dolbeau, Wynter Blyth, Wharton and Stillé, Woodman and Tidy, Quimby and Elliott —these and others were enquired into and mastered till even Clarke felt satisfied that his researches had been thorough.

Steeped in the facts, primed with technical knowledge, inspired by the conviction that his client was innocent—no advocate has ever been better equipped for a defence than was Edward Clarke when, on the first day of the trial, he walked into the packed and expectant Old Bailey and took his seat on leading counsels' row. He was a few minutes early, but that was intentional. "I made a point," he said afterwards, "of being in my place every morning before the judge came in, so that when the fragile, pale little woman came up the prison stairs to take her place in the dock she should see in the crowded court at least one friendly face."

Every eye was turned in that direction as the two accused, with their retinue of warders, slowly filed into the legendary dock. With the courtroom crammed and alert with curiosity, their bearing was subjected to a stern and painful test. They responded somewhat differently. Mrs. Bartlett, in widow's black, looked drawn but perfectly composed; the Reverend Dyson displayed signs of strain and fidgeted uneasily. It was observed that, though he sometimes stole a covert glance at her, she gazed straight ahead as if unconscious of his presence. . . .

The customary awestruck hush accompanied the appearance of the judge. Though an extremely able lawyer and a recognised authority on circumstantial evidence, Mr. Justice Wills is now chiefly remembered for his brutal sentence upon Oscar Wilde, and the fierce, hysterical terms in which he couched it. He was indeed fanatically puritan, and the mere thought of sodomy deprived him of all balance. The Bartlett case, where the charge was merely murder, did not outrage his instincts to the same degree, and while often expressing horror and disgust, he tried it without prejudice or partiality. . . .

Before the trial opened, the Attorney-General (who was leading for the Crown) announced a decision that changed its shape and course.

Frank Lockwood, Q.C., counsel for the Reverend Dyson, had applied on his client's behalf for separate trials. The lawyers present had been expecting some such move. Statements by one prisoner are not evidence against another (unless made in the other's presence and hearing), but in a joint trial, when such statements are put in, it is hard to maintain that principle in practice. There was a risk that statements made by Mrs. Bartlett might injure the Reverend Dyson. There was an even greater risk that statements made by him might injure her, and Clarke accordingly supported Lockwood's application.

It was all unnecessary. The Attorney-General rose, not to object nor to reply, but to apprise the court of an impending metamorphosis. "After anxious and careful consideration," he declared, "we have come to the conclusion that there is no case to be submitted to the jury on which we could properly ask them to convict George Dyson, and after his arraignment we propose to offer no evidence against him."

By this single sentence the Reverend Dyson was transformed—from prisoner himself on trial for his liberty to potential witness against prisoner on trial for her life. The onlookers were taken completely by surprise. They had got their first big thrill before they had expected.

For a moment the court rocked and murmured like the sea.

The judge was appropriately circumspect. "I think," he said, "that the proper course, for every reason, is that I should reserve any expression of opinion until the case against the other prisoner has been investigated."

The court moved through the long-established ritual. Both prisoners were arraigned; each pleaded not guilty; the jury were sworn and the prisoners given in their charge; the Attorney-General briefly repeated his intention of offering no evidence against the male accused; thereupon the judge directed the jury that it was their duty to say at once that Dyson was not guilty; the jury's foreman stood up in his place and pronounced the formal verdict of acquittal.

The Reverend Dyson was free. Eagerly and thankfully he hastened from the dock, without a word or even a glance behind. No bond survived between his former love and him, and yet somehow his departure made her seem still more forlorn as she sat amid the gaolers to face her trial alone.

This was, on the whole, by no means a disadvantage, viewed coldly and heartlessly from the tactical point of view.

The Attorney-General, by virtue of his office, is titular leader of the English Bar. Since political considerations influence his appointment, he is not necessarily the country's leading counsel. The Attorney-General of this period, however, stood pre-eminent in every respect; he was not merely the Crown's chief law officer by preferment, he was also the Bar's outstanding figure by acclaim. For the rôle of Mr. Attorney in April, 1886 was filled by no other than the great Charles Russell, in the fullness of his powers and at the summit of his fame.

That the Bartlett trial involved a clash between Russell and Clarke considerably added to its fascination. Though not as yet upon the same high pinnacle, Clarke was rapidly climbing to a place in which he would be Russell's regular opponent, and with him would constitute the first of those famous pairs that have been such a striking feature of our courts. Like those that followed later—Carson and Isaacs, Simon and Smith, Hastings and Birkett—Russell and Clarke abounded in sharp contrasts. One was born for strife, one for conciliation; one was caustic and impatient, one courteous and suave; one relied on power, one upon persuasion. And yet each somehow avoided the defects of his qualities; Russell's brusque manner seldom alienated juries, and Clarke undoubtedly possessed an inner toughness that enabled him to defy adversity or fatigue.

When both men were at their best and given equal opportunities, Russell was beyond all question the superior. But in the trial of Mrs. Bartlett only Clarke was at his best, and only Clarke could deploy the full range of his gifts. Russell's forte was cross-examination, but there was not a single witness for him to cross-examine. Moreover, no counsel can be at the top of his form if there is anything on his mind besides the case in progress, and the Bartlett trial happened to coincide with the first Commons reading of Mr. Gladstone's first Home Rule Bill, in which Russell, as Irish nationalist and English politician, was patriotically as well as professionally involved. His long and tiring days in court were followed—and preceded—by equally long and tiring evenings in the House, and it is permissible to assume that even as he spoke of Dr. Leach or Mrs. Bartlett at the back of his mind hovered Morley or Parnell.

The effect on his performance as an advocate was marked. It became apparent in the early stages of his opening, which was neither so forceful nor so well-knit as his reputation promised. He was handicapped by imperfect acquaintance with the facts, being not infrequently pulled up by Clarke or prompted by his juniors. It is doubtful whether Russell ever made another speech in which the introductory phrase "I think" occurred so often; he used it manifestly to insure against involuntary mis-statement.

But however much inhibited by uncertainty on detail, Russell was incapable of vague and cloudy speech. Though his opening was in no way memorable or brilliant, it furnished a clear outline of the prosecution's case. He gave a brief history of the Bartletts' marriage and established the Reverend Dyson's relation to the pair. He described how Mrs. Bartlett had asked Dyson for the chloroform, and pledged himself to prove that her "reasons" were all lies: Edwin Bartlett had had no internal ailment; neither that nor any other disease was shortening his life; she had never obtained chloroform from the nurse Annie Walker, nor had Annie Walker ever been abroad. He pointed out that Mrs. Bartlett only put forward the "extraordinary story" that she told to Dr. Leach after she had learnt of the analyst's report.

"And now," said Russell, emerging with some relief from the complex web of fact, "I come to what you will probably find is the real question in this case. You will probably have no difficulty in coming to the conclusion that the deceased died from the effects of chloroform, which chloroform somehow found its way to his stomach. *How did it get there?*"

How, indeed? Russell submitted that there were only three alternatives. It might have been suicide, but, he said, "you will find nothing to support that suggestion. Edwin Bartlett was in returning health, in improved spirits, and before going to bed had made arrangements for his breakfast." It might have been an accident, "but it is in the highest degree improbable that, on putting the glass or tumbler to his lips, a man would not at once perceive the mistake that had been made." And, Russell added, "Taken with the intention of committing suicide or taken accidentally, the pain it would cause would be so acute that no amount of self-control which anyone can suppose to exist could restrain the paroxysms of pain, followed by contortion and by outcry and by exclamation, which could not have failed to attract attention."

Russell frankly admitted that this must also be expected if the chloroform was administered by any third person. "There would be the same outcry, the same acute pain, and so forth—provided that the administration into the stomach was not *preceded by some external application* of chloroform, which might lull into a stupor or a semi-stupor; and in that condition it might be possible—and in that condition alone, as the medical men think, probable—that it could be conveyed to the stomach without it being followed by circumstances and occurrences which must have attracted attention."

Here, then, was the Crown's third and last alternative—the alternative of murder. The theory was that Mrs. Bartlett had first, in the popular acceptation of the word, "chloroformed" her husband until he was insensible, and afterwards poured liquid chloroform down his throat.

The Crown elected to stand upon this theory as the only one consistent with the facts.

The Attorney-General's speech occupied most of the first morning. During much of the afternoon Edward Clarke was cross-examining old Bartlett.

This Dickensian villain, part Quilp, part Silas Wegg, had made up his mind from the start that Edwin Bartlett had been murdered by his wife. Assiduously he worked to procure evidence. "This cannot pass," he had cried dramatically as he stood in the room of death with Dr. Leach. "We must have a post-mortem, doctor, a post-mortem." While bestowing a father's last salute on the forehead of the corpse, he had cunningly sniffed the lips for the smell of prussic acid. He had tried the pockets of Mrs. Bartlett's cloak before she departed in it from the house—an occasion on which the cynical old fraud made a point none the less of kissing her goodbye. ("It calls unbidden to one's lips," his lordship was to comment, "the name of Judas.")

Old Bartlett had done his best to get her charged. Now, there can be no conceivable doubt, he intended to do his best to get her hanged.

There was little of real substance in the evidence of Old Bartlett; he never touched the main line of the prosecution's case. He had set himself the task of fomenting suspicion, of building up an atmosphere, of conveying to the jury by a host of minor incidents that Mrs. Bartlett's behavior in itself bespoke her guilt. For instance, he was "refused" (at her command) to see his son while he was ill; for instance, though he had particularly asked, she would not tell him who was his son's doctor; for instance, despite his earnest supplication, she would not call in a physician "from London" to advise. "We cannot afford it," she had said. "You had better afford it," Old Bartlett had said amiably.

Such evidence, though without roots and inconclusive, if allowed to stand unchallenged might influence a jury. Clarke did not intend to take the slightest risk. He had enough ammunition to annihilate Old Bartlett—and though this might not bear on any major issue, it would at least mean the defence had been launched under good auspices. The demolition of a witness, even a mere auxiliary, always benefits the side against whom he is called.

Clarke rose to begin his cross-examination immediately the court reassembled after lunch. The air was electric, as it always is in any great trial at the first real clash of swords.

Clarke wasted no time in preliminary sparring; his opening questions struck straight at the heart.

"Mr. Bartlett, I believe you were not present at your son's marriage to the defendant?"

"I was not."

"Did you disapprove of that marriage?"

No attack was ever more direct. Old Bartlett played for time.

"I was not asked," he said.

"Not asked to the marriage or not asked whether you approved?"

"I was not asked whether I thought she was suitable or not."

"As a matter of *fact*, did you disapprove?"

Old Bartlett, who was anything but a fool and fully understood the drift of this, tried to make his answer noncommittal.

"Well," he said, "I did not much approve of it, but I did not disapprove of it."

"Were you asked to the marriage?" Clarke enquired.

"No."

"Why not?"

"Because they knew I was busy," Old Bartlett answered.

The most gullible jury wouldn't swallow that. Clarke had established his first important point—that Old Bartlett had never been well disposed towards his daughter-in-law.

He proceeded at once to build on this foundation.

"When did you go to live with your son?"

"1877 or 1878."

"Do you tell the jury that you enjoyed the complete confidence of your son and his wife after that time?"

"We lived on most friendly terms," Old Bartlett said, but Clarke preferred to keep to his own wording.

"Do you say you enjoyed the complete confidence of your son and his wife?"

Old Bartlett—foolishly—plunged.

"I believe so."

Clarke's face darkened in reprobation of the lie.

"Very soon after Mrs. Bartlett came home to live with your son did you have to write an apology for the things you had said about her?"

"I signed an apology," Old Bartlett admitted, "but I knew it to be false."

"What, sir?"

The ring in counsel's voice might have checked a cooler witness. But Old Bartlett was aflame with his own malice. He went on:

"When I signed the apology it was to make peace with my son. He begged me to sign it because it would make peace between him and his wife, and I did."

Clarke spoke with the utmost gravity and distinctness. Each word fell separately into the hushed court.

"You say that, because it would make peace with your son, you signed that apology, *knowing it to be false?*"

"Yes," replied Old Bartlett, hard-pressed but defiant.

"Did your son make use of that apology, and have it printed?"

"At her suggestion."

"I should think so," snorted Clarke, permitting himself one of his rare lapses into comment.

The cross-examination was not five minutes old, but already Old Bartlett wore a very different aspect. It was clear—all the more so from his efforts to conceal it—that his hatred for the prisoner was venomous and abiding. It was clear that his hatred did not merely lie dormant, but found a vent in backbiting or calumny. It was clear that he was not above affirming what was unveracious—for either the apology he had signed was false, or else he had lied in saying that it was.

One more question and the picture was complete.

"Have you entered a caveat," asked Clarke, "against the will in which your son left everything to his wife?"

"I have," Old Bartlett reluctantly acknowledged.

So to the hatred and the lying had been added powerful motive —the most powerful that could operate on a man of such cupidity. Only Adelaide stood between him and his son's fortune. . . .

Having discredited the witness with admirable economy, Clarke now turned to his specific allegations, and these, too, soon assumed a different complexion. The old man had to admit that, though he had been "refused" to see his son on one occasion, on at least one other he had been expressly asked to come—by Mrs. Bartlett herself, in one of several letters that she wrote to keep her father-in-law apprised of Edwin's state. He had to recant his earlier assertion that he had "particularly asked" for the name of Edwin's doctor. ("She seemed reluctant," he told Clarke, "to say much about the doctor." "Tell me what you asked her?" "I didn't ask her anything.") He had to expand and clarify his story about the prisoner's unwillingness to take a second opinion; Clarke confronted him with a passage from another of her letters—"I am expecting another doctor, so you must excuse this note."

"Take that letter," Clarke said. "Was it written before or after you had suggested a physician?"

Old Bartlett knew that he was tied down by the dates.

"Well, I suppose after."

"When you saw Mrs. Bartlett soon after that letter did you ask if the doctor had been?"

"They told me that he had."

"Did you ask his name?"

"No."

"Did not Mrs. Bartlett tell you?"

"I won't undertake to say."

"Was it not Dr. Dudley?" Clarke said with sudden sternness.

"Yes, it was Dr. Dudley," Old Bartlett answered grudgingly.

There was nothing left now; neither credit nor character nor even trumped-up charges. The despicable old man slunk out of the box, conscious that he had wholly failed to promote his wicked purpose. "Fortunately, as it seems to me," Mr. Justice Wills said later, "very little depends on the evidence of the senior Bartlett. With the sole observation that, from the hour of his appearance after his son's death, Mrs. Bartlett lived under suspicious eyes, I think I may dismiss him from the scene."

That evening, back at home in his quiet library, Clarke could review his first day's work with modest satisfaction. The downfall of Old Bartlett had been crashing and spectacular; an event to rouse the feelings and stir the imagination. But Old Bartlett, after all, had been no more than an outrider. No one knew better than he who was defending that the Crown's main forces were yet to be engaged.

To dispose successfully of the these main forces demanded a carefully calculated plan. In advocacy, tactics should be flexible and resilient, strategy almost always definite and fixed. The swift improvisations when new dangers develop, the dramatic counter to an unexpected thrust, the dazzling riposte to the damaging reply, the neat turning movement to protect a punctured flank—such agile and dexterous manœuvres, incomparably exciting in the throbbing heat of court, lack none the less a substance and a purpose unless integrated in a general design.

Having heard Russell's opening speech, sketching the Crown case,

Clarke could project his own campaign with something like precision. Russell had said there were but three alternatives, and had then discarded two; Clarke would seek to show that one of the latter—suicide —was not at all unfeasible. Russell had admitted that the administration of liquid chloroform was extremely difficult; Clarke would seek to show that for the medically unskilled it was virtually impossible. Russell had cast scorn upon the explanation Mrs. Bartlett gave to Dr. Leach on 26th January; Clarke would seek to show, out of the mouths of others, that that "extraordinary story" was substantially correct. (This was not the least important point, and maybe the most delicate. Juries seldom accept purely scientific evidence if it seems in conflict with everyday horse-sense. "What did she want the chloroform *for?*" and "Why did she *lie* to get it?"—these would be the questions preoccupying their minds; questions to which her answers, unless in some degree corroborated, invited rejection as outrageously farfetched.)

Such were the lines Clarke laid down for himself, and which were to guide and govern his handling of the case through the swelling climax of the next five days.

The second day's proceedings were entirely dominated by the Reverend Dyson's appearance in the box.

The Reverend Dyson remains a constant puzzle. It is impossible to reconcile his conduct with his character. We know him to have been a weak, timorous caricature of a man, in love with himself and yet afraid of his own shadow—the last individual to play the smallest part in forwarding a plot to murder in cold blood. Assuming that the Crown case was well founded and that Mrs. Bartlett wilfully took her husband's life, I should still be disposed to rule out any suggestion that the Reverend Dyson was privy to the crime.

And yet how furtive, how sly, was his behaviour at the time—illaccording with his subsequent displays of injured innocence. At every step he laid himself open to suspicion. He deliberately distributed the purchase of the chloroform, visiting three different local chemists' shops in turn. From each he bought a small amount, to each he told a lie ("It is for taking out grease stains," he had casually remarked). At home he poured the aggregate into a larger bottle which he gave to Mrs. Bartlett the following afternoon—gave it to her, not in the house at Claverton Street, but when they were out strolling on the Embankment by themselves.

Under the pitiless glare that beats upon the witness box the Reverend Dyson recounted these events. The judge did not conceal the effect it made on him.

"You were asked to purchase a medicine bottle full. Why didn't you ask for it straight out at the first chemist?"

"I do not remember," said the Reverend Dyson wretchedly. "I do not remember what was in my mind at the time."

As at the inquest, so at the trial, the Reverend Dyson spared Mrs. Bartlett not at all. While he had at the last moment regained status with the law, he had still to clear his reputation with the public and to re-establish beyond a shade of doubt his eligibility as a minister of God. If in so doing he destroyed Mrs. Bartlett, that would be distressing but it just could not be helped. It was she, after all, who had brought this misfortune on him. . . .

"She asked me. . . . She told me. . . . I did what she wanted. . . . I was puzzled. . . . I was perplexed. . . . I was alarmed"—the exculpatory phrases poured forth in abundance. Incessantly the Reverend Dyson sang his brave refrain: It was she, not I; it was she, not I. Compulsively the spectators glanced from witness box to dock. Mrs. Bartlett sat bolt upright and gazed into the void. . . .

When the Crown had finished examining the witness, and Edward Clarke rose to his feet, from the purely emotional point of view the case had reached its zenith. Mrs. Bartlett's champion now came face to face with the man whose intervention had placed her where she was. His mode of giving evidence could have done nothing to mollify the prisoner's angry feelings, and many expected her counsel to exact a retributive penalty in cross-examination.

It would have been easy enough—easy to crush and blot out the Reverend Dyson if Clarke had been of such a mind. As in the earlier instance of Old Bartlett, ample material lay ready to his hand. An hour or two's questioning on certain hostile lines and the Reverend Dyson might have found few to believe that his association with Mrs. Bartlett was platonic or that his purchase of the chloroform was free from bad intent. You are in holy orders, are you not? And expected to maintain a high standard of propriety? Do you consider it proper that you should regularly spend many hours as the sole companion of a young married woman? *I did not ask whether Mr. Bartlett thought it proper, sir, but whether you did.* Then why did you do it? Is it usual for clergymen to act in this fashion? To comfort the wives of their absent congregants with kisses and embraces? Or to present them with love poems? Why did you buy the chloroform in three separate lots? Was it not to disguise the fact that the amount was large? Why should

you try to disguise it if you thought the transaction was straight-
forward? What were you afraid might come to light? . . . The questions are easy to devise but difficult to answer, as the Reverend Dyson
would have soon discovered. Like many a better man before and since,
this selfish weakling would have learnt how frail a shield is innocence
when folly, mischance and indiscretion have marked a human being
for their own.

It was open to Clarke to send Dyson from the box broken, disgraced
and ruined beyond repair. But how would this avail? Clarke's business
was not to avenge his client's shabby treatment but to gain her acquittal
on a capital charge. Unrestrained attack upon the Reverend Dyson
would frustrate rather than promote this end. The more sinful he, the
more sinful she; the more evil he knew, the more there was to know.
By painting his situation at its blackest, one might win a battle and
then lose the war.

The cross-examination therefore called above all else for tact—a
quality with which Clarke was liberally endowed. If the destruction
of Dyson had been what was required, Russell would have done it
with more brilliance and panache. But no one could have judged and
carried out with greater nicety the delicate performance that promised
most reward.

Clarke began his questioning in a quiet, even tone. The spectators
—and perhaps the Reverend Dyson too—waited for the storm that
never was to break.

"Whatever your relations were with regard to Mrs. Bartlett, they
were relations that were known to her husband?"

"Oh yes."

"And did you down to the last day of his life endeavour to re-
ciprocate his friendship and to deserve his confidence?"

"I did."

"Were you sincerely solicitous for his welfare?"

"I was."

"And do you believe that every day of that illness you and his wife
were both anxious for his welfare and tried to serve him?"

"I do."

All these answers could be forecast with moral certainty. In the
Reverend Dyson's eagerness to clear himself, Clarke had perceived
an element of which he could make use. While the witness would
not hesitate to incriminate Mrs. Bartlett if it appeared to offer an advantage to himself, he would be equally ready to speak up in her

favour where his own interests were intertwined with hers. More than
once during the cross-examination Clarke properly exploited the points
of such identity.

"You became aware at a very early period of your acquaintance
that Mr. Bartlett had peculiar views on the subject of marriage?"

"Yes."

"Did he ask you whether you thought the teaching of the Bible was
distinctly in favour of having one wife?"

"He did."

"Did he suggest to you that his idea was that there might be a wife
for a companionship and a wife for household duties?"

"He did."

"He suggested to you that a man should have two wives?"

"Yes."

"That would have struck you as a most outrageous suggestion, would
it not?"

"A very remarkable suggestion."

The scandalised judge could not restrain himself.

"Did it not strike you," he asked, "as an unwholesome sort of talk
in the family circle?"

"Not coming from him, my lord," the Reverend Dyson answered.
"He was a man who had some strange ideas."

This answer to the Bench was of immense value to Clarke. It
furnished the first support for the "extraordinary story" which Mrs.
Bartlett had told to Dr. Leach. Before anyone could make his mind
receptive to that story, he would have to be independently and thoroughly convinced that Edwin Bartlett had had some very strange ideas
indeed.

"Did he ever make reference," Clarke asked the Reverend Dyson,
"to marriage between you and Mrs. Bartlett after he should be dead?"

"He made statements which left no doubt in my mind but that he
contemplated Mrs. Bartlett and myself being ultimately married."

In strict accordance with his policy of steering clear of any head-on
clash, Clarke made a studiously indirect approach to a dangerous part
of the Reverend Dyson's evidence—his assertion that he had been
told by Mrs. Bartlett of an internal ailment which caused her husband
spasms and was shortening his life. Clarke neither contested nor admitted this assertion. He simply took steps to demonstrate that such
statements might have been made innocently.

"You told my learned friend that you have seen Mr. Bartlett put
his hand to his side and complain of some convulsive pain?"

"Yes."

"On more than one occasion?"

"Yes."

"When his wife has been there?"

"Yes."

The first point was made. Clarke moved swiftly on.

"Did he ever mention the possible duration of his life?"

"I think he did."

"When?"

"I cannot say."

"Was it not when you were on holiday at Dover?"

"I cannot swear that."

On matters which did not implicate him personally, the Reverend Dyson was scrupulous to a fault.

"At Dover did he mention something about his condition?"

"I think so."

"What was it?"

"He said he was not the strong man he once was."

"Did he say what was the cause?"

"He attributed it," the Reverend Dyson said, "to overwork."

Second point made. If the prisoner had indeed talked of an internal disease, there had been overt signs that might excuse such a conclusion; if she had indeed talked of its shortening his life he himself had also been disturbed about his health.

Her remarks—if ever made—no longer seemed so damning.

Clarke now struck the preliminary notes of what has been previously catalogued among his major themes. He began to set the stage for his theory of suicide.

"You were with Mr. Bartlett, were you not, at the very beginning of his illness?"

"I was."

"Before this time, had he appeared to you to be getting into an ailing and low condition?"

"He seemed very much worn out at night when he returned."

"Very weary, very depressed, complaining of sleeplessness?"

"During the actual sickness, yes."

"As that sickness wore on, did he become more depressed?"

"He varied," the Reverend Dyson said.

"You've seen him crying, have you not?"

"Once."

"When was that?"

"The Monday in Christmas week."

"All that time was he talking about not recovering?"

"He spoke very little."

Clarke tried another way round.

"Is it not the impression on your mind that at that time he thought he would not recover?"

"Yes, I have that impression."

"When you went on the following Sunday, was he not even worse?"

The Reverend Dyson demurred.

"No, I thought he was brighter. But . . ."

"But?"

"He . . . contradicted himself."

"How?"

Then it came out: the perfect answer for Clarke's purpose.

"Well, he asked me whether anyone could be lower than he was without passing away altogether."

In print, the author can italicise or underline. In court, counsel must use other means for emphasis.

"He asked you whether it was possible for a man to be lower than that without passing away altogether?"

"Yes."

"According to that expression, he was thinking of himself as one actually on the edge between life and death?"

"Yes."

Thrice had the Reverend Dyson said it; threefold had been its impact on the jury.

Very grave, very firm, but still without heat or rancour, Clarke now drew the witness to the central point of all. His questions on this subject were deliberately few and heavily insured against an unexpected answer.

"Did you mention to *Mr.* Bartlett that you had got the chloroform?"

"Mr. Bartlett? No."

"You understood that Mrs. Bartlett did not desire it to be mentioned to him?"

"Not specifically the chloroform," replied the Reverend Dyson, "but the affliction for which she wanted it."

The opening was no larger than a crack, but the able cross-examiner needs no more.

"Then she never asked you not to mention you had got the chloroform?"

"No. But I think," the minister characteristically added, "I ought to state, in justice to myself, that there was a visitor there and I could not give it her in his presence."

The Reverend Dyson's urge to clear himself had intervened again. Now the trick was on the table for the taking.

"At all events, *she* had not asked you to keep it secret?"

"No."

Although he would have hardly dared to hope so at the time, the Reverend Dyson's ordeal was drawing to a close. One further matter and Edward Clarke had done.

"You said, did you not, that you threw away the bottles you had bought from the chemists' shops on Tooting Common as you were going to church on January the 3rd?"

"I did."

"Were you then in great anxiety and distress about your position?"

"I was."

"You were afraid the effect of your having bought the bottles might get you into trouble?"

"Precisely."

"You had in your mind what might happen to yourself?"

"What might have been the cause of Mr. Bartlett's death."

"What might happen to yourself?" Clarke quietly insisted.

"The thought was in my mind," the Reverend Dyson said, "that possibly the chloroform I had bought had been the cause of Mr. Bartlett's death."

"And you thought you would be ruined if the matter came out?"

"I thought I would be ruined if my fears were true."

"That is, if *you* were associated with the matter?"

"Yes," said the Reverend Dyson, "I saw that danger."

Here was another solid gain for the defence. For Mrs. Bartlett also had thrown away a bottle—the larger bottle into which the chloroform was poured. She had disposed of this bottle—so she told the Reverend Dyson—through the window of a railway train on January 6th. That was a suspicious and incriminating action which might have been construed as consciousness of guilt. But, Clarke could now say, what of the clergyman himself? This man, against whom the Crown presents no case; this man, against whom I have made no imputation—he too hastily got rid of every article that might tend to connect him with Edwin Bartlett's death. His motive? The fear of false interpretations. Why should Mrs. Bartlett's motive not have been the same? . . .

By the only criterion that could be reasonably applied—the effect upon the interests of the woman in the dock—Clarke's handling of

Dyson richly justified itself. The spectators, it must be confessed, were somewhat disappointed. There had not been any fireworks; it had all been so subdued.

For exactly the same reason the Reverend Dyson felt intensely gratified. There had not been any fireworks; it had all been so subdued. He had passed through the crucial test comparatively unscathed, and now his protracted agonies were over. Breathing a prayer of thanksgiving he vanished from the box, from the court, from the case, to lose himself for ever in the nameless multitude.

Dr. Alfred Leach, L.R.C.S., of Charlwood Street, Pimlico, had come to curse the day when Mrs. Bartlett invited his attendance on her husband. He was a modest family doctor and had no aspirations to be a Willcox or a Spilsbury. Indeed his scientific attainments were but average and no one was likely to ask him to give evidence as an expert. But because of his short association with the Bartletts, because at all material times he had been the deceased man's medical attendant, because he had been the first qualified physician to appear upon the scene after Edwin Bartlett died, because he had been made the recipient of Adelaide Bartlett's "extraordinary story"—because of these things he found himself, not merely a witness, but a key performer in one of the most sensational trials of the century.

It was not a rôle for which he was well fitted, either by abilities or temperament, and of this Dr. Leach himself was painfully aware. For weeks before the trial he worried himself sick. Obsessed by an anxiety to tell the exact truth, he continually went over every detail in his mind and wrote out long accounts of what he thought had taken place. In the flurry of court he tried to bring to mind these documents, with only intermittent and variable success. Abrupt and disconcerting lapses of memory, irrelevant and unrequested bursts of recollection, a passion for futile and interminable periphrasis, a visible terror lest he might leave something out, a suggestion that he had learnt his evidence by heart—this awe-inspiring combination of defects made honest Dr. Leach the very archetype of bad witness. Sorely he tried the patience of barristers and judge. "This perpetual self-consciousness," complained the latter at one juncture, "detracts from the value of what you have to say."

It was unfortunate that he should cut so miserable a figure when he tried so hard and undeniably meant well. No one recognised his shortcomings more frankly than himself. "I'm sorry I'm such a bad witness," he once remarked remorsefully—which would have been disarming in a less austere assembly. Counsel seldom apologise for being bad advocates, nor does his lordship for being a bad judge.

Largely through his own fault, Dr. Leach was in the box a good deal longer than any other witness. He was called in the middle of the third day of the trial; his examination-in-chief (conducted by Russell, whom he soon provoked to frenetic irritation) dragged on into the later stages of that afternoon; his cross-examination had only been begun when the judge adjourned proceedings for the day. Clarke's further questions, and a re-examination of unusual length—and tone —occupied the whole of the morning session following. Dr. Leach's patients, back in Pimlico, must have been almost as fretful as the lawyers.

Clarke's cross-examination of this unhappy man is the kind of masterpiece that the lover of dramatic coups so often overlooks. Even its author did not seem to rate it high. In later years he confessed some merit in his tackling of Dyson; of his duels with the experts he felt justifiably proud. But about Leach never a word. And yet in cross-examining this upright, worried doctor Clarke built up one of the main walls of his defence. He made the case for suicide.

He opened with a few broad and general questions, designed to form a frame for what was to come after.

"So far as you could see and judge, during the whole of the time was Mrs. Bartlett tending her husband with anxious affection?"

"So far as I could see and judge, decidedly."

"Could you have wished for a more devoted nurse for him?"

"No. It is only right that I should say that emphatically."

"You were told that, night after night, she had sat and slept sitting at the foot of the bed?"

"Yes."

"Was it obvious to you that she needed rest and was suffering in strength?"

"It was."

Clarke added nothing more by way of preamble. Now—though the fact was not immediately apparent—he embarked upon a great and sustained effort to show that Edwin Bartlett had been ripe for self-destruction. He did not—could not—claim that in those three weeks of December he was on the verge of death. He could—and did—invite the doctor's collaboration in composing a portrait of a man who might well have *wished* to die.

Clarke started by eliciting a sickening description of the conditions which the illness had created in the mouth.

"When you first saw him on the 10th December, doctor, what attracted your attention?"

"He had a blue line round the edge of his gums, and the gums themselves were red and spongy."

"By the 14th was the blue line beginning to give way?"

"Yes—to a grey sloughing margin."

"Was that when his sleeplessness got bad?"

"Yes, his teeth were beginning to pain him then."

"On the 16th and 17th he had some teeth out, and a number of loose roots?"

"Yes."

"Were they all very decayed and horrible?"

"That fairly describes them."

"Was there a foul fungoid growth at the roots?"

"In some later extractions, there was."

"On the 17th were the gums still bad?"

"Yes. In front the grey slough had sloughed off, leaving a jagged margin."

There was nothing novel about any of these facts, nor had Dr. Leach the least desire to hide them. They were, quite literally, there for the mere asking. The artistry lay in their presentation and arrangement; in the way they were linked to make a cumulative impact, which in turn was linked to others as the advocate went on.

"Was it on the 19th you began to talk to him about getting out of doors?"

"Quite as early as that."

"Did he refuse?"

"He said," Dr. Leach replied, "that it would kill him."

The doctor, who had so far been more relevant and concise in answering Clarke than he had been with Russell, now once again got the bit between his teeth. "He really was so obstinate about going out of doors that he almost at one time made me believe that I had overlooked something serious in him. He was—"

"Doctor—"

"—so reasonable on some points that I—"

"Doctor—"

"—could scarcely have put it down to sheer folly."

"Just listen to me, doctor. At that time did Mrs. Bartlett tell you before her husband that he still talked about dying?"

"It was about that time probably; I'm not sure but that she said it more than once."

"Did you promise that if he went to Torquay for Christmas you would take him down and place him under the care of a medical man there?"

"Yes; I said I would take him down and I mentioned Dr. Dalby because I thought he would like to feel that he would be looked after. He—"

"Doctor—"

"—required no looking after practically."

"You wanted him to stay in Torquay alone?"

"Oh yes."

"Why was that?"

"Because he was practically a hysterical patient at the time, and his wife petted him very much."

"He was getting better physically?"

"Oh yes."

"Then on the 23rd did something happen that upset the whole thing?"

"Yes. He passed a worm."

"Was he much depressed and shocked?"

"Yes. He thought it had proved there was something wrong with him."

"Did he say he now thought there was more mischief about him than you had found out?"

"Yes."

"Did he tell you a day or two afterwards that he felt worms wriggling up his throat?"

"Yes, the next day, I think, and he kept to it."

"It was a delusion, I suppose?"

"I don't know." Dr. Leach was nothing if not fair—to the Crown, to the defence, to the dead. "I don't know. Two or three days ago I saw a worm that did wriggle up a patient's throat and was vomited."

Delusion or fact, it was all the same to Clarke.

"Then he may have felt that?"

"He may, but in his case I think it was a mistake."

"The upset imagination of a very nervous man?"

"Yes."

"And he was in a more depressed and troubled condition after that time, was he not?"

"For a day or two."

Clarke paused for a moment before putting his next question. His words were measured.

"During that next day or two did a very curious matter take place with regard to mesmerism?"

Dr. Leach flew into one of his not infrequent panics.

"I cannot fix the date of it from memory," he said. "I think I have notes of it somewhere. I think the Treasury have them. I think I must have parted with my original copy." He fumbled desperately among his sheaf of notes—most of which, so far, he had not been allowed to read. "Oh yes, here it is. It was on the 26th; he told me an extraordinary tale."

"About the possibility of being under somebody's influence from a distance?"

"Yes; he thought he and his wife had been mesmerised by a friend. Shall I relate what he said?" the conscientious doctor asked.

"Do, please."

"I went to see him that morning and said, 'Well, Mr. Bartlett, how have you slept?' He said, 'I could not sleep. I was nervous and restless when I saw my wife asleep in the easy chair, so I got up and went and stood over her like *this!*'"

The doctor held up his arms in demonstration.

"He was very excited. 'I was like this,' he said, 'for two hours, and I felt the vital force being drawn from her to me. I felt it going into me through my finger tips, and after that I laid down and I slept.'"

The ungovernable murmur of astonishment in court testified to the effect created by this narrative.

"Did you imagine," Clarke enquired gravely, "that he had stood over her for two hours extracting the vital force from her?"

Dr. Leach was moved to unaccustomed raciness.

"I did not imagine," he said, "that Mr. Bartlett would stay two hours doing anything. . . ."

It was growing late and upon this answer ended the third long day of Mrs. Bartlett's trial. The participants went their several ways to private meditation: Clarke to his home, where, buttressed and surrounded by his books on chloroform, he prepared to do battle with the Crown experts on the morrow; Mrs. Bartlett to prison, where she passed the torturing night in a turmoil of thoughts that must for ever remain secret; the jury to the quarters which of necessity they shared, where they could ponder at leisure a new-born possibility—that in his last days Edwin Bartlett had been mad.

Next morning Clarke resumed his cross-examination and completed his sketch of Edwin Bartlett's mental state. So neurotic, so hysterical did this now seem to have been, so eccentric were his sayings and so unbalanced were his acts, that there was no surprise when Clarke put into words the idea that was floating through everybody's mind.

"Had you suspected him of insanity?" he asked.

"At one time I did," Dr. Leach admitted.

The doctor had not benefited from his night's repose, if indeed he had been able to get any. It is much more likely that he lay awake for hours, wondering why he had proved such a tiresome witness and planning to give greater satisfaction in the morning. Whatever the cause, he was even more diffuse and long-winded than before; he added to his harvest of judicial reproofs; and it took Clarke two more hours of patient, expert questioning before he had taken him through all essential points.

That which is essential is not necessarily decisive. But one short passage, which appeared that morning of only minor consequence, was destined, in conjunction with the scientific evidence, to play a major part in influencing judgment.

"Did Mrs. Bartlett wish," Clarke said, "to have the post-mortem made as quickly as was possible?"

"She certainly did," answered the doctor. "She chafed at the delay till next day. When I told her that the eminent pathologist we wanted couldn't come that afternoon, she said, 'Can't he be persuaded?' "

"Persuaded to come so that he might make the post-mortem on that very day?"

"On that very day."

"So," said Clarke, "if the pathologist had been able to come the post-mortem would have taken place on the afternoon of death?"

"Yes."

The majority in court may have wondered at the time whether Clarke was not labouring a secondary matter. But it was not secondary, and he had good reason to make sure it was remembered.

Like tigers travelling in the wake of a rabbit, the Crown experts were due to follow Dr. Leach. Matters of pure science would have to be thrashed out with them. But Dr. Leach after all had academic knowledge and practical experience; here was a chance of reconnoitring the ground.

Clarke picked his steps warily.

"Just a few questions on a different subject, Dr. Leach. Have you ever at any time seen a case of death from poisoning by liquid chloroform?"

"No."

"It is extremely rare, isn't it?"

"It has occurred, of course; it is rare."

"Have you yourself administered chloroform from time to time?"

"Yes; about two hundred times."

"Is it an operation that requires to be very carefully and skilfully done?"

"It is an anxious one."

"Of late years has ether been substituted for chloroform in anæsthesia?"

"Yes."

"Do you know why?"

"Because it is less dangerous."

"Not only less dangerous," suggested Clarke. "Are not some things incidental to chloroform less often found with ether—vomiting, for instance?"

"Yes, quite so."

"Is vomiting constantly found with inhalation of chloroform?" the judge interpolated.

"The patient usually vomits afterwards," Dr. Leach explained, "and even during the administration."

"In many cases," Clarke asked, "does the vomiting begin almost immediately?"

"It depends."

"On the condition of the stomach?"

"Oh yes; if food has been given previously."

"I was going to say, if you had made up your mind to administer chloroform to a patient, you would take care with regard to diet six hours or so before?"

"At least four," said the doctor, feeling a slight revival of confidence now he was being asked to judge instead of being judged. "At least four, and that must only be beef tea or some liquid easily digested."

"Suppose you had any indigestible substance in the stomach, such, for instance, as a substantial quantity of mango chutney." (Evidence had been given that Edwin Bartlett had had mango chutney with the last meal of his life, and the remains of it, *half digested*, were observed at the post-mortem.) "That would almost certainly produce vomiting, would it not?"

"It might," said Dr. Leach.

"It *would*, would it not?"

The doctor still hesitated.

"I should not like to say it *would*."

Clarke saw how close he was to yielding. He lowered his demand by a fraction.

"I should not like to ask you to prophesy, but you would *expect* it to?"

It was sufficient. Dr. Leach accepted the compromise.

"It is a very likely suggestion," he said.

Russell, seeing the way that things were moving, irritably tapped his celebrated snuff-box. He had staked his case at the outset on a theory: that the administration of liquid chloroform had been preceded by external application. Only thus, he had admitted, could "the medical men" explain how the liquid was administered without causing cries and paroxysms of pain. And now here was one of his "medical men" (though Russell when he had used the term was certainly not thinking of small fry like Dr. Leach) giving Clarke one reply after another that tore up the platform on which that theory stood.

Still, the experts will be able to put it in perspective. If only we could get this blundering fool out of the box. . . .

But the defence had advanced further before Edward Clarke sat down.

"Have you ever administered chloroform to an adult in sleeping?" he had asked.

"No," said Dr. Leach.

"Have you ever heard of an authentic case of its being done?"

"No," said Dr. Leach. . . .

The re-examination (by one of Russell's juniors) was extraordinarily long and extraordinarily contentious. At times it seemed that everyone forgot by which side the witness had originally been called.

At lunch-time Dr. Leach was released at last from purgatory to dedicate himself afresh as a healer of mankind. Few men have run inadvertently into such a sea of troubles or contributed so innocently to their exacerbation.

The way was now clear for the prosecution experts to speak in support of the Attorney-General's opening and to back, by the weight of their considerable authority, his reconstruction of the way the crime was done.

The cross-examination of scientific experts falls into a peculiar and isolated category. Others are called to testify to *facts*, and opposing counsel is generally concerned to show that they are either untruthful or mistaken. The experts lead the way into the realm of *theory*, of analytical dissertations and deductive reconstruction. Any contest with them may ultimately turn upon niceties of wording or the shape of formulæ.

Some surprise is occasionally expressed because so many acknowledged experts prove unimpressive witnesses; they are moulded like wax by the cunning hands of advocates who do not rival them in specialised erudition. That is because their mastery of the subject under review is not matched by a mastery of the art of giving evidence. They may be profound, but not quick; thorough, but not selective; accurate, but not lucid. They may find it easier to express themselves on paper; they may find the laboratory more congenial than the court. They may be witnesses who are Experts, without being expert Witnesses.

Few have been both in superlative degree; not more than two or three in any generation. But one such, unquestionably, was Dr. Thomas Stevenson, and it was he who had performed, at the Home Office's request, the analysis of Edwin Bartlett's remains. Professor of Medical Jurisprudence at Guy's Hospital, one of the leading consulting physicians of the day, a toxicologist of international repute, Dr. Stevenson was above all a tough, shrewd witness; honest and fair enough in forming his opinion, but not easily moved to qualify his blunt expression of it. He could not be rattled and he would not be cajoled.

In the Bartlett trial Dr. Stevenson appeared amid distinguished colleagues, each of whom contributed a viewpoint of his own. But on all sides he was considered as their leader, and when on the fourth afternoon he stepped into the box everyone present saw in him the instrument of destiny.

Stevenson was not the man to exploit by style or manner the drama inherent in his situation. He gave his evidence with matter-of-fact composure. He told of finding chloroform in the contents of the stomach, and fixed the quantity at $11\frac{1}{4}$ grams. He described an inflamed patch on the stomach itself—"at the usual spot," he said, "after swallowing irritant poison." He declared unhesitatingly that the chloroform discovered had been the cause of death.

"Could he take a fatal dose," asked Russell, "and suppose he was taking some innocent thing?"

"No," replied the witness, "I don't believe he could."

"Is it possible to put liquid down the throat of a person who is insensible, in the sense of being unconscious, but still having the sense of feeling?"

"Yes; you can put liquids down the throat of a person who is fairly moderately under the influence of inhaled chloroform."

"Would it be difficult?"

"Not if the man was lying on his back with his mouth open."

Thus was filled in Russell's sketch of the Crown theory. There would be "no great difficulty" in pouring the *liquid* down if *inhaled* chloroform had taken "moderate" effect.

But could a person untrained in medical technique produce such a condition, or recognise it when it had been produced? This was the main point Clarke was to take in a cross-examination which he himself regarded as the trial's turning point. . . .

When Russell sat down, Clarke got slowly to his feet.

In front of him was a rampart of massive medical books, the paper markers drooping like a sea of flags becalmed. The moment had arrived—the moment when the close research of many days would bear or stint its fruits.

Signs of the strain inseparable from a long capital trial showed momentarily on the defender's face as he put his first questions.

"Dr. Stevenson, you have for many years given your attention to subjects of this class?"

"I have."

"And you have had a long experience of the administration of chloroform?"

"I have."

"And you have also given study to the experience of other doctors?"

"Yes."

"And you have edited *The Principles and Practice of Medical Jurisprudence,* by Dr. Alfred Swaine Taylor, who is well known as one of the greatest authorities in that branch of medical science?"

"Yes."

"And so far as your skill and experience have enabled you, have you taken care that it is complete in the subject with which it deals?"

"Yes; it is fairly complete, I think."

Deliberately Clarke was reinforcing Stevenson's prestige. Deliberately he was projecting him as the Supreme Authority; the Expert of Experts; the man who, in dealing with chloroform, knew all there was to know. Now he asked the question for which this had dressed the ground.

"Can you refer me to *any* recorded case, *anywhere,* of murder by the administration of liquid chloroform?"

Stevenson answered as Clarke knew he must.

"No," he said, "I know of none."

So if Mrs. Bartlett had killed her husband by giving him liquid chloroform, she had performed a feat that was apparently unique.

"There are no recorded cases of murder in this fashion," Clarke went on, "but have there not been deaths from the swallowing of chloroform by accident?"

"Yes," said Stevenson.

"How many?"

"About twenty have been recorded."

So, by the test of statistics, accident was a more feasible hypothesis than murder.

"You say that liquid chloroform could be administered while a person is under the influence of chloroform inhaled?"

"Certainly."

"You know that the brain appeared normal on post-mortem?"

"I have heard so."

"But when chloroform has been inhaled just a short time before death would you not expect a distinct odour in the ventricles of the brain?"

"Not always," Stevenson said, adding, "It has been observed."

"Come," Clarke persisted. "Is it not one of the most prominent symptoms recognised?"

"Not according to my observations." Clarke's hand reached out among the books. The witness anticipated the coming thrust. "I am speaking from my own observation," he re-emphasised.

"I do not want to challenge your book by any other," Clarke remarked politely, "but you know *Guy and Ferrier?*"

"Yes."

"Is it a book of substantial authority?"

"Yes."

Clarke opened the volume at a place already marked. Stevenson waited, outwardly impassive.

"I am at page 550 of *Guy and Ferrier*." Clarke began to read. " 'The odour of chloroform is perceptible on opening the body. It is especially observable in the cerebral ventricles.' "

He paused enquiringly. Dr. Stevenson's response was not entirely unevasive, nor did it possess his usual rigid relevance.

"Asphyxia usually arises from giving too much chloroform," he said. "There you would expect to find the smell more prominent."

Clarke seized his advantage.

"I quite agree it may be a question of quantity, but what I am putting to you is—if you are looking for post-mortem indications of chloroform having been inhaled, the odour in the cerebral ventricles would be one of the principal ones?"

"Oh, I should certainly look for it," Stevenson conceded.

All this, though highly useful, was subordinate. It set the scene; it provided Clarke with a favourable background against which to open the decisive interchange.

"You spoke earlier," he said, "of administering chloroform to persons while in sleep?"

"Yes."

"Did you speak of adults?"

"Yes."

"As a matter of your own practice?"

"No," said Stevenson, "I have not done it myself."

"You are speaking of recorded cases?"

"I am."

"In the case of adults, is it the fact that the attempt to administer chloroform by inhalation during sleep almost invariably wakes the man?"

"Not almost invariably," Stevenson jibbed at the phrase, which was indeed a little strong. "Not almost invariably. If I may refer to the largest number of experiments that have been carried out by one individual—Dolbeau—he found that three awoke to one that was chloroformed."

Clarke extracted another volume from the stack.

"Do you know Wynter Blyth's work on poisons?"

"I do."

"I am reading from page 136. 'Dolbeau has made some interesting experiments in order to ascertain whether under any circumstances a sleeping person might be anæsthetised. The main result appears to answer the question in the affirmative, at least with certain persons; but even with these *it can only be done by using the greatest skill and care. This cautious and scientific narcosis is not likely to be used by the criminal classes, or, if used, to be successful.*'"

Clarke stopped. Dr. Stevenson nodded slightly, but made no spoken comment. . . .

The afternoon had lengthened into evening, and still this intensive questioning went on. It was conducted entirely on the plane of general principle; no references were made to the case that was being tried. The talk was not of Mrs. Bartlett, but of Wynter Blyth and Dolbeau; not of the man who died at the house in Claverton Street, but of patients in Scotland or the United States; not of what the prisoner had or had not done, but of what, in the light of science, it was possible to do. Yet Clarke's purpose was most relevant and consistently maintained. Each question was directed to the self-same urgent end: to show that the operation which, on the Crown theory, Mrs. Bartlett had performed would test the powers of a qualified physician and be utterly beyond her capacity and knowledge.

Toe to toe, counsel and doctor fought the matter out. As book after book was produced and scrutinised, as successive authorities were cited and discussed, the Old Bailey seemed transmuted into some scholastic forum where learned professors contended for the truth. But there was one who sat apart, in her sombre widow's garb, to bear constant reminder of the stake upon the outcome.

At last the advocate pushed the books aside. They had served him, and he had used them, well. The witness was not in any way discredited—this would have been the reverse of Clarke's intention—but he was tied, as a result of the long interrogation, to certain important medical premises. On the basis of these Clarke could now venture upon a series of dramatic, and indeed decisive, questions which related all that had transpired to the case before the court, and garnered the harvest he had so astutely sown.

"Let me put it again," he said to Stevenson, and there was that in his voice that made everyone alert. "Let me put it again. You say there is a particular point in the process of chloroforming at which the patient would be able to swallow, though he was sufficiently under the influence of chloroform not to suffer from the pain?"

"I do."

"How would you yourself ascertain that that time had arrived?"

"By the reflex of the eye. I would not like to pour down the throat if the reflex had been abolished."

"How would you test it?"

"By touching the eye and watching for the closure of the eyelid."

"Would you mind touching your own eye; just show us how it is done?"

The jury watched the doctor's practised fingers.

"Like this. You separate the eyelids, see? And . . . just touch the conjunctiva."

Clarke bowed in acknowledgment.

"I am much obliged. That is the test to ascertain if the sensation of pain has gone?"

"Yes."

It was time for the concluding strokes.

"Suppose you had to deal with a sleeping man and it was your object to get down his throat without his knowing it a liquid which would cause great pain; do you not agree it would be a very difficult and delicate operation?"

The eye; the reflex; the precise stage of anæsthesia. Stevenson had to bear them all in mind. He replied in somewhat guarded terms.

"I think it would be an operation which would often fail, and might often succeed."

He had gone far enough; Clarke could afford to insist on his own phrase.

"Would you not look on it as a *delicate* operation?"

Stevenson yielded.

"Yes, I should look on it as delicate; I should be afraid of pouring it down the windpipe."

"If the patient got into such a state of insensibility as not to reject it, it would go down his windpipe and burn that?"

"Some of it might."

"If it did so, it would leave its traces?"

"I should expect to find traces."

As the whole world knew, no such traces had been found. The cross-examination appeared to have reached its culminating point. But Clarke was to add a final, unexpected twist.

"If the post-mortem examination had been performed, *as we know from Dr. Leach that Mrs. Bartlett wished,* on the very day upon which death took place, there would have been a better opportunity of determining cause of death?"

"There would," said Dr. Stevenson.

Clarke sat down amid a buzz of murmurs which leapt into a hubbub as the hearing was adjourned. The cross-examination had been admirably managed, the closing phase spectacular in triumph.

The effect that it produced upon the jury may be gathered from what took place next morning when the court resumed.

A word ought to be said about the jury that now held Adelaide Bartlett in their charge.

Notwithstanding official pronouncements to the contrary by those whose high attainments must command respect, a number of juries called to modern murder trials have shown themselves perverse or unintelligent or both. The Bartlett case provided an opposite example. The jury were fair-minded and notably acute, closely following the intricacies of scientific argument and not at all averse to doing some thinking on their own. This was already patent from questions they had put to various witnesses as the trial progressed.

Nine times out of ten an interfering jury is an even greater bane than an interfering judge. But the Bartlett jury earns complete exoneration. Their interventions were, without exception, strictly to the point; they were cast in language that was clear and yet exact; they usually led, and were always meant to lead, towards elucidation of some obscurity. Anyone who, remembering the trial of Mrs. Thompson or of William Herbert Wallace, feels inclined to regard the jury system with despair, may take fresh heart from the sagacity and diligence of the twelve London citizens who tried Mrs. Bartlett.

On the night of Dr. Stevenson's cross-examination they must have talked it over at length among themselves. In the course of their discussion they found that there was something more that they would like to know. . . .

First thing next day Dr. Stevenson went back into the box for the inevitable anti-climax of his re-examination. It did not last long, and he was about to step down again when the foreman of the jury stood up in his place.

"My lord," he said, "there are one or two questions *we* should like to ask," and he proceeded to ask them in a style of which no barrister need have felt ashamed.

"We desire," he began, "to be perfectly clear upon this point." There was none of that hesitation, that unintelligible stammering that serves to characterise the muddle-headed. Here was a man who knew what he was about. "If an unskilled person administers chloroform down the throat, must he not do it very gradually for fear of choking?"

Dr. Stevenson took a second or so to turn the question over.

"In some cases," he said, "I don't think it would be difficult to do it quickly."

"But the chances are that some portion of the chloroform would remain in the mouth for a little time?"

"A *very* short time."

"But it must remain there for a little time?" The foreman stuck to his point with the tenacity and coolness of a seasoned silk who has been cross-examining witnesses these five and twenty years. "It must remain there for a little time, doctor, must it not?"

"Some of it might. If the person were unable to swallow, it would be likely to remain at the back of the throat."

"And then it will show some signs of having been there, in the same way as if it lay in the intestine?"

The court was following with rapt attentiveness. Such a scene was rare between juryman and witness.

"It would show some sign," Dr. Stevenson repeated, "if the patient were unable to swallow."

"You would expect more signs if a person could not swallow than if he were drinking medicine quickly off?"

"Yes."

"What signs?"

"If a person could not swallow, the chloroform would remain at the upper end of the windpipe, and upon the post-mortem I should expect to find irritation or inflammation."

"If taken suddenly, you would not expect to find either?"

"I should not."

The foreman glanced round at his fellows much as the seasoned silk would glance round at his juniors. That what we wanted?

They nodded their assent. . . .

On those rare occasions when a jury speaks, none pays heed more anxiously than counsel; it makes a chink, however slight, in that blank wall of silence that normally conceals the tenor of their thoughts. Clarke weighed and weighed again the purport of the foreman's questioning. He was too wise and circumspect to build hopes on it unduly. But as a straw in the wind he observed it and felt thankful; it proclaimed that the jury had understood his case and that their minds were at any rate not closed.

From this he could justifiably derive encouragement as he braced himself for the greatest of his tasks.

The Crown case had closed. Clarke had intimated that he would call no evidence. Russell, who, as a law officer, could claim a prescriptive right to the last word, showed that he meant to do so by remaining in his seat. On that fifth morning, therefore, in a court not less expectant than it had been on the first, Clarke uttered the first words of what was destined to become a classic of forensic eloquence—the closing speech on behalf of Mrs. Bartlett.

He began by referring to Russell's exercise of his "anomalous privilege" and made legitimate capital out of his own disadvantage. "Although I call no witnesses," he declared, "although I have to content myself with comments on the evidence before you, when I have finished I shall be answered by the leader of the English Bar. He will have an opportunity—I do not say that he will use it—but he will have an opportunity of pointing to topics which I may not have appreciated.

If he were to make his statement now I should hear his comments and might be able to answer them, but they will come to you when my lips are closed."

The beautifully modulated voice—one of the most melodious and expressive that has ever graced the courts—assumed a note of challenge as this protest was developed.

"I hope an Attorney-General may be found some day—unless the law is altered, as it should be—to abandon the exercise of a right which does not seem to me defensible." As Russell's underlip jutted forward in ill-humour, Clarke was exquisitely disarming. "I know that my learned friend will endeavour to be as fair in his reply as he was in his opening. But I know so well, by my own experience of forensic combat, how an instinct of antagonism is aroused in which the strongest determination to be impartial could not be trusted by any of us to clear him from prejudice or passion." Then came a telling stroke. "My learned friend, *coming from a country distinguished far more for its advocates than for its judges,* may import the combative instinct into the conduct of this case."

Russell's Irish blood may well have boiled, but he was temporarily rendered impotent. What valid objection could one take? Courteously but firmly, with absolute propriety but infinite finesse, Clarke had spiked the guns he was to fire hereafter.

As a pendant to this preliminary theme, Clarke warned the jury that his speech must be a long one since he had to bear in mind that Russell was to follow him. "That consideration obliges me to deal with all the topics that are before you, because otherwise I should run the most grievous risk—not for myself," he added parenthetically, "for it is a matter of no moment to me what comment might be made on my speech or on my advocacy—but risk to one whose interests are present to me at this moment in far higher degree than any consideration that could attach to myself."

A look of pathetic gratitude flickered for a moment across the sad young face of the woman in the dock.

The jury would not be in any wise dismayed at the prospect of a long and comprehensive speech from Clarke. They had followed the evidence with unfaltering attention; they earnestly desired to reach a just decision; they would gratefully welcome assistance in their task. And—to adopt a less disinterested approach—recompenses are not lacking for those who find themselves caught up in the grip of a great orator.

The jurors leaned forward receptively as Clarke invited them to hear his grounds for claiming an acquittal.

By way of exordium he summarised the case in a devastating sentence—a sentence that, with one possible exception, was not open to criticism in a single phrase or word, but which held compressed within its narrow compass almost every circumstance in favour of his client. "You are asked to believe," he said, "that a woman who for years had lived with her husband in friendship and affection; who, during the whole time of his illness, had striven to nurse him and to help him; who had tended him by day, and had sacrificed her own rest to watch over him at night, simply sleeping at the bottom of his couch that she might be ready to comfort him by her presence; who had called doctors, that by no possibility should any chance be lost of ascertaining what his trouble was and having the quickest means to cure it; who had watched over him, had tried to cheer him, had talked lightly when they were together before the doctor in order to give him spirits—that woman, you are asked to believe, on New Year's Eve was suddenly transformed into a murderess, committing crime not only without excuse, but absolutely without object, by the execution of an operation which would have been delicate and difficult to the highest trained doctor."

In theory, Clarke had been outlining the case for the Crown; in practice he had outlined the case for the defence. It was like a simple plan or chart to guide the jury through the multitude of detail, and show how each part was related to the whole.

Perhaps because he knew that it was uppermost in their minds, he elected to deal with the scientific evidence first. He reminded them that there had never been a murder in this fashion— "Though there have been murderers equipped with all the medical experience." Had the unskilled Mrs. Bartlett established a grim precedent? Let them realise what such a verdict must involve. . . .

It had been admitted by the Attorney-General that an unwilling person could not be made to inhale chloroform; nor could it be poured down the throat of such a person unless inhalation had first made him insensible. "And I do not think," said Clarke, "that my learned friend will suggest that Mr. Bartlett acquiesced."

"Certainly not," interpolated Russell from beside him.

"Very well," Clarke rejoined, his gaze still on the jury. "Now let us see what step this is that you are asked to take." He recalled the Crown's theory of the double operation: that Mrs. Bartlett had first "chloroformed" her husband, and then poured the liquid down his un-resisting throat. "That is the suggestion," he said, and shook his head. "But it is a suggestion which is almost an impossibility."

He supported this assertion by plain and forceful reasoning. Experiments had shown, as agreed by Dr. Stevenson, that if an attempt was made to "chloroform" a sleeping person he was overwhelmingly likely to wake up and resist. And these experiments, Clarke shrewdly pointed out, were made by skilled chloroformists under the best conditions. "Is it not," he asked, "in the highest degree improbable that an unskilled person would *ever* be able to administer chloroform in sleep without waking the person subjected to the process?"

But it did not finish there. If chloroform was inhaled shortly before death one would expect to find signs of it in the brain; no such signs were remarked at the post-mortem. Again, one would expect to find signs of it in the heart; the examining pathologists declared the heart was normal. And again, as a general rule, chloroform caused vomiting; there was no evidence that Edwin Bartlett had vomited at all.

"I am going by steps, gentlemen," Clarke said. "I have shown you the enormous—may I not say the almost insuperable?—difficulty of administering chloroform to a sleeping person without waking him. But now let us assume this . . . *miracle* has been worked."

He rapped out the word "miracle" with electrifying effect.

"What happens next? There may be a time, the duration of which no one can measure, the conditions of which it is scarcely possible for the most careful doctor to predict—there may be an instant of time or a few instants in which the second part of the operation might be done. For Dr. Stevenson, with all his experience, such an operation would be difficult and delicate." And what was the allegation of the Crown? "That one absolutely unstudied in the ways of medicine; who knew little of chloroform, the mode of its administration, the objects it would serve—that she, alone in the room with her sleeping husband succeeded in performing this difficult and delicate operation, and so succeeded that no trace, no spilling of chloroform by the nervous hand, no effects through contact with the soft passages, no signs in the post-mortem condition of the body, remained to reveal the fact that she had done it."

This constituted the strongest argument at Clarke's disposal. It was founded on the success of his cross-examination, and he had hammered it home with clarity and power. But now there were the general issues to be faced; the string of suspicious incidents, the lies to get the chloroform, the marital relations between Bartlett and his wife in the crucible of which her credibility would be judged.

Clarke had been speaking for the best part of two hours. He had barely reached the fringe of this less favourable ground when the adjournment came.

The mounting pressure was taking toll of all, and for the chief actors lunch was a token meal. Each was preoccupied and worn with private cares. Russell felt conscious that he had not been at his best, and that the case against the prisoner could have been more aptly put; as senior Crown counsel he deplored this situation and ransacked his resourceful mind for a means to rectify it. Mrs. Bartlett, lodged below the dock for the fifth successive day, reflected that the sixth must surely seal her fate, and wondered for the thousandth time where she would spend the seventh. Clarke, aware that this was now suspended by a thread, summoned up his last reserves of nervous energy and strength. He dreaded, as every sensitive man in his position must, that calamity might result from some shortcoming on his part.

When he re-entered court so large a flock of barristers had crowded in to hear him that it was only with some difficulty he got back to his seat. The public galleries, which had been crammed to bursting-point throughout, now appeared to have accomplished the impossible and packed in even more than had been there hitherto. It is doubtful, though, whether this made much impression upon Clarke. He was not an actor with an audience, but an advocate with a jury, and his absorption in his client's interests was complete.

That afternoon session was entirely his. From beginning to end he remained upon his feet, striving without cease for possession of the jury. Flinching from nothing, ventilating all; commenting, interpreting and placing in perspective; using the facts to illuminate psychology and using psychology to illuminate the facts; allying simplicity of substance with nobility of style, he composed such a picture of this melancholy case as could never be forgotten by those who saw it done. . . .

Very still he stood; pale from his exertions, but straight and sturdy as a pillar, as he opened the last phase of his tremendous fight.

Already he had dealt with what he called "the smaller matters" of suspicion: the fire that had seemed freshly tended in the middle of the night ("With a patient suffering from sleeplessness it would be the manifest duty of the person watching to build this fire up and make it last for hours"); the conversation about chloroform with the landlord's wife ("That day Mr. Bartlett had had a tooth drawn. . . . He had taken gas"). These "suspicious" circumstances, Clarke had declared, "do not survive examination," and Russell himself was later to concede that they were "insignificant." But now Clarke met the challenge of a much more serious matter—the excuses for requiring chloroform that Mrs. Bartlett was alleged to have concocted.

He reminded the jury that this matter depended on the evidence and recollection of the Reverend Dyson, and adroitly utilised the Crown's endorsement of his innocence. "I accept the conclusion at which the Crown arrived. There was really no case to be submitted to you against him. But"—and Clarke's voice rang out in indignation—"when you are asked to use against Mrs. Bartlett the untruthful statements which she has made, and which come to you on Mr. Dyson's evidence, does it not occur to you that if matters of this kind are to have great weight, how fortunate Mr. Dyson is that he is not standing in the dock himself?" He took pains, though, to make it crystal clear that he was demanding equity, not denouncing Dyson. "I beg you to note," he emphasised again, "that I do not impeach his innocence in the least. But supposing *his* case were before you, what would you have? Suppose someone who knew him had seen him fling away the bottles on Tooting Common and had had the curiosity to pick a bottle up; suppose it had come out, at the first meeting of the inquest, that he was a habitual visitor at the house, that he had been in the habit of walking out with Mrs. Bartlett, that his relations with the Bartletts were of an exceptional character; suppose it had come out by enquiry at the chemist's (whose name is on the label) that when Mr. Dyson asked for the chloroform he had told him a falsehood—what would have been Mr. Dyson's position?"

Between accused woman and exonerated man the parallel was indeed remarkably exact. "I use it," said Clarke, "to show you that where against him, *an innocent man,* a falsehood told for the express purpose of getting this poison might have been proved in the witness box, it would be hard indeed that a statement from the lips of the very man to whom Mrs. Bartlett told a story which was not wholly true to explain her desiring to possess this chloroform—it would be strange indeed if that were allowed to weigh upon your minds as a serious element of suspicion against *her.*"

The form of this plea was singularly persuasive. Dearer to a jury than the most flawless syllogism is the traditional tag concerning sauce for the goose.

Recalling, in studiously temperate terms, that "there is very good ground for the suspicion that he has been anxious to protect himself without much regard to the actual truth," Clarke declared it would be unsafe to rely on "the entire accuracy" of the Reverend Dyson's statements. But—he reinsured himself lest the jury should think otherwise—suppose that Mrs. Bartlett *had* departed from the truth. Could she have told Dyson what she later told Dr. Leach? Could any woman of delicacy have done so? "She gave him some reason for wanting the chloroform," said Clarke. "Mr. Dyson's idea, he says, was that she would sprinkle drops upon a handkerchief and use it for the purpose of soothing Mr. Bartlett. Well, it is not far from the explanation she gave to Dr. Leach; and is it not perfectly intelligible that she should desire to veil by that sort of account the real truth which she could not be expected to communicate to Mr. Dyson?"

Perfectly intelligible—always provided that the real truth *was* contained in the story Mrs. Bartlett had told to Dr. Leach. The difficulty of making that story even credible—a difficulty that did not exclude its authenticity—had haunted Clarke since before the trial began, and he cannot have been wholly free from qualms as he came to grips with this least tractable of problems.

He spoke, though, as ever, with a burning sincerity that was the mirror of his faith in Mrs. Bartlett's innocence. Her story, he said, had received corroboration at every point where it was possible to test it. It was in evidence that Edwin Bartlett had held strange views on marriage, and had harboured the idea that a man might have two wives. It was in evidence that he had fostered, as far as he was able, the growing affection between Dyson and his wife. It was in evidence that he had written to the former expressing his "thankfulness" for "the loving letter you sent Adelaide today," and subscribing himself "yours affectionately, Edwin." Clarke attached great importance to this letter, which he roundly described as the key of the whole case. "Of all the strange things that this court has heard," he exclaimed, "there has been nothing stranger than that letter, where "yours affectionately, Edwin," is with apologetic humility thanking the man who had written a loving letter to his wife."

Moreover, Clarke insisted, Mrs. Bartlett's story was entitled to the greater credence as she had never intended nor expected it to be made public. "I claim for that statement this: it was not a statement offered to an accusing world as an explanation of circumstances that had cast suspicion on her; it was a private communication of the most private matter to the physician in whose skill she was trusting for her treatment. It was a statement which comes to you in such circumstances as to bear with it the almost irresistible presumption that it is true."

It is instantly apparent when a jury has lost sympathy with counsel, when they find an argument entirely unacceptable even at the very moment of its exposition. Their concentration breaks. They begin to fidget. They glance at one another and occasionally exchange conversation in a whisper. They are again twelve separate, unrelated individuals instead of twelve members of an integrated team.

Subconsciously, but none the less intently, Clarke watched for any of these signs while he steered through this most perilous passage on his course. There were none. The jury, whatever they might later come to think under stress of other pleas and after time for meditation, were at present following him without hint of resistance. They sat quiet and almost motionless, absorbed in every word, their eyes never departing for an instant from his face.

Heartened, he moved on to the theme of suicide. (It had never, of course, been incumbent upon him to offer the jury an alternative solution, but he knew very well that the absence of one would inevitably operate to his client's prejudice.) He recited the now familiar catalogue of Edwin Bartlett's disabilities and woes: the overwork, the illness, the depression, the insomnia, the visits to the dentist, the appearance of the worm. But to these Clarke linked, as a potential climax of the husband's anguish, Mrs. Bartlett's confession about the chloroform. "She told him to what extremities she had been driven, and gave the bottle into his hands. . . . On this night, when he has suffered during the day, when he has undergone this operation, and must undoubtedly have suffered from his condition, he is told by her, substantially, that the consent which he has given with regard to Dyson is regarded by her as an irrevocable decision, that she has taken him at his word."

This led him into a vivid reconstruction of what took place upon that New Year's night. A pictorial gift is invaluable in advocacy; pictures stay in the mind after abstractions disappear; and Clarke's superbly evocative account, rooted in fact but crowned with imagination, must have fought a mighty battle for his client in the jury room. "Suppose," he said, "that Mrs. Bartlett had left the bedroom as usual to wash, and he had placed the bottle of chloroform on the mantelshelf. There was a wineglass there, the glass that was found afterwards, and while she was away it was perfectly easy for him, without leaving his bed, to pour some chloroform into this wineglass and to drink it off. If he swallowed it quickly, there would not be—as there were not— appearances of long exposure of the softer substances of mouth and throat." Thus Clarke took up the point the jury themselves had made.

"Having drunk it, he reassumes his recumbent position; the chloroform passes down his throat and reaches the stomach." (No word, though, of the predicated agony and uproar.) "Within two or three minutes after that he might be passing into a state of coma. . . . Then she herself goes to sleep, and her husband's coma deepens into insensibility, and insensibility passes into death. . . . The hours go by. She has heard them, happier than she, in the other parts of the house speaking to each other of the brighter hopes of the New Year that is beginning, but the first thing she awakens to in that New Year is the sad consciousness that the husband who might not fully have deserved the love that he received, but who, at all events, had treated her with affection, with confidence, with the desire to protect her—she awakens to find that husband apparently cold and dead."

His delivery quickened with the narrative. "She springs to his side. There is close to the end of the mantelshelf—for we know it—the wineglass from which he has taken that fatal draught; the woman's instinct is at once to administer brandy in hopes to restore him. She pours into the glass some brandy and tries to pour it down his throat. I am not sure she does much; with shaking hand she spills some brandy on his chest which the doctor smells afterwards. It is no use; she puts back on the mantelshelf, where it was found when they came into the room, this wineglass with the brandy in it. The landlord, on smelling the glass, may well have detected the odour of chloroform, though it was only brandy it contained."

The momentum of the speech was now almost irresistible. It tore along torrent-wise, engulfing and sweeping forward everything in its path. "There was no scientific miracle worked by the grocer's wife. There was unhappily the putting within reach of a man who was broken by illness, and upon whom there had come this disappointment, there was the putting within his reach of the poison which he might have used, and probably did use; but there was nothing more, and from that moment there was not a word of hers, there was not an action, not a look, which was not the look or the word or the action of the loving wife who had nursed him through his illness to this point, and who now found him suddenly gone for ever."

The end of Clarke's stupendous effort was in sight. For weeks he had worked and lived for Mrs. Bartlett, hardly allowing himself one extraneous thought, but soon he would be powerless to lend her further aid. This was his last chance, and the strong flame of his advocacy burned white as he spoke his final words for the client whom he believed.

"This woman has not had the happiest of lives. She has been described to you as a woman who had no friends. But she had one friend —her husband. In his strange way he stood by her and protected her. He was affectionate, and when her reputation was assailed he defended it as only her husband could. And to her at this moment it may seem most strange that he to whom she had given persistent affection should be the one of whose foul murder she now stands accused. And if he himself could know what passed among us here, how strange, how sorrowful, it might seem to him—how strange that such an accusation should have been formulated and tried in court in spite of the efforts which he made to prevent it—efforts which he perhaps defeated by his own despairing act."

It was a bold and moving image, giving rise to the memorable appeal which was to be his close.

"Gentlemen, that husband has gone, but she is not left without a friend; she will find that friend here today in the spirit which guides your judgment and clears your eyes upon this case. It is a great responsibility for men to be called suddenly from their business and their pleasures to decide upon matters of life and death. I believe that, as a case like this goes on from day to day, there comes into your hearts a deep desire which is in itself a prayer that the spirit of justice may be among us and may guide and strengthen each to play his part. That invocation is never in vain. The spirit of justice is in this court today to comfort and protect her in the hour of her utmost need. That spirit will speak in firm and unfaltering voice when your verdict tells to the whole world that in your judgment Adelaide Bartlett is not guilty."

He had finished, after speaking for close upon five hours. As he sat down the strength ebbed out of him; he felt almost dazed by an onrush of fatigue. He closed his eyes and rested his head for a moment on his hands, barely conscious of a sound seldom heard inside the courts—the billowing thunder of tumultuous applause.

For all practical purposes the trial was at an end. The defence, which from the start had made uninterrupted progress, exceptional in hardfought trials outside the realm of fiction, had now attained the peak. Clarke had started with a case that it was generally expected he would lose. With his cross-examination of Old Bartlett the adverse current, which had been flowing fast, was stemmed. With his cross-examination of the Reverend Dyson, he reversed the tendency and was no longer losing. With Dr. Leach he began to win, though he was not yet winning. With Dr. Stevenson he was winning, though he had not yet won.

The speech clinched all. There was still another night for the jury's second thoughts, there was still another day for argument and review, but the spell of that eloquence persisted unimpaired. Whether they knew it or not, whether they minded or not, the twelve were no longer free to make their own decision.

A thirteenth member had been added to the jury.

This only becomes clear, however, in the light of history. Until the verdict all remained in doubt, and the tension prevailing in the last hours of the trial was even greater than had gone before.

Clarke himself was a prey to deep misgivings. "I do not think," he said afterwards, "that anyone who has not been through it himself can realise the mental strain of the last day of a trial for murder upon counsel for the defence. As he listens to the reply for the Crown, and to the judge's summing-up, he finds little comfort in the thought that he has done his best."

Outwardly calm but with every nerve on edge, the defender perforce sat silent hour by hour in the court that yesterday had been quickened with his voice. He heard Russell's reply, vigorous and pithy, only marred by a last-minute attempt to substitute a brand-new theory of the murder for that which had been so badly blown upon. He heard a careful summing-up of exemplary fairness, though the judge did not disguise his personal opinion that the proper verdict would be to convict. And ever and anon he heard the shouting and the clamour from the huge throng waiting in the streets outside. . . .

The jury retired a few minutes before three. An hour passed, an hour of restless agony. Just before four they came back into their box—but merely to ask the judge to verify some minor points of detail, which being done they once again withdrew.

They were out a further hour. It was precisely five o'clock when the rustling and whispering of an overwrought assembly died upon the instant as the jury reappeared. They bore themselves as men do who have reached a great decision, but what decision few then would have ventured to predict. . . .

The prisoner was brought back into the dock and the figures were disposed for the most nerve-racking of ceremonies. Mrs. Bartlett showed an iron self-control, but it was hard to determine whether she or her counsel looked more white and strained.

The Clerk of the Court rose with due formality.

"Gentlemen, have you agreed upon your verdict?"

"We have," said the foreman.

"Do you find the prisoner guilty or not guilty?"

Nobody breathed. Time stood still. Then the foreman began to read from a sheet of paper.

"We have considered the evidence," he said, "and although we think grave suspicion is attached to the prisoner—"

The qualifying clause told all. A spontaneous cheer went up and could hardly be suppressed.

"—we do not think there is sufficient evidence," the foreman continued, "to show how or by whom the chloroform was administered."

The dock door opened, Mrs. Bartlett stepped forth to freedom, and for the first and last time in his fifty years of practice Edward Clarke broke down in court and wept.

And now the cheers burst forth again, and would not be denied. In vain did the ushers scurry to and fro; in vain did the judge speak of insult and of outrage. His remonstrances were drowned in the ever-growing din, which spread like wildfire through the corridors and courtyard, and was presently being echoed back from the overflowing streets.

This demonstration was not for Mrs. Bartlett. It was Edward Clarke who was the idol of the hour. It was he for whom the jury waited by the steps to shake his hand before he left the court for home; it was he who, as his carriage passed out of the gates, found it surrounded by a demonstrating crowd which ran alongside all the way down Holborn where passers-by called tribute from pavement and from bus; it was he who, on attending a theatre that same evening, was immediately picked out and accorded an ovation.

So in a more leisurely and spacious age than ours was homage paid to the triumph of a great counsel.

For Russell a less exhilarating sequel lay in wait.

Three years later he was to figure in a not dissimilar case that acquired equal notoriety—the trial at Liverpool of Mrs. Florence Maybrick. She too was charged with murdering her husband; she too was alleged to have used poison; she too drew the scientific fire of Dr. Stevenson; she too had to endure a minute scrutiny of her private life. But there was this striking contrast between the plight of the two women: Mrs. Bartlett had Russell ranged against her, Mrs. Maybrick had Russell enlisted on her side. That the evidence against Mrs. Bartlett was stronger than that against Mrs. Maybrick is, in my opinion, not open to doubt. Yet Russell, the most formidable counsel of his day, failed to obtain a conviction against the former and failed to secure an acquittal for the latter.

The one woman was as luckless as the other fortunate. Mrs. Maybrick had cause to curse the fate that gave her a perverse jury and a mentally sick judge. Mrs. Bartlett had cause to bless the gods that laid at her disposal the selfless endeavours and persuasive voice of Edward Clarke.

15

Robert Wood

SINCE the beginning of this century many London districts have completely changed their character. Such is not the case with Camden Town. There are superficial differences, of course, but in essentials it remains what it was in 1907, the year of the murder distinguished by its name. It is a place where underfed and overcrowded thousands wage perpetual battle on the poverty line; where dubious lodging-houses jostle modest homes and working folk commingle with shady fly-by-nights; where squalor animates as it deforms, and lends to ugliness a crude enchantment; where social commerce flourishes in the steamy pubs from which couples, casually met and matched, depart each night at closing time to furtive privacy. It is a place of pungent contrasts—of dull monotony and indiscreet adventure, of dingy greyness and flashy colour, of gay excitement and unrelieved despair. It is a place that provides its own escape from its own horror. It is the poor man's West End.

Even in this restless spot, however, there are backwaters and byways where at least on the surface life is lived at slower tempo. One of these may be found behind Royal College Street by anyone turning eastward at The Eagle. He will pass under some railway arches, dank and cavernous; over a crossing where traffic lights strike a solitary modern note; and thence into a long ascending road along which a few trees import a faintly rustic air. Known as St. Paul's Road in its days of notoriety, this thoroughfare has since been unaccountably re-christened.

The houses in St. Paul's Road now are mostly bruised and battered. A cheerless tale of penury or indifference can be read in the missing gates and broken gateposts, in the numbers rudely chalked on splin-

250

tered doors, in the rubbish dump that fills the space intended for a garden. Few make St. Paul's Road their permanent abode; it is a temporary stop on the way up—or the way down.

In appearance, Twenty-nine does not differ from the rest. It has the same depressing, unattractive air. Children may clamber up and down the steep stone steps; a couple of milk bottles may stand upon the sill; but these indications of harmless domesticity, while tempering the gloom, accentuate the commonplace. Not a house, you would think, to draw anyone's attention, to be worthy of the slightest notice from the passer-by. And yet there are still those who would make a special journey just to gaze on Twenty-nine—and particularly at the window of the first floor front.

That window grips and chills and terrifies. Fancy likes to make of it an eye that constantly looks inwards, scanning the room it has learnt to know so well. The scene there, one imagines, never changes to the Eye; it is frozen into a macabre tableau, and has been so now these many, many years. Whole generations have passed through it un-heeded—have lived, loved, quarrelled, worked and died; to the Eye they were but phantoms, it is the tableau that is real.

You and I, if privileged to penetrate this room, might see a large family at the ritual of tea; the Eye sees only empty liquor bottles and the broken meats of a supper laid for two. You and I might see a lively bunch of youngsters, playing on the floor with their cheap and simple toys; the Eye sees only the steady drip of blood, soaking through the bed into the boards below. You and I might see a genteel widow, toast-ing at the fire, while outside beats the hubbub of a golden afternoon; the Eye sees only a torn and naked girl, motionless in the silence and the slate-cold light of dawn.

For the Eye sees the room in which The Murder was committed; the Camden Town Murder that destroyed Phyllis Dimmock and came within an ace of destroying Robert Wood. It is a room that has held its secret more than forty years; a secret shared with none—except the murderer and the Eye.

The women of the streets draw a sharp distinction between prosti-tutes (prompted solely by the profit motive) and whores (who, while not indifferent to monetary reward, practise promiscuity because they relish it).

Phyllis Dimmock was a prostitute who had turned into a whore. Born into respectable poverty at Walworth, and christened more prosaically Emily Elizabeth, she grew up into a pretty, pleasant-mannered girl.

The combination of good looks and bad prospects set her upon a well-worn and platitudinous course. First as a factory worker flirting with her "boys," then as a domestic servant flattered by her "followers," she quickly learnt how to exploit the fascination it was in her power to exercise over the other sex. Economic pressure, combined with youth's predilection for the raffish, ensured that this power was in due course capitalised, and Phyllis abandoned irksome thriftiness for the relative prodigalities of the prostitute's half-world.

Few who tread this demoralising path ever get a chance to retrace any of their steps. Phyllis Dimmock furnished an exception to the rule. At the age of twenty-one, already a veteran of the brothels and the streets, she made the acquaintance of a man named Bertram Shaw, who was employed on the railway as a dining-car attendant. Despite the corrupting effects of her profession, Phyllis still retained considerable charm and Shaw was stirred to more than passing interest. The girl being not unwilling, a liaison was established. Perhaps because of his knowledge of her past, Shaw would not enter into a contractual alliance, but in every respect save that of legal ceremony he conferred on Phyllis Dimmock the status of a wife.

They lived together in modest but agreeable apartments, dividing responsibilities as married couples do. Phyllis got the meals and did the household chores. Shaw earned the money and paid the household bills. It was an orderly existence and, as Shaw was a steady man and genuinely fond of her, Phyllis could look forward to a protracted partnership. Even if the menage was not, technically, respectable, at least it offered her escape from the degrading accompaniments of haphazard harlotry.

But Phyllis, being Phyllis, did not see it in that light. Harlotry was not only a trade, it was a pleasure. The joint home with Bert was quite convenient in its way—as a base, a jumping-off ground, the tranquil centre of a wild and vicious vortex. Though she did not despise the comforts of the new life, she lusted after the excitements of the old.

The nature of Shaw's work presented her with a solution. Most afternoons he went out at four o'clock, travelled north during the evening with his train, slept at Sheffield over night, and travelled back next morning, arriving about noon. This gave Phyllis freedom and immunity during the hours that for her purpose counted most. In one regard she was better off than she had been before; provided that she acted with reasonable caution she had now what her sisterhood refers to as "a place," without the necessity of settling the rent.

So night after night, as the unsuspicious Shaw expertly manœuvred down the rocking restaurant car, Phyllis set forth from the sombre street she lived in, seeking places better served with noise and light— and men.

Her favourite hunting ground was the pavements and the public houses of the Euston Road.

Any one of several reasons may prompt a man to cultivate the company of those whose morals and behaviour are less seemly than his own. It may be curiosity; a consuming thirst for first-hand knowledge of phenomena absent or suppressed in his habitual milieu. It may be titillation; the undeniable stimulus of entering a world where normal values are inverted or annulled. It may be a pernicious taste for coarse debauchery that appears to be endemic among the most fastidious; this weakness is exemplified by Oscar Wilde and Dowson, and has been dramatised by Emlyn Williams and Pinero.

There is reason to surmise that all three motives combined in Robert Wood. He was a well-educated, intelligent young man, with an inquisitive and restless disposition. He had a high degree of talent as an artist and designer, betokening a temperament responsive to impressions. And though he held a well-paid post with a reputable firm, and though he lived with the most virtuous of parents in a middle-class environment of unpretentious worth, from very early manhood Wood had shown a propensity to seek out the companionship of public courtesans.

For some time this propensity was largely satisfied by his association with a girl named Ruby Young—a name that he was presently to make for a brief space almost as familiar and notorious as his own. Ruby described herself as an artist's model, but like numerous other ladies in that estimable profession she spent most of her evenings on the prowl in Leicester Square. Wood was well aware of this; it may indeed have kindled rather than subdued his ardour; certainly he and Ruby maintained a close relationship hardly distinguishable from that of any courting couple—save perhaps in the omission to contemplate a marriage, and in the readiness with which favours were demanded and bestowed.

It was Wood, though, not Ruby who first tired of the arrangement. It seems likely that the kindly, amiable artist had a fancy to inspect more thorough-paced depravity. When at last Ruby moved from Liverpool Street, King's Cross (which was only a few yards from his home off Gray's Inn Road) and withdrew to the less accessible region of Earl's Court, Wood seized the chance to start a gradual cooling off.

He saw Ruby less and less, and frequented more and more a stratum of the half-world in comparison with which the girls of Leicester Square constituted an élite.

His favourite hunting ground was the pavements and the public houses of the Euston Road.

The precise date and hour at which the artist Robert Wood and the harlot Phyllis Dimmock first crossed paths on their common hunting ground was the subject of vigorous contention at the time and can now never be finally determined. It may be that, as some of the girl's associates asserted, it occurred as early as April, 1906, and that thenceforward for a space of eighteen months the pair met frequently on the friendliest of terms. It may be that, as Wood consistently maintained, it did not occur until September,1907, and that their brief acquaintance mainly hinged on fortuitous encounters. Whichever version is accepted, of this there is no doubt: whether by chance or whether by design, Robert Wood was in Phyllis Dimmock's company on four of the last six evenings of her life.

Phyllis was murdered early on Thursday, 12th September. On the previous Friday, Wood was with her at The Rising Sun. On the Saturday he was with her at The Eagle. On the Monday he was with her at The Rising Sun again. On the Wednesday once again he was with her at The Eagle.

On this last occasion they stayed at least an hour. They were not, however, narrowly observed. The bar was full, and others were busy with their own affairs. No one gathered any clue to their precise relationship; no one noticed whether they left singly or together. Even the watchful staff could only say that, before the closing hour, both of them had gone.

That Wednesday night when Phyllis Dimmock stepped out of The Eagle to all intents and purposes she stepped out of this world. A gap begins—a gap in which nothing can be learnt of her actions or companions save by reconstruction both laborious and fallible.

The gap extends for twelve hours; then terminates abruptly.

At half-past eleven on the morning of the Thursday, Bertram Shaw, refreshed by his short walk from St. Pancras, came striding briskly up the slope of St. Paul's Road. He was in excellent spirits. His train had been on time. The day had turned out sunny. His afternoon was free.

He whistled as he trotted up the steps of Twenty-nine, latchkey in hand, ready to open the front door.

Usually Phyllis ran downstairs to greet him. Instead the landlady met him in the hall.

"Oh, Mr. Shaw," she said, "your mother's just arrived."

His mother lived some sixty miles off at Northampton, and her advent in London was entirely unexpected. She had in fact made the journey on a sudden impulse, being eager to inspect the lately acquired "wife" whom her son had mentioned in his letters.

The Fates never acted with more cynical brutality than in prompting the poor lady to choose that very day. . . .

"I'll go right up," Shaw said.

"She's below," said the landlady. "I took her to my room."

"Why?" Shaw asked.

"Because," said the landlady, "we can't get into yours."

Shaw looked puzzled, as he was; puzzled and inquiring; but before he could give his perplexities a shape his mother had appeared and hurried to embrace him. The reunion banished the matter from his mind.

"Come up and meet Phyllis," he said, without a qualm.

Chattering lightheartedly they climbed the stairs together.

The apartment Shaw and Phyllis shared consisted of two rooms, linked and divided by a pair of folding doors. They had a key to these and to the door on to the landing, but it was not their habit to lock either.

Shaw tried the landing door and found it would not open. He rattled the handle. He banged upon the panels. He called Phyllis's name, loudly and repeatedly. He pressed his ear to the narrow slit and listened. Inside there was not a stirring, not a breath.

All Shaw's unformed misgivings now returned in sharper outline. Leaving his mother bewildered, he tore downstairs again. In a moment he was back with the landlady's spare key.

What Shaw expected to see when the door opened depended on his idiosyncratic mental make-up. Each of us in such circumstances fashions his own nightmare.

What Shaw actually saw was but the prelude to a nightmare. The sitting-room had been incontinently ravished; furniture shifted, drawers upset, the contents overturned. But there was no human occupant —none, alive or dead. Beyond, the folding doors stood shut, blankly non-committal.

They also were locked. But Shaw had grown too apprehensive to be patient. He used his sturdy shoulders and cracked the doors by force.

It was then that he saw what he must now have feared to see; the nightmare itself, stark and unforgettable.

The police moved fast. In a matter of hours they believed themselves on the verge of an arrest.

All their data pointed in the same direction. The medical evidence —based on the advance of rigor mortis—fixed the girl's death between four o'clock and six. Nothing suggested that there had been a struggle; her face was peaceful; her body lay at ease. And since Shaw could produce an alibi from his colleagues and employers; and since enquiries soon established beyond a shadow of a doubt that Phyllis had been bringing men home almost every night, smuggling them in after the landlady's retirement and smuggling them out again early in the morning, the police were irresistibly impelled to this conclusion—that it was one of these stray visitors who had murdered Phyllis Dimmock; taking her unawares—maybe as she slept—and, with one tremendous slash from a sharp and powerful weapon, cutting her throat from ear to ear right back to the spine.

So investigation turned to the taverns she had haunted and among whose patrons she had angled for admirers. Foremost among these was The Rising Sun, and here straightaway the police came upon a man acutely conscious of his own predicament.

He was a ship's cook, lately paid off from a voyage. In accordance with the mariner's immemorial tradition, he had set out to spend his accumulated wealth upon a round of amorous conviviality. In pursuit of this aim, he fell in with Phyllis Dimmock, meeting her first in Euston Road on Sunday, 8th September. The couple having made themselves sufficiently acquainted, they drank together in The Rising Sun; thereafter the ship's cook escorted Phyllis to her rooms, where he remained with her till seven the next morning. This programme proved so profitable to one and so enjoyable to both that it was repeated on the two succeeding nights. . . .

Sunday, Monday, Tuesday.

"And Wednesday?" the police asked.

"Oh no," said the ship's cook, instantly defensive. "I never saw her Wednesday; not after I left her at her place in the morning."

"Where were you Wednesday night?"

"In The Rising Sun," the ship's cook answered promptly. "But Phyllis wasn't there; she didn't come in all night. I stayed till after twelve; anyone'll tell you that."

"And where did you go from there?"

"To the place where I'd been stopping; it's a temperance hotel. I walked back with a friend—a chap; he was staying there too. The old girl let us in and she locked the front door after us."

"What's the name of the hotel?"

He told them, and they hurried off to verify his statement. It was confirmed and vouched for by unchallengeable witnesses. Had it been otherwise the ship's cook might have paid high for his pleasures—in the shape of a trial and maybe a conviction. It would not have been the first time that an innocent man was hanged.

As it was, the police acknowledged the inevitable and crossed off the only name upon their list of suspects. They may be pardoned if they did so with professional reluctance. For lately the ship's cook had almost monopolised the girl and thus reduced the number of potential candidates. In those last few days, what other men had been around with Phyllis?

Some frequenters of The Rising Sun did speak of a man: a man with a long, thin face and sunken eyes; a well-spoken man; a man of education. He had been in with her more than once, they said, in the days before the murder; but they had never seen him since and did not know who he was.

Wood worked hard to make certain that they never should. As the Camden Town mystery filled the columns of the press and excited speculation both in public and in private, the artist with the long thin face and sunken eyes took steps to cover up the tracks that linked him with the victim.

Provided he kept well away from Camden Town there was only one person he had valid cause to fear. That was Joseph Lambert, a bookseller's assistant, whom he knew on pleasant terms but only seldom met. By an irony of the Fates (different in kind but comparable in degree to that which timed the visit paid by Mrs. Shaw to London), one of these rare meetings between Wood and Lambert had occurred in the bar of The Eagle public house on the evening of Wednesday, the 11th of September. Lambert had dropped in by chance. Wood was with Phyllis. He introduced her by her first name to his friend, and before Lambert left they all had a drink together.

Nine days later, when photographs of Phyllis were appearing in the papers, Wood called at the shop where Lambert worked. He took the latter aside and asked him if he had heard about the Camden Town affair. "Yes." said Lambert, "I have, but what about it?" He had not, after all, recognised the photographs, and was somewhat mystified that

Wood should seek him out for an idle conversation about a shocking crime.

Wood might have refrained from committing himself further. But the hue and cry was dangerously insistent; at any moment more and better pictures might be published; Lambert's enlightenment might only be postponed. Better that his friend should hear who Phyllis was from him—and hear at the same time his reasoned plea for silence.

He went straight to the point.

"I want you to do me a favour. That night I saw you in the pub—last week—remember?" Lambert stared, nonplussed by Wood's urgency of manner. "Well, if anyone says anything to you about it, say we met and had a drink. But leave out the girl."

"Leave out the girl," Lambert repeated.

"Yes," said Wood.

Lambert cast his mind back. He recalled that curious meeting at The Eagle, and the little group the three of them had formed; himself, Wood and the girl—the girl, on whom he had never since bestowed a single thought. He had forgotten her; she whom he was being entreated to forget. His response was human; he tried to recollect her. Tall, slender, a rather pretty face. . . . *Have you heard about the Camden Town affair?*

The two men looked steadily at one another. No word passed; but at that moment Lambert knew—and Wood perceived he knew.

"She was Phyllis," the latter said at last. "That girl was Phyllis Dimmock."

"Yes," Lambert said. There didn't seem anything else to say.

"Of course, I don't want to get mixed up in this affair," Wood continued. "Think of the publicity. Think of my people."

Lambert did so. He thought of Wood's father, lately in poor health; thought of how he would take a public revelation that his well-respected son had been a prostitute's familiar. With the gentle and likeable Robert Wood before him no theme more sinister entered Lambert's head.

"I can rely on you?" Wood asked.

"That'll be all right," Lambert said.

Wood pressed his hand and left. . . .

But this was only the negative side of Robert Wood's precautions. On the positive side he enlisted his old sweetheart, Ruby Young.

Ruby Young was in love with Robert Wood. She had been so from the start; she remained so to the end; it complicated equally her actions and reactions, and drew her, unwilling, to the center of the stage. She is indeed the third tragic figure in this drama, and her sufferings, though less conspicuous and fearsome, are not one whit less pitiful than the sufferings of the pair that underwent a crucifixion more spectacular.

By the September of Phyllis Dimmock's murder, Wood's alliance with Ruby Young was virtually quiescent. A quarrel in July about another woman—Ruby was inclined to be jealous and possessive—precipitated a breach that had already been foreshadowed. Since then they had only seen each other once, and that through an accidental meeting in the street. But Ruby still hankered after her former flame and when, out of the blue, on the 20th of September she received a telegram asking her to meet him at their old rendezvous, she decked herself out in all her finery and went to the appointed place in pleasurable elation.

Wood's greeting was flatteringly warm, but his subsequent behaviour proved a little disconcerting. He showed gallantry, affection, remorse for his neglect—but seemed to be obsessed by an undisclosed anxiety. He could hardly wait till they had sat down in the teashop before he appealed to her to help him in his "trouble."

"But what sort of trouble is it?" Ruby asked.

"Remember this," he said, side-stepping the query: "if any questions should be put to you, say you always saw me on Mondays and on Wednesdays." He patted her arm tenderly. "On Mondays and Wednesdays. Will you?"

"But what for?" she demanded.

"Will you do it?" he said.

Ruby felt resentful. If he didn't trust her, if he didn't want to tell her what he had been up to—very well, he needn't; that was as he liked; but then why should she put herself out to help? "And it's sure to be something to do with a girl," she bitterly reflected.

"Will you do it?" Wood repeated gently.

It was on the very tip of Ruby's tongue to say she wouldn't—and thereby to save them both unutterable torment. But as she looked at him, her mood suddenly changed. Here was the way to conciliate the loved one; once she had this hold upon him he would have to see her— see her often to make sure of her goodwill. "And if I can only see him," Ruby thought with the female's timeless faith, "if I can only see him, I know I'll win him back."

"Well," said Wood, "will you do this for me?"

Ruby heaved a sigh.

"Oh, all right," she said. . . .

Having muzzled truth and sown the seeds of falsehood, Wood could face the future with less disquietude. Day by day he went about his business, patiently waiting for the tumult to die down.

So it might well have done had not the ship's cook, dead end of one trail, opened up another.

He told the police a story that could not be disregarded. Before he left Phyllis on the Wednesday morning—after the third and last of his nightly visits—he had picked up a letter that had come with the post and been thrust under her door. She took it, read it, then showed part of it to him. That part he remembered. "Dear Phyllis," it had run. "Will you meet me at the bar of The Eagle at Camden Town 8.30 tonight, Wednesday—Bert." He was sure about that; sure of the very words— just as he was sure that Phyllis had struck a match, set fire to the letter, and thrown it in the grate.

What impressed the police most about this revelation was the fact that it could be at least partially confirmed. Some charred paper had been salvaged from the grate, and such writing as could be deciphered seemed corroborative. One could say no more than that; it was too vestigial to be read consecutively—or to furnish a fair sample of the correspondent's hand.

There remained, however, a further chance of coming by the latter, and here once again the ship's cook was instrumental. Phyllis had had a hobby; she collected picture postcards, most of which she kept in a big, old-fashioned album. She had shown him one such card, the ship's cook said, immediately after she had let him see the letter. At her prompting he had read the message written on it—another, not dis- similar, request for an appointment, somewhat unexpectedly signed with the name "Alice," and charmingly embellished, by whoever sent it, with an expert little pencil drawing of a rising sun. The ship's cook was certain that the writing on postcard and letter were the same.

The police could now indulge in an attractive chain of reasoning. If you knew who wrote the postcard, you would know who wrote the letter. If you knew who wrote the letter, you would know who was with Phyllis on Wednesday at The Eagle. If you knew who was with Phyllis on Wednesday at The Eagle, you would know who took her home. And if you knew who took her home . . .

This chain might not seem flawless to a trained logician, but in a case almost devoid of other clues it made a hopeful basis for renewed investigation, or would have done if the police had not been frustrated from the outset.

The postcard itself was nowhere to be found.

Methodically they sifted the contents of the album—pathetic little trophies of a brief and sordid life; mostly contributed by sometime paramours dispersed among the ports and docks and barracks of the world. There were cheap comic cards, cheap sentimental cards, cards with ardent postscripts, cards with waggish innuendoes—but none that was signed "Alice" and none that had been decorated with a rising sun.

The police thought they knew why. Indeed, the very absence of the postcard might explain a feature of the crime that had been so far inexplicable. When Shaw burst through the folding doors that morning he found the shutters of the bedroom window incompletely closed; the gap admitted a narrow shaft of light trained exactly on the dead girl's sewing machine. On the top of that machine was the album, lying open; some of the cards lay scattered on the floor below it. It now seemed nearly certain that, before he left, the murderer had recalled to mind the card that might betray him, that might serve as proof of his connection with the girl; that he had had the nerve to search for it, the good fortune to find it, and the prudence to destroy it or take it out of reach. . . .

Another trail was closed. The days passed. The tumult lessened, and at last began to die.

Bertram Shaw was packing up. He had not slept here since the night it happened; always up North, or at an hotel, or with friends. Now, thank God, he had got another place.

He packed rapidly, keen to get it over. Shirts, his weekend suit, some personal belongings—he crammed them into the bag just as they came to hand. Phyllis's few possessions had already been removed. Soon no visible trace remained of either to show that they had ever occupied the room—except a sorrel stain which no scrubbing would erase.

Shaw took a quick look round to make sure nothing had been left. Mindful how small articles like studs and links secrete themselves, he felt under the paper lining of the drawers. He found no studs nor links; only a picture postcard, signed with the name "Alice," and charmingly embellished, by whoever sent it, with an expert little pencil drawing of a rising sun.

The flagging hounds revived; once more the hunt was up. Next Sunday, at the wish of Scotland Yard, a replica of the postcard was displayed in national newspapers, backed by an appeal to the civic

spirit of anyone who might chance to recognise the writing. Reinforcing this inducement, one enterprising paper made an offer of one hundred pounds reward.

One may wonder whether there has ever been another postcard
delivered to the breakfast table of so many millions. They studied it
with the care befitting its credentials ("believed to have direct bearing
on the case of Phyllis Dimmock"); examining the postmark ("9 Sept.
4 a.m."); reading and re-reading the now notorious address (Mrs. B.
Shaw, 29 St. Paul's Road, Camden Town"); brooding over the seemingly innocuous invitation ("Phyllis darling, if it pleases you, meet me
8.15 p.m. at the—" and there the words gave way to the celebrated
drawing: a perky, rather bibulous sun coming over the horizon, one
eye closed in a Rabelaisian wink); musing solemnly on the facetious
close ("Yours to a cinder, Alice").

Fired with the zeal of amateur detectives, eager to assist in track-
ing down a malefactor, the millions were baffled; they did not know
the writing.

But Ruby Young knew it—knew it the moment her eye fell upon
the paper.

"It *is* your writing, isn't it?" she said, even before the front door had
been closed.

"Of course it is," Wood answered.

He spoke almost lightly, but Ruby shrank back as if she had been
struck.

"Why have you come? What has happened?" she whispered. "Oh,
Bob, what have you done?"

Wood smiled reassuringly.

"Have patience," he said. "Let's go up to your room, and I will tell
you all."

Ruby had passed through a day of mental torture, beset by thoughts
she hardly dared to form. The newspaper, unread, was folded back
to show the postcard, and every few minutes she stared at it again.
So this was the "trouble" in which Wood had sought her help; this was
why she had to say she always saw him Wednesdays; this, too, was
the reason for his renewed attentiveness—the kisses, the gifts, the
visit to the play. He had been keeping the right side of her, fostering
her devotion, using every trick to make his shield secure.

Not even fear and horror and foreboding insulate a woman from
the pangs of wounded pride. . . .

She sat down and waited. He paced about a little, then suddenly began.

"Ruby, it's just sheer bad luck," he said. "I'd only met the girl a week before, and all we ever did was pass the time of day. I was nothing to her and she was nothing to me."

"Then why," Ruby asked, "did you send her a postcard asking her to meet you?"

"I didn't," Wood exclaimed. "That's the terrible part about it. It was meant as a joke." He shook his head slowly. "It all happened on the Friday before . . . before the murder: meeting her, and the postcard, and everything."

He stopped, as if to see whether he was being heard with sympathy.

"Go on," Ruby said.

"I was with a friend of mine and, entirely by chance, we went in The Rising Sun. There was a girl there; she asked me for a coin to start the electric organ. I gave her one, and—well, naturally, next time I was ordering I stood her a friendly drink."

"And that was Phyllis Dimmock?" Ruby asked.

"I just knew her name was Phyllis; you know what it is in a pub."

"And you'd never seen her before?"

"Never in my life."

"What about the postcard?"

"I was just coming to that. After my friend left—he had to catch his train—a boy selling postcards came into the bar. They were rubbishy stuff, and I happened to have some really good ones in my pocket—some I'd brought back from my holiday at Bruges. So when I saw Phyllis was going to buy one from the boy I suggested she choose one of mine instead. She had a look at them, she picked one out, and she said, 'That's pretty; send it me and write something nice on it.' "

"How did you know where to send it?"

"She dictated her address."

"And why did you write . . . what you did?"

Wood ran a hand through his hair.

"Well, Ruby, what *was* I to write? Something nice, she said. I used the first thing that came into my head. Before my friend left I'd arranged to meet him again at The Rising Sun, so I wrote down the words of that appointment, and drew a picture to make it more amusing. It didn't seem to matter. I was going to sign my name, only she said, 'Don't; the governor might cut up rough; put "Alice"—that's the name of a woman that I know.' I put 'Alice,'" Wood said, throwing wide his arms, "and now you know the story of this miserable post-card that looks as though it's going to bring me to my ruin."

Ruby's heart was growing lighter. He didn't do it, then; of course he didn't do it; her deepest instincts had told her all along. He was the prey of circumstances, and as such to be pitied—but he was still not absolved for his duplicity with her.

"What happened next?" she said, coldly inquisitorial.

"I hadn't a stamp," Wood said, and smiled forlornly, "so I said I'd post it later. I finished my drink, I said good night, and I walked out of the pub."

"Did you see her again?"

"I saw her on Saturday—next day. I was up in Camden Town, on business, and I met her in the street. She said, 'You haven't sent my postcard,' and she was right, I hadn't; truth to tell, I'd forgotten the whole thing. I promised I would, and we talked for a bit, and then I left her. I posted the card next night."

"Did you see her again?"

Wood hesitated.

"Once more—on the Monday. She was in The Rising Sun. She came over to speak to me; I stood her a drink; then she said goodbye and joined some other men. That was the last time—the last time I ever saw her."

"She was murdered on the night of the Wednesday," Ruby said. Her voice was strained.

"I know." Wood looked graver now than he had done throughout. "I know, Ruby. That's why you must stand by me. I was out walking by myself that Wednesday night, and I can't bring anyone to prove just where I was. *You must say I was with you.*"

There was a pause. They were both very still and quiet.

"It might get me into dreadful trouble," Ruby said, "if other people proved that I was . . . somewhere else."

"No, no," Wood insisted. "Your word and mine together, we can defy the world."

"If you went to Scotland Yard—" Ruby began.

"—they wouldn't believe me. Not without a witness." He sat down beside her. "I know I can trust you, Ruby."

"I'm not the only one who knows your writing," Ruby said.

"They won't spot it at home," Wood said, "and you're the only other one who knows it well enough." He put his arm about her. "You'll be my own girl, won't you? Promise me, dear? Promise?"

Ruby gazed straight ahead.

"I promise," she said at last, and her lip began to quiver as the burden of the day's events grew more than she could bear.

During the months that were to come Ruby Young was widely regarded as a female Judas. This judgment—based in part upon the incorrect assumption that she had betrayed Wood for the newspaper reward—was wickedly unjust to one taxed beyond her strength. Initially she did more for Wood than could have been expected. Having given her promise, she was resolved to keep it; having entered into conspiracy, she meant it to succeed; and it was actually Ruby, not Robert Wood himself, who constructed in detail the mendacious alibi. That she later was the cause of Wood's exposure is a fact; that she became so deliberately is unwarrantable inference. Hers was not a case of broken faith, but of breaking nerve.

There were two phases in the process of attrition. At first she was in a continuous state of dread lest someone else should have recognised the writing. But in this respect Wood's optimistic surmise proved well founded; no one else apparently formed even a suspicion—except one business colleague, a Mr. Tinkham, who was satisfied when Wood gave him the selfsame explanation, and about whom Ruby Young did not even hear. But as her justifiable and substantial fears receded Ruby conceived others, not less grim because less tangible; fears of some unforeseeable contingency in which they themselves would effect their own undoing. Her distress was not diminished by Wood's understandable but harassing insistence on their compact. "Be true," he would adjure her each time that they met. "Yes, yes," she would say, "but don't bother me; it's getting on my nerves."

Ruby's ultimate concession to this pressure followed precedents established by her sex. She sought the solace of a confidant. Her choice was unwise—indeed, calamitous. Thinly disguising it as someone else's story which was being presented for its academic interest, the foolish girl recounted the whole episode to a man whom she described as "one of my gentleman friends." This friend in turn had a friend who was a pressman; next day the latter was brought into this oblique discussion; he grasped its real significance—and also its potential value to himself. Almost before Ruby realised what she had done she found herself being questioned by an officer from the Yard.

There was then no alternative; she had already gone too far; Ruby had to admit that she knew Robert Wood to be the author of the postcard. But as full comprehension of her grievous blunder dawned, and she foresaw the consequences it might have for Wood, the anguish of remorse completely overcame her. She could not go on; she could tell them nothing more.

For the police, however, that was temporarily enough. Dropping dark hints about what can happen to accessories—especially accessories who don't repent in time—that afternoon they took Ruby with them to wait for Wood as he came out from his work.

It was a painful scene. The girl, half stunned by now with misery and terror, stood near the office door in accordance with her orders. The police kept watch from a short distance away. When Wood appeared, Ruby, leaden-footed, moved into his path.

He smiled at the sight of her.

"Sweetheart," he said, and put his arm through hers, "this is nice. I'm glad to see you. You're pale, though; what's the matter? You've not been crying, have you?"

Ruby almost choked.

"Of course not," she said. "I . . . I'm all right."

"Well, you look a bit downhearted," Wood said chaffingly. "Come on, we'll go and have some tea and cheer you up."

Still arm in arm, they walked along together. A burly man came from an alley opposite and moved towards them purposefully. Wood tightened his grip on Ruby's arm.

"See that fellow there?" he muttered. "I believe he's a detective."

"Take no notice," Ruby said. She was going through it compulsively, as one does through a bad nightmare.

The burly man approached.

"Mr. Wood?" he asked.

"Yes," said Wood.

"I am a police inspector and I wish to speak to you."

"Certainly," said Wood.

The two men withdrew a little.

"I've been making enquiries into the murder of Phyllis Dimmock," the inspector said, "and I have reason to believe that a postcard sent to her was written by you."

"Quite right," said Wood.

"Then I shall have to detain you pending enquiries into your movements on the night of 11th September."

Wood was perfectly calm. Had he not an unassailable alibi?

"Very well," he said. "You will allow me to say goodbye to my young lady?"

The inspector nodded. Wood went to Ruby and took her in his arms.

"I have to go with him," he said. "Don't worry, dear."

Ruby was like stone.

"Goodbye," he said again, and kissed her on the lips.

It broke her strange, somnambulistic trance. She began to sob, loudly, hysterically, clinging to him as though she would never let him go.

"Don't cry," he whispered, greatly touched. "Don't cry. But be true, dearest. Be true."

Wood's belief that Ruby would be "true" led him still deeper into the morass. Invited to recount how he had spent the evening on 11th September, he strictly adhered to their concocted alibi. He told the police that he had been out with "Miss Ruby Young, my sweetheart"; that they had had tea together in a Holborn café; that they had afterwards strolled about in the West End; that it was late before he parted from her outside Brompton Oratory—all upon the confident assumption that Ruby, when questioned, would tell this story too.

But meantime the police were hard at work on Ruby, who was pitifully demoralised and almost unresisting. Between passionate storms of weeping she confessed what had been done, and Wood's carefully plotted alibi became a boomerang.

The whole flock of lies and subornations and suppressions now came home to roost. The police discovered Lambert. They discovered Tinkham. And from the former—as Wood's friend, an unimpeachable source —they learnt that their man had been with Phyllis on Wednesday at The Eagle. . . .

On the 6th October—two days after his original detention—Robert Wood was formally charged with murder. His employers instantly and generously donated a handsome sum earmarked to meet the expense of briefing counsel. His solicitor was thus without restriction in his choice; he could select the man best fitted to the task; and so was brought into the case its most potent element—the giant personality of Edward Marshall Hall.

The legend of Marshall Hall is the strongest ever woven round a figure at the Bar. With his impressive height, handsome face and superbly stalwart bearing, his burning eloquence, selfless courage and manifest sincerity, he fulfilled, better than any before or since, the popular conception of the ideal advocate. As Spilsbury in his time was undeniably The Pathologist, so Marshall Hall was undeniably The Barrister—and for many so remains, and so will remain for ever. When history is forgotten, legend is remembered.

No purist, shocked by Marshall Hall's unorthodox performances, can blot out or invalidate the long tale of his triumphs. To specify the gifts he lacked is to stress those he possessed. One should not, therefore, hesitate to say that there were serious flaws in his technical equipment. One might disregard an imperfect acquaintance with the law, which he never attempted to disguise, and which was not a major handicap in his usual sphere of work. But even as an all-round jury advocate he never reached the very highest rank—that sparsely tenanted and exclusive rank where Russell, Carson and Rufus Isaacs stand. Marshall Hall fell short of these because he suffered the defects of his great qualities. The eloquence could degenerate into indiscreet loquacity; the courage could induce a mood of fierce recklessness; the absolute belief in the cause for which he fought could lead to quarrels with an unsympathetic bench and to bitter feuds with influential parties —quarrels and feuds that did not always serve his client while frequently inflicting injury on himself.

This made Marshall Hall a variable and uncertain asset in ordinary cases—even when playing his destined rôle of criminal defender. But there was one situation that hardly ever failed to evoke his highest powers, and in which he surpassed most of those who were otherwise his superiors. Place him in a trial where the outcome must depend upon probing and interpreting the springs of human conduct, put into his care the interests of a prisoner struggling in the net of State or circumstance, make the prospects dark and the stake his client's life— and then Marshall Hall could be a champion beyond praise. In such an atmosphere and such a setting his faults appeared trivial, his virtues magnified; errors of tact or judgment were offset and wiped out by his magnetic intensity and dynamic force. Marshall Hall was at his best where some are at their worst—fighting back to the wall in a dramatic murder case.

That he should take up Robert Wood's defence was altogether fitting, but that he would be offered the opportunity was no foregone conclusion. For several years, as a result of friction with the appellate courts and a long-standing conflict with a newspaper proprietor, Marshall Hall had been in comparative eclipse, and though by 1907 his fortunes were reviving he had not yet regained his former eminence.

It so happened, however, that Wood's solicitor was one of his staunch adherents. He took the course suggested by both loyalty and sense, and presently Marshall Hall, zealously assisted by the young men in his chambers, was delving deep into the details of the case—the case which (says Edward Marjoribanks, his biographer) was to restore him to his old position at the Bar.

It is obvious why the trial of Robert Wood caused a tremendous popular sensation. It is not, however, easy to see why—unlike most sensational murder trials—it became a fashionable society event. No member of the clergy was involved, as in the earlier case of Mrs. Bartlett. No member of the wealthy classes was accused, as in the later case of Mrs. Barney. There have been settings as shocking, crimes as grisly, mysteries as inscrutable—and the modish world has been content to read of them in the papers. But a desire to attend this trial, to be present in person at the Old Bailey, gripped the best derived and the most distinguished.

The court, in consequence, presented an unusual spectacle. When on the first morning Marshall Hall took his seat in counsels' row and cast a quick glance round him, he found that his eyes could hardly turn to any spot without lighting on some celebrated face. Leading actors, like George Alexander; leading novelists, like Hall Caine; leading playwrights, like Pinero; leading journalists, like George R. Sims; dozens of nameless and yet well-established figures from the landscape of St. James's Street and the pages of Debrett—they squeezed against each other in uncomfortable congestion, and their presence somehow added to the tensions that had drawn them.

No one felt these tensions so much as Marshall Hall. At all times a man of highly strung temperament, with nerves of almost morbid sensitivity, he reacted to the strain of a capital defence more perhaps than any other advocate. This was one reason—maybe not the least— why he generally excelled in conducting such defences; his own emotions grew so heavily charged that they doubled and trebled his impact on the jury. It is also a reason why he was prone on such occasions to indulge in outbursts of anger and excitement; the smallest episode, immaterial and irrelevant—a whisper overheard, the grimace of a spectator—might have entirely incalculable effects upon a man keyed up to such abnormal heights.

In the trial of Wood, partly because of its intrinsic characteristics, partly because of the atmosphere created by the audience, Marshall Hall was keyed up to these heights before the start. He maintained himself upon them throughout six arduous days, and the results—in every way—were what might have been expected.

As leading counsel instructed for the Crown, Sir Charles Mathews was for those six days the defender's chief opponent.

In appearance and physical endowments Mathews might have served as Marshall Hall's antithesis. He was short, in contrast with the other's towering stature; spare and slight as his adversary was massive; unenvied possessor of a high-pitched voice that grated unpleasantly on the cultivated ear. Even so, his quality as an advocate was high. He had a lucid mind, a firm grasp of essentials, an immense capacity for assimilating facts. In an age when cross-examination still ranked as an art, Mathews was one of its most notable exponents. Moreover, he and Marshall Hall, otherwise such opposites, shared one gift of immeasurable importance. Each had a strong yet subtle sense of drama. Marshall Hall backed his with his natural advantages; Mathews backed his with his natural defects. The crouch which gave him a semblance of the dwarfish; the draping of the black gown upon the spindly form; the skilful use of that diabolical voice so that it rose on words like "kill" and "death" to a bloodcurdling shriek—these were not to be despised among the attributes that had made Charles Mathews leader of the Old Bailey Bar. Marshall Hall was the last man to underestimate him.

One who was by nature so prone to histrionics might easily have made an over-zealous prosecutor. But though colourful in style, Mathews knew how to be fair, and his opening address was moderately couched. None the less, it was a formidable indictment. The Rising Sun postcard, the fragments of the letter, the lies, the false alibi, the tampering with witnesses—these, as ingredients of a single composition, acquired a force far greater than their sum as separate parts. They produced an effect upon that overcrowded court hardly diminished by Mathews's acknowledgment that there was ample testimony to Wood's good character—especially as the prosecutor did not deny himself a slightly acid comment. "Whether those who thought so highly of him," he said, "knew the way in which he spent his leisure time is doubtful."

These already familiar inculpations did not exhaust the Crown's case against the prisoner. It was proposed to put the issue wholly beyond doubt; in due course the jury would hear the evidence of a man who, shortly before five o'clock on the morning of the murder, *had seen Robert Wood leaving Phyllis Dimmock's house.* "His name is Robert MacCowan," Mathews said. "He is a carman, who was unemployed and had gone out early that day in the hope of finding work. As he went up St. Paul's Road he saw a man coming out of Twenty-nine. MacCowan doesn't pretend that he could see his face, but he noticed an odd peculiarity in his gait—a curious jerk of the shoulders as he walked—and this peculiarity held MacCowan's attention. . . . Now the accused has just such a peculiarity in his walk. The police will tell you that. Ruby Young will tell you that. And several weeks later, at an identification parade, as soon as the men assembled were required to walk, MacCowan without hesitation picked out Robert Wood. 'There,' he said, 'that is the walk of the man I saw that morning.' . . ."

To Marshall Hall, as he sat listening to that unmelodious and yet compelling voice, the shape of his own tasks became clearer momentarily. First, he must convince the jury that all Wood's desperate and dishonest efforts to conceal his association with the girl might feasibly be ascribed to a natural anxiety that no one should know the kind of company he kept. Secondly, he must convince them that the burnt pieces of paper from the grate (although it could not be denied that they bore his client's handwriting) were not necessarily part of a letter of assignation—nor indeed part of any letter at all. Finally, he must knock MacCowan right out of the case.

By his very first intervention in the trial Marshall Hall began to move towards fulfilment of this latter aim.

Mathews hurtled to a strident climax and sat down. His junior rose and called the name of Arthur Grosse. A plainclothes detective, carrying some papers, progressed importantly to the witness-box.

It is customary for a prosecution to introduce its formal evidence first. Photographers and surveyors prove their photographs and plans; officers specially detailed for the purpose tender the fruits of their expert observations. There is thus often created, between prologue and first act, an unintentional but marked breathing space in which spectators can relax, counsel scan their notes and reporters thankfully rest their aching wrists.

But in the trial of Wood such intermission was short-lived. While Mr. Grosse apprised his lordship and the jury that it was precisely one mile three hundred and eighteen yards from Twenty-nine, St. Paul's Road, to The Rising Sun, and that opposite Twenty-nine, parallel with the street, was a railway siding lighted up by arc lamps, Marshall Hall was seen to be studying intently a copy of a plan that the witness had put in. The more he gazed on it the darker grew his brow. Now and again, with a gesture of displeasure, he would point out some particular feature to his juniors.

When Mr. Grosse ran out of information and junior counsel for the Crown had no more to ask, Marshall Hall withheld the usual gesture of dismissal. Instead he stood up and confronted Mr. Grosse with an expression on his face that was far from cordial. The reporters instinctively again picked up their pencils.

"When was this plan prepared?" asked Marshall Hall. The ring of challenge in his voice was plain.

"Last week," said Mr. Grosse.

"Was the object of it to show how the light from the railway lamps affected St. Paul's Road?"

"It was."

"Do you think this is a fair plan?"

"I do."

"What?" Marshall Hall shook Mr. Grosse's work contemptuously. "I put it to you, have you ever seen a more misleading plan in your life?"

The detective withdrew into complacent silence. "Shout away," his look implied; "you won't get anywhere with me."

"Wouldn't anybody, looking at this plan, conclude that the light from the railway siding was reflected on the front of Twenty-nine?"

"Not on the front," said Mr. Grosse, "but in the neighbourhood."

"Look at it!" Marshall Hall commanded. "Look at it, sir! Is there anything to show that on the opposite side of the road, between the siding and Twenty-nine, there stands a continuous row of dwelling houses?"

"It is not continuous."

"Not continuous? Do you say that there are not houses all the way along?"

"They are in pairs," said Mr. Grosse. "There are spaces in between."

"But from the optical point of view," put in the judge, "would the line not be continuous?"

"Yes," Mr. Grosse reluctantly admitted.

"Of course!" Marshall Hall cried heatedly. "And therefore the only light would have to be projected above the building and down into the street. Wouldn't it? . . . Wouldn't it?"

It took Mr. Grosse some time again to answer yes.

"There is a tree right in front of Twenty-nine?"

"Yes."

"You know that, on the morning of the 12th September, the street lamps were extinguished before twenty to five?"

"Yes."

"So if MacCowan was there just before five the street lamps would be out?"

"Yes."

"Yes." The defender's voice was very hard. "And, that being so, you were specially asked, weren't you, to prepare a map that would show sufficient light to be coming from the railway—the railway which is forty feet below the level of the road?"

Mr. Grosse was once more silent, but his complacency had gone. The body blows now landed thick and fast.

"Have you heard it was a dark and muggy morning?"

"Yes."

"That would reduce the reflecting power of the arc lamps to a minimum?"

"Yes."

"Is there by the railway a wall that's nine feet high?"

"Yes."

"Is that shown on the plan?"

"No."

Marshall Hall, who all this time had been holding the plan stretched out between his hands, now crumpled it up and threw it pointedly aside. . . .

By this cross-examination he achieved a dual effect. He had not only prepared the way for discrediting MacCowan. He had also in some measure discredited the Crown. Their very first piece of evidence had made a bad impression; if not actually manufactured and contrived, it appeared deliberately prejudicial and tendentious. Henceforward the jury could never repose full faith in the prosecution's impartiality. Their suspicions were aroused; they were on their guard, taking nothing upon trust; they were far more receptive than they might otherwise have been to Marshall Hall's subsequent charges of distortion and mis-statement.

One doubts whether there has ever been a trial of similar prominence in which cross-examination of an apparently formal witness gave the defence such a brilliant flying start. It is an example to advocates —and a warning to detectives.

The advantage had been dexterously seized. It was Marshall Hall's problem to retain it and exploit it.

After that first fierce fusillade he husbanded his fire while several unprovocative witnesses came and went. From the landlady—stock figure of respectable dismay; "in *my* house, indeed"—he asked nothing at all. From the doctor he sought only some slight clarifications. From Bertram Shaw, who was candid and forthcoming, he obtained what he required without appreciable trouble.

"What is the name by which you are known to friends?" he asked.
"Bert," answered Shaw.
"And that was the name that Phyllis always called you?"
"Yes, it was."

This short passage, seemingly so trivial at the time, was to prove a powerful weapon at Marshall Hall's disposal when, in the waning hours of that December afternoon, he attacked again with unrestricted force. His prey was the ship's cook.

The defender's interrogation of this witness—a classic instance of a man who was bent upon secretiveness being driven from his covert and pitilessly exposed—owed its form and method of approach to one whose name does not appear in the official record. But naturally the brief in any important case is read by all the juniors in leading counsel's chambers. The Wood papers, indeed, had been particularly earmarked for the attention of Marshall Hall's youthful "devil," Wellesley Orr, who was later himself to win distinction at the Bar and become stipendiary magistrate at Manchester. It was Orr who, by a blend of industry and intuition, hit upon a point that had eluded Marshall Hall, and without which the latter's attack on the ship's cook could not have been one half as devastating.

The danger in the ship's cook's evidence was patent. If, at St. Paul's Road on the Wednesday morning, he had really seen a letter such as he described, then Wood's meeting with Phyllis in the evening was not accidental but had been pre-arranged. Honest mistake in such a matter was unlikely; might the story, though, be deliberately untrue? The ship's cook himself had been under suspicion: had he tried to transfer that suspicion somewhere else? It would be easy enough, of course, to suggest that he had done so, and that this had led to his perversion —or invention—of the letter; but the suggestion would doubtless be indignantly denied and, as things stood, could not be carried further. What the defence sought was some definite sign that the ship's cook in his fright had taken active steps to ensure that the murder would not be pinned on him.

Wellesley Orr found such a sign—in an unexpected quarter. Among those interviewed during police enquiries was one May Campbell, who had known the murdered girl. She had made a long statement, highly damaging to Wood. She claimed to recognise in him a person called "Scotch Bob"—Wood was Scottish born and retained a slight Scots accent—who had been going with Phyllis and had frequently ill-used her. May Campbell said that Phyllis, on the day before her death, talked of a letter she had had from Scotch Bob, asking her to meet him; that Phyllis expressed anxiety because Scotch Bob had a great grievance against her; that Phyllis also volunteered the information that she had shown a part of Scotch Bob's letter to a sailor who had slept with her upon the previous night.

This statement of May Campbell's had been passed as an act of courtesy to the defence; but the woman herself was not being called by the Crown because much of what she said was demonstrably false —not least her account of the talk she had had with Phyllis, which she fixed at a time when the latter was with Shaw. It thus became possible, and even probable, that she didn't see Phyllis on the Wednesday at all.

As May Campbell was not to be a witness, as nothing that she said would be brought before the jury, many barristers would have thought it wasting time to bother about her and her statement any further. But Orr was thorough, patient and intellectually inquisitive. Constantly he turned the matter over in his mind. Why had May Campbell— whom it did not seem to benefit—gone out of her way to be vindictive towards Wood? How did she know, if Phyllis didn't tell her, that the girl had had a letter and that a sailor saw it? The answer to the second question had imposed itself: she must have got it direct from the ship's cook—although there was no evidence that they were acquainted. But Orr's imaginative stroke was in perceiving that the answer to the second question really solved the first—that the ship's cook must have confided in May Campbell and enlisted her help in shifting the suspicion. They pooled their knowledge and acted in concert. Hence her vindictive lies. Hence his story of the letter.

So Wellesley Orr construed the situation and he struggled to convince Marshall Hall that he was right. The great defender first resisted and demurred; it was too remote, it was too suppositional, there wasn't enough to go on. But Orr, strong in his belief, continued to argue stubbornly and at last converted Marshall Hall to his own view.

Had Orr proved wrong, the attack upon the ship's cook would probably have failed, with consequences that one cannot calculate. But Orr proved right; and his flash of inspiration, turned to full account by a matchless fighting advocate, developed into one of the great forensic coups of history. . . .

The ship's cook was a tough and hefty fellow—not at all the type to be easily overawed. He answered Sir Charles Mathews with dogmatic assurance. Yes, Phyllis had shown him the postcard and a letter; yes, he had read all of one and a portion of the other; yes, he could remember that portion very well. He recited it to the jury as he had done to the police: "Dear Phyllis, Will you meet me at the bar of The Eagle at Camden Town 8.30 tonight, Wednesday—Bert." The Crown lawyers, following him in the depositions, observed he was word perfect.

"Just look at those." Mathews handed up a slide; secured in the glass were some wafery shreds of paper—all it had been possible to rescue from the grate. "Do you know what they are?"

"Yes," said the ship's cook. "They're pieces out of the letter that I saw."

When Marshall Hall got up to cross-examine he stood for several moments before putting any question. Under his penetrating gaze, that might well strike fear into the heart of one who had not been wholly frank, the ship's cook straightaway seemed ill at ease. He shuffled his feet and tried to turn his eyes elsewhere.

The crowd in court was absolutely quiet, as if instinctively aware of an impending crisis.

"Tell me," said Marshall Hall at last, "do you know a woman called May?"

The effect on the ship's cook was extraordinary. His jaw dropped; his fingers twitched; a perceptible tremor shook his bulky frame.

"No, no," he stammered. "No."

It needed no psychologist to tell that he was lying. That was apparent to everybody present, though why and what it portended most could still only conjecture. But Wellesley Orr's heart beat a little faster as he noted the frightened appearance of the witness and knew he was going to be vindicated right up to the hilt.

"Think again," said Marshall Hall. "And think hard. Do you know May Campbell?"

The ship's cook looked almost stupefied.

"May Campbell?" he repeated.

"May Campbell." Marshall Hall never relaxed that hard, relentless gaze. "Do you know her?"

The ship's cook hesitated long.

"By sight," he faltered.

The first—and the most difficult—obstruction had been cracked. Now, one by one, the barriers tumbled down.

"Have you ever spoken to her?"

"Yes."

"Where?"

"In The Rising Sun."

"When did you first speak to her?"

"I think it was the day of Phyllis Dimmock's funeral."

"Did you talk about the case?"

"It was common talk."

"Did *you* talk about it?"

"Yes."

"Did May Campbell give you a description of a man who, she said, was known as a friend of Phyllis Dimmock's?"

"Yes."

"Did that description correspond very much with the description of the accused?"

"Yes."

"And after that you picked him out as a man you had seen with Dimmock?"

"Yes."

The success of this reconstruction transcended expectations, and it stands for all time as a superlative example of the relationship that may temporarily exist between star advocate and inconspicuous "devil"— if the one is resourceful and the other receptive. It is the relationship between every playwright and his virtuoso actor. Wellesley Orr could not have done it quite like that himself; without him Marshall Hall would not have done it at all.

The defender continued, on the swell of a fast-running and favourable tide.

"When you heard of the murder," he asked, "were you not in a great fright?"

"No," said the ship's cook, though he was certainly in one now.

"You knew that the habitués of The Rising Sun were well aware that you had been with this woman on the Sunday, the Monday, and the Tuesday nights?"

"Yes."

"It was a very unpleasant situation," observed Marshall Hall. "Wasn't it? . . . *Wasn't it?*"

How did you contradict this dominating man, who knew every detail of your personal affairs?

"Yes," the ship's cook admitted. "It was unpleasant, yes."

The witness had undergone a metamorphosis and was now cutting a very different figure with the jury—the figure of one who was, or had been, afraid for his own skin and whose evidence must be weighed and valued in that light.

"On the Wednesday morning," Marshall Hall went on, "you say the girl showed you a letter she had just received?"

"Yes."

"And gave you The Rising Sun postcard to compare with it?"

"She did."

"Why on earth should she want you to compare them?"

"I don't know."

"You don't know." Marshall Hall echoed him satirically. "Look at the slide again; look at that piece of paper. You say that is part of the letter that you saw?"

"Yes."

"Do you see the faint blue lines upon it? . . . Look."

The ship's cook looked as best he could; his hand was not too steady.

"Yes, I see them," he said.

"Isn't that paper torn from a notebook, from a scribbling book?"

The ship's cook perceived what was coming. He was desperately uncomfortable.

"Well, I saw the letter," he mumbled, with head bowed.

"Look up, man!" thundered Marshall Hall. "Look up and speak up! We are in a court of justice. I put it to you that the story of this letter is an invention, and that the fragment you have there might have come from anywhere and certainly never come by post."

"It did," maintained the ship's cook, but the sweat poured from him.

"You say the letter was signed 'Bert'?"

"Yes."

"Where did you get that name?"

"It was in the letter, I tell you."

"Did you know that the man whom Phyllis lived with was called Bert?"

"Only after the murder."

Marshall Hall spoke very slowly.

"If it had been the object at that time to put suspicion upon *him*, to say the signature was 'Bert' would have been useful, wouldn't it?"

The defender waited, but no answer ever was forthcoming. With a faultless sense of timing, the curtain forthwith fell, both on the ship's cook and on the first day of the trial.

The second day's proceedings revolved round the evidence given by MacCowan. He was the one Crown witness who could hang Wood by himself. If the jury thought him honest; if they trusted in his powers of observation; if these twin conclusions led them to believe that he had indeed seen a man leaving Phyllis Dimmock's house shortly before five on the morning that she died, and that he was able to identify him afterwards as Wood—why, there would be the virtual finish of the matter. For it was certain as anything can be in this world that if MacCowan had seen anyone leaving Twenty-nine, it was Phyllis Dimmock's murderer he saw.

MacCowan was a wiry little man, bred in the country, seasoned in the town; his face reflected his mental composition—a curious admixture of naïveté and cunning; he had heard all about these lawyers, especially Marshall Hall, and he was ready for 'em, any time they liked. They'd best not try any of their gammon upon him.

He replied to Sir Charles Mathews with the cheerful air of one who believes that his evidence is incontrovertible. "I was going through St. Paul's Road at twelve minutes to five," he said. "As I passed Twenty-nine I saw a man leaving the gate. His left hand was in his pocket, and he jerked his right shoulder forward as he walked. I turned round several times; I had him in sight for thirty yards."

Left hand in pocket, right shoulder jerking forward; they were the very words that had been used by Ruby Young in describing to the police the walk of Robert Wood—words that the Crown would invite her to repeat when her turn came to go into the box.

It is not always possible, even in retrospect, to pick out the real turning point of a lengthy trial. In this case, however, there can be little doubt. It came when Marshall Hall joined battle with Mac-Cowan. . . .

Unlike the ship's cook, MacCowan did not quail as the defender rose to face him. He, after all, had no underhand transaction to conceal. Nor had he been in court during the former's overthrow, which—notwithstanding his own less vulnerable position—might have exercised a chastening effect.

As it was, he began the engagement almost perkily.

"Did you know at the time," Marshall Hall had asked him, "that the gate from which the man came out was the gate of Twenty-nine?"

"No," said MacCowan, as if it didn't matter in the least. "I read it in the papers and identified it afterwards."

"Did you say before the coroner that you were passing Twenty-nine at *five* minutes to five?"

"Yes."

"And the same before the magistrate?"

"Yes."

"And yet you now say it was not five minutes, but *twelve* minutes to five?"

"That's right," said MacCowan. "I knew I'd left home at twenty to, and I've stepped it out since then and found that I was wrong."

"Oh, you were wrong, were you?" Marshall Hall's voice suddenly deepened. "Didn't you alter the time because you were cross-examined before the magistrate as to when the street lights were put out?"

"No," said MacCowan, a trifle more defensively.

"*Were* the street lights out when you were passing Twenty-nine?"

"No, they were in."

"Do you know we have had evidence in this court that they were put out that morning before *twenty* to five?"

"They were in," MacCowan persisted.

"When you made your original statement to the police did you say you saw a man coming not out of the gate but *down the steps* of Twenty-nine?"

"No."

"Did you not? Wasn't your statement read over to you after you had made it?"

"Yes."

"It was?" Marshall Hall read aloud from his own copy. "'I looked round and saw a man coming down the steps of Twenty-nine.' . . . Did the police invent that?"

For the first time MacCowan showed signs of harassment.

"When we go to make a statement," he protested, "we aren't so fly as when we come to be cross-examined."

"'Fly'? 'Fly'?" repeated Marshall Hall in anger. "What do you mean by 'fly'?"

"I wasn't so particular," MacCowan said defiantly. "I didn't listen particularly to what was being read over."

Never was advocate offered such a gift. Never did advocate accept one more wholeheartedly.

"You were 'not so fly,'" said Marshall Hall with stinging scorn. "Do you mean to say that, knowing a man's life might depend on your description, you did not take particular notice of what was read over to you? Have you no regard for human life?"

MacCowan had had time to realise his blunder. He tried to extricate himself by misplaced flippancy.

"One life is as good as another," he retorted.

He could hardly have made a more inopportune observation. Those in court looked almost fearfully at the defender, anticipating another outburst of explosive wrath. But with sound tactical and keen dramatic sense Marshall Hall restrained what must have been his natural feelings. He was to make full use, though, of the episode later on—in his final speech, when he would stigmatise MacCowan as "not only a careless, but a callous, witness."

Meanwhile he still held in his hand the latter's statement. He displayed it ostentatiously as he resumed his questions.

"According to your story you only identified the man by some peculiar twitching of the shoulder?"

"The peculiarity of his walk," replied MacCowan warily.

"The peculiarity being this twitching of the shoulder?"

"Yes."

"Did you mention that peculiarity when you first talked to the police?"

The sheets of typescript fluttered a clear warning.

"No," said MacCowan, "but I did tell 'em that the man had a swaggering walk."

"Oh," said Marshall Hall. "Do you wish the jury to understand that when you said 'swaggering walk' you meant 'a peculiar twitch of the shoulder'?"

"Yes," said MacCowan. His rather impudent and cocksure manner had passed into one of uncertainty and mistrust.

"Did you describe the man you saw as one of stiff build with broad shoulders?"

"Yes."

"Wood, stand up. . . ."

The stage folk present must have watched the resulting scene with envy. No production effect, no theatrical contrivance, no arrangement of curtains or of mirrors or of lights could have occasioned so sudden and intense a concentration as that which now was focused on the figure of the prisoner. No one had eyes or thought for anyone but he as he got slowly to his feet from his chair inside the dock.

He looked very serene, very self-possessed—and very narrow-shouldered.

Nobody spoke. Nobody moved. Marshall Hall waited till the silence was oppressive.

"Now," he said. "Do you describe *that* man as broad-shouldered?"

MacCowan was on the run, but would not capitulate—not because of any animus he felt against the accused, but rather because of his own uncompromising pride. He was an egotistical man who conceived the whole trial in terms of a joust between himself and the defence. And, though he was getting the worst of it, he wasn't giving up; he meant to get one back on this lawyer fellow yet.

"He'd look broader if he wore his overcoat," he said.

"Then he *shall* wear it," Marshall Hall declared.

The overcoat was brought; the prisoner put it on. It made very little difference. His slim, almost puny build could not be concealed.

"Would you describe *that* man as broad-shouldered?" asked Marshall Hall again.

MacCowan made one last throw.

"He has broader shoulders than I have," he contended.

"Would you call a bluebottle an elephant," said Marshall Hall instantly, "because it is bigger than a fly?"

Not even the Old Bailey's sombre setting could deaden the effect of this annihilating thrust. A gale of laughter swept across the court—a gale in which MacCowan and all his high pretensions were tossed derisively before being blown away.

That second day, marked by such a signal triumph, had also a less satisfactory side for Marshall Hall. It brought the first overt and unmistakable sign of a strained relationship between the defender and the judge.

Marshall Hall's weakness for wrangling with the Bench has already been noted, together with its source—that state of hypertension and emotional absorption that possessed his whole being throughout the longest trial and made him the outstanding advocate he was. One may accept this explanation without being blind to the fact that in these wrangles Marshall Hall was very often wrong, and was sometimes gratuitously offensive in addition. But when he fell foul of authority during the trial of Wood, Marshall Hall was almost invariably right; and if he did put his points with greater vehemence than respect, one must say in fairness that authority had asked for it.

Mr. Justice Grantham was a keen sportsman and therefore popular with the public, a learned lawyer and therefore admired by learned lawyers. There are, however, attributes of which a High Court judge stands more in need than readiness with a gun or even proficiency with precedents. One is an open mind; another a regulated tongue. Grantham possessed neither. He was prone to form strong and stubborn preconceptions, which he would freely ventilate in the hearing of the jury. He was equally prone to garrulous interruption which more often confused than elucidated issues.

It is not surprising that there was no love lost between him and Marshall Hall, and those best acquainted with their past encounters had probably expected trouble to begin before. In the early stages, though, both men were on their best behaviour: Grantham silent and seemingly impartial, Marshall Hall directing all his salvoes at the witness-box.

It was the judge who brought this period of concord to an end. . . .

Marshall Hall was cross-examining that friend of the ship's cook who had returned with him on Wednesday night to the temperance hotel. The defender did not essay to break this alibi, but to stress and expand his previous suggestion that the ship's cook had been seeking cover for himself.

"How long had you known him?" he enquired of the witness.

"Since the eighth of September."

"What, only the Sunday before the murder?"

"Yes."

"After the murder did he tell you he was very anxious to prove where he had been on the Wednesday night?"

"No."

"Did you *think* he was anxious to prove it?"

"No."

The man clearly supposed that the ship's cook himself still stood in danger of the gallows and intended to do all he could to help his new-found friend.

With a master's intuitive sense of what was coming, Marshall Hall cast his next question in peculiar form.

"Did you hear," he asked, "that he had slept with Phyllis Dimmock on the Monday, Tuesday and Sunday nights?"

"Yes," said the witness. He knew that the ship's cook had admitted so much all along.

"Did he tell you in the course of conversation?"

"Yes."

"A curious conversation," Marshall Hall went on, "to hold with a man who had only known you for three days—curious, wasn't it, for him to tell you he had passed the three previous nights in such a way?"

One may logically deduce the next step contemplated: a suggestion that these intimate matters came to be discussed only because the ship's cook was expressing apprehensions, and that the preceding denials of this witness had been false. But, as events befell, that step was never taken, for at this point the witness suddenly caught fright. Whether he, too, could anticipate developments and foresaw some difficulty in explaining things away; or whether, puzzled by Marshall Hall's transposing of the days and his subsequent reference to "the three previous nights," he wrongly believed he had been trapped into admitting that the ship's cook had said he slept with Phyllis on the *Wednesday;* or

whether, for some other reason more obscure than these, he decided
to repudiate what he had already sworn.

As he hovered on the brink of this effrontery, Marshall Hall pressed
for an immediate reply.

"Curious, wasn't it?" he repeated, "for him to tell you he had spent
the three previous nights in such a way?"

"He didn't say that," said the witness shiftily. "He just mentioned
he'd been with her."

"But for three nights?"

"No."

Marshall Hall flared up at the barefaced lie.

"Why, I put the three nights to you specifically. I placed them in
the wrong order so as to mark the question."

"I never heard it," said the witness.

For some moments the judge had been irritably fidgeting. Now he
sprang to the witness's support.

"No, nor did I," he said.

If Mr. Justice Grantham was speaking the literal truth—and any
other view would be less charitable still—he had simply not been paying the requisite attention. One may sympathise with Marshall Hall
if his self-control was taxed.

"I'm absolutely positive," he shouted. "I'm as sure I put that question
as that I'm standing here. We shall see soon enough from the shorthand note. I call for the shorthand note."

Even the judge, who had suffered before from Marshall Hall's quick
temper, looked taken aback by the storm that he had roused. He sat
in sour silence as the shorthand writer turned over the pages of his
book. The jury, and indeed most other people in the court who had
been listening more closely than Mr. Justice Grantham, felt fairly certain that Marshall Hall was right, but awaited final demonstration by
the record.

The shorthand writer found the passage. He read aloud haltingly,
made nervous by his unexpected leap to prominence.

" 'Question: Did you hear that he had slept with Phyllis Dimmock on
the Monday, Tuesday and Sunday nights? Answer: Yes. Question: Did
he tell you in the course of conversation? Answer: Yes.' "

Marshall Hall swung round in triumph towards the jury. They had
their heads together and were talking in low tones. The judge observed the spectacle with obvious displeasure.

"Very well," he said, "if the witness misunderstood it, I misunderstood it too."

This singularly graceless piece of sophistry at once brought Marshall Hall back into the fray.

"But your lordship has heard the note read," he said sharply, "and I mentioned the three nights."

"There's no need to get excited," said the judge in cold reproof.

The injustice of this stubbornly unreasonable attitude might easily have driven the impetuous advocate into some excess of speech that could not have been repaired. It probably would have done so had there seemed no other recourse open in the interests of his client than an outright accusation of judicial unfairness. But however impassioned Marshall Hall became, one part of his mind automatically registered the slightest signs of feeling exhibited by the jury. He knew that so far in this dispute he had their sympathy. He knew that one intemperate act might throw it all away.

There was a short and tense pause while judge and advocate regarded one another with unconcealed hostility. Then the latter turned towards the witness, who was patently dreading a resumption of his questions.

Marshall Hall addressed him quietly and gravely.

"Will you base the truth of your evidence," he said, "on the statement that I did not ask you about those three nights?"

"Yes," said the witness, who now had only one idea—to get out of the box.

"Very well," said Marshall Hall, "I will ask you nothing more."

As he sat down he remarked with satisfaction that the jury had once again put their heads together.

None the less, that evening Marshall Hall brooded over the incident, and though he could find little or nothing with which to reproach himself, he could not altogether suppress a flicker of disquiet.

No matter what the rights and wrongs may be, there are always dangers lying in wait for any advocate who gets involved in repeated conflict with the judge. His lordship holds cards not available to barristers. A jury, looking on at a continuous rebellion, may gradually turn against the rebel whom they once admired. Above all, the added pressure may adversely affect counsel's discharge of his prime responsibilities.

So it seemed to Marshall Hall, meditating in the calm repose of his own room, that any further clashes must at all costs be eschewed. He still bitterly resented Grantham's mischievous intervention, and would certainly not sit passive if there should be more. But the prisoner's cause could best be served without them altogether, and Marshall Hall made up his mind to promote this end. Although the injured party, he shelved his personal pride and planned a generous gesture to make peace with the judge. . . .

Next morning when the court resumed he shaped his course accordingly.

"My lord," he said, "may I mention a purely personal matter?" Everyone leaned forward. "There appears to have been an impression," Marshall Hall went on, "that there was some friction yesterday between your lordship and myself. I would like to make it clear that I had not the smallest intention of questioning anything that was said from the Bench."

The olive branch had been held out without a reservation. Grantham, who in private was not an ill-natured individual, seemed willing to accept it.

"It is not for me to assume there is any friction," he said affably.

"Friction with the witness," said Marshall Hall, "I don't repudiate, but I am most anxious to repudiate friction with your lordship."

"I don't think you should take the trouble," said the judge.

Upon this friendly and agreeable exchange was ushered in the third day of the trial—a day on which discord between the two men reached its peak and produced at least two scenes of uninhibited antagonism.

In the first of these the fault again entirely lay with Grantham.

The Crown had called Wood's departmental chief. This gentleman agreed with Marshall Hall that the prisoner had been on his staff throughout the past five years; that he had not the least peculiarity in his walk; that on the 12th September he came to work as usual and showed no trace of perturbation or excitement; that he was an exceptionally amiable, upright and industrious young man.

"Do you know anything," asked Marshall Hall, "that would lead you to believe he was capable of committing a dreadful crime like this?"

"Most certainly not," the witness said emphatically.

Such evidence should never count for more than it is worth; dreadful crimes are committed not infrequently by those who would have been deemed incapable of them by their friends. A so-called "double life," of body or of mind, is not by any means an exceptional phenomenon. To some degree Wood himself was a confessed example; by day he earned golden opinions of his rectitude, by night he amused himself with the lowest sort of trollop. The judge was fully entitled to demonstrate this point.

"At the works you thought him a high-minded man," he said. "Had you any idea of the immoral life you have now heard he was leading?"

"No," the witness said.

Whether "immoral" was an entirely justifiable word, whether "disreputable" would not have been better, might now be considered at least open to debate. At the time, however, to demur would have been fruitless. Mr. Justice Grantham's chosen epithet was backed by the ethical criteria that obtained in 1907. Whatever he may have thought, Marshall Hall kept silent.

"It is admitted," the judge continued, "that, though nominally under Shaw's protection, this woman was receiving men. *Had you any idea that Wood was living with such a woman?*"

This time there was no question; Mr. Justice Grantham had gone very much too far. In his eagerness to drive home what was a legitimate point against the prisoner—to whose case he was now displaying himself consistently inimical—he had lapsed into flagrant error and injustice. No witness had been called, no witness would be called, to say that Wood had ever lived with Phyllis Dimmock. It was the purest surmise presented as proved fact.

In an instant Marshall Hall was on his feet.

"I do not understand your lordship's question," he declared.

"Are you addressing me or the jury?" Grantham replied irately. "If you are speaking to me, I wish you would not look at them."

Many counsel—and Marshall Hall was undoubtedly among them—incline to watch the jury, when, by strictest etiquette, their eyes should be elsewhere. This habit on occasion may merit a rebuke—but not, perhaps, most fittingly at a moment when the judge himself has just done something infinitely worse.

"I am addressing your lordship," said Marshall Hall, unflinching. "I said that I did not understand your lordship's question."

"I am taking the accused's own statement," Grantham barked, and as Marshall Hall, still standing in protest, endeavoured to fathom this astonishing assertion, the judge repeated his injurious blunder.

"Had you any idea he was living with such a woman?"

The situation was intolerable. Marshall Hall broke in without ceremony.

"There is not a tittle of evidence—"

"I am addressing a witness," said the incensed judge. "Counsel must not interrupt when I am putting questions on the evidence in the interests of justice."

"In the interests of justice—"

"I must ask you not to argue with me."

"My lord—"

"I shall permit no argument," decreed Grantham with fierce finality, "as to the way I am putting my questions to him."

The conflict of wills had reached a pitch which did not admit of compromise. One or the other must now accept defeat.

It was not to be Marshall Hall.

"With great deference," he said—and Grantham, despite himself, felt constrained to listen—"I only wish, *in the interests of justice,* to point out that there is not a particle of evidence that the accused ever stayed with the girl or had improper relations with her."

When he had finished, and only when he had finished, the courageous and resolute advocate sat down. The judge glared at him but said nothing more.

As the witness was suffered to retire, Marshall Hall boldly turned his face towards the jury.

The personal ascendancy that Marshall Hall had won stood him in good stead a little later on.

Wood's friend Lambert had been into the box to tell of his meeting with the prisoner and Phyllis at The Eagle. He was followed by one of The Eagle's barmaids who, though able to identify the girl she saw as Phyllis, could only say that she had come in with "a man" and that presently "another man" had joined them.

"Did you hear her speak to this second man?" asked junior Crown counsel.

"She said, 'Excuse me being untidy; I had to come and meet—'"

"I object," interposed Marshall Hall, and the court, barely recovered from the last pitched battle, was plunged again into a fever of excitement. "I submit that since the witness has identified neither of the two men who were with Phyllis Dimmock, her statement as to what Dimmock said cannot be evidence."

Marshall Hall was invoking the rule that, in the process of a prosecution, one person cannot report another's words unless those words were uttered in the hearing of the accused. You have not proved Wood was there, the defender argued; therefore the conversation is not admissible.

But we *have* proved he was there, the Crown retorted; we proved it earlier through the mouth of Lambert. "And," counsel added, "Lambert's statement as to what Dimmock said was to the same effect."

"No, it was not," said Marshall Hall, jumping up once more.

The Judge's displeasure was immediately revived.

"Do you want me to decide against you without further argument?" he said.

"No, my lord."

"Then you had better sit down." The pedagogic reprimand soothed Grantham's pride, still smarting painfully from his previous rebuff. "We can soon see what the witness Lambert said." He searched his notes, turned up the place, and frowned. Marshall Hall, so it appeared, was right again.

"Lambert said that Dimmock's remark was: 'I hope you will excuse my dress, *as I have just run out.*' That *is* different," the judge conceded.

"Very different," said Marshall Hall, "and I submit you cannot accept the evidence of this witness."

It raised a delicate point on adequacy of proof. The judge thought it over.

"I do not agree," he said. "I think the evidence is admissible."

Marshall Hall was not content.

"Will your lordship make a note of my objection?"

"Yes."

The defender appeared to think the judge's tone perfunctory.

"I implore your lordship to note that this witness has *not* identified these men—"

"You have said that before." Grantham tried to close the matter. "I have not forgotten it."

"I thought," said Marshall Hall deliberately, "your lordship did not *appreciate* it."

And once again he was left with the last word.

The *atmosphere* of a trial is as important as its substance. It determines the mental and the moral standpoint from which—and by which—the accused is judged. It determines the interpretation of his mind and character. It determines whether, given two alternatives, a good or bad construction will be placed upon his acts.

Due in large measure to the work of Marshall Hall the atmosphere in Wood's case had gradually changed. Where earlier had mostly been antipathy or indifference, now there was a sympathetic feeling for the prisoner. The scales against him had seemed unfairly weighted; too many, for motives perceptible or otherwise, had disclosed concern

to encompass his destruction. The effect was not diminished by those
bringing up the rear—Ruby Young (often in tears, but fulfiling her
bitter rôle), and an unsavoury set of prostitutes and brothel keepers
whose bias against Wood was as plain as their depravity. The privileged
spectators crushed inside the court, the crowds that loitered every day
in the surrounding streets, the masses that followed the proceedings
from afar—all, or nearly all, were modifying their views. Without
necessarily holding that Wood *ought* to be acquitted, they found themselves irrationally *hoping* that he would be.

Maybe a mood of optimism engendered by this atmosphere induced
Marshall Hall, when the prosecution closed, to submit to the judge
that no case had been made out.

There is always some danger in a submission of no case. That is because the jury—who must perforce sit listening—seldom comprehend
exactly what is going on. Upon these occasions the defender is contending that there is no evidence on which one could *possibly* convict; that
the Crown has made out no case even calling for an answer; that, in
fact, the prosecution has utterly collapsed. But juries, unfamiliar with
the niceties of procedure, are apt to suppose that the judge is being
asked whether *he* believes the prisoner innocent or guilty. Consequently, if his lordship turns down the submission, though he is saying
no more than that the jury must decide, the latter body often too
readily assumes that he is giving them a broad hint to find the prisoner
guilty. "Ah! the judge thinks he did it," they whisper to each other.

It follows that such submissions ought not to be made unless they
enjoy a solid prospect of success.

Only one of Marshall Hall's sanguine disposition could have dis-
cerned such a prospect in the trial of Robert Wood. He argued with
all his usual urgency and warmth. There was "an absolute and utter
want of any evidence" that the accused was ever seen at Phyllis Dimmock's house; the evidence of identity was "weak beyond thought, of
a kind to which no attention should or can be paid"; no motive had
been attributed to Wood, "not one iota even of a suggested motive.
I ask your lordship to say," he concluded, "that the accused ought not
to be put in any further peril."

No fault could be found with the judge's decision nor with the way
in which it was pronounced.

"Taking all into account," he said, measuring his words, "I cannot
say there is no case to go to the jury. I cannot say that there is no case."

"As your lordship pleases." Slowly Marshall Hall turned towards the

jury-box. He looked like a man who had been labouring in chains but
was now suddenly freed. "Gentlemen." His voice rang out almost triumphant. "Gentlemen, for four days you have heard the prosecution.
Now, at long last, I can open the defence."

In any trial this was Marshall Hall's great moment.

Some counsel regard the jury as lay figures, impersonal and inanimate accessories of the court, only springing into temporary life when
ultimately called on for their Aye or Nay. Such counsel neither feel
nor seek a close relation, even when going through the motions of addressing them. Like actors wholly absorbed in the performance, they
hardly heed their audience until the end.

Marshall Hall lay at the opposite extreme. From first to last, from
the moment that the jurors took the oath in turn until they finally withdrew upon their solemn business, he was acutely conscious of their
presence; conscious of them, not only as a corporate entity, but also as
defined and separate individuals; conscious that any single one of them
might come to hold the key to his client's fate; conscious that at any
time the smallest incident might sway their judgments and tip the balance either way; conscious above all of his own responsibility for
charging both their emotions and their thoughts. That, rather than any
reprehensible intention, was the cause of his constant preoccupation
with the jury, to which Mr. Justice Grantham had objected. That, too,
was why he felt his powers run highest when he could legitimately meet
them face to face; when he could talk to them directly, not obliquely;
when, without diversion by opponents or by witnesses, the jury passed
into his absolute possession.

"His tall, commanding figure," one reporter wrote of him while the
Wood trial was in progress, "his outstretched arm, his white set face,
communicated his spirit of intensity to the court." Never was this
more manifest than in his opening speech. All the pent-up forces of
that energetic nature were released and fused in one tremendous effort
to sweep his client clear of the hazard that beset him.

He began by adroitly turning to account his various embroilments
with witnesses and judge. "You may have thought," he said, "that, now
and then, I was pressing unduly, that I took an unfair advantage, that
I asked a question that might appear unworthy. If I seemed to exceed
the proper limits I implore you to forgive me; my whole anxiety was
for my client. Gentlemen, his life is at stake. I cannot rob the Crown
witnesses of theirs. *They* have far less to lose at *my* hands than *he* has
at *yours*." There followed a passage of sustained and brilliant rhetoric

in which he dramatised with harrowing vividness the duty which they were sworn to discharge. "I am proud to boast myself a member of the Old Bailey Bar, to whom are entrusted the lives of their fellow citizens of London. . . . This burden has been lying very heavily on my shoulders. Gentlemen, it will pass to yours all too soon."

He turned now to the facts, and told them at once what all were keen to learn. "Wood is going into the box.* He will speak for himself and it will be for you to judge his story." Boldly the advocate faced and grappled with his chief remaining task. "Gentlemen, I do not close my eyes to this. We will put him in the box, but he will go into it tainted —tainted because he has spoken untruths in the past. It was wrong; it was unfortunate; the man has suffered greatly for it, heaven knows —but is there not a simple and a natural explanation?

"Assume his innocence; then everything becomes clear." Superbly Marshall Hall rose to the height of his own challenge. "Think of it, gentlemen; think of it. He knew that within a few hours of his leaving that young woman she had been foully done to death. He foresaw that his name would be dragged through the public press as one who had been in company with a prostitute. He foresaw the ruin of his reputation. He foresaw the injury to his father's health. So he did what many other foolish folk have done before. He thought a lie would be better than the truth. He asked his sweetheart to save him—not to prove that he did not commit the murder, but to prevent him being publicly inculpated with a harlot.

"That isn't mere surmise. You can test it for yourselves. *The Ruby Young alibi does not cover the crime.* Phyllis Dimmock was killed between four and six a.m.; *we* know this from the doctor—*but the murderer, whoever he is, has known it all along.* Now Wood asked Ruby Young to say that he was with her until eleven o'clock—a useless alibi for the murder, but a perfect alibi for the meeting at The Eagle."

This very effective point—obvious enough once attention has been called to it, but how many of us would perceive it for ourselves?—produced a visible impression on the jury. More, perhaps, than any other feature of the case, it lent colour and convincingness to the proposition that the charitable view of Wood's behaviour was correct.

Having thus dealt with his greatest difficulty—for, as the judge was to remark in summing up, "the main evidence against the accused is his own conduct in endeavouring to get people to tell lies"—Marshall

---

* Although prisoners had been permitted to give evidence on their own behalf since 1898, the practice had not yet become almost obligatory.

Hall swept on to amplify his earlier gains. The burnt paper in the grate? Wood himself would tell them how the girl could have acquired these fragments of his writing; they might be the remains of some scribbling and sketches he did in the public house to amuse himself and her. Certainly they were not the remnants of a letter; there had never been a letter; there was no one but the ship's cook to assert otherwise, and the ship's cook—thanks to Wellesley Orr this could be said with confidence—was palpably a man who did not always tell the truth. MacCowan? His was the flimsiest evidence ever presented in any court of justice in the world. Put aside his chopping and his changing, his barefaced prevarications, his disregard for accuracy when life might hinge upon it; even without these no one could believe that a murderer, with the body of his victim lying in the house, would choose to come out—and to come out, according to MacCowan himself, under the full glare of the electric lamps—at a moment when somebody's feet were clattering past.

Under this slashing and spirited attack the Crown case assumed a new and sicklier complexion. Marshall Hall was well aware of it; in all these matters he felt infinitely strong, buttressed as he was by his cross-examination. But there still remained for him one source of some anxiety, although it lay beyond the strictest boundaries of relevance. Throughout he had been considerably perturbed at the possible effect of his client's admitted laxity. Wood had not scorned the society of prostitutes; one (Ruby Young) had undeniably been his mistress. To what extent would this be held against him by the jury? There were some melancholy precedents—notably Mrs. Maybrick, only recently released from gaol after serving fifteen years—of persons convicted upon a murder charge where the evidence was plainly insufficient but their sexual morals had been open to reproach. True, this vindictive and inequitable sanction was more often imposed on women than on men. But even male prisoners could not hope to be immune from the vengeance of a puritan society—for any group of twelve, however tolerant individually, forthwith becomes society in miniature.

Marshall Hall firmly grasped this nettle in the concluding passage of his speech. "He may have been immoral," he said very earnestly. "His relations with women may not always have been pure. In that respect, gentlemen, do not let us be unworldly; in that respect he is only one of many thousands. But what has it to do with the case that brings you here? Nothing; precisely nothing. Were he twenty times as immoral as he is, that would not even begin to prove he was the author of one of the most atrocious and skilful murders of our time."

The speech had done more than project the prisoner's case. It had equally projected the prisoner himself. Over and over again, in a variety of ways, Marshall Hall brought Wood and the jury into contact. "The murderer was mad. Does *he* look mad?" he once demanded, pointing dramatically at the figure in the dock. (It was like an echo of Governor Robinson's famous stroke—'Gentlemen, does she look it?' —in the Lizzie Borden trial.) The jury found themselves, at Marshall Hall's behest, glancing from client to advocate and from advocate to client—that unruffled client who, under their survey, did not interrupt his sketching of celebrities in court.

This increased awareness of Wood as a human being, not merely as a bloodless cypher in a mystery tale, had one immediate and one remote result. The latter was to make them more reluctant to convict. The former was to make them still more eager for the moment when Wood would tell his own story from the witness-box.

Their eagerness survived the intermission of a night. It survived the succeeding morning, during which Wood's father, brother and a neighbor swore that he came home at midnight on September 12th; they were patently honest but confused in recollection, and Mathews expertly cast doubt upon the date. It survived the advent of a St. Paul's Road resident who had gone on early shift at five on the morning of the crime; he attributed to himself "a peculiar swinging walk" and Marshall Hall announced him as the man MacCowan really saw. It survived attestation by two Rising Sun habitués that they had seen Phyllis Dimmock with a man not the accused at half-past twelve upon the night she died. It survived all this and indeed delay fomented expectation, not more among the jury than among those looking on.

The feelings of the latter finally found expression through an incident unique in British criminal trials. When at last, towards mid-afternoon on the fifth day, Marshall Hall called the name of Robert Wood, a breathless hush descended on the court. Then, as with one accord, the whole assembly rose, and the prisoner picked his way from dock to box like some high priest amid his reverent congregation.

How a prisoner is received when he goes into the box is primarily the business of his advocate. How he fares while he is there is primarily his own.

From a lawyer's standpoint a "good" witness is one who answers briefly the questions that are asked, does not volunteer unsolicited information, and above all refrains from argument or comment. Any sort of histrionics are regarded with peculiar apprehension and abhorrence.

It was soon apparent that, by these criteria, Wood's merits as a witness were very, very few. Refinement he possessed, and a certain delicate charm that made the notion of him as a brutal murderer incongruous. But with this charm went affectations and conceits that could easily be construed as a technique of evasion.

Right from the start he gave trouble to his counsel.

"Did you kill Phyllis Dimmock?" Marshall Hall had asked him.

This classical propounding of the theme invites one, and only one, response—a simple and unhesitating "No." But Wood chose to decline the obvious lead. Instead he thrust his hands out in mute expostulation, flung his head back, and rolled his eyes to heaven.

This foolish exhibition caused acute embarrassment. The jury shifted awkwardly, and Wood's friends looked at one another in dismay.

"Did you kill Phyllis Dimmock?" Marshall Hall repeated with expressive emphasis.

Wood arched his brows theatrically.

"Ridiculous," he said.

Obtuseness of this kind on the part of his own client is the recurrent nightmare of every barrister. It raises difficulties almost insurmountable. You are forbidden to put the appropriate answer in his mouth; you cannot subject him to cross-examination; you can hardly seek to treat him as a hostile witness.

Marshall Hall went as far as settled practice would permit.

"You must answer straight," he told Wood solemnly. "I will only ask you perfectly straight questions. . . . Once again—did you kill Phyllis Dimmock?"

"No," Wood said belatedly, "I most certainly did not."

There was an audible sigh. Even those indifferent to the outcome somehow felt relieved. . . .

This, though, was but the first of many occasions. Wood refused to tread the path his counsel indicated. He paltered; he digressed; he struck melodramatic attitudes ("If I am lying, I hope God will destroy me at this moment."); he threw off chatty and intimate asides to the twelve men who were engaged in trying him ("I dare say some of *you* will know what goes on in public houses"). "I wish you would answer me and not talk to the jury," said Marshall Hall in fruitless remonstrance; as imperturbable as he was mannerised, the accused would not alter nor modify his course. Perhaps he could not; perhaps his personality forbade; perhaps this was the price that he paid for being "artistic"—which, many people noted, was his favourite adjective.

Only by patient and arduous endeavour did Marshall Hall succeed in drawing from his wayward client something that resembled a coherent narrative. Before he had finished it was almost evening. The single-handed duel between accused and prosecutor—one in which the parties seemed pathetically unequal—was postponed until the sixth and last day of the trial.

If Mathews had seemed subordinate so far to Marshall Hall and had not competed with him as the focus of attraction, that was largely due to the restrictions of his rôle. Now most of those restrictions were temporarily cast off; next morning as he stood up in his place, hands upon his hips, eyes piercing as needles, shrewd mouth very tight-lipped and determined, he made a powerful bid for mastery of the court.

He at once passed up to Wood the celebrated postcard, without which there would have been neither prisoner nor trial.

"Look at that postcard, if you please. Look at what is written on it. On its face it is a note of assignation, is it not?"

The harsh voice rasped the nerves like tearing metal. Of all who heard it Wood seemed least affected, although today he looked fatigued, as well he might. A week may be more restfully spent than on trial for your life, with a Mathews lying in wait for you almost at the close.

"It looks like a note of assignation, does it not?"

"Yes," agreed Wood, wearily resigned. We've been through this, his manner hinted, so many times before.

"A note that was written by you unquestionably?"

"Yes."

"And addressed to the woman by the name in which she lived?"

"Yes."

"At the house where she was killed?"

"Yes."

"You posted it on the night of the Sunday?"

"Yes."

"You would expect it to reach her on the morning of the Monday?"

"Yes."

Mathews drew his gown about him ominously.

"Did you keep the assignation made upon that postcard?"

Wood hesitated. The court was still and soundless.

"I did go to The Rising Sun on Monday night," he said, "but later —later than 8.15, it was."

"Do you suggest that the appointment which you kept was not made by that postcard which you wrote?"

The facts had not changed, yet somehow they now wore a different aspect. Wood felt uncertain of his ground. He stumbled badly.

"There was no *seriousness* attached to it," he said. "It was immaterial to me."

Mathews pounced.

"My question is not directed to materiality. It is directed to fact. Did you keep the appointment made on the postcard?"

There could be no turning back.

"Well, it was hardly a promise," Wood protested.

"An understanding?"

"So mild," said Wood, "that it was only by the way."

But an admission that the message on the postcard had implied even the mildest "understanding" was in open contradiction to what Wood had said before—that the words were utterly meaningless and empty; only set down, as the first that came into his head, when Phyllis had asked him to "write something nice on it."

It had, of course, no direct bearing on the crime; it disclosed another lie, but he had confessed to many lies; none the less, this enforced reversal of a statement that he had made only yesterday on oath could not be considered a hopeful augury.

Wood did indeed quickly go from bad to worse. Mathews turned next to the fragments from the grate, which the Crown still maintained were the remnants of a letter. He gave Wood the slide, asked him to examine it, and pointed out a half-decipherable sequence: ". . . ill you . . . ar of the . . . e . . . Town . . . Wednes . . ."

"Take that in your hand," the prosecutor said. "Let us try to reconstruct this passage." Memories went back to what the ship's cook said he saw: Will you meet me at the bar of The Eagle at Camden Town 8.30 tonight, Wednesday.—Bert. "It seems to begin 'Will you,' does it not?"

"I'll give you the 'w,'" Wood said, "if you wish."

"Then there is something illegible followed by 'ar.' Tell me, as it originally stood, didn't this run: 'Will you meet me at the bar?'"

"Are you imagining that?" Wood ironically enquired.

"No, no." Mathews rapped out a sharp repudiation. "No, no. I am imagining nothing. I am asking you, who admit you were the writer, what the wording originally was. Can you help me?"

"No, I can't."

"Well, I don't propose to dismiss it quite so readily." Once more the deadly little man pulled and flapped his gown. "Please look at it again. I put it to you that it originally ran: 'Will you meet me at the bar of The Eagle.'"

'You are imagining it,' Wood reiterated. "I didn't even know then what the place was called."

"The public house where you went with Dimmock on the Saturday?"

"Yes."

"You say you didn't know its name?"

"I have been to many houses in my life," said Wood, "but I didn't know and I don't know the names of all of them."

That was not implausible. Mathews astutely reverted to the slide.

"You see that next is a blurred space, and then follows the word 'Town.' Didn't 'Camden' come before the word 'Town' in the letter?"

"Sir Charles, it was *not* a letter."

"And next is 'Wednes . . .'—obviously 'Wednesday'?"

"Yes."

Mathews deliberately paused.

"Wasn't the Wednesday referred to the 11th of September?"

"Not to my knowledge."

"Consider. You had only known this girl, you say, for five days altogether, beginning on the Friday before she met her death?"

"Yes."

"She died early in the morning of Thursday, 12th September?"

"So I understand."

"Mustn't the Wednesday referred to here be September the 11th?"

A flat denial was now virtually impossible.

"It might have been," Wood said.

Mathews folded his arms.

"So these words which remain, when critically read, are consistent with the making of an assignation?"

"That's what *you* suggest, Sir Charles."

"Let us see what *you* suggest." The words shot out with the speed and militancy of machine-gun bullets. "Did you say that it was something you had written in her presence?"

"I said it might be. I honestly can't make head or tail of it. I can only imagine it was something of the sort."

"Something of what sort?"

"Oh, just sketches and amusing phrases."

"Can you find any sketches on it?"

"No."

"Or any trace of a sketch?"

"No."

"Or any amusing phrase?"

"No."

"Or anything which might conceivably be part of one?"

Wood turned the slide between his fingers helplessly.

"No."

"When do you say you gave that document to Dimmock?"

"I don't know that I gave her anything."

"Then where do you suggest she got it?"

"I don't know . . . except that she looked through the letters from my pocket when I pulled out my sketch book in the bar."

"Do you suggest she *took* it?" Mathews asked icily.

"Yes," Wood said, then added pitifully. "She was very forward. Those girls are. . . ."

All that morning Mathews kept Wood upon the rack. Fashions change, even in the practice of the law, and such remorselessness by counsel for the Crown might not pass uncriticised today. No one, however, could reasonably complain that, as such, the cross-examination was improper. Mathews never stooped to a questionable device; he was inexorable but scrupulous, hard-hitting but correct. His triumph over Wood—for triumph, by any measurement of scoring points, it was— seemed the proper due of a brilliant cross-examiner whose gifts had dazzled everyone in court.

But while the limelight thus beat on his opponent, the defender did not retreat far into the shade. It is a peculiar attribute of the greatest advocates that they can exert authority by their very presence. During the three hours in which Mathews questioned Wood, Marshall Hall uttered hardly a dozen words. But he was there; a vibrant, active force, refusing to cede the dominion he had won. Not for a moment were the jury permitted to forget him—nor what he had said, nor the cause for which he stood.

The general public now was with Wood to a man. It furnished ample proof of the defender's grip upon them that Mathews, despite his virtuosity, had not been able to reverse this favourable trend. Within and without the crowds seemed of one mind; they were no longer sympathetic, they were frankly partisan; they were not merely hoping for but *willing* an acquittal. As the minutes of the afternoon ticked by, and the trial steadily drew towards its close, this emotion sometimes passed out of control; hysterical demonstrations took place in Newgate Street, and when the judge, who had begun his summing-up in a manner markedly adverse to the accused, unexpectedly said something in his favour, the notabilities in court forgot themselves and cheered.

No jury could have been insensitive to the pressure of this mass anxiety. But that did not necessarily mean the jury shared it, nor that they would feel any compulsion to give way. Between those who are free from responsibility and those upon whom responsibility is thrust the approach to a verdict may be radically different. It is of no avail to carry thirty million with you if you fail to carry the adjudicating twelve.

Marshall Hall need have entertained no fears. His conquest was to be complete. By a memorable feat of all-round advocacy, in which his splendid talents were extended to the full, he had transformed the losing battle of a week ago into the winning battle of today. He had saved Wood from the gallows and the processes of justice from the shame of grievous error. . . .

It was exactly eight o'clock when the jury returned after fifteen minutes' absence. A few seconds later pandemonium broke loose.

That night, though, the Old Bailey was the quietest place of all.

The town was running wild. Men shouted and waved hats; women wept and fluttered handkerchiefs; groups formed impromptu processions of rejoicing; traffic was held up in scores of streets. It seemed, said Marshall Hall with surprising understatement, less like the end of a trial than the result of an election.

But the court, after its frenzied climax, stood silent and empty. Those who had daily gathered there were gone their separate ways—the actors to their theatres, the journalists to their papers, the authors to their studies, Robert Wood to a new life under a new name, Marshall Hall to the next of that long line of cases which was to keep him in the limelight for a further twenty years. The Camden Town drama was at last played out and abandoned for good by its cast of characters.

Only one was bound to it for ever; one who had not been present at the trial at all. She lay now, as she lay then, six feet underground, and her throat had been cut from ear to ear right back to the spine.

16

Elvira Barney

EVERY outstandingly successful advocate is to some degree the creation of his age. By natural instinct or by conscious acquisition he reflects the temper and the ethos that prevails among the society in which his work is done. Failing this, no technical equipment will attain the topmost heights.

Patrick Hastings—who unquestionably takes rank among the greatest jury advocates who have ever adorned the Bar—is the supreme example of a forensic master precisely attuned to the requirements of the time. In any generation his exceptional talents would have won acknowledgment: his extraordinary acuteness as a cross-examiner; his agility and resourcefulness in argument; the vigour of his quick and lucid mind, keenly intelligent rather than deeply intellectual, which made him more at home—as befits a jury advocate—with people and affairs than with theories and ideas. But to these was added a decisive factor that served to set the lasting seal on his success and fame: a worldly knowledge that was rooted in the moment. This worldliness, this fund of contemporary sense, directed his approach to every case he undertook; to those for whom he fought, to those he fought against, to those upon whom rested the outcome of the fight. That approach can be defined in a single word, used in its best and most recent connotation. More than any other counsel of comparable eminence, Hastings was a *sophisticated* advocate—in fashionable practice when fashionable people were setting new standards in advanced sophistication.

Sophisticated people do not care for strident emphasis; they stand on guard against assaults on the emotions; they like effects to be subtle and power to be concealed. In the language of the theatre, they prefer to have their dramas underplayed.

Hastings introduced, or at any rate perfected, the art of underplaying in the English jury courts. He utterly discarded the barnstorming technique; nobody has ever been more unlike Marshall Hall—nor, one suspects, more pleased to be unlike him. Hastings never stormed nor shouted; never waved his arms about; never gave any sign that he felt at all excited nor that he wished to cause excitement among others. And yet, in the sphere of high life litigation, there has never been a more exciting advocate, nor one who could exert a more mesmerising spell. The personality, cool, self-contained, rather offhand, slightly cynical; the voice, no organ throb moving listeners to tears, but smooth and even purring with an undertone of sarcasm; the manner, informed with that assurance and that ease which, in a public performer, masks the highest art—they enthralled and fascinated London Special Juries, particularly in the years between the two world wars. Here was an advocate whose individual style accorded with current cultivated taste. Hastings was a portent and an influence at the Bar analogous with and parallel to du Maurier on the stage.

Like du Maurier, and for not dissimilar reasons, Hastings' professional home was the West End—which includes, for these purposes, the east point of the Strand but does not extend as far as the Old Bailey. During his great years in the very highest flight, when he was seldom missing from a civil *cause célèbre*, Hastings engaged in little criminal work and hardly ever accepted a capital defence. "I have always hated trials for murder"—so he wrote after retirement; and one might well imagine that such trials would repel a genius of his type and temperament.

This did not mean, though, that were he once involved he would not defend a murder case with dazzling ability. Especially a murder case falling, however remotely, into his chosen province; a murder case with a sophisticated setting and, at least upon the surface, a sophisticated twist.

Murder is rarely a sophisticated act; and suspicion of murder is generally aroused by the presence of unsophisticated passions. Greed, hate, jealousy and lust—these are universal impulses to action; but in a highly civilised and sceptical community one expects them to remain under reasonable control. It is therefore not surprising that, in contrast to the Borgias of fourteenth-century Italy and to the Medicis of six-teenth-century France, the well-to-do classes of twentieth-century Britain did not go in for killing, except with motor cars. Their murder rate was low, their murder charges few, even in proportion to their restricted numbers. During the last two decades of their existence—for since 1940 they have been virtually wiped out in the redistribution of property and wealth—they found ample employment for their favoured advocates by libel, slander, probate squabbles, and divorce.

This had become such a convention of the epoch that its one great murder trial which did involve the rich came to many as a bolt out of the blue. It gave an entirely unexpected handle to those who disliked and denounced sophistication, but had formerly had no grounds for connecting it with violence. Even now, unless qualified, the implication was unwarranted. For the tiny band of debauchees and profligates that formed the human background to the case of Mrs. Barney was no more than a foul offshoot, a leprous excrescence, of true sophistication. They enjoyed—either at first or second hand—the wealth so helpful to sophisticated living; they used what passed for sophisticated language; the simple were deceived by their sophisticated front. But theirs was sophistication that had run riot and turned rotten; sophistication that had gone into reverse. Idle, drunken, emotionally unstable, crude in conduct as they were coarse in spirit, they made a natural forcing bed for frenzy and convulsion.

Out of the rank soil of this Mayfair saturnalia sprang the most vivid murder trial of 1932. It gave the upper strata of society a shaking, seized the undivided attention of the lower, and involved all England in a passionate debate about the character and morals of the woman they accused.

Life had showered many favours on Elvira Barney. She was well-bred; her titled parents, with their house in Belgrave Square and their country seat in Sussex, occupied a position of dignity and respect. She was affluent; money raised no shadow of a problem and her pleasures never had to be curtailed through lack of means. She was attractive in the style her contemporaries preferred—a face that was pleasing rather than beautiful; large grey eyes; a tip-tilted nose; blonde and fluffy hair; a boyish figure (though by the time of her trial, when she was only twenty-six, both figure and face were paying for indulgence). She had animal energy and natural intelligence. All these assets she threw heedlessly away.

From her very early womanhood the writing on the wall grew steadily more visible. The existence she led, the diversions she sought, the friends she cultivated—every one was trivial, rackety and exhausting. For a period she did toy with the idea of being an actress, and once even appeared on the stage of the Gaiety in some tiny part in a musical play; but hard work enticed her less than superficial glamour, and she did not press ahead with a theatrical career. She married, with characteristic levity and caprice, a cabaret singer who had performed at a function in her father's house and whom she decided she had fallen in love with at first sight; this marriage turned out badly— Mrs. Barney later spoke of it as "hell"—and the couple separated, never to re-unite. Mr. Barney returned to the United States whence he had come, and contributes nothing to this story but his name.

The break-up of her marriage expedited Mrs. Barney's downward course. London's Bright Young People claimed her for their own. You still sometimes meet survivors of this long extinguished set; they are mostly male and now almost invariably perverts. Gin-soaked, fish-eyed, tearful with self-pity, these middle-aged derelicts haunt the bars of Kensington and Chelsea, calling down curses on their present lot and feebly lamenting the gay days that are no more. It is hard to believe, looking at them now, that anyone could have ever found them tolerable. But youth, while it lasts, is a potent alchemist, and for Mrs. Barney certainly they were not without appeal. Her home in William Mews, near Knightsbridge—a converted cottage—became one of their recognised resorts and her black and red two-seater an addition to their transport. There were many parties; there was much dashing to and fro; there was a brisk traffic in sexual partnerships, from which Mrs. Barney did not hold herself aloof.

Her lover, who had no genuine occupation (he vaguely described himself as a dress designer), rented an apartment room on Brompton Road. Everyone called him Michael, although that was not his name. Like Mrs. Barney herself, he was respectably derived; but his father, a prominent magistrate and banker, in disgust at his son's conduct, had cut off his allowance; Michael had lately kept himself supplied with cash by "borrowing" alternately from his mother and his brother. He was now apparently quite content to be kept by his new mistress.

There were several other things besides good family and a taste for dissipation that Mrs. Barney had in common with this handsome wastrel. They were exactly the same age. They both drank far too much. And each was prone to sudden fits of jealousy, his petulant and sulky, hers unbridled and consuming.

As in all the circumstances could have been foreseen, their relationship was marked by wildly fluctuating phases. There were times of mutual rapture, all the more intense for being so perilously poised; times when they made love with fierce abandonment or wrote each other tender letters in the idiom affected by adults when addressing infants. There were also times of mutual agony, when they tore them-

selves and their shallow love to tatters; times when they had painful
and degrading scenes in public and quarrelled bitterly far into the
night. Neighbours in the mews, mostly chauffeurs and their wives, suffered whichever condition was prevailing; the din of recrimination and
dispute was matched by the din of exultant celebration. Resentment
aroused by these continual disturbances was not without its bearing
upon subsequent events.

If that resentment fixed upon the woman, not the man, the causes
were manifest and comprehensible. She, not he, was the tenant of the
cottage. She, not he, was in constant residence, the human storm spot
of a peaceful neighbourhood. And she, not he, was the dominating
partner; even the least discerning could perceive that at a glance. Hers
was the more possessive and explosive nature; the more self-willed; the
more accustomed to impose itself on others. Of Elvira Barney it might
be said with literal truth that she would rather die than be deprived of
her own way.

One has forgotten the smart jargon of 1932, so it is impossible to
say whether the party Mrs. Barney gave on the 30th of May was divine
or marvellous or super or terrific. There were, however, abundant
indications that it gave great pleasure to the persons who attended, and
it presented the neighbours with a further opportunity of studying
their social betters at close range. From shortly after six the racing cars
rattled and roared into the mews; their occupants, loudly shouting to
each other, vanished one by one through Mrs. Barney's door; the hubbub floating through the windows steadily increased as the female
voices grew more shrill, the male more stentorian; sometimes a solitary
guest, appearing overtaxed, came out into the mews for a few minutes'
fresh air; and once or twice, keen-eyed observers noted, a couple would
emerge, drive off in one of the cars, and, half an hour later, return and
go inside again. Mrs. Barney did nothing by half measures; she entertained her friends in the style to which they were accustomed.

By half-past nine, though, all of them had gone. Michael—who had
been handing drinks assiduously—and Mrs. Barney—who had been
assiduously taking them—now sat alone amid the residual débris. They
drank some more—he faster, in order to catch up. When they had put
themselves entirely in the mood they set off together on their usual
nightly round.

Soon after ten o'clock they were seen having dinner in the Café de
Paris. Soon after eleven they were seen at a well-known night resort
in Dean Street—the management of which indignantly complained

when the papers so described it in the days and weeks that followed. ("We are a high-class social rendezvous and members' club.") Soon after twelve they left this club and so far as is known went straight back to William Mews.

They were certainly there at three, when yet another of their quarrels broke the silence of the summer night. Sleepers in the mews reluctantly awakened; swore at the nuisance; prayed it would die down. But instead the uproar gathered force and swelled in volume. Woman's voice; man's voice; woman's voice; man's voice; separate and distinct at first, then jumbled together. The mews pulled its sheets round its infuriated head; but could not shut out this obliterating row. Groans, abuse, tears, entreaties—and was that the sound of a struggle, of a fight?

Somewhere about four there was a piercing crack. People sat up, startled. No, it couldn't be. Crazy as that woman was, it couldn't be. . . .

Most of them had dropped off again to sleep before the doctor's telephone began to ring.

"I have been cautioned that I am not obliged to make this statement. I have known Michael for about a year. We were great friends, and he used to come and see me from time to time.

"He always used to see me home. He did so last night as usual. Immediately we got in we had a quarrel about a woman he was fond of.

"He knew I kept a revolver in the house. I have had it for years. It was kept in various places. Last night it was under the cushion of a chair in the bedroom, near the bed. I was afraid of it and used to hide it from time to time. He knew where it was last night.

"He took it, saying, 'I am going to take it away for fear you kill yourself.' He went into the room on the left. I ran after him and tried to get it back.

"There was no struggle in the bedroom. It was outside in the spare room, in the doorway. As we were struggling together—he wanted to take it away, and I wanted to get it back—it went off. Our hands were together—his hands and mine. . . .

"I did not think anything had happened. He seemed quite all right. He went into the bathroom and half shut the door, and said, 'Fetch a doctor.'

"I asked, 'Do you really mean it?' I did not have the revolver then. I think it had fallen to the ground.

"I saw he looked ill, so I rang up a doctor, but no one answered. I went upstairs again and saw him sitting on the floor.

"I was upset and began to cry. I again rang up the doctor and he said he would come. I went upstairs again. Michael asked, 'Why doesn't the doctor come? I want to tell him what happened. It was not your fault.'

"He repeated that over and over again. I tried to cut his tie off, put a towel on his chest and got towels. I again rang up the doctor, and they said that he was leaving.

"I again went upstairs and saw he was dead and just waited. I don't remember what I did afterwards. I was so frantic. I am sure—as far as I know—there was only one shot fired.

"Michael and I have quarrelled on previous occasions, but not often."

Mrs. Barney leaned back. Her face was ashen and her breath came heavily. While the Inspector read over her statement in official monotone, for the first time she allowed her eyes to wander over the bleak and bare police station room.

The foolscap sheets were put in front of her. Mechanically she signed.

It was morning, almost ten o'clock in the morning, after a night packed full with horror and distress. When the doctor arrived in response to Mrs. Barney's summons ("There has been a terrible accident; for God's sake come at once!") he beheld a scene that might have been pleasing in a mystery novel, but was apt to harrow the steadiest nerves when encountered in real life. Michael sprawled at the top of the stairs, a bullet through his lung; it was obvious to the doctor that he was already dead. Close beside him lay a pistol; it contained five cartridges, two of which were spent. Mrs. Barney herself was uncontrollably hysterical and only intermittently coherent. "He cannot be dead, he cannot be dead," she cried time and again. "I will die too; I want to die. I loved him so. I loved him so." As the doctor, stooping low over the corpse, confirmed his initial melancholy conclusion, she ran aimlessly to and fro, calling the dead man's name and trying to explain what had occurred in disconnected fragments.

The arrival of the police (whom the doctor as in duty bound immediately informed) seemed to drive the unhappy woman clean out of her mind. She said afterwards that she had no recollection of this episode, and quite conceivably she was in some sort of delirium; if not—whether innocent or guilty—her conduct would have surely been less hurtful to her cause. She cursed and fulminated against the officers, calling them "vile swine" and ordering them to leave; when they used the telephone, she snatched it from their hands; when told that she must go to the police station for further questioning, she gave her interrogator a blow across the face. She shrieked, stamped, laughed and wept alternately. She was, said the doctor, absolutely frenzied. . . .

No spark of frenzy lingered in Mrs. Barney now. It had died when they took her away from the cottage that had been her home and where now her lover's body lay. Thenceforward she was calm but patently exhausted; what woman could be otherwise who in so few hours had passed through so many prostrating events? While she made her statement, under the horrified eyes of her distracted parents who had been apprised and had hurried to her side, Mrs. Barney must have been close to collapse from sheer fatigue.

The clarity of her account thus becomes the more remarkable. Moreover, it entirely corresponded in essentials with all she had so far said and all she was yet to say. There were one or two omissions, probably deliberate. It would have been painful to reveal in the presence of her parents that she and Michael had been lovers many months; that the quarrel had developed after they had gone to bed; that Michael had threatened to leave her, got up again and dressed; that it was then she had talked of committing suicide. She hoped—no doubt expected—that the matter would soon drop without necessitating these intimate disclosures. But substantially the story that was outlined in her statement was the story that the doctor had already pieced together from her paroxysmal and confused ejaculations; nor was it changed in that excruciating hour when, with two prison wardresses beside her, she told it to a packed and palpitating court. . . .

The police conferred together. Her own statement exculpated Mrs. Barney, and they had no evidence yet to suggest it was untrue.

"Very well," said the Inspector, "we will not trouble you, madam, any more just now. You are free to go."

"She will come home with us, of course, Inspector," said her mother. . . .

The respite was a short one. Only three days afterwards, as the troubled family prepared for dinner, the police came visiting the house in Belgrave Square. They had now been able to make a full investigation and, as a result, were no longer satisfied. Data in their possession could not be made to tally with the statement that the lady gave them earlier in the week.

That evening Mrs. Barney, who had said she wished to die, stood in grave danger that this wish would be fulfilled.

From the moment of her arrest the popular press was in full cry; their headlines sometimes read like a satirical burlesque. "West End Flat Mystery," "Society Tragedy Sensation," "Mayfair Beauty in Shooting Drama," "Banker's Son Dead after Cocktail Party," "Knight's Daugh-

ter on Murder Charge"; variations revolved round these titillating words
—save in one instance, where a banner frankly promised "Mrs. Barney:
The Biggest Thrills." The prisoner herself, on her first appearance at
the preliminary proceedings in the police court, unintentionally added
to the atmosphere of melodrama by falling to the floor of the dock in
a dead faint.

Mrs. Barney had good reason to feel deeply apprehensive. The police had not at all overstated their position; the new evidence—if accepted—made her story of an accident untenable. One female neighbour was fully prepared to swear she had heard Mrs. Barney shout
"I'll shoot you" just before the shot. Another female neighbour was
equally prepared to swear that she had heard more than one shot
being fired (an assertion that appeared to gain considerable force from
the presence of a bullet mark on the cottage bedroom wall). Both
women also spoke of an incident some days earlier when, as they declared, Mrs. Barney from the window fired at Michael in the mews.
And to all these presumed facts was added the opinion of two exceptionally influential experts, Churchill the gunsmith and Spilsbury the
pathologist; each independently had come to the conclusion that Mrs.
Barney's version of the shooting was improbable. The former attached
special significance to the type of pistol. "It requires both a long and
heavy pull," he said.

The Crown thus had a formidable case and the prisoner sore need
of a formidable defender. For once in a murder trial money was no
object. The brief for Mrs. Barney was offered to Patrick Hastings.

One may surmise that that distinguished advocate, then a little over
fifty and at the very peak of his dazzling career, thought hard before
he undertook this burden. It was in the middle of the summer term,
and a dozen heavily marked briefs were on his desk. He was representing one of the great trusts in a claim for £60,000 from one of the
great banks. He was retained by a leading theatre management in a
suit for damages brought by a leading lady. He was concerned for the
co-respondent in an aristocratic divorce with Eaton Square addresses
and an adultery charge at Cannes. He was also concerned in a big
probate action (disposed of four days before the Barney trial began),
in a newspaper libel on a popular peeress (settled three days after the
Barney trial concluded), and, as leader of a string of eminent counsel,
in an appeal by the directors of a company against a verdict of £250,-
000 imposed upon them for conspiracy and fraud. (This last case
actually started on the final morning of Mrs. Barney's trial, and continued uninterruptedly thereafter for a fortnight.) There were certainly

ample demands on Patrick Hastings—and there was, of course, his confessed dislike of capital defences.

Nevertheless, he did not decline the Barney brief, and this without doubt was artistically fitting. Here at last for the sophisticated advocate was a murder case that had at least grown out of his own world.

Any murder trial at any time tends to attract spectators if only because the stake is human life. A sensational Victorian trial like Mrs. Bartlett's or a sensational Edwardian trial like Robert Wood's was not only sure of a continuously packed court, but also—as has already been remarked—would draw and hold great multitudes in the adjoining streets. More recently this latter phenomenon had been rarely seen. It reappeared, however, at the trial of Mrs. Barney, which, on 4th July and the two succeeding days, made the Central Criminal Court like a fortress under siege.

The military metaphor is far from inappropriate. For in one respect, at least, the crowds on this occasion easily surpassed all their predecessors. They were less demonstrative than some, partly because of the changed bent of the time, partly because at no point was there anything approaching unanimity of view upon the case's merits. But they were surely unique in ferocity and resolve. The waiting crowds of earlier years may have envied those within; they did not themselves seek entry by violence and brute force. But many of those who stood and stared at the walls of the Old Bailey, hour after hour while Mrs. Barney was being tried, only accepted this second-best sensation after a pitched battle in which they were repelled.

The queue had begun to form on Sunday afternoon, more than twenty hours before the court was due to sit. Well before midnight it had grown so long and deep that the police decided it ought to be dispersed. Those who had already waited nearly half a day did not receive this decision with good humour. There were loud cries of protest; heated disputes developed; one poor old lady burst into bitter tears—she had been there since two o'clock and now her last train had gone.

The police, however, insisted on their orders being obeyed, and reluctantly the crowds withdrew from their vantage-ground. Some gave up altogether and went home. Some took refuge in the all-night cafés, where they debated plans for making a fresh attempt. But the majority merely split up into groups of two or three, who walked and stood and squatted in the neighbourhood all night and took up posts next morning within sight of the court door like so many beasts of prey around a water-hole.

These omens were not lost upon the police, and a strong protective cordon was established before giving the signal that the queue might be re-formed. Strong, but not strong enough to seize immediate control. From all directions men and women flew towards the spot with an impetus as if they had been shot from catapults. The cordon swayed, retreated and at one point finally broke; the mob hurled themselves madly at the gap; and that first afternoon the newspapers had pictures of police and civilians struggling on the ground.

Only a handful of these warriors gained admission to the court, where most of the space had been allotted in advance by tickets bearing the full name of the successful applicant. But there, too, disorder threatened, though a different kind. Many of the tickets had somehow been obtained by young, well-dressed and frivolous-minded women who regarded the trial as a theatrical first night and proceeded to behave like the audience at one. They giggled and chattered with indecent zest as they waited, all agog, for the performance to begin.

At any intimation of weakness on the Bench this animated bevy might have got right out of hand. There was no such intimation. "If there is any more of this," remarked his lordship coolly, when the female babble broke out for the first time in his presence, "the whole court shall be cleared."

Thenceforward silence reigned. Even the silliest could see that Mr. Justice Travers Humphreys was a man who meant exactly what he said.

Hastings had come into court just before the appointed hour. After one contemptuous glance at the gay parade of fashion, he took his place without ostentatious fuss and sat there very straight and very quiet and very still. Those present who had witnessed Marshall Hall's volcanic entries on similar occasions, and the indisputable gallery play that followed them, could hardly fail to be struck by the sharp contrast. One thing only the two men had in common—a personality magnetic and commanding. Without the slightest effort—almost as though it were contrary to his wish—from the very moment when he first appeared Hastings dominated the entire Old Bailey scene. Long before he had said a single word, even during the opening statement for the Crown, the eyes of the jury were straying constantly to him. . . .

A practised observer can usually detect when a prosecutor feels full confidence in his case. If he harbours any serious doubt himself, being imbued by his training with the salutary doctrine that the prisoner must receive the benefit of a doubt, this is almost sure to be reflected in his speech. He will pitch his argument in a lower key, sprinkle it with exceptions and provisos, leave the issue conspicuously open. In short, he becomes more narrator than accuser.

Nothing of this kind occurred at the trial of Mrs. Barney. Percival Clarke, leading counsel for the Crown, gave the jury at the outset a strong and clear lead. His manifest integrity—befitting a son of Mrs. Bartlett's great defender—lent his comments additional effect. Some of these consisted of direct denunciation. Of the prisoner's hysteria on the arrival of the doctor he said: "Perhaps she realised then what she had done." Of her assault upon the police: "You see what sort of temper this woman gives way to on slight provocation." And of the actual shooting he spoke in these uncompromising terms: "The medical evidence can definitely establish the direction in which the revolver was held when fired. You will learn from that that it is practically impossible for the man to have caused this injury to himself. If he did not, who did? There was only one other person there. If you are forced to the conclusion that she shot him, you will have to consider whether she did it by accident or design. In that connection you will bear in mind her admission of the quarrel. You will bear in mind what she shouted before the gun was fired. You will bear in mind that she had fired the gun during another quarrel on a previous occasion. Members of the jury, is there any explanation consistent with common sense which will enable you to understand how that man met his death unless this woman *deliberately* fired?"

To the lawyers in court—and there were a great number, some even disposing themselves upon the floor—it became more apparent as each minute passed that the prosecution were not pulling any punches. Obviously they believed in their case and they were both seeking and expecting a conviction.

The chief witnesses called on the first day of the trial were Mrs. Barney's much-enduring neighbours from the mews.

There were three altogether; but the last, a chauffeur, was of little consequence. It was the two women who mattered—the women, each of them a decent chauffeur's wife, who had had their lives made wretched by Mrs. Barney's escapades. The defence could not hope to find them favourably inclined, and their cross-examination needed infinite finesse.

One important gain, though, Hastings made without exertion; simply by watchfulness and tactical restraint. The first chauffeur's wife was being examined by the Crown. She had given her account of the earlier incident in the mews, describing how Mrs. Barney leaned out of the window; how she was holding "something bright" in her *left* hand; how there was a report and witness saw "a puff of smoke." Now she had come to the night of Michael's death, and to the one real point at which she might have thrown some light upon it.

"So you heard the sounds of their quarrelling," Clarke said. "Were there any words—any *important* words—you could pick out?"

"Yes," she replied. "Just before the shot I heard Mrs. Barney say, 'Get out. I'll shoot. I'll shoot.'"

Now "I'll shoot" is not at all the same thing as "I'll shoot *you*," which was what the woman had originally told the police; otherwise Clarke would not in turn have told the jury. "I'll shoot" is as consistent with a threat to commit suicide as a threat to commit murder. If the evidence stood thus—and no other witness claimed to have overheard this passage—it need no longer conflict with the prisoner's own story.

"You heard her say 'I'll shoot'?" Clarke repeated interrogatively.

The rules of British procedure do not permit counsel to put leading questions on matters in dispute to any witness that he himself has called. A leading question, one should point out, is not—as common usage would suggest—a question peculiarly probing or embarrassing; it is one so framed as to indicate the answer that the questioner desires or expects. It is not "leading" to ask "Where were you yesterday?"; it is "leading" to ask "Did you go yesterday to Brighton?" It would certainly have been "leading" had Clarke at this juncture asked the witness "Did you hear the prisoner call out, 'I'll shoot *you*,'" and Hastings, though he sat with folded arms, looking straight ahead, was poised to intervene with an immediate objection. But it did not prove necessary. Clarke bowed to the inevitable and passed to something else.

Hastings carefully refrained from mentioning the matter in cross-examination. Any attempt at that stage to emphasise the witness's cardinal omission ("So, after all, you only heard the prisoner say 'I'll shoot'?") might prompt her to reconsideration and retraction ("She *first* said 'I'll shoot,' and then after, 'I'll shoot *you*'"). There would be a later and a safer chance to enlarge on this discrepancy. Meanwhile prudence prescribed leaving well alone.

But there was still of course the earlier shooting to be dealt with, and the court now got its first glimpse of Hastings in full action.

He began in a tone so soft, so conversational, that spectators in the gallery held their breath for fear of missing a single word.

"This incident in the mews—it happened late one night?"

"Yes."

"About eleven o'clock next morning did you see the young man again?"

"Yes."

"Was he then leaving the cottage?"

"Yes."

"Was Mrs. Barney with him?"

"Yes."

"Did they seem friendly?"

"Yes."

"On the best possible terms?"

"Yes."

Marshall Hall would have paused there and stared hard at the jury. Hastings would no more emphasise a point in such a fashion than Noel Coward would wink at the stalls to stress a witty line.

The questions continued; terse, pithy—and exact. They left no room for evasion or misunderstanding.

"You saw this earlier incident while standing at your window?"

"Yes."

"And the young man was below you in the mews?"

"Yes."

"Did you give evidence at the police court?"

"Yes."

"Did you say there that immediately after the shot was fired the young man spoke to you?"

"Yes."

"And in the police court there the matter ended?"

"Yes."

"But now," said Hastings, "I want you to tell us what he said."

That he had touched a highly sensitive spot was attested by the quickness of the Crown's reaction.

"My lord, I object." Percival Clarke had at once sprung to his feet. "I submit that what this witness and the young man may have said outside Mrs. Barney's hearing cannot be admissible. That is why it was not tendered at the police court. And if it cannot be evidence for the crown, equally it cannot be evidence for the defence." *

He sat down. The judge cast an inquiring look at Hastings.

"In all my experience at the Bar," declared the latter, "I have never

---

* Clarke was pleading the same rule, but for Crown instead of prisoner, as Marshall Hall had done concerning the barmaid from The Eagle. (See p. 288.)

heard such an objection made before. The prosecution ask a question in the lower court and then they don't allow it to be answered." It was a perfect example of his gift for deadly ridicule, for deflating opposition in one swift, colloquial phrase. The jury, unversed in procedural technicalities, must have rejoiced in this attractive simplification—well calculated to excite their sympathy if the evidence should be ultimately excluded.

But the defence was very anxious that the evidence should be heard, and this depended not upon the jury but the judge.

Travers Humphreys listened attentively, impassively, as Hastings made his submission on the law. "Here the prosecution have proved a fact. They have proved there was the firing of a revolver from a window and that the deceased man *at that moment* made a statement to a witness. I submit it is always admissible to give evidence of any statement accompanying such an incident."

It was in fact a question involving much more doubt than might have been deduced from the defender's confident air. The judge, although an unsurpassed authority in this field, reflected deeply before giving a decision. "The matter is not free from difficulty," he said. "I think the objection was quite properly taken. But"—and the lawyers knew then the defence would get their way—"but . . . I do not think this evidence ought to be excluded."

The reason why both sides had treated this as a prime issue soon became apparent when Hastings, armed with sanction from the Bench, resumed.

"What conversation passed," he asked, "between you and the young man?"

"I told him to clear off," said the first chauffeur's wife, "as he was a perfect nuisance in the mews."

"What did he reply?"

"He said he didn't want to leave Mrs. Barney because *he was afraid that she might kill herself.*"

To the defence this admission was of immeasurable value. If Michael had previously confided to a stranger that he suspected Mrs. Barney of suicidal tendencies, what was more likely than that, prior to going away, he would at least try to dispossess her of the pistol? And if he did, what more likely than that a woman of her temperament, whether genuinely contemplating suicide or not, should struggle fiercely to defeat him in this purpose lest her expressed intentions should appear frustrated? . . .

It was the beginning, this—the beginning of a long series of scores

by Mrs. Barney's advocate that gradually cemented what had seemed
a flimsy case.

One such score was to be added before this witness left the box.

The defence were not going to disavow the earlier shooting, when
Mrs. Barney was upstairs and Michael in the mews. But they were
going to deny that she had fired *out* of the window, maintaining she
had fired, for effect, *inside* the room.

Others had seen Michael; others had heard the shot; but only this
lady spoke of seeing Mrs. Barney with the pistol in her hand at the
moment it was fired.

There was ground for supposing an imaginative faculty occasionally
influenced her powers of observation. Hastings brought this out into
the light.

"When the shot was fired," he said, "you say you saw a puff of
smoke?"

"I did."

"How big was it?"

The witness knitted her brows.

"Well—"

"As big as that?"

Counsel extended his hands about a foot apart.

"Oh no; not as big as that."

"How big, then?" Hastings asked encouragingly.

The witness spread her hands in turn.

"As big as that?"

"Yes."

Hastings nodded slightly. His next two questions seemed to come as
afterthoughts.

"I suppose you didn't know that Mrs. Barney's revolver contained
cordite cartridges?"

"No." The witness answered with indifference.

"And I suppose you don't know either," Hastings added casually,
"that cordite cartridges don't make any smoke?"

The ten men and two women on the jury may have known nothing
of the properties of cordite; but they did know, by applying ordinary
sense, that so shrewd a counsel would not make such an assertion if
it were open to subsequent disproof by the Crown. The puff of smoke
disappeared into thin air. . . .

The second chauffeur's wife seemed to have seen a good deal less,
but heard a good deal more. It was she who thought that on the night

of Michael's death more than one shot had been fired, and that they came in quick succession. If the jury thought so too, the outlook for Mrs. Barney would be bleak indeed.

Once again Hastings sought his ends without direct attack. Keenly aware of psychological resistances, he made no suggestion that the lady had been wrong. Instead of pressing her to cut down the number of the shots, he almost appeared to help her run them up. In no time at all she had sworn to hearing *five*.

"Quite a fusillade," observed defending counsel, absently fingering the barrel of the pistol, from which only two bullets had been fired in all. . . .

Few yet realised exactly what had happened. They felt instinctively that this sardonic advocate, restrained but masterful, was having his own way and getting what he wanted; they did not at once perceive how much he had wanted nor how far he had gone. There had been none of the orthodox phenomena associated with a crisis in a murder trial; the rising voices, the deepening gravity, the open conflict between witnesses and Bar. All they had heard were some crisp and simple questions asked in the most natural and unpretentious style. But where now was the mews evidence—the shouting and the shots?

It was like a conjuring trick—but a conjuring trick performed without any drum rolls or spotlights or hey prestos. Nor did the conjurer bother to take a formal bow.

The witnesses from the mews, for all essential purposes, constituted the whole of the Crown's evidence of *fact*. But in a trial the emphasis may be more upon *opinion*—the opinion of experts formed after the event.

Many have gone to the gallows in consequence of these. Would Norman Thorne have been hanged but for Spilsbury's opinion that no cord was ever passed round Elsie Cameron's neck? Would Seddon have been hanged but for Willcox's opinion that Eliza Barrow died from acute, not chronic, poisoning? Would Rouse have been hanged but for Colonel Buckle's opinion that the nut in his carburettor pipe was purposely made loose?

This is not written in disparagement of experts—none will deny that Seddon and Rouse, at least, were rightly hanged—but simply to recall again their influence and power. A famous name, an authoritative style, the mystique of science and the glamour of detection—these may combine to produce such an effect that juries on occasion find it almost irresistible.

Unless, of course, the glamour can be stripped off and the mystique penetrated.

The experts in the Barney trial were called on the second morning, and Spilsbury was the first to go into the box. He made his usual excellent impression: suave, sure of himself, with every detail at his finger ends, he took great pains to make the jury understand that Michael could not possibly have committed suicide. He made play with the pistol. He explained the nature and direction of the wound. He told of experiments he had made upon a skeleton. It was all immensely neat and competent; it bore on every word and movement the authentic Spilsbury stamp.

As the pathologist went through this demonstration Hastings preserved an appearance of detachment. "A most interesting performance," his expression said; "remarkably learned, extraordinarily instructive, it has nothing whatever to do with Mrs. Barney or with me." None the less, he was following most intently—waiting for any attempt on Spilsbury's part to dismiss as impossible the real defence of accident.

Although the point might not have struck the ordinary observer, no such attempt was ever made in positive terms. Whatever may have been the general tenor of his evidence, Spilsbury did not rule out accident in so many words. The omission, it seems certain, was one of policy. Both the Crown and their star witnesses doubtless expected events to trace a long familiar pattern; they thought defending counsel in cross-examination would try his utmost to get Spilsbury's blessing for his client's story. Better to hold direct comment on that story till then. Better leave the accident defence till it was raised.

But Hastings was a subtle and unorthodox tactician; he did not mind forgoing the slight chance of Spilsbury's blessing, provided he had not incurred his expressed condemnation.

The crowd was waiting eagerly for a titanic struggle between two such masters in their respective spheres. When Spilsbury's interrogation by the Crown was over, and Hastings was seen to be rising in his place, heads craned forward and hearts beat faster. People felt on the brink of an historical event.

Spilsbury watched Hastings narrowly as the first question was put.

"To qualify yourself to show how the bullet was fired into the body, you had to examine the skeleton of someone else?"

"I had to *confirm* it on the skelton of someone else," said Spilsbury.

"Does each human body differ in formation?"

"Yes, in the formation of the bones."

"And the best way to see how a bullet is fired into a body . . . is to look at it, I suppose?"

"Yes," Spilsbury admitted.

They had quickly got to grips. The spectators resettled themselves for a long and thrilling tussle.

The next thing they knew was that, incredibly, unaccountably, Hastings had sat down.

"Sir Bernard Spilsbury," he observed later to the jury, "gave no shred of evidence to suggest that the young man's death could not have been caused in the way that Mrs. Barney has always said it was. . . . He did not affect my case. I had no questions to ask him."

This neutralising of the country's crack professional witness was ultimately justified by the strictest of all tests. Meanwhile those in court received a shock of non-fulfilment, the kind of shock you get when you put your foot on a step that isn't there.

A more spectacular battle, however, was to come—a battle fought out toe to toe with every move in view, a battle in which the art and flair of Hastings were displayed so that laymen no less than lawyers could admire. . . .

Robert Churchill, who followed Spilsbury, was also a leading expert and a seasoned witness who had figured prominently in numerous murder trials. Whenever in a shooting case anything seemed to turn upon the bullets that were fired or the weapon that was used, more likely than not Churchill would be called on by the Crown. Level-headed, matter-of-fact, a savant in his sphere, he shared with Spilsbury an enviable legend of impregnability in cross-examination.

Upon that legend a chill wind was now about to blow.

Churchill had examined Mrs. Barney's pistol and gave his views about it with definite conciseness. It was one of the safest revolvers ever made. It could only be fired by the exercise of considerable strength. Therefore the idea of it going off accidentally when no one wished to fire certainly did not commend itself to him.

The defence could not skirt gracefully round such evidence as this. It struck at the essentials of Mrs. Barney's story. This time when Hastings rose it was no false alarm.

He placed the revolver on the flat of his hand and held it out before the witness and the jury.

"Do you seriously say," he asked, "that this is one of the safest weapons made?"

"I do," Churchill replied.

"Where is the safety device?"

"There isn't one."

"Isn't there one on most good hammerless revolvers?"

"Yes," said Churchill. "What I meant was that it's safer than a revolver with a hammer, safer than an automatic pistol."

"I see." Hastings suddenly grasped the pistol and held it up aloft. His finger pressed the trigger. Click-click, click-click, click-click it went continuously, with little more resistance than a child's cheap toy. "It doesn't seem to require any terrific muscular strength?"

"It would require more," said Churchill, "if the weapon were held loosely."

"Would it?" Hastings promptly changed his grip and held the revolver as the expert had suggested. "Would it?"

Again he pressed the trigger, quickly and repeatedly, with disdainful ease. And again it was the only sound in the hushed and listening court: click-click, click-click, click-click, click-click, click-click.

"Well," said Churchill, speaking as best he could in competition with the pistol, "I still say it's safer than an automatic."

Hastings kept on pressing the trigger almost languidly. Churchill watched him, a shade uncomfortably. The incessant sound of clicking only ceased when it had imprinted itself on every mind.

The defender laid the pistol on the desk before him.

"You know the sequence of cartridges found in this revolver?"

"I do, yes."

"Did they go like this—discharged, live, discharged, live, live?"

"Yes."

"The two discharged cartridges represent shots fired?"

"Yes."

"Somehow one chamber in between had been passed over?"

"Yes."

"Have you noticed something peculiar about this revolver—that if you only half pull the trigger the pressure just rotates the cylinder?"

"Yes."

"Rotates it, without firing?"

"Yes."

"It looks, doesn't it, as though some time after the first shot had been fired *something* had happened to press the trigger, but not to the full degree?"

"The cylinder had certainly been moved," said Churchill guardedly.

Hastings took care not to press the point further, not to involve

himself in argument as to what that "something" was. He relied upon
the quicker-witted members of the jury; they would not fail to realise,
in present circumstances, that a struggle for the weapon, with fingers
clutching at it indiscriminately, was more likely to give rise to a half
pull at the trigger than anybody's genuine attempt to fire a shot.

He again picked up the pistol and meditatively pressed the trigger
once or twice.

"Supposing a person had got the revolver and another person came
and there was a struggle, it is extremely likely that if they continued to
struggle and the revolver was loaded it would go off?"

"Yes," said Churchill.

"And it is quite impossible for anyone who was not there to know
exactly how the revolver in these circumstances would go off?"

"Yes," said Churchill.

"And if one person has the revolver in his hand and the other person
seizes it and the revolver is pointing towards him, it is certain it will
go off if it is pressed hard enough?"

"Yes," said Churchill.

"And if he happened to be there, opposite the revolver, he would
be certain to be killed?"

"Yes," said Churchill. "Yes, he would; of course."

How exactly had they reached this situation? The witness himself
might have found it hard to say. He had answered yes to a short series
of questions, none of which sounded very deadly in itself and each of
which hardly allowed of any other answer. And yet, at the end, he
seemed to have agreed that no flaw could be pointed out in Mrs.
Barney's case. Or hadn't he?

Anyone who shares this slightly puzzled feeling should study those
four questions phrase by phrase and word by word. Their deceptive
facility masks perfect craftsmanship.

That afternoon Mrs. Barney went into the box.

It is highly doubtful whether she had been able to form any clear
impression of her trial or any distinct notion about how matters were
going. In the first hour or so she had taken copious notes, but mainly
with the object of occupying herself, and the effort of concentration
soon became too great. Thereafter, most of the time, she had seemed
pathetically remote. Now and again a sob, immediately stifled, had
shown an awareness of what was being said; she could never hear,
without betraying emotion, any direct allusion to her lover's death. For
the rest she had sat back in her chair, her grey eyes fixed on some

point above the bench, ceaselessly twisting a handkerchief through
visibly trembling hands. She had been, as many prisoners mercifully
are, partially numb from suffering and anguish.

But now, having taken the oath, as she turned to face the court she
beheld her situation in cruelly sharpened outline. The judge, who
seemed so frighteningly close; the rows of counsel in their austere black
and white; her father's bowed head and her mother's piteous face up-
turned—all were assembled on her account. She, Elvira Barney, was
being tried for murder, and the punishment for murderers was death.
Her nerve momentarily snapped, and absolute breakdown threatened
just when her life might turn upon her self-command.

Perhaps this challenge, dimly apprehended, lent her strength. Perhaps she drew comfort from her famous counsel, who spoke to her
with reassuring informality, putting questions so specific yet so simply
framed that she could easily follow them notwithstanding her distress.
Perhaps the instincts of a quondam actress stood her in good stead
during this critical performance. Certainly she fought and overcame
her panic; only the first few answers came in choking whispers; soon
she was pouring out the tale of her afflictions in a voice not less audible
for being pleasantly low-pitched.

The order of her narrative—imposed, of course, by Hastings—was
skilfully judged in its cumulative power. She began by describing the
miseries of her marriage and the physical brutality exhibited by her
husband; this might reasonably be expected to arouse—in all probability for the first time in the trial—a modest degree of compassion for
the prisoner, and go a little way at least towards extenuation of the
vicious and discreditable life she had led since. She went on to say
that she had sought divorce, but she had been advised of legal difficulties,* and that she had earnestly desired to marry Michael; this put
the liaison in a rather better light and made her appear less contemptuous of good morals. She explained her possession of the loaded pistol
—not normally a young woman's dressing-table adjunct; it had been
given her several years ago by an army friend she named, from whose
country house they used to go out rabbit shooting; she had always
kept it with her in the cottage, which was easy game for burglars and
where she often was alone.

Then Hastings guided her to the first mews episode. She told how
she and Michael had quarrelled over money; how she had refused to
finance his gambling; how he had walked out of the cottage but would
not stay away, returning to create a scene in the middle of the night.

* Viz., that Barney being an American, she was a domiciled American herself.

"I was so unhappy," Mrs. Barney said, "I thought I would make him think I was going to commit suicide. So, when he was outside, I fired the pistol at random in the room. Then I thought if he really believed I'd killed myself he'd go and fetch people, so I looked out of the window."

"When was the bullet mark made on the bedroom wall?" Hastings asked.

"On that occasion," answered Mrs. Barney.

She maintained the mastery of her rebellious nerves even when asked about the night of Michael's death. Again she went through all the agonising details, from the start of the party early in the evening to the finish of it all in the shining summer dawn. Only when she spoke of Michael's last few living moments and of the last few words that she would ever hear him say, her will-power proved insufficient to the task and a storm of weeping broke upon her unrestrained. . . .

She did not give way to the same extent again, but by the day's end, after being searchingly and closely cross-examined, Mrs. Barney was not far from emotional exhaustion. But there was one more unexpected test for her to undergo.

"I want the revolver," said Hastings, "put on the ledge of the box exactly in front of the witness."

Everyone watched the usher carry out counsel's direction. Then their eyes moved back to Mrs. Barney. She was gazing down wretchedly at the source of all her griefs.

Hastings faced the judge. He seemed about to address him. Suddenly, almost violently, he turned.

"Pick up that revolver, Mrs. Barney!"

His voice rang out, deliberately harsh. That it gave Mrs. Barney a surprise and shock was manifest to all; it was beyond her meagre acting skill to simulate such a jump. She picked the pistol up at once—picked it up with her right hand.

There was a mighty throb in court as people realised that the first chauffeur's wife had said she fired it with her left.

The Crown, though, were neither disconcerted nor deterred. Clarke, it is true, could hardly have foreseen the exact trend of events during the past two crowded days—otherwise so sound an advocate would have modified his opening—but he had patently not wavered in his own view of the case nor in his expectation of its outcome. All along he had shown unabated confidence, and now, winding up at the end of the second afternoon, he sounded like a man merely clinching a decision. He pointed to Mrs. Barney's jealousy: "What was more likely to make her lose control?" He pointed to the peril in which she knew she stood: "What stronger motive could there be for colouring her story?" And that story itself? "It is incredible," he said. "If you can believe it—*if* you can believe it—of course, members of the jury, you will be happy to acquit. But"—and here the prosecutor spoke with solemn emphasis—"if you weigh the evidence carefully and dispassionately, I submit that you will find the accusation proved."

At this stage many, perhaps most, were ready to agree. I personally believe that if the verdict had been taken there and then Mrs. Barney would not have been acquitted. The jury must have been keenly aware of the defence successes, so brilliantly accomplished and accented by her counsel, but the relation of these successes to each other and their implication when considered as a whole were as yet almost certainly beyond them. They could only be made plain by a feat of argument— not of eloquence, nor imagery, nor pathos—but sheer hard *argument*, explicit and translucent, which would convince the reason and satisfy the mind.

Such a performance was forthcoming on the morrow when Patrick Hastings made his closing speech.

That speech contains no quotable passages of rhetoric. It will never be a feature of collections or anthologies. For perfection of phrase and elegance of form it cannot compare with more sumptuous orations, such as that of J. P. Curran on behalf of Justice Johnson or that of John Inglis on behalf of Madeline Smith. It was never designed nor intended so to do. It can only be judged within the context of the trial; by its aptness and response to the immediate demand; by its value in advancing the cause of the accused. The test of advocacy, in the last resort, is functional and empiric—and by that test Hastings' speech for the defence of Mrs. Barney will hold its own in the most exalted sphere. . . .

There were no eye-catching preliminaries; no pose adopted, no attitude struck, to mark the imminence of a big occasion. As soon as the court sat next morning he got up and began.

"Members of the jury, I shall not indulge in flights of oratory or dramatic surprises such as are supposed to be the attributes of an advocate. They may be amusing, but we are not in this court to amuse."

The note had been struck at once. As he stood facing them, almost motionless, hands clasped behind his back, he gave due notice that he meant to launch no emotional appeals. This was a serious matter, to be seriously considered, and not obscured by ill-timed histrionics. It was implied not more by his words than by his manner as he uttered a warning preface to his theme.

"I beg of you not to be unduly influenced by the first simple story that was put before you by the Crown two days ago. We know now that a great deal of it was . . . not absolutely accurate."

There was a sharp and icy edge to this restrained impeachment. It cut deep into the prosecution's case as Hastings backed it straight away by factual illustration.

"Do you remember how counsel for the Crown described Mrs. Barney—took great trouble to describe her—as a lady who lived in an extravagantly furnished flat?" Percival Clarke searched among his notes; he had indeed made use of this expression, and many of the newspapers had found it to their liking. "An extravagantly furnished flat—I wondered at the time why it was necessary to discuss the furniture. I am still wondering. I also wondered what evidence would be produced to bear out this assertion. That point, at any rate, does not remain in doubt.

"We have now heard that evidence—evidence given by witnesses for the Crown. Downstairs there was a sitting-room with one or two armchairs. Upstairs there was a front room with a divan bed in it and a back room with practically nothing in it at all. That," remarked Hastings in cool, even tones, "was the extravagantly furnished flat in which Mrs. Barney lived."

Needless to say, Clarke's blunder had been entirely innocent. He was probably misled at a much earlier stage when he learnt that the cottage had a fitted cocktail bar. This apparatus, though, must have enjoyed priority in the eyes of Mrs. Barney and did not typify the rest of the appointments. Hastings was fully justified in emphasising this, even if, as he said himself, the point was secondary.

"But the next thing is rather more dangerous than that." He recalled Clarke's reference to Mrs. Barney's ugly behaviour with the police, and the inference the jury had been desired to draw—that such was the sort of temper she customarily exhibited upon slight provocation. What was this "slight provocation"? Hastings asked. "It was this: that she was a young woman, entirely by herself, without the support and comfort of her parents or her friends; that within a few yards of her lay a dead body—the body of the man she obviously loved; that she was surrounded by a group of officers who were proposing to remove her to the station. That, says counsel for the Crown, is 'slight' provocation; a 'slight' strain upon the temper and the nerves. I wonder," added

Hastings, looking gravely at the jury, "what provocation he would class as serious."

The third and final thrust of this introductory phase had long been deferred until the appropriate hour. The Crown knew it was coming; its shadow had hung over them since early in the trial, but there was nothing they could do to parry or prevent it. The prosecution had to sit in silence while the wound was opened with a surgeon's neatness and dispatch. "Three separate times during the opening for the Crown you were told that Mrs. Barney had said 'I will shoot *you.*' People had heard her; they would say so in the box. . . . A good many people have been into the box, but not a single one has said anything of the kind."

The prologue was over. The defender had made it clear that the Crown had overcalled their hand. Now he was to bid upon the merits of his own.

"There are cases," he said, "in which advocates feel in such despair that they are driven to plead for mercy for their clients and to urge that they are entitled to the benefit of the doubt."

It was rarely indeed that Patrick Hastings raised his voice. He raised it now, and the effect was all the greater.

"I am going to do nothing of the sort. I am not going to ask you for the benefit of the doubt. I am going to satisfy you that there is no doubt. I am going to show you that there is no evidence at all."

As he set out to implement his pledge he held the jury in the hollow of his hand. Just as the supremely naturalistic actor makes his audience forget that they are looking at a stage, so this supremely naturalistic advocate almost made his audience forget they were in court. They were not conscious of listening to a speech, delivered upon a ceremonial occasion. They were engrossed in what was being said as people are engrossed in private conversation when matters of life and death are being decided. Their absorption was too complete for them to be aware of it.

The whole twelve followed in absolute surrender as Hastings came to deal with the earlier shooting in the mews. He first defined its precise relation to the case. "The prosecution ask you to believe that Mrs. Barney tried to murder on this previous occasion; that she shot at Michael then and that her purpose was to kill." Three witnesses had said they *heard* the shot on this occasion; only one—the first chauffeur's wife—had said she *saw* it fired. Her evidence alone conflicted with Mrs. Barney's description of the incident. And what exactly did her evidence amount to? How much confidence could be reposed in it? "She says she saw Mrs. Barney holding something bright. You can see for yourselves—this is a perfectly black revolver. She says she saw a puff of smoke after hearing the report. This revolver does not make any smoke. She says Mrs. Barney held whatever it was in her left hand. You will remember that I asked her to pick up the revolver at the conclusion of her terrible ordeal here in the box. She picked it up—like this—with her right hand." Displayed in counsel's grasp, the black lustreless pistol told its own tale to the jury. "It would be very odd indeed," Hastings quietly commented, "if the only time that Mrs. Barney used her left hand was when it is alleged she tried to commit murder."

So swiftly and decisively was punctuated the direct, visual evidence relating to this matter—the evidence of what was supposed to have been seen and done. But Hastings had not yet finished with the subject. He turned now to the indirect evidence—the things that were not seen and the things that no one did.

"Supposing *you* had been shot at, what would you have done? Wouldn't you have taken very quickly to your heels? Michael never budged. We have heard that he still stood about there in the mews, talking up at Mrs. Barney in the window—this man who, according to the Crown, stood in great and imminent danger of his life.

"Supposing *you* had been a witness of the scene, and you had believed this woman was trying to murder the man below—what then would you have done? Something, I'll be bound. What did these people do? Nothing whatsoever. They all went back to bed, and—as the police told me when I asked them yesterday—not a living soul ever lodged any complaint. Can you imagine that any of them thought that the revolver had been fired *out* of the window?

"And if it had, wouldn't you expect to find some trace of the bullet in the mews? I asked the police about this too; you'll recollect the answer; they made a thorough search but not a sign of it was found.

"This is not surprising, for the mark of that bullet was on the bedroom wall; it showed that Mrs. Barney had fired *inside* the room, to make this man whom she adored think she was so unhappy."

Any evidence there was against the prisoner on this incident had now been torn to shreds and irremediably scattered. The Crown indeed would have had a stronger-looking case without it. They would at least have been spared the scathing observation with which Hastings finally dismissed this episode. "If you think," he said, "that the prosecution have merely tried to bolster up their case by something of which there

is no evidence at all—well, then, it may help you to see with some
clarity what is the real position on the charge itself."

The real position on the charge itself—this Hastings now proceeded
to size up. He had been speaking for an hour, and the utter silence
waiting on his voice was the measure of the grip that he had gained
upon the court. "Not a sound," said that evening's paper, "broke the
steady stream of words, which seemed to hold everybody in a spell.
The jury, it was noted, eagerly leaned forward."

In calmly level tones, sometimes faintly shot with irony, Hastings
anatomised the night of Michael's death, scoring point after point in
Mrs. Barney's favour. The marks on the revolver had been too blurred
for fingerprints to be deciphered, just as one would expect following
a struggle; "if Mrs. Barney's fingerprints *had* been detected on it,
counsel for the Crown would have said it was conclusive—but is this
tremendous artifice of science only to be used when it helps a prosecution?" Within a few hours of the tragedy Mrs. Barney had made three
separate statements—to the doctor, to the police at home, to the police
at the station—but no question had been put to her in cross-examination suggesting that anything she had said in the statements was a
lie; "I don't think counsel for the Crown has mentioned that, so I am
venturing to supplement his speech." Everything denoted that Michael
was the object of her passionate devotion; "in all her distress and anguish, she wanted to kiss the man who was dead."

Mrs. Barney stared up at the high dome of the court. The reference
had produced its invariable effect; her mouth trembled, and presently
her face was stained with tears.

The compact argument flowed on uninterrupted. "Put yourself in her
position. Put yourself in that box with the wardresses beside you. Suppose yourself under thorough questioning by the Crown, with the
thought in your head of what each question might mean; not knowing
what you were going to be asked, not knowing what construction might
be placed upon your answers. Would you give your evidence like Mrs.
Barney did if what you were saying wasn't true? Was she caught out
anywhere? Was there any discrepancy between what she told you
and what she told the doctor and the police? Members of the jury,
was that woman lying?"

Was that woman lying? The question was not posed in the traditional Old Bailey style of fierce defiance ("I dare you, I challenge you,
to say this woman lies!"), but with the quiet assurance of one who

has forged a solid chain of reasoning which will lose rather than gain from declamatory effects.

This was really the climax of the speech. It was the point at which the advocate would gather himself for his touching peroration, if touching peroration there was going to be. But Hastings remained faithful to the undertaking with which he had begun. Both temperament and technique caused him to recoil from anything remotely resembling a harangue. Nor was Mrs. Barney's case one where sympathy, as such, could readily be roused; unlike that of Madame Fahmy, which had been heard in the selfsame court nearly nine years before, and was now being frequently recalled and quoted as a parallel. In each a young woman of good breeding and good station was charged with murdering the man whom she had loved. In each a revolver was the instrument of death. In each, oddly enough, Percival Clarke was prosecuting counsel. But Madame Fahmy, a Parisian lady of faultless morals and gentle disposition, had married a rich Egyptian prince whose suave drawing-room manner concealed a savage cruelty and perverted appetites; for several years before the shooting incident—in respect of which her successful plea fused self-defence and mishap— she had patiently borne great suffering at his hands. Mrs. Barney, on the other hand, had engaged in an illicit and unsanctified relationship with the young man she was accused of having killed; her general standards of behaviour fell somewhat short of strict; her disposition was volatile if it was not violent; and any suffering there may have been she voluntarily endured, and in all likelihood commensurately repaid. With an English jury the differences were radical.

Notwithstanding, it is of interest to compare Hastings' conclusion to his speech for Mrs. Barney with Marshall Hall's conclusion to his speech for Madame Fahmy, if only as an object lesson in contrasting advocates. "Members of the jury," Marshall Hall had said, after an address in which he imitated an oriental crouch, pointed the pistol at the faces of the jury, and threw it on the floor with a horrifying crash, "I want you to open the gates where this western woman can go out, not into the dark night of the desert, but back to her friends, who love her in spite of her weaknesses; back to her friends, who will be glad to receive her; back to her child, who will be waiting for her with open arms. You will open the gate, and"—here Marshall Hall pointed to the skylight—"you will let this woman go back into the light of God's great Western sun."

It was symbolical, romantic, picturesque—an unashamed and undiluted play upon the feelings. If Hastings had defended Madame Fahmy it is certain that he would have attempted nothing of the kind. It was doubly certain in the less propitious atmosphere of Mrs. Barney's trial. Either the jury were won over by his reasoned argument or they would never be won over at all. Hence the simple finish to his magnificent defence. "I claim that on the evidence that has been put before you Mrs. Barney is entitled as a right to a verdict in her favour. I ask of you, as a matter of justice, that you should set her free."

On the evidence. As a right. As a matter of justice. These—and not references to suns or gates or deserts—were the demands that Hastings formulated for his weeping client.

For a brief interval after he sat down there was no sound save that of Mrs. Barney's anguish. Then, forthright in phrase and business-like in manner, the judge embarked upon his summing-up. . . .

On Travers Humphreys the public and the legal profession could for once agree. Both rightly considered him the best British criminal judge of his generation. In this place of high regard he was succeeding Horace Avory, whose last years upon the Bench Humphreys overlapped. And, like Avory, Humphreys had assumed judicial office admirably equipped for the rôle he had to fill—equipped not merely with theoretical knowledge of criminal law, but by constant engagement at the Bar in criminal work. As Treasury counsel—an appointment that he held for more than twenty years—Humphreys had taken part on one side or the other in a high proportion of the epoch's best remembered cases. In his twenties he had been concerned with the defence of Oscar Wilde; in his thirties with the defence of Kitty Byron; in his forties with the prosecutions of Crippen, Seddon, Roger Casement and Brides-in-the-Bath Smith; in his fifties with those of Horatio Bottomley and Mrs. Thompson, and with the defences of Colonel Rutherford and the financier Gerard Bevan. A remarkable catalogue of sensational cases, and it is only such cases that stand out, like the visible fragment of an iceberg, above the obliterating waters of remoteness. They act as indicator to several thousand more, now quite forgotten and sunk beneath the surface, that combined to produce the vast experience of the judge who, in his middle sixties, was to try Elvira Barney.

If Humphreys' career bore resemblance to Avory's, the men themselves were of very different mould. Avory was credited with a vein of callousness, a pitiless contempt for human frailty; Humphreys was never lacking in a disciplined compassion. Avory reasoned in the abstract as if all men were alike; Humphreys allied logic with imaginative insight. Avory forced life into the plaster cast of law; Humphreys made law serve the purposes of life. In a word, he had that precious attribute, humanity.

He was therefore merciful—but not indulgent; understanding—but not sentimental. He was invariably firm, and could be extremely stern once he had made his mind up that sternness was demanded. And in making up his mind he showed a penetrating shrewdness, bestowed on him by nature and sharpened to perfection by the manifold activities of his busy life.

Humphreys was the first man to appreciate a good point, but he was also the last to be hoodwinked by a bad one. Nor did he deal in compliments unless they were sincere. That being so, the first words he uttered to the jury paid Hastings a tribute that has seldom been surpassed. "You have just listened," he said, "to a great forensic effort. I am not paying compliments," went on this great veteran of so many famous trials, "when I say it is one of the finest speeches that I have ever heard delivered at the Bar."

The speech, deliberately aimed not at the heart but at the head, had indeed been of a kind to win the judge's admiration. It was, he went on to impress upon the jury, "free from anything like an appeal to sentiment and, one should add, of all the more assistance to you because it consisted of careful and accurate analysis." Moreover, before the summing-up had progressed very far it began to be apparent that in one vital respect Humphreys himself had been convinced by Hastings' argument—or had at least been thinking along very similar lines. He did not try to *impose* any opinion of his own, holding the balance with that scrupulous precision which is the mark of judges who believe in trial by jury. He warned them against shrinking from a disagreeable task. "If you are satisfied on the evidence as a whole that it is proved that she did intentionally fire the revolver, pointing it at the body of the man, and so caused the bullet wound from which he died, then she is guilty of the crime of murder, and no feeling of pity, no feeling of regret, should deter you from the duty you are called upon to do." But the judge gave an indication of his personal view in a form that almost echoed Hastings' chief contention. "What right have we to say her story is untrue?" he asked. "If it is not inconsistent with the facts that have been proved, a rejection of it would be simply and solely on the ground that it was told by a person under trial." He was judge, not jury, and took great care not to usurp the function of the latter. None now could doubt, though, that in Humphreys's judgment the prisoner's story was not demonstrably false—and unless that story was demonstrably false a conviction for murder could only be perverse.

There remained, however, another alternative to acquittal which had so far received no mention in the case. "Counsel," observed Humphreys, "have said nothing about manslaughter; on the facts there was nothing that they could have said. It is for me to direct you on the law concerning this. Manslaughter is the *unlawful* killing of another without any *intention* of either killing or of causing serious injury." Having established the formal definition, he immediately applied it to the case that was before them. "It amounts to this," he said. "If the prisoner threatened to commit suicide—suicide, let me remind you, is a crime —and the deceased man removed the revolver in order to prevent it, and she, in order to carry out her intention, struggled with him and so caused the revolver to go off she would then be guilty of manslaughter and answerable for that offence at law."

The sting in this passage was delayed until the end, when it suddenly dawned upon the judge's listeners that his manslaughter example exactly corresponded with Mrs. Barney's own account of what had taken place. . . .

When a judge, in the rightful discharge of his office, presents an assessment of the case for acceptance or rejection, he is sometimes said to be summing-up *for* a particular verdict. The expression is a loose one. But if one did venture to use it in respect of a well-nigh faultless jury charge, one would say that Humphreys summed-up for a manslaughter decision.

That the twelve men were not in any way obliged to follow suit had repeatedly been emphasised by the judge himself, and the outcome of the trial still appeared entirely open. No finding could be summarily ruled out. It was possible—some believed it probable—that they would convict the prisoner of murder; public disgust at the background of the case had been crystallised in a justifiable reference by the judge to Mrs. Barney and her lover as "these rather worthless people"—and a jury's natural reluctance to destroy a useful life can sometimes tip level scales in a defendant's favour. It was possible that they would, by voluntary process, arrive at the manslaughter verdict which the judge had mooted. It was possible, after Hastings' great performance in the morning, that they would do neither and instead acquit outright. . . .

The jury retired at five minutes to three. Judge and counsel also withdrew to their respective rooms. Mrs. Barney left the dock like some automaton; it required two pairs of hands to pilot her below. The spectators remained in court, where long-pent-up excitement at last found release in feverish discussion.

The sensation of suspense, greater than any crime reporters present could remember, intensified as the jury's absence was prolonged. Half-past three; quarter to four; four o'clock; a quarter past—they had been conferring now for an hour and a half. Everyone had his own views on the delay. They could not decide between manslaughter and murder; they could not decide whether to add a mercy rider; they could not decide about convicting her at all. Some held that this length of time precluded an acquittal; others that each added minute favoured the defence; yet others that everything presaged a disagreement. Slowly moved the clock and fast the ferment rose.

At a quarter to five the speculative tongues were stilled. The jury had reappeared at the entrance to their box.

Officials hurried in. Counsel came back, the defending side with deeply anxious faces; according to one observer, Hastings was "almost haggard." The judge resumed his seat amid the crowded bench; close to him his clerk held the dread black square in readiness. Last of all, the wardresses brought up Mrs. Barney; her feet dragged so that the shuffling sounded oddly through the court, and her white, manicured hands clutched the dock ledge for support.

"Do you find the prisoner guilty or not guilty of wilful murder?"

"Not guilty," said the foreman of the jury.

"Do you find the prisoner guilty or not guilty of manslaughter?"

"Not guilty," said the foreman of the jury.

The crowd heaved a great sigh; someone laughed hysterically. Mrs. Barney cried out, "Oh!" and put her handkerchief to her mouth. Just beside the dock her mother, who had sat there through the trial, laid her head upon her arms and very quietly fainted.

It was a triumph, of course, but what was its especial nature? What were the elements that made Hastings worth every penny of his fee— which was certainly one of the largest ever marked upon a brief to defend a charge of murder?

First, the rare capacity to judge a case's impact on contemporary life, and thus upon the jurors empanelled to decide it. Second, the requisite technique to act upon this judgment in setting the tempo and the key of his performance. Third, the delicate but devastating fashion in which he handled hostile witnesses. Fourth, the cool sense of his realistic plea.

These were the practical contributions of this fascinating advocate to a result that might have easily been different. For the student of forensic style, one point must be added. In the Barney trial the Bar's du Maurier tackled Sir Giles Overreach and, while strictly faithful to his own distinctive method, showed that he could play it as well as any Kean.

17

Jones and Hulten

DURING 1944 I was working at the B.B.C. and my duties often took me to the Service ministries. To avoid the crowds in Regent Street, I made a habit of using the narrow lanes lying parallel as a quick walking route from my office to Whitehall.

About three o'clock one bright spring afternoon, I had got within a long stone's throw of Golden Square when I heard the sounds of an approaching rumpus. Presently an American soldier came round the nearest corner at a lurching trot. It was obvious from a glance that he had been drinking heavily. His head was bandaged and there were fresh bloodstains on his tunic: traces of some brawl or scuffle earlier that day. In his arms he carried several unopened liquor bottles. Behind him, at a distance, followed a shouting crowd of Soho Italians, Cypriots, and Greeks, presumably led by the owner of the shop that had been robbed. They made no attempt, however, to overtake the thief, for a good reason that was soon apparent. Every few yards, he turned unsteadily and hurled one of the bottles back at his pursuers. They jumped and dodged in terror as the glass cracked and the wicked fragments flew.

I stepped into a doorway and waited for this perilous operation to pass by. When the soldier was level with me, though, he threw into the air his last remaining bottle, and the exultant crowd now rushed swiftly forward. But still more swiftly did they halt and dive for cover. Because, deprived of simpler weapons, the soldier drew a gun, and aimed it at them sightlessly as he went lumbering on.

Whether it was loaded or not, I never knew. In due course the soldier disappeared from view, the hue and cry was cautiously resumed, and I continued on my way towards Whitehall as if nothing in the least out of the ordinary had occurred. In a sense, nothing had. For this was London's West End during those hectic months when the American military invasion reached its peak, and the atmosphere prevailing in some respects resembled that of a Yukon boom-town in the gold rush of the 'nineties. This atmosphere affected, in varying degree, elements of both invaders and invaded. It generated a racing pulse of unhealthy excitement. It imparted a contempt for civilized conventions. It prompted countless minor sins of recklessness or licence. And it gave rise to at least one major act of evil—that which was popularly called The Cleft Chin Murder, but which legal records less dramatically designate the case of The King versus Jones and Hulten.

Karl Gustav Hulten was twenty-two years old. Swedish by birth but American by upbringing, he was trained as a paratrooper in the United States and ultimately dispatched with his regiment to Britain in order to assist in liberating Europe. Instead he preferred the path of a deserter. Wearing an officer's uniform (to which his rank did not entitle him), using the bogus name of "Lieutenant Ricky Allen," driving about in an army truck he had contrived to make his own, Hulten on the run possessed in goodly measure what he afterwards described as "a build-up" for himself.

The precise form of his "build-up"—*anglice,* shooting a line—depended on his estimate of persons that he met. But as he carried a fully primed revolver at the ready—that is, with both the safety catch and the hammer back, so that it could be fired at once at any time—it was easiest for him to sustain the rôle of desperado, whenever that might seem advantageous or attractive. Thus his "build-up" was predetermined when he fell in with the girl whose name is now forever linked in infamy with his.

Elizabeth Marina Jones (the Marina had been Maud) was still younger than Hulten—a few months past eighteen. Most of her life had been spent in the Neath district of South Wales, against a drab background of industrial depression. Eventually she escaped to London where she worked in turn as barmaid, waitress, cinema usherette, and what is euphemistically termed a strip-tease artist (in which capacity she performed at several third-rate nightclubs for an average reward of four pounds ten a week). She lived in one small room in King Street, Hammersmith, and took most of her meals at a local eating-house. London hardly gave her the flamboyant life she craved—neither the colour nor the throb nor the sensation—but at least it was not Neath, and at least she could assume a smart name like Georgina Grayson, and at least there was the shoddy glamour of the dancing floor. Above all, there were the Yanks. To the little strip-tease artist, as to countless other girls, America was identical with glittering Hollywood, and every farmer's boy from Tennessee or South Dakota appeared potentially a Gable or a Crosby. Better still, perhaps, a Cagney or a Bogart; the romance of brutality was very much in vogue, and Georgina Grayson responded to it ardently. Thus her course was predetermined when she fell in with the man whose name is now forever linked in infamy with hers.

Their first encounter, so powerfully charged with ruin and not only for themselves, took place on October 3, 1944. They were introduced to one another in a café. This is Georgina Grayson; Georgie, this is Ricky. Pleased to meet you, Ricky. Hiya doin', babe? All right, how's yourself? Okay, okay; like to take a ride tonight? What you got to ride in? I got it, don't you worry; pick you up eleven-thirty, by the cinema. Where'll we go, Ricky? Most anywhere you like. . . . Each kept the appointment, and shortly before midnight they were speeding in the stolen truck along the Great West Road.

As they drove they talked, finding out about each other. Hulten, as always, was eager to show off, and he very quickly sized up his new acquaintance. He remarked in casual fashion that he was a gunman, and that back home in Chicago he ran round with a mob; then noted complacently how his callow lie immediately won the girl's naïve admiration. You a real gangster? Sure I'm a real gangster—why, if you wanna know, I'm boss of a gang that's operating over here right now. What, over here in London? Yeah—but take it easy, Georgie; don't you go round telling no one about this. . . . He took a hand from the wheel and groped inside his belt; the strip-tease artist gasped and thrilled—she saw the gun.

Interactions became fast. The man's conceit was flattered by the girl's enraptured awe, the girl's imagination stirred by the man's parade of toughness. To feed his conceit and her imagination further, by separate process each conjured up the same unreal world; a world that they undoubtedly derived from the same sources; a world where they were partners—a gunman and his moll. It was a platitudinous fancy, and had it ended there—he concocting tales and boasting, she receptive and enthralled—the phenomenon need not have been malignant; it would not even have been especially unusual. Make-believe is a more common adult pastime than is supposed, and play-acting the part of villain may be harmlessly cathartic. What made this pair remarkable and dangerous, forcing society to strike out in self-defence, was the way they translated their conception of themselves from the plane of air-drawn fancy to the plane of solid fact. For although neither had previously committed an offence involving any kind of physical assault, within a few hours of their meeting in the café they embarked on a positive debauch of violent crime.

Later, when each of them came to tell the story of the ensuing orgiastic days, their two accounts did not wholly correspond. The girl maintained that she was terrified of Hulten, and had only done the things she did from fear: Hulten maintained that it was she who made the pace, she who urged him on. Their respective defences were shaped accordingly and, as a result, at their subsequent joint trial at the Old Bailey, the two prisoners set about attacking one another with far more ferocity and far more virulence than a rightly temperate Crown exhibited in attacking either. Their mutual hostility was indeed so marked, and the effort of each to destroy the former ally so relentless, that they almost invited comparison with the classical "cut-throat" cases; Millsom and Fowler, for instance, or Browne and Kennedy. Such behaviour on the woman's part was at any rate comprehensible; in perpetration —as distinct from inception and idea—she, it was not gainsaid, acted merely as auxiliary; making things as black as possible for Hulten offered her, albeit faintly, a prospect of escape. Hulten, however, had not even this practical excuse. On his own admission, his was the active hand; if—which he denied—criminal intention lay behind it, he was doomed; by implicating the woman, he stood to gain precisely nothing —except the doubtful luxury of malice satisfied. Nonetheless, his inculpations surpassed hers. Between the two conflicting and irreconcilable versions, that of the timid girl bullied by the brutal male, and that of the simple boy made the designing female's puppet, the jury of mankind is left to choose one—or neither.

The trial, therefore, is a dubious and indeterminate guide to the development of their personal relationship during the period in which they ran amok. But concerning broad essentials there can be no real dispute. They turned into a pair of vicious, predatory beasts. They made expeditions almost nightly in the truck, with highway robbery as their express object. They offered lifts to unsuspecting walkers; they molested cyclists on lonely country roads; they tried to hold up cars. They were absolutely ruthless and cold-blooded. One girl, whom Hulten had struck with an iron bar and afterwards half-strangled, they threw like a discarded dummy into the Thames to drown. That in fact she survived they neither knew nor cared. There could be no looking back as their wild campaign of banditry tore towards the inevitable climax.

It came on the fourth night of their association. At half past eleven, Hulten whistled outside the girl's lodging. She came downstairs, and joined him in the street. Where's the truck, Ricky? Ain't brought out the truck. What we going to do, Ricky? Let's go get a cab. . . . She had no doubt about the underlying innuendo. "I knew the meaning of his words," she admitted to the police. "He wanted me to go with him to rob a taxi-driver."

They walked along Hammersmith Road and stood together in a doorway. A grey Ford car leisurely approached. Hi, taxi, taxi. The grey Ford pulled up opposite. You a taxi? Private hire; where d'you want to go? What d'you say, top of King Street? That'll be ten bob.

Strictly, a private hire car should not pick up casual fares. But the driver of the grey Ford was not punctilious. He had had a slack night —and didn't everybody dodge the regulation anyway? So when the American officer agreed to his somewhat exorbitant demand, he grinned affably, emphasizing the hollow in his chin—a feature that was shortly to fascinate the headline-writers, after his corpse had been discovered in a ditch near Staines.

Hulten and the girl got in, and sat in the back seat. The car moved off. Nobody spoke a word. Bored by the silence, the driver whistled softly through his teeth. He didn't specially like the look of his two passengers, and wasn't sorry when they reached their destination. Here's the top of King Street. Yeah, that's right, bud, but I wanna go further on. You said top of King Street; further on'll cost you more. Take it easy, bud; I don't mind what I pay.

On they went again, past the darkened houses, over the roundabout, into the open road. The driver grew irritable, even a shade uneasy. This near where you want, guv'nor? Yeah, it's near; go slow. We come a tidy way, guv'nor. Okay, we'll get out here. . . . As the car came to a standstill, Hulten was holding in his hand the fatal gun.

The driver leaned across to open the nearside door. Then the final madness supervened. Without warning, without prelude, Hulten fired into his back. The driver moaned, and slumped over to the left. Hulten jumped into the front, and drove rapidly away. The driver ceased to moan and his breath came chokingly. As he died, the girl was going through his pockets.

The cleft chin murder—for which Hulten was hanged and the girl, reprieved at the eleventh hour, condemned to a life sentence—is not of special interest to criminologists; the minds of both criminals were crudely commonplace. It is, however, of surpassing interest to social chroniclers, for no murder has ever been more firmly rooted in its age. At any time Frederick Seddon might have poisoned his lodger. At any time Jack the Ripper might have slashed his prostitutes. At any time Alfred Rouse might have kidnapped his unknown. But for the Cleft Chin crime there could be only one occasion; the occasion when it happened; the occasion when the characters responsible had been transported by events and transformed by one another.

The brash American, physically strapping but of stunted mental growth, consigned by army order to an unfamiliar land, sought to impress the natives with his own superiority by aping the habits of a gunman or a thug. The poverty-stricken adolescent refugee from Neath, frail alike in body and in mind, vaguely aspiring but completely talentless, sought a pitiable escape in fantasies inspired by the spurious appeal of gangster films. A world convulsion brought this pair together, at a moment when life was cheap and violence sanctified; under such conditions the union was deadly. It was like holding a lighted match to dynamite, having first ensured that the latter was exposed.

And so the hapless car driver, whose facial marking gives the case its name, may be written down no less a casualty of war than those who met a death more orthodox from shell or bomb.